Praise for *Charles*

"A much-needed, very welcome reminder of the genius of Charles Walters, whose work has been too long neglected by historians and students of American film. Phillips offers a lively, convincing argument that Walters should take his place alongside such greats of musical film as Vincente Minnelli, Stanley Donen, and Gene Kelly."— William J. Mann, author of *Kate: The Woman Who Was Hepburn* and *Tinseltown: Murder, Morphine and Madness at the Dawn of Hollywood*

"An extremely significant contribution to film scholarship, full of very precise detail about Walters's multifarious contributions to the show business world in which he operated, demonstrating throughout a serious commitment to its subject—a great director whose life and work have been grievously overlooked until now."— David Ehrenstein, film critic for *Keyframe* and *Cahiers du Cinéma*

"Brent Phillips makes a staggeringly persuasive case that Charles Walters is one of the most underappreciated directors and choreographers in the annals of film history. The book also brings to light the trailblazing Walters did by living openly as a gay man during an era when such things were strictly taboo. Exhaustively researched and impeccably written, this addictive treatise made me rabid to rediscover and reassess Walters's entire oeuvre. It is absolutely essential reading!"— Sam Irvin, author of *Kay Thompson: From Funny Face to Eloise*

"Chuck Walters was Hollywood's best kept secret. Thankfully, his days as an overlooked and underappreciated artist are finally over. In this informative and engaging biography, Brent Phillips examines the life and legacy of the multitalented director, dancer, and choreographer who brought his special brand of showmanship to every production. From Fred Astaire and Judy Garland strolling along Fifth Avenue in *Easter Parade* to an invincible Debbie Reynolds on the road to somewhere in *The Unsinkable Molly Brown*, Walters was responsible for some of the most beloved images in American film. Through careful consideration of Walters's work on Broadway and in Hollywood, Phillips reclaims a life and career worthy of much greater attention."— Mark Griffin, author of *A Hundred or More Hidden Things: The Life and Films of Vincente Minnelli*

"Brent Phillips has provided anyone with a passion for the golden age of Hollywood musicals a much-needed and wonderfully informative biography of director Charles Walters. Phillips makes an excellent case that Walters, who hitherto has been dismissed as a mere company man, was actually a genuine artist whose taste and skill not only shaped his own films but also made enormous contributions to films directed by other better-known directors. Phillips also writes sensitively and not sensationally about Walters's private life and how a brave, talented gay man could swim through the rough waters of homophobic Hollywood with his integrity intact."— Charles Busch, actor and playwright of *The Tale of the Allergist's Wife* and *Die, Mommie, Die*

Charles Walters

CHARLES WALTERS

THE DIRECTOR
WHO MADE
HOLLYWOOD DANCE

BRENT PHILLIPS

UNIVERSITY PRESS OF KENTUCKY

Copyright © 2014 by The University Press of Kentucky
Paperback edition 2017

Scholarly publisher for the Commonwealth,
serving Bellarmine University, Berea College, Centre College of Kentucky,
Eastern Kentucky University, The Filson Historical Society, Georgetown
College, Kentucky Historical Society, Kentucky State University, Morehead State
University, Murray State University, Northern Kentucky University,
Transylvania University, University of Kentucky, University of Louisville, and
Western Kentucky University.

Editorial and Sales Offices: The University Press of Kentucky
663 South Limestone Street, Lexington, Kentucky 40508-4008
www.kentuckypress.com

"I Wanna Be a Dancin' Man," by Johnny Mercer and Harry Warren,
copyright © 1951, 1952. Used by permission of the Four Jays
Music Company.

Frontispiece: Charles Walters Caricature. Used by permission
of artist Michael Willhoite.

The Library of Congress has cataloged the hardcover edition as follows:

Phillips, Brent.
  Charles Walters : the director who made Hollywood dance / Brent Phillips.
    pages   cm — (Screen classics)
  Includes bibliographical references and index.
   ISBN 978-0-8131-4721-5 (hardcover : alk. paper) — ISBN 978-0-8131-4723-9 (pdf) —
ISBN 978-0-8131-4722-2 (epub) 1. Walters, Charles, 1911–1982. 2. Motion picture pro-
ducers and directors—United States—Biography. I. Title.
  PN1998.3.W355P55 2015
  791.4302'33092—dc23
  [B]
                        2014032911

ISBN 978-0-8131-6971-2 (pbk. : alk. paper)

This book is printed on acid-free paper meeting the requirements of the
American National Standard for Permanence in Paper for Printed Library
Materials.

Manufactured in the United States of America.

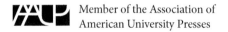

Member of the Association of
American University Presses

For Mom, for believing
And in memory of Mark Goldweber, my chum

Contents

Contents

Illustrations follow page 130

Preface
What a Swell Party

The underrated fellow at M-G-M was Chuck Walters, who did such great work. All the other performers will tell you the same thing, although he wasn't the big name the rest [of us] seemed to be.

Gene Kelly

When the much-vaunted magic of the Hollywood musical is discussed—specifically the magic of the M-G-M Hollywood musical—certain iconic sequences are inevitably embraced. Among the most timeless are a tuxedo-jacketed Judy Garland imploring an audience to forget their troubles, and Judy dressed in her Sunday finest for an Easter morning stroll down Fifth Avenue with Fred Astaire. Add the wide-eyed Leslie Caron as she harmonizes "a song of love" with a carnival puppet; recall the tipsy Frank Sinatra and Bing Crosby as they tunefully skewer the swells of Newport; include the rambunctious Debbie Reynolds as she tackles high society in Colorado. These prized celluloid moments, capturing nonpareil performers at their unqualified best, possess one thing in common: each sprang from the imaginative mind of Charles "Chuck" Walters—dancer, choreographer, director. Yet despite his more than four decades of continuous contribution to Broadway and Hollywood entertainment, Walters routinely has been overlooked in most histories of dance, theater, and film. This exclusion, coupled with the filmmaker's lifetime disinterest in self-promotion, has resulted in an undeserved obscurity across the years.

Historian David Quinlan acknowledged this as early as 1983, a year after the director's passing, when he wrote: "It seems amazing that when film fans, even some musical aficionados, have the names of [Stanley] Donen and [Vincente] Minnelli at their fingertips, that of Charles Walters escapes them. But any director whose work includes *Good News, Easter Parade, Lili, Dangerous When Wet, The Tender Trap, High Society,*

Ask Any Girl, The Unsinkable Molly Brown, and *Walk, Don't Run* has to be counted in the front flight."[1]

Such neglect seems even more baffling when one reviews Walters's entire career. Throughout the 1930s he was one of Broadway's most celebrated dancers; his debonair appeal and lively technique were integral to such hits as *Jubilee, I Married an Angel,* and *Du Barry Was a Lady.* In 1942 he traveled to Hollywood, joining Metro-Goldwyn-Mayer as a dance director, and spent the next five years creating musical sequences for *Best Foot Forward, Girl Crazy, Meet Me in St. Louis,* and *Summer Holiday,* among others. When promoted to full-fledged director in 1947, Walters went on to deliver some of the most enjoyable and profitable Metro pictures during that studio's golden era and beyond. He earned a Best Director Academy Award nomination for *Lili,* and ten of his films won coveted premiere engagements at Radio City Music Hall.

Away from the studio, Walters lived contentedly—if carefully—as a gay man; in retrospect, this makes his accomplishments seem even more significant. He had come of professional age when homosexuality was a criminal offense and its exposure could threaten (if not destroy) a career, especially during the conformist McCarthy era of the 1950s. Certainly there were other preeminent gay directors during the years of the studio system, yet most of this small but vital subset caved to the circumspect code that governed the industry. Walters, on the other hand, was discreet but not dishonest. He bucked the status quo by living unapologetically with his partner and agent, John Darrow, from the time of his arrival in Hollywood. (Even ultra-conservative columnist Hedda Hopper became a regular at the couple's Malibu beach home, and her pen remained forever supportive.)

During a 1976 conversation with film critic Arthur Knight, Walters alluded to the difficulties he had experienced and the tactics he had adopted to combat Hollywood's mores: "I *had* to work harder. I couldn't do the social thing, and play the game the others were playing. I had to work that much harder and hurdle the 'evils' by doing good work."[2] Because of his unwillingness to participate in heterosexual masquerades (along with the unrelated but infamous nepotism that ruled M-G-M), Walters worked with greater obedience; seldom would he decline a project or refuse to lend a hand.

Quick-witted, ever resourceful, and supremely tactful, Walters gained respect and strong affection from his colleagues. When interviewed for this book in 2008, Leslie Caron was asked, "What is your immediate reaction when you hear the name Chuck Walters?" Her face was instantly alight, and her eyes shone as she replied, "I smile."[3]

Given his background as an entertainer and the teach-by-example techniques he perfected as a choreographer, Walters was well prepared to guide his performers. Assistant director Bill Shanks observed the director actively coaching Doris Day on the *Jumbo* set and recounted: "Here's the way he works: He'll say, 'Doris, you stand by the camera, and I'll show you what I want.' Then without any self-consciousness, he'll take her place and give a brilliant performance. Because [Chuck] knows about acting, and what he wants an audience to feel, he could show Doris the mood and what she had to do to portray it. Actors understand him."[4] In turn, Walters certainly understood his actors. He liked to boast, "You have to know the stars better than they do themselves."

What is problematic, then, is pinpointing a consistent cinematic style for Charles Walters. His fellow M-G-M compatriots included Vincente Minnelli (the artiste), Busby Berkeley (the surrealist), George Sidney (the colorful adapter), and the team of Gene Kelly and Stanley Donen (the dynamic duo). By comparison, there is an unpredictable, kaleidoscopic quality to Walters's twenty-one feature films. He tended to blur the borders between genres—his comedies often seem like musicals, and his whimsical tales are rooted firmly in tragedy. The director lightly dismissed any claim to a singular vision in his movies, focusing instead on the storytelling: "I would look for the heart and the honesty that I could glom onto; I think that was my basic principle. I'd throw jokes over my shoulder if they got in the way of honesty. I think drama has to be amusing, and comedies have to have some drama. That's the way life is." In his 1963 *Film Culture* appraisal of American directors, critic Andrew Sarris agreed that Walters was difficult to categorize and ranked him as "Likeable but Elusive."[5] The director considered that label, then commented, "You're supposed to be backstage. You can't star yourself—*that* is the danger."[6]

Charles Walters retired from moviemaking in the mid-1960s and could look on as his "likable but elusive" style was hailed by some, yet neglected by the majority. (French filmmakers Eric Rohmer and Jacques Rivette both publicly claimed partiality for Walters over critics' darling Minnelli.)[7] By any analytical standard, however, it remained difficult to align the low-key, modest man with the diversity of his accomplishments.

The director himself found it easy to appraise his contributions. He offered: "My films were made to entertain, pure and simple. And that's really all I wanted to do."[8] In that goal, he succeeded as few others did, before or since.

This is his story.

I

The Anaheim Hoofer

He was born to dance. The expression is a cliché, uttered virtually every time an infant intuitively bounces to a musical beat. Yet in the case of Charles Walters, the overused idiom is remarkably accurate. He could not help himself; dance was within. This predisposition, he'd relate, started "even before my birth. . . . [M]y mother said that when she was pregnant, each time she went to a concert she had to leave before the end because I danced the whole time."

Far from distressing, such mild discomfort made Winifred Taft's first pregnancy all the more memorable. Only recently had the twenty-four-year-old uprooted herself from Tomah, Wisconsin, with the idea of starting a family. She was joined by fellow Tomah native Joe Walter, two years her junior and ready for something new. "His family just seemed to have a jinx fastened to it," Walters later said. "After a series of accidents had caused the loss of three sisters and a brother, Dad decided a change of scene was needed."[1]

That scene proved to be Southern California. Heading westward circa 1910, the unwed couple got as far as Seattle before funds ran low. They took rooms at an inexpensive boardinghouse; Winifred found work as a stenographer, and Joe, following in his father's footsteps, discovered his talents as a salesman. Solvent once again, they continued their jour-ney to Pasadena, where the climate convinced them to settle. The two were married (apparently during the winter of 1910–1911), and Winifred soon discovered she was to begin the family she wanted.

Arriving on November 17, 1911, Charles Powell Walter was born at 325 South Grand Avenue, quite possibly the residence of a Pasadena midwife. Although the parents were newly married, the birth certifi-cate makes it clear that his was "a legitimate birth."[2] Joe named his son after his own father, but even from the beginning the baby was called

Chuck. (The surname was later amended to Walters when Chuck—tired of misspellings—affixed the final *s*. This didn't occur until the 1930s, but for the sake of clarity, he will become Walters from this point in the narrative.)

Little is known about the Walter family dynamic, though Chuck later described his parents as "square and untheatrical." Joe reportedly was a lively man, while Winifred was more subdued.[3] She valued music and, from the outset, instilled that love in her son.

By the time Chuck was two, Joe had moved his small family south to Anaheim, taking a modest one-story home on Center Street. "We classed Anaheim as a very enviable place to live," recounted longtime resident Howard Loudon. "It was a beautiful, very satisfied, independent community that had a lot of culture behind it. They had a concert series—people like Madame Schumann-Heink and Jascha Heifetz . . . were brought into the community, which was quite unusual for a town of ten thousand people. I would say Anaheim could be classed as a very wealthy, well-educated, farming community that enjoyed life immensely."[4] This was the comfortable, neighborly world in which Chuck Walters was raised.

As a salesman, Joe was a natural. He peddled cigars to billiard parlors, then bettered his situation by aligning himself with the burgeoning automobile industry. (As late as 1917, horse and buggy remained the principal mode of transportation in and around Anaheim.) He began in partnership, establishing Walter & Day, a tractor and auto dealership that provided Anaheim residents with a garage and service station. His skills were such that he soon opted to go it alone as J. E. Walter & Company, proudly distributing the "smartest new auto models": Jordans, Willys-Knights, and Overlands.[5] It was a fortuitous decision. The city soon paved over its dirt streets, autos were in demand, and Joe saved enough to make a down payment on a better home in a better neighborhood. By 1922, when Chuck was eleven, the family was living well in a two-story house at 120 South Kroeger.

"That was a fun area," remembers boyhood compatriot Elmer Thill. "I can just see that old street. There were lots of trees on it. My family lived on the corner, and the Bushard boys—Joe, Chance, and Earl—lived across the street. Chuck was three or four houses down. He was a likable fellow and would let me tag along. Being the youngest of the bunch, I looked up to the older guys. Oh, we'd sit on the curbs joking, shooting blackbirds with an air rifle, and making each other laugh. We laughed a lot."[6] Within the Kroeger Street gang, a tight camaraderie developed between fair-haired Chuck and darkly handsome Joe Bushard. Both confessed a fondness for musical entertainment, and conveniently—not too far from their homes—stood the California Theater, Anaheim's 735-seat vaudeville house.

"My oldest memory of dancing," Walters recounted in 1972, "is from when I was really very small. [My parents] would get me out of bed, bring me down to the parlor, play the electrophone so that I'd dance for the guests, and finally put me back to bed."[7] These nocturnal recitals, he'd joke, could be counted as his first personal appearances. More significant is that he was a hit.

As Chuck matured, so did his appreciation of dance. On Saturday afternoons he nestled down in a seat at the California, and the technique of every visiting hoofer spurred his fascination. Those on the vaudeville circuit were bringing a broad terpsichorean spectrum, from cooch to cakewalk, Irish jigs to clog dances, ballet to ballroom. Every style seemed to make an impression. "Of course, in those days, live vaudeville was quite common," explains Thill. "Chuck would see routines and try to teach us, and we would have these songfests. We'd do tunes like 'Yes, We Have No Bananas' and 'Mr. Gallagher and Mr. Shean.'"[8]

For most of the neighborhood boys, the shows were a good way to pass the time. But for the now hopelessly stagestruck Walters, performing meant something more. "I got the notion I'd like to be a dancer [while] hanging around with the gang at the corner drug store Saturday nights," he said. "I recall dancing the Charleston to a pipe organ and entering street dancing contests."[9]

Anaheim offered no professional dance academy, leaving Chuck to his own creative devices. Private hours increasingly were spent teaching himself numbers, and sometimes he was known to fashion a few surprises. "I remember he used to come out every once in a while all dressed up as a female," says Thill. "He'd kinda dance around, and you really couldn't tell if he was male or female. He was truly clever at that."[10] (In later years, Walters's ability to mimic lady performers would prove a great asset when he coached female entertainers.) Because there was nothing overtly effeminate in Chuck's manner and appearance, these improvisatory performances barely raised an eyebrow. "His dressing as a girl was really interesting to us. Nobody thought anything of it, really."[11]

Nobody, that is, except perhaps Chuck himself, who was on the cusp of adolescence and inwardly beginning to feel that his schoolboy interests were different from those of his mates. Neither Babe Ruth's batting average nor the golden gloves of Jack Dempsey commanded his attention; instead, it was soigné ballroom dancer Clifton Webb who most impressed him. "Clifton was so damn elegant!" Walters later praised, recalling the well-mannered entertainer's brief engagement in Anaheim. "He'd finish a number, take out his cigarette case, tap out a cigarette, light it, and then just saunter off." Such élan was a revelation, providing initial passage to Chuck's own identity and professional aspirations. In his immediate circle, however, this was a lone reaction: "Who had heard of Clifton Webb in Anaheim? Nobody. So I was a freak, more or less; a man just didn't dance in those days. At least not in Anaheim."

Joe and Winifred's parenting technique was not without purpose. Their boy learned that success in life stemmed from discipline and high objectives. Young Chuck slipped effortlessly though elementary school, graduating from St. Catherine's Military Academy with a sound academic foundation and an assured work ethic. When it came time for high school, he was enrolled at Anaheim Union High, a public institution imperially fronted by a Parthenon-like colonnade. Well funded and well attended, the high school maintained stringent standards while offering a wide selection of music organizations: an "advanced" orchestra, a marching band, a Mozart Club, and two glee clubs—operetta for the girls and Negro minstrelsy for boys. (The latter lasted only briefly, undone perhaps by Anaheim's growing problems with the Ku Klux Klan in the mid-1920s.) Drama classes were also available, and several one-act plays were prepared for school assemblies and various local social groups. It was, however, the Royal Order of the Grand Drape—the school's honorary dramatics club—that most captured Chuck's attention.

Drape members were a select group; a student had to earn his or her placement by participating in underclassman plays. Hopefuls who had accumulated sufficient stage experience could audition, and if they were successful, they went through a (supervised) initiation that included a paddling delivered by Drape superiors.

Chuck went to work. On Friday, December 9, 1927, in his sophomore year, the sixteen-year-old surprised a packed house of students, families, and faculty at the annual Christmas pageant by performing a self-designed clog dance. It was perhaps his first official stage performance, and although he had to follow the glee club's uproariously received blackface antics, his solo was described by the school newspaper as "a novel feature [that] received great applause."[12]

From that point on, Anaheim High's young hoofer was unstoppable. In February his star performance as a Gypsy won accolades for *The Rim of the World,* a "three-act fantasy" presented by his dramatics class. *Not Quite Such a Goose* followed later that spring, and he "took considerable honors" as a boy who disliked girls and tennis.[13] During junior year he landed the title role in the 1928 Christmas pageant *The Beau of Bath* and scored the lead in the end-of-term comic mystery *The Rear Car.* "Walter's clever comedy did not require the help of his Sherlock Holmes hat and tie to amuse the audience," observed the school's theatrical critic of the latter production; "neither did he stand in need of his pistol to create suspense."[14] (Summarizing his adolescent obsession many years later, the adult Walters would self-mockingly joke: "I was very big into dramatics—*if you can imagine.*")

Although he may have considered himself a "freak," Chuck nonetheless proved popular with his fellow classmates. He joined the track team, and at other sporting events he and Kroeger Street pal Joe Bushard served as the school's "yell leaders." Away from the field, he was elected vice president—and later president—of the forty-member Spanish club, El Circulo Español.

Chuck's supreme victory, however, came when he pledged the Grand Drape. The initiation luncheon was held during the spring semester of his junior year. ("Cocktails were served—*fruit,* that is," the school paper dryly noted.)[15] Joe Bushard, a year older and already a Drape member, led the cheers when Chuck performed his clog dance audition. Unanimously accepted, the delighted new recruit received the obligatory oaken paddle on his backside with pride.

Anaheim was only miles from Hollywood, but the future motion picture director often joked that he spent his youth "trying to get out of California."[16] Just prior to his senior year, Chuck received his first real opportunity for independence when family friends came to visit. "They said if I would drive them back to Oregon, they would send me back by ship," he recounted. "Now *that* sounded exciting!" On the voyage home, he met Aida Broadbent, a young ballerina from the Ernest Belcher classical troupe. His time aboard was spent listening to Broadbent tell tales of her profession. (Three years earlier, Broadbent's balletic ability had won her a brief spot in Metro-Goldwyn-Mayer's *La Bohème*.) This was heady stuff for a motivated dreamer like Walters. Upon docking, the two agreed to stay in touch.

Chuck returned to Anaheim High with halfhearted enthusiasm. He narrowly lost the election for class president but was crowned chief executive of the Royal Order of the Grand Drape. With that mantle, the eighteen-year-old Chuck Walters was poised to demonstrate his true potential. "The senior class play was to be of my choice," he told. "We'd never done a musical, and *Good News* was very popular at the time. So I said, let's do *Good News*! We got the high school orchestra, and then we found out that we couldn't afford the rights. So the dramatic teacher [Faye Kern Schulz] and I used the same storyline but different popular music." Their initiative, according to Anaheim High historian Louise Booth, led to "the first musical comedy to be given at the school" after years of dusty operetta.[17]

Chuck plunged into his first real attempt at entertaining the public on a grand (if local) scale. He gave his *Good News* knockoff the spirited title *Heigh-Ho* and tended to every aspect of "putting on a show": writing, choreography, costume design, scenic construction, advertising, and performing. Weeks were spent coaching his dancers to perfection and then adding the school orchestra into the mix. With fifty-seven amateur thespians at his command, he also managed to play the lead role of football hero Bob Trent. "That," he later said with a smile, "was my *starring* vehicle."

The musical played two sold-out evenings in November 1929, and the school paper prominently featured the front-page headline "Heigh-Ho Is Success."[18] The paper continued, "Partial student direction was a feature of the performance as the choruses bore the very professional mark of Charles Walter's training in their dancing. A black-and-white version of the 'Breakaway' proved a particular hit."[19] Although relying primarily on instinct, Walters had already demonstrated two traits essential to a director: he carried to completion a unifying vision for his production and effectively communicated his goals to his co-workers. Hailed as Anaheim High School's "general entertainer supreme," Chuck was overjoyed.[20]

Seventeen years later, the collegiate *Good News* would make an unanticipated return to his life, providing yet another significant turning point.

It was during rehearsals for *Heigh-Ho* that Black Tuesday hit Wall Street. The implosion of the stock market sent a ripple of fear across the nation, but as Walters's classmate Richard Fischle Jr. explained: "Our agriculture held up [Anaheim's economy] longer than other areas of the East Coast."[21] Confirming this, the 1930 federal census reveals that Joe Walter, now selling insurance, earned an impressive $18,000 that year. This was more than double the net of other well-off neighbors.

Still, some degree of hardship remained inevitable. By mid-1930, more than five hundred U.S. banks had collapsed, and Joe and Winifred were adamant that their son's theatrical aspirations should continue as a leisure pursuit, not a career goal. "They finally insisted that I go to the University of Southern California after I graduated from Anaheim High," said Chuck. Law was to be his choice of study—"and all I wanted to do was dance."

During the 1930–1931 academic year, he attended USC law seminars and pledged Kappa Sigma. But nothing dulled Walters's appetite for performance. He grew somewhat starry-eyed when he was befriended by Leonard Sillman, a colorful (if temperamental) twenty-three-year-old entertainer appearing in the short-lived L.A. production *Temptations of 1930*. Sillman's credits included Broadway and vaudeville (where he toured with George and Ira Gershwin's baby sister, Frances). He'd replaced Fred Astaire in the 1924 touring company of *Lady Be Good*. His celebrity friends included Howard Dietz, Tallulah ("Taloo") Bankhead, and even Clifton Webb. It all seemed so impressive.

Chuck soon ditched campus life ("I thought, 'To hell with this'"), moving back home to consider dance options. "I had stayed friends with Aida Broadbent," he recounted, and in the summer of 1931 the ballerina was working as a choreographer for Fanchon Simon and Marco Wolff. The former sister-and-brother dance team had become impresarios with their "prologues"—short live entertainments that preceded feature film presentations in movie houses from coast to coast. "A [Fanchon and Marco] unit was going out on tour," he recalled, "and they needed a replacement. Aida said, 'I think maybe I can coach you enough, teach you the time step, teach you some of the basic things.' It was an army unit, and I had been to military school as a boy. The gun drill part was easy enough for me, but I didn't know the time step."

Once hired and on the road, Chuck found everything a learning experience. His typical day consisted of a stage rehearsal, multiple performances, and travel to the next location. Hotel rooms were communal; new prologues were added regularly, with themes developed on the spot.

Walters later defined his time with Fanchon and Marco as the "best training for a young artist."[22]

From city to city, however, he maintained an increasing handwritten correspondence with Leonard Sillman, insisting, "There is no one in the company that I can or care to talk with—seriously."[23] Chuck mixed his acute homesickness with obvious adoration.

From the Coronado Hotel in St. Louis:

Leonard, what can I do to improve myself? As you know, I have nothing now but plenty of ambition. It seems as though there should be some way I could accomplish something and have something to show when I get back. I suppose I could get steps & things from the fellows in the show (all old hoofers from way back), but I hate just plain hoofing, buck dancing, wings & that sort of stuff—in other words, just dancing from the knees down. I like easy rhythm work that requires as much, if not more, body movement as foot movement. That's why I admire your work so much; it's so far from "hoofing." . . . You know, since I received your last letter, I have been wondering why you should be interested in me and write, etc., after all you don't even know me (I hope you won't be disappointed when you do), but some day I will show you and prove my appreciation, that's that!

From the Hotel Royal Palm in Detroit:

Why haven't you written? I expected to hear from you before we [left] for Toronto. . . . Don't let anyone see this letter, kid, . . . 'cause I'm stinkin' drunk for the last three days on account I wish I were in Hollywood . . . I think we'll be in New York about eight weeks from now—probably during the holidays. Leonard you've got to be there or I'll die—Christmas away from home will be to[o] much for me—I know—do you think there's any chance—we could get dead drunk, kid, and forget its Xmas or New Years & I want to. Forgive me for writing under the circumstances, Leonard, but you have been so damn nice to me. I think you are so swell that it gives me a good excuse to say so. I'll probably have to write to you tomorrow (if I remember) and apologize for this, but I mean it anyway, kid, so good-night and

God knows how I hope you will be in New York *eight* weeks from now.

On a train leaving Toronto:

> Thanks a lot for the cigarettes, they certainly came in handy—in return I am sending you a nice cold Canadian beer which I hope you will also enjoy.... Seriously, I think it was swell of you to offer to give me letters to people in New York, and I would appreciate it more than anything I know. I have always wanted to see N.Y. so I will probably be in a complete daze when we get there.... You know, I wish I had a chance to talk with you before we left—you probably could have told me how to get the most out of this trip besides just average stage experience (there must be something more). But I am trying to keep my eyes and ears open (sort of a struggle to keep my eyes open at present due *only* to two sleepless nights).
>
> Please write soon, Leonard.

Although Chuck's letters reveal a propensity for typical youthful angst, his presence with the troupe did have its perks. "I was six months on the road with Fanchon and Marco," he remembered, "making $33.60 a week. Some of these kids would come back *owing* Fanchon and Marco and have to go out the next season. I thought, 'Oh boy, I'm not going to do that.' I saved $500."

Walters returned to Hollywood in early 1932 and began to make the rounds. Sizing up his competition, he considered himself more practical than most other aspirants, but future movie heartthrob Tyrone Power was different. "Tyrone was always the best mannered," Chuck observed. "That drew me to him early. He was a young gentleman, and I like to think I was, too. It attracted us to each other. He had more class and breeding than the others."[24] On a continuous cycle of auditions, they faced the challenge of remaining solvent while looking dapper. "We loaned each other sweaters mostly. If we'd worn one four times to see an agent, we'd borrow somebody's blue alpaca or maybe a suit."[25]

Although Power was a dependable companion, Chuck earnestly pursued his association with Sillman. From Anaheim he wrote: "Dear

Leonard, Back home sweet home. . . . Sorry you couldn't come down this week-end—I watched for you and sort of expected you. Please write."[26] Though performing in the unspectacular revue *Hullabaloo* at the Pasadena Community Playhouse, Sillman remained in steady communication with Walters; his datebooks from 1932–1933 indicate that the two frequently met for dinner.

By early spring 1933, however, Sillman's well-known temperament had all but blacklisted him as an entertainer. He later admitted, "The only way I could get a job as a singer and dancer [was] to be a producer and hire myself."[27] The twenty-five-year-old announced plans to mount his own revue at the Pasadena Playhouse, a folly titled *Low and Behold*. "Ninety percent of my cast," he promised, "will be talent that I definitely feel has great brilliance and unfound qualities: [both] young and experienced people that have not had anyone to take them and bring them out the way they should be brought out."[28] Twenty-four performers were gathered to support Sillman—plus one young hoofer from Anaheim he had "tentatively in mind."

"When Chuck had first swum into my ken," Sillman reflected, "he'd been a juvenile with a handsome face and a pair of marvelous feet—and less animation than a corpse. All through rehearsals of *Low and Behold*, I had bullied him into dancing with everything he owned—his arms, his neck, his head, his smile."[29]

Beyond improving Walters's limited technique, Sillman took aim at breaking his impeccable behavior. "It's amazing about Chuck, because he had, at that time, no imagination. . . . He was a charming boy with a delightful personality and a good dancer—but square, completely square. No humor at all, and no imagination, no sense of imagery."[30]

If Sillman's recollections are accurate and Walters then presented little of the wit or creativity that would become his hallmark, working alongside *Low and Behold*'s colorful cast must have helped draw it out of him. The show's roster included chubby female impersonator Larry Armstrong (a former bootlegger for Sillman's father), Paal and Leif Rocky (aka the Rocky Twins—flashy, effeminate brothers from Norway), funny lady Eunice Quedens (who within two years would change her name to Eve Arden), and jazzy vocalist Kay Thompson. At the Pasadena Playhouse, Walters later proclaimed, "*the* star was Kay Thompson." Rehearsing among these eclectics brought Chuck into an entirely new world, and he reveled in the often gay atmosphere. He became far more outgoing, far more accessible, and, as Sillman notes, a far better performer: "By the time the show opened, he was dancing all the way from head to toe."[31]

The transformation wasn't reflected in Walters's salary—a mere dollar a week during rehearsal—but even that sum seemed a gold mine to the unemployed Tyrone Power. "He was really starving," said Walters. "I wasn't doing too good either, but he was really on his ass. As we would learn the routines, I would teach them to him. He wasn't a dancer, but he was young and energetic and attractive. As we were rehearsing, I found they needed another kid in the chorus. I said I had a friend who knows the routines."[32] It took very little to convince Sillman to hire the dark beauty and later retain him as his personal chauffeur. "He couldn't sing, he couldn't dance, and he couldn't act," said Sillman. "But he was positively beautiful."[33]

Chuck and Ty carpooled daily to the Highland Avenue rehearsal hall and spent weekends in Anaheim. On occasion Ty would bring along his girlfriend, and even though this was 1933, Joe and Winifred were apparently open to the idea of the young couple sleeping together. "We were just kids," Walters would laugh. "How broadminded my parents must have been to let them share a room."[34]

Despite the goodwill of the cast, *Low and Behold* almost closed before it opened. The Depression by now had permeated the country, and the usually affluent Pasadena Playhouse had to scrape together the means for the show's gala opening on May 16, 1933. Movie favorites Tom Brown, Anita Louise, and Frank Morgan, along with M-G-M director Edmund Goulding, were on hand to enjoy Sillman's pastiche, and the *Los Angeles Times* declared the production "an arresting if not always attractive" evening's entertainment.[35] The revue was retained for a three-week run.

Chuck appeared in fifteen of the nearly forty sequences, including a novelty that opened the show, "Things They Told Us Not to Do in Pasadena." For this he joined Thompson and Power as they humorously demonstrated all that was forbidden. While not singled out by the California critics, Walters won a positive response from his co-workers, whose professional opinion mattered most. He had reason to believe he had found his niche.

2

A "New Face" in Town

Flush with moderate success (and despite Pasadena Playhouse opposition), Sillman took his *Low and Behold* to the Hollywood Music Box. He justified the move by saying that the new venue would give the underpaid performers "their only chance to show their talents to production and casting agents" in Los Angeles.[1] Soon after, Kay Thompson warned that she would remove herself from the encore engagement if people didn't stop saying "hell" and "God damn" around her. "When I asked her what the hell had gotten into her," Sillman recalled, "she quit."[2] Chuck and Ty almost followed suit when offered full scholarships by the Pasadena Playhouse, then one of the finest dramatic schools on the West Coast. "We talked about accepting them," Walters recalled, "but neither Ty nor I could wait that long. We were both too ambitious—we had to make a career, and we had to get going."[3]

Low and Behold reopened July 10, 1933. If it was a modest hit at the Playhouse, the revue proved a major flop at the Music Box. Sillman remembered that for five lonely weeks, the production "drew friendly relatives and strays from the street who could be persuaded to come in and sit down."[4] Given the lack of interest from casting agents, Walters decided to self-promote. He became a regular at the Musso and Frank Grill, a famed movie industry watering hole not far from the theater.

"Chuck said he loved going to Musso and Frank," remembers Mary Whiteley, later Walters's assistant when he returned to USC to teach in the early 1980s. But with a weekly salary of $8.92, "he couldn't afford the place. All week he would save his money, and on Sundays he'd go and get the cheapest item on the menu, which at that time was flannel cakes. He'd stay for hours eating these flannel cakes just hoping to get noticed."[5] Luckily, *Low and Behold* performer Teddy Hart had a munificent older brother named Larry who could lend support.

At that time, Broadway lyricist Lorenz "Larry" Hart was dutifully writing movie scores with melodist Richard Rodgers at M-G-M. From these rigors the thriving Los Angeles nightlife became a necessary escape. Hart, though privately uncomfortable with his homosexuality, was the life of the party and the soul of generosity when out on the town with pretty young men. Chuck and Ty frequently joined his entourage, as did others from *Low and Behold*. They were escorted after the show to the nearby Christie Hotel, where female impersonator Jean Malin—a favorite of the lyricist's—appeared nightly at the New Yorker club. The late-night revelry reportedly continued either at Malin's home or at the Malibu beach house of movie actor Lew Cody. "They weren't orgies," noted a male dancer who often accompanied Hart. "Nobody got raped. . . . If someone showed up and was shocked by what was going on, he left."[6] Such clandestine evenings, however, were not to be discussed the next day. Per one *Low and Behold* cast member, "Most of the dancers must have known that the people they worked with were also gay. But there was a paranoia at the time . . . you played it straight."[7]

Whatever the after-hours socializing, Chuck never lost sight of his new career path, which he now hoped would lead to the screen. "I wanted to go to M-G-M," he admitted. "For me, there weren't any other studios." The "dream factory" of Louis B. Mayer and Irving Thalberg then was the most successful studio in Hollywood and the only one making a profit—nearly $8 million in 1933. In early August, Walters thought he'd won his chance. It's now impossible to determine if his screen test was arranged by Larry Hart or came through Sillman's connections with M-G-M directors George Cukor and Edmund Goulding. (In 1933, Metro doors opened to Sillman—who appeared in the Jean Harlow comedy *Bombshell*—and to the Rocky Twins, who ended up in Goulding's *Blondie of the Follies* with Marion Davies.) Unfortunately, Chuck's test with *Low and Behold* co-star Peggy Neary yielded no contract for either dancer, prompting Walters to consider other means of gate-crashing.

"My whole reason for going to New York in the first place," he said, "[was] that this was the time you had to be discovered in New York to be *brought* to Hollywood."

Leonard Sillman was poised to help. *Low and Behold* may have misfired in Los Angeles, but it could also boast an impressive last-minute attendee. "In the final week," recounted Sillman, "I found out the great Lee Shubert, high mogul of the Broadway theater, was in town. I did not know the man, but . . . I called him and invited him to the show. Contrary to the warnings of his doctor, who *had* seen the show, he came."[8] Afterward Shubert made an unexpected visit backstage and offered to back a Broadway transfer. Sillman later acknowledged, "The one member of the cast I wanted in the New York production was Chuck Walters . . . and I arranged for him to meet us [there]."[9]

Larry Hart, true to form, took it upon himself to lend an additional hand. Walters recalled, "Larry was very sweet and gave me a letter of introduction to John Murray Anderson," one of the most respected director-producers of musical extravaganza.

Whether the journey east included (as Chuck liked to claim) weeks of "thumbing my way across country" is unclear, but there is little doubt as to his determination.[10]

"I went to New York, with about ten letters of introduction—period," he said later. "Didn't know a soul. *From Anaheim!* When people say, 'If I could be twenty-one again and know what I know today . . .' And I say, if you were twenty-one and knew what you knew today—the luck [needed], and being at the right places—you wouldn't want to get out of bed!"

Despite a severely fractured economy, there was still much advance excitement about the 1933 autumn season. Between September and December, Broadway would boast the premieres of *As Thousands Cheer*, in which tunesmith Irving Berlin joined scenarist Moss Hart to bring to life the headlines of the day; *Ah, Wilderness!*, playwright Eugene O'Neill's paean to small-town Main Street; *Roberta*, Jerome Kern and Oscar Hammerstein II's musical comedy take on couture; and *Let 'Em Eat Cake*, the Gershwin brothers' sequel to their Pulitzer Prize–winning *Of Thee I Sing*. Star vehicles for women included Helen Hayes's royal transformation in *Mary of Scotland* and Miriam Hopkins's resurrection of the Old South in *Jezebel*.

The latest installment of the *Ziegfeld Follies* raised its own expectations. This would be the first edition of the long-established revue since the death of impresario Florenz Ziegfeld in 1932. Fortunately, the show was now under the direction of John Murray Anderson. Holding Lorenz Hart's letter of introduction, Walters made his way to the Winter Garden. "I just bought a record, rented a portable phonograph, and danced for him. Afterward, John Murray asked, 'Have you got enough money to get home? Back to wherever it is?' I said, 'No, Mr. Anderson,' which was true. He said, 'Well, I wouldn't give you a job in one of my choruses. . . . Either go home or take some lessons.' And he walked out." (In later years Walters would shake his head in embarrassment. "How could I have *dared* to present myself only knowing how to get by?") Worse, it soon became obvious that letters of introduction helped open doors on Broadway but were no guarantee of employment. "I was so 'new,'" he said, "that when I finally began to get auditions, I was afraid to go to them. I was afraid that I wouldn't know what to do."[11]

Walters was ready to cut his losses, but his attitude changed when Sillman arrived in town. "Chuck had been out of my clutches," said the director. "I was twenty-two and Chuck was about twenty-one, but I considered him my protégé. I'd spent long hours working with Chuck, and I had no intention of seeing those hours go to waste."[12] (In truth, their ages were a bit more advanced: twenty-five and twenty-two, respectively.) The two took a room together at the Algonquin Hotel.

Musical revues remained popular in the 1930s; in addition to the *Follies,* audiences could enjoy *Earl Carroll's Vanities, George White's Scandals,* and the Shuberts' *Passing Show.* Sillman knew he had to distance his approach to song and satire from these more lavish spectacles. Envisioning himself as a sort of modern-day Svengali, he planned to cast only "unfamiliar" young performers, polishing their fresh talent and introducing them as his "New Faces." Walters had his ticket to Broadway.

As ever in New York, there were plenty of new faces looking for work. An unknown arrived to audition and announced himself as Henry Fonda. "He had to spell it for us," Sillman later said, "because none of us had ever heard the name before."[13] Chuck was paired with a pixyish girl whose comical name, Imogene Coca, later became synonymous with American comedy when she starred on the 1950s television program *Your Show of Shows.*

Rehearsals for *New Faces of 1934* began on December 12, 1933, in a small apartment at 427½ East Fifty-Second Street. Three days later, the complaints of neighbors forced the troupe to relocate to the living room of a cast member's mother at 1 Gramercy Park. The setting didn't matter. Creativity overflowed, and cockeyed songs, dances, and burlesques were fashioned. One sketch spoofed Walt Disney's then popular Three Little Pigs in their attempts to perform the dramatic *Ah, Wilderness!* and *Tobacco Road;* another offered a sly send-up of a movie star's rumored temperament in "Katharine Hepburn Gets in the Mood for *Little Women.*"

Despite the imagination on display, Lee Shubert unexpectedly pulled out. This forced the determined company into a winter of arduous backers' auditions—a reported 137 in all. A new angel finally hovered when Sillman enlisted funds from former movie actress Mary Pickford. ("Not for nothing was she known as 'America's Sweetheart,'" enthused Sillman.)[14] But it all came together when Broadway entrepreneur Charles Dillingham ("that great gentleman") lent his support—and his name.[15]

For Walters, this production process provided a crash course in the tenacity and joint effort required to mount a Broadway show. "If you can't go through the front door," he would later optimistically reflect, "go around to the side door—or use the back door. Or go underground!"[16]

An easygoing friendship developed between Walters and Coca during *New Faces* rehearsals. When watching her perform, he marveled that her seemingly timid offstage persona was supplanted by a knock-down, drag-out comic. "[Imogene] was a *helluva* actress and comedian," Walters commended. Working opposite her, he witnessed how Coca got around her limited terpsichorean ability by mimicking popular dancers of the day: "She could make herself look dandy." The result was a theatrical ruse, but an entirely effective one. It proved a valuable lesson in how imitation could help an untrained performer give the illusion of proper movement. In future years as a dance director, Chuck would impart this trick to a wide assortment of actors of varying capabilities.

Walters and Coca partnered for three *New Faces* routines, but the enduring symbol of their association was a camel's hair coat. Walters had purchased the fashionable full-length garment to ward off the cold of his first New York winter, but he soon deemed it as thin "as my skinny California blood." In rehearsal, however, the man-sized garment proved to be an effective coverlet for his elfin partner. Sillman noted, "It was a cold, damp, bitter day, and nothing gets colder, damper, and more bitter than an empty stage." Coca borrowed Walters's coat against the chill, and in the process of improvising dance steps with Marvin Lawlor and Alan Handley, she looked every bit the wide-eyed little girl enveloped in Daddy's clothing. Sillman was delighted by Coca's attire and told the trio he had four spots where the curtain would have to close while scenery was changed. To fill the time, they would perform out front. "Imogene, you'll wear that coat," he instructed.

Chuck was dumbfounded. "That's my only one!" he shouted.

Sillman shot back, "I'll rent it."[17]

Much to the performers' surprise, their director's plan worked beautifully. "[On] opening night," Coca explained, "[the three of us] went out in a file, turned, faced the audience—no expression at all—did these little steps, walked off. And there was a kind of murmur. Second time we came on in the first act, the audience started to laugh. They applauded when we left. The third time they applauded our entrance. And the fourth time—wang! We were big hits. And . . . that was really literally doing nothing."[18] A few years later, Coca would be hailed for doing a mock strip-tease while bundled tightly in a long woolen overcoat. It became a trademark.

New Faces of 1934 premiered at the Fulton Theatre on March 14, 1934. According to Sillman, it "was one of the most amazing openings that Broadway ever had. One-third of the audience came to laugh, knowing of this growing legend of these twenty-two kids giving hundreds of auditions. Another third came out of respect to Charles Dillingham, and the other third were just plain theatre-goers. Before five minutes [had passed], the show was in. I have never . . . heard an audience go so completely berserk as that one did. In the front row sat Katharine Hepburn, Mary Pickford, Louis Bromfield, Tallulah Bankhead, Libby Holman and many others. Tallulah was so excited that she smoked through the entire performance without knowing it."[19]

Certainly some of the crowd's jubilation grew from their first exposure to the talented new faces themselves. In the show's *Playbill*, Sillman replaced the customary "Who's Who?" with "Who's *New*?" and detailed the origins of each debuting artist. He kidded the tanned Walters for having "a face so new that it still bears Hollywood pallor."[20]

In its review, the *New York Sun* observed that "a deliriously responsive audience rewarded the slightest flicker on the stage with screams of delight, and no performer could so much as make his entrance without bringing down the roof."[21] The equally enraptured *New York Evening Journal* critic John Anderson proclaimed, "These youngsters may not be the best dancers and singers in town, but they do sing and dance violently, as if they were actually interested in entertaining the audience."[22] Robert Garland from the *New York World-Telegram* bestowed backhanded approval on Coca and Walters, deciding they "dance effectively. It is a pity they see fit to sing."[23] Despite the minor swipe, the duo's accomplishment had been singled out.

Word of mouth kept *New Faces* playing for a respectable 149 performances, until it was closed by the early summer heat. Never knowing when to quit, Sillman relocated his opus to the Castle Theater, a dying movie house on the boardwalk in Long Beach. For much of August 1934, Walters and company played to beachcombers and drifters, a situation patently reminiscent of the empty houses that had greeted *Low and Behold* in Hollywood. "It was there, for the history books," Sillman observes, "that the first *New Faces* really died—not on the stage of the Fulton in New York, but in a sick nickelodeon somewhere by the beautiful sea on Long Island."[24]

Pure love of the theater fueled both *New Faces of 1934* and Chuck Walters. His Broadway baptism had exposed him to the perseverance the profession required. Years later, in a majority of his movies, he would champion theatrical dreamers like his *New Faces* castmates, showcasing their optimism, unbending persistence, and backstage travail.

Keeping company with brilliant members of the opposite sex was a significant feature of Charles Walters's life. He didn't tolerate show-offs, temperament, or pretension, but if a woman possessed intelligence, genuine talent, and a sense of humor, he was hers for the duration. In Pasadena, Kay Thompson matched this template, as did Imogene Coca in New York. (Later there would be Audrey Christie, Gloria Swanson, Lucille Ball, Nancy Walker, Joan Crawford, and Judy Garland.) When Sillman hired Dorothy Kennedy Fox as one of Broadway's *New Faces*, Walters was instantly drawn.

A dark and slender St. Louis girl, Fox initially was bent on becoming a "dance artiste." She took seriously her studies with the Denishawn School, Isadora Duncan, Mary Wigman, and Martha Graham but could also delightedly use what she learned to poke fun at what she called the "grab-at-a-vase" style of interpretive movement.

So immediate and strong was the Walters-Fox rapport that the two decided to combine talents as a dance team, and once *New Faces* closed, they swung into action. The repeal of Prohibition in December 1933 meant the hasty reinstatement of nightclubs in major hotels, many vying for promising acts. After fourteen years of speakeasies and vaudeville, however, the cabaret terrain was forgotten territory. "Everybody said we were crazy [to go that route]," Dorothy remarked a few years later, "but we worked hard."[25] (At this point—convinced the name "Fox and Walters" had harmonious appeal—Chuck once and for all adopted a final *s* for his surname. He was now Charles Walters.)

Tryout gigs led the duo to "Philadelphia for our first *real* job" at Howard Lanin's Town Club.[26] Shortly thereafter, Fox and Walters returned to Sillman (as did Imogene Coca) for his prophetically titled *Fools Rush In*. This calamitous summer revue was first presented aboard the Floating Theater "Venture," a Mississippi riverboat facsimile that traveled the often tempestuous Long Island Sound. ("We were storm-tossed and seasick and beset by strange hazards of the deep," moaned Sillman.) In autumn 1934, the company launched rehearsals and revisions in Manhattan. Billed as a "new *intimate* revue," *Fools* attempted forty-eight numbers over the course of two protracted acts.

Near the top of the show, Walters reunited with Coca for "I Want to Dance," but he stayed at Dorothy's side for the remainder of the presentation. Then, he recalled, "they needed a spot 'in one' [i.e., before the closed downstage traveler curtain] for a scene change. Leonard said, 'I think I'll give Chuck a solo.' A boy out of the chorus getting a solo—it was the thrill of my life. Rehearsing, rehearsing, rehearsing, and then Leonard said, 'I've got a brilliant idea. I think you should be in all black, black curtain, black hood, and we'll illuminate just your shoes and put a strobe light on them. It'll be just feet flying around.' Well, I was heartbroken, because as a personality, I couldn't smile and be charming!"

With an announced opening on December 25, 1934, *Fools* found itself in direct competition with the premieres of three other shows. Sillman wanted his work observed by the first-string critics, and rather than struggle against such a schedule, he unwisely invited reviewers to a December 23 run-through. It proved disastrous, with Walters's solo a major misfire. Sabotaged by an inattentive lighting man who failed to turn on the strobe, Walters would later laugh at the indignity, summing up his first Broadway solo as "a five minute lull—*in one!*"

By Christmas night—and after some salient doctoring by Moss Hart—*Fools Rush In* was in fine shape. But reviews described the dress rehearsal, and the show closed fourteen performances later. Smarting over his latest failure, Sillman opted thereafter to play it safe. He relentlessly offered Broadway audiences new editions of *New Faces* in 1936, 1943, 1952, 1956, and 1968. Chuck, however, was a "new face" no more. In later years, he would reconsider Sillman's competence, calling him "impossible—hysterical and a big ham. I [thought] he knew what he was doing. . . . [L]ooking back, I'm not so sure."

19

Nevertheless, the two remained in sporadic contact. Sillman reminisced with historian Ronald L. Davis about a reunion in 1978, "a big alumni party given for me on the Coast. There was a girl in [*Fools Rush In*] that [Walters] danced with, Dorothy Fox, a wonderful dancer. She was his partner for years, and they hadn't seen each other. She came early, and when he arrived—she had quite a few drinks under her belt—and before I even had a chance to say 'hello' to him, they flew into each other's arms and did a tango dance. She lost her balance, and he fell and hit his head on a huge jardinière [and] cracked his head open! They had to take him to the hospital, and that's the last time I saw Chuck," he recounted.

"He was all right, though."[27]

3

Beginning the Beguine

Fox and Walters wasted no time mourning *Fools Rush In.* Less than two weeks later, in January 1935, they set sail aboard the SS *Statendam,* appearing nightly throughout a West Indies cruise. On their return, they received an invitation to appear at the Versailles, then one of New York's trendiest supper clubs. The duo took private delight in knowing they had auditioned for the swanky establishment in a wardrobe priced at no more than twenty-five dollars. "My gown," said Fox, "cost exactly seventy-five cents."[1]

By a bit of luck, they had already met Virginia Volland, future Broadway costume designer of *Sunrise at Campobello* and *A Raisin in the Sun.* Volland had never dressed dancers but was eager to learn. "These youngsters needed a lot of clothes," she wrote later, "had no money, and [asked] could Dorothy pay me off as Versailles paid her? . . . [She said she] needed, to begin with, a long, concealing, and yet fluid and sexy garment that would break away and reveal [her] gorgeous figure hampered by nothing but a minimum of black lace. I said yes, not having the foggiest notion what a breakaway was."[2]

Fox and Walters made their Versailles bow on March 14, 1935, in a set that combined elegance with some subtle cheekiness. Their rather pointed "Serenade to a Wealthy Widow" scored an unexpected hit with the black-tie and ermine-clad audience, and the two-month booking was a triumph.

It also led to one of the most fortuitous encounters of Walters's career, as he and Dorothy were seen by Robert Alton, Broadway's rising—and soon to be busiest—choreographer. Alton was quick to offer Fox and Walters a "specialty" spot in *Parade,* the upcoming political revue he was about to stage for the Theater Guild. "I learned so much from Bob Alton," Walters later praised. "Style . . . fluidity . . . and [he was] so amenable."

Unquestionably, Alton came to wield considerable influence on Chuck's early career, affecting his artistic development and, in time, encouraging and ultimately enabling his choreographic ambitions. Their friendship would extend over twenty years as they collaborated on four Broadway shows and four motion pictures.

Born Robert Alton Hart in Vermont in 1902, Alton was just beginning his active redesign of musical comedy dancing when he and Walters first met. In shows such as *Anything Goes* and *Life Begins at 8:40* (both 1934), Alton rejected old-style line patterns. Instead, he flooded the Broadway stage with movement, "jiving" ballet, refining tap, and swinging modern dance in the process. "Everything we know about staging a musical number," insists venerated Broadway choreographer Donald Saddler, "comes from the work of Robert Alton."[3]

Despite the birth of their son, Alton's three-year marriage to dancer Marjorie Fielding ended in divorce in 1929, most likely because of his homosexuality. (By 1940, Alton was living with dancer Bernard Pearce.) Some journalists since have theorized that the choreographer's initial interest in Walters was romantic as well, although this remains speculative. "They were close, absolutely," asserts dancer Don Liberto. "Whether there was anything more, who knows?"[4]

Intimate or not, Alton and Walters shared an intense camaraderie. Chuck enjoyed the older choreographer's campy sense of humor and remained in awe of his agility—as did most who worked with him. "Bob Alton used to make me so mad," laughs Liberto. "I don't know if he ever warmed up, but he'd come to rehearsal and would say, 'I want your leg like this,' and his leg would go up higher than the girls' legs!"[5] Dancer Lewis Turner retains similar fond memories of Alton's legendary limberness: "When everybody else was exhausted, he would take his right foot in his hand, lift it above his head, and say, "All right, everybody do *this*."[6]

While revues such as *New Faces* and *Fools Rush In* offered pure escapism for Depression-weary audiences, the Theater Guild's *Parade* opted instead for astute social commentary about that turbulent time. Summarizing the end result, Brooks Atkinson at the *New York Times* dismissed the endeavor as "a strange brew of dance abstractions, strident music, and political mummery."[7] Opening May 20, 1935, the show folded one month later. Walters concurred with the disapproving critics, remarking at the time, "Lots of dancers have an idea they have a message. Even ballroom dance teams cherish the curious illusion they are putting over some sort of an idea when they go through a charm routine in a nightclub—all of which seems to me so much horse-feathers. The stage is like any other business, and the function of actors and entertainers is to give the public what it wants, not what they think it ought to have."

Broadway scuttlebutt of this era had barely considered *Parade*. Devotees instead were gripped by rumors of a project being fashioned during a Southern Hemisphere cruise aboard the Cunard Line's *Franconia*. Songwriter Cole Porter, playwright Moss Hart, and actor-director Monty Woolley set sail from New York on January 12, 1935; by the time they returned on May 31, their much-anticipated *Jubilee* had been crafted. "All of a sudden, while I was in *Parade*," remembered Walters, "rumors started that [producer] Sam Harris was out front to see me. Then it was Woolley. Then Porter. Then Hart. Each was out front to see *me*. [Finally,] about three or four weeks later, there are agents at the stage door saying, 'Look, if you sign with me, I think I can get you an audition for *Jubilee*.'"

Confused but curious, Walters knew whom to turn to for information: "The chorus kids get *all* the dirt." Those dancing detectives reported that tap star Paul Draper had been the first choice for *Jubilee*'s juvenile but was being reconsidered because of his unfortunate stutter. Walters himself was in awe of the headliner, insisting Draper was "the most elegant tap dancer" he'd ever seen: "He tapped to Mozart and Brahms, and it had never been done before." Given the circumstances, Chuck found it difficult to believe that he would be considered as an alternative. "Draper was the big hot shot dancer in New York, and I'd only been a dance team!" he marveled.

Disbelief turned to panic when Walters was summoned to the Music Box Theater to meet both Harris and director Woolley. The latter tossed the *Jubilee* script to the dancer, and they adjourned to one of Harris's offices to read through the juvenile's scenes. "He came out," Chuck later recapped, "and in that *Monty Woolley voice,* said, 'He's all right.'"

"Mr. Walters," said Harris, "we'd like you for the part of Prince James and can offer $350 a week." There was a considerable pause, after which Chuck quietly declined. "I'm very sorry, but I have a partner, and it's not fair that I leave her," he told them. "We've worked hard and are doing very well."

Clearly, this was not the reaction Harris had anticipated. He countered, "Well, if you care to split your salary, we'll give your partner a solo spot in the second act."

With that guarantee, Walters signed a contract to appear in one of the most anticipated productions in recent Broadway history. "That one *really* started off my career," he noted.

Dorothy accepted the news graciously. Before *Jubilee* rehearsals began, the two crammed in a series of last-minute engagements, including a return to the Versailles. Hollywood also took notice. Paramount Pictures hired Fox and Walters for its *Big Broadcast of 1936,* a bizarrely plotted catch-all in which George Burns and Gracie Allen try to sell a television set stored inside a suitcase. "When the picture was finished there was no picture," explained assistant director Arthur Jacobson. "It was a lemon. [Producer] Barney Glazer came up with the idea that to save the picture we'd find the best acts we could, put them on that television thing, and when the picture started to sag, [we'd] cut to that. They signed up Ray Noble and His Orchestra, who in those days were *it.* We got Amos 'n' Andy, and Fox and Walters, a great dance team. . . . In order to do this, we all had to go to New York. Those people could not leave their jobs and fly [to California]."[8]

Fox and Walters were stylishly showcased for their film debut—glossy parquet floor below, crystal chandeliers above. To their disappointment, their classy pas de deux failed to make the movie's final cut. But with dance sequences supplied by Bill Robinson, the Nicholas Brothers, and the ensembles of LeRoy Prinz, there simply may have been too much Terpsichore for one Burns and Allen comedy to accommodate.

When the rehearsals for *Jubilee* began, the chorus members went through their paces at the Imperial (where the show would premiere), while the principals were ensconced at the adjacent Music Box. Sitting at the piano was the fashionable Porter ("very cold," per Chuck), while Woolley ("very pompous and ominous") paced the aisles. Working alongside Melville Cooper, Margaret Adams, and the irrepressible Mary Boland in the musical, in which Porter's music blended seamlessly with Hart's story about a quirky royal family who flee castle life to pursue some incognito adventuring, Walters remained in a state of anxiety. "I'd never *really* sung!" he'd later confess. "[Dorothy and I] were what you call a 'dumb act': you just dance—no singing, no acting. You *just dance.*" Adding to his insecurity, he now was paired with M-G-M movie starlet June Knight, playing the chanteuse who snares herself a prince.[9]

For the minor role of Prince Peter, producers engaged the beautiful and beautifully mannered fifteen-year-old Montgomery Clift. Offstage, the adolescent actor shadowed his "older brother" Walters, which initially pleased mother Sunny Clift. "[Monty] and his mother latched onto me," Walters recalled, "and she said to Monty, 'I want you to be just like Chuck. That's what I want you to be like.'"[10] Sunny Clift eventually reconsidered her instruction, fearing that her impressionable son was becoming too enamored of the attractive older man.

Prior to that, Walters had offered career advice to young Monty. "Take dancing lessons, take singing lessons, take acting lessons," he counseled. "Take it all. It doesn't matter if you use it. It's exercise. It's part of your business." Later, Chuck would find great amusement in his own hypocrisy: "[Meanwhile,] *I'm* not doing anything, you know. I'm [just] doing eight shows a week. But I could tell *others* what to do!"

He could have heeded his own counsel, as Chuck admittedly lacked acting ability. "When I started as an actor, *nobody* helped me, and I was left floundering. I'd say [my line], 'Oh, Mother, I think it would be a marvelous idea to go to Feathermore' and [then] would think, 'Now, I haven't got anything to say for about a minute-and-a-half.' So I'd be scratching my ass, or thinking what I'm going to have for dinner, and, oh, I have another line. [Then I'd] go back into my disdainful coma." Knight, groomed by Metro's stellar training, privately reminded her "prince" to stay present and sustain the scene. "I thought, 'Now why wouldn't someone [else] tell me that. Moss Hart . . . or Monty Woolley? Why wouldn't they help me?'" Walters quickly gathered that most directors did not teach actors to act.

Mercifully, he felt more at home in dance rehearsal with choreographer Albertina Rasch. Though renowned for her popular Hollywood and Broadway ballet troupe—which largely consisted of chorines en pointe—Rasch also valued technique and encouraged personality. Walters earned both her attention and her allegiance. "When I say I never had a dancing lesson," he'd later clarify, "well, I was getting paid, per se, for lessons [by] Rasch and [later] George Balanchine."[11]

Jubilee would be the first of four major Broadway or Hollywood musicals to connect Walters and Cole Porter. As Prince James, Chuck introduced three original Porter compositions. "A Picture of Me Without You" was staged as a post-coital dance with Knight, the duo clad in pajamas.[12] More notably, "Just One of Those Things" dramatized the prince's farewell to his new playmate. Rasch staged the lovers' fragile final moments rather melodramatically, as the despairing Knight attempted to disengage from and flee her partner. (Despite the efforts of choreographer and dancers, "Just One of Those Things" took years to become a standard song. Critic Robert Garland—who'd earlier dismissed Walters's warbling in *New Faces*—complained in his review of *Jubilee:* "With no singer who can sing at the Imperial Theatre, there is no whistle-as-you-walk-out melody ripe for its pucker-up endeavors."[13] On the other hand, columnist Elita Wilson judged Walters "a divine dancer with a surprisingly pleasant singing voice.")[14]

The third Knight-Walters offering was hailed as *Jubilee*'s intoxicating masterwork. Rasch, perhaps hesitant about staging a too-seductive pas de deux, ceded the choreographic reins for "Begin the Beguine" to Tony De Marco and his wife, Renee, arguably the best exhibition dancers in their field. Set in a chic nightclub, "the dance would become one of the memories of the age," states Broadway historian Ethan Mordden, "choreography in art deco."[15] De Marco's tailored movement followed Porter's melodic lead, building to emotional peaks and falling back to virtual stillness. The climax saw Walters and Knight perform a series of syncopated arm movements, and the vitality of their execution brought spontaneous applause, both onstage from club onlookers and from the actual audience. Future songwriter Ralph Blane, though several years away from his own professional collaboration with Chuck, made repeated visits to the Imperial to enjoy "Begin the Beguine," later commenting, "It was such a *spectacular* number."[16]

In mid-September the *Jubilee* cavalcade traveled to Boston for a warmly received tryout. ("Charles Walters is well-cast as the prince," said a local paper, "and unloads a few steps that make his audience want more.")[17] Word of mouth was good and brought the industry's own imperial brigade out in full force for the show's October 12 opening in New York. "Not since 1929 [has] there been such a convocation of ermine, mink, Russian sable, diamond dog collars and star sapphires," offered radio commentator Mary Margaret McBride.[18] Attendees included Lillian Gish, Helen Hayes, Marilyn Miller, Laurette Taylor, Edna Ferber, Tallulah Bankhead, Jerome Kern, Franchot Tone, Sophie Tucker, George Burns and Gracie Allen, George S. Kaufman, and Joan Crawford arm in arm with Loew's president Nicholas Schenk.

"[For me], the opening night of *Jubilee* will remain a terror forever," Walters confessed. "I got out on the stage, my feet moved in correct rhythm, but my jaw was frozen. I remember the stage manager gave me a ghastly grin from the wings, and after a few parched syllables, I got into my stride. I think it was a vision of returning to the West Coast that finally straightened me out."[19]

The primarily positive reviews effusively praised Mary Boland and accorded Chuck approving nods. John Anderson noted that "[Walters] dances with extraordinary agility and good humor,"[20] while another critique likened his "ease and skill" to that "of an Astaire."[21] The less declarative Brooks Atkinson simply labeled him "a modest prince,"[22] while the *Daily News* seemed half impressed: "Walters . . . dances better than he reads lines."[23] "Begin the Beguine," on the other hand, garnered universal raves. The *Hollywood Reporter* proclaimed it a "sensation" and went on to say, "[As] executed by Knight and Walters, it is a contagious rhythm, and the terpsichoreans stopped the show with it."[24] *Women's Wear Daily* frankly advised its readers that the sequence alone was "worth the price of admission."[25]

Every critical comment, however, paled by comparison to the *New York Times*'s reassessment when its reviewer returned to *Jubilee* several months later: "Mr. Walters is certainly to be counted among the best of the light-footed gentry of the revue world. He lifts what might easily be mere hoofing into the precincts of excellent theatrical art by reason of the very simple fact that he is a born dancer."[26]

4

The Show Is On

Reveling in his newfound celebrity, Walters began 1936 at socialite Elsa Maxwell's New Year's masquerade ball at the Waldorf-Astoria. He appeared with Knight on a bill that additionally featured Beatrice Lillie, Ray Bolger, and Adele Astaire. It was obvious to him just how far he had traveled since his Leonard Sillman days.

Throughout the five-month run of *Jubilee,* Fox and Walters did some moonlighting as well. They were praised by the *Times* as having "made such sensational strides in the past year," and they were the final dancers to appear at the Central Park Casino before it was replaced by a playground.[1] Yet, busy as Walters had become, his world wasn't all work. He had met and fallen for John Darrow, ultimately the most important man in his life.

A former movie actor, Darrow was an imposing presence. As much athlete as matinee idol in appearance, he possessed wavy black hair, a broad jaw, and arched eyebrows that framed smiling eyes. Seven years Chuck's senior, he was born Henry L. Simpson on July 14, 1904, in Leonia, New Jersey. His two years of high school in New York segued into work in Washington, D.C., where he became known as "the handsomest page-boy in the Capitol."[2] After minor stage success, Darrow traveled to Hollywood, where his older brother Allan was already working as an actor. Paramount Pictures grabbed John for its silent feature *The High School Hero* (1927), and seven films and four years later, he had one of his best opportunities as a young German in the acclaimed war saga *Hell's Angels.* Director Howard Hughes had noticed John and "made sure there were an extraordinary number of body and face shots of [the] glowing Adonis," notes Hughes biographer Charles Higham. "Given the fact that Darrow was a magnificent physical specimen, clear-skinned, broadshouldered, muscular, an American dream of masculinity, Hughes, as a bisexual, would have to have been superhuman to have resisted this golden youth."[3]

Darrow then passed from studio to studio in a string of forgettable pictures. He managed, however, to maintain a viable Hollywood presence through his deepening friendship with director George Cukor. Ever the host, Cukor had amassed a good-looking mélange of Movieland's most charming "confirmed bachelors," and his Sunday afternoon soirees became the stuff of whispered conversation throughout the industry. (The gossip later grew into Hollywood legend.) Comparatively quickly, John discovered a classic truism: instant fame built on youthful looks is fleeting. He appeared in five inconsequential films in 1935, then abandoned his performing career after receiving tenth billing in Paramount's *Annapolis Farewell.*

Darrow was savvy enough, however, to see who was making money in the industry. Taking lessons learned as a working actor, John moved back to New York and swiftly became a respected and successful talent agent. His early list of clients ranged from choreographer Alton to designer Raoul Pène Du Bois and actor William Eythe. Darrow also signed a disciplined young hoofer from Pittsburgh and planned to rename him Frank Black. But Gene Kelly insisted his own name was good enough.

"John," says dancer Don Liberto, "helped launch the careers of many. He was certainly beneficial to Chuck, who always seemed to have work."[4] Whether they first met professionally or socially is uncertain, but Darrow and Walters began a committed relationship about which they were comparatively unguarded. Such candor was rare, even within the liberal New York theater circles of the 1930s.

Jubilee played its 169th and final performance on March 7, 1936, and the end of the show also marked the end of Fox and Walters. Dorothy launched a solo career, while Chuck (with John) set sail in June aboard the SS *Europa.* He'd accepted an offer from young Romanian producer Felix Ferry, whose self-referentially titled *Ferry Tales of 1936* was London-bound with a multi-star cast. "It was my first trip to Europe," Walters recalled, "and I didn't see a thing. I went from the ship into rehearsal and was sailing back almost before I could realize that I had been there!"[5]

During the show's Manchester tryout, he and co-stars Ruth Etting, Lupe Velez, Lou Holtz, Ford "Buck" Washington and John Bubbles (aka "Buck and Bubbles"), and Dorothy Dare learned that the inexperienced Ferry had exhausted an ample budget on the extravagant Marcel Vertes production design. Key financial backer James Donahue, a Woolworth heir, temporarily closed his wallet, and salaries went unpaid. Etting wasted no time before sniping to the press, "Only little birdies sing for free," but Walters remained silently annoyed about Ferry's fiscal mismanagement, learning a lesson in the process.[6] A budget, he'd later say, was something to be respected. "I wasn't extravagant with my own money, so I was that much more careful with somebody else's," he remarked. (It was a trait that would eventually endear him to theatrical producers and film moguls alike.)

On October 2, 1936—without the benefit of an onstage rehearsal—the retitled *Transatlantic Rhythm* premiered at London's Adelphi Theater. A mob of international journalists joined the capacity audience, intrigued by reports of unpaid American performers. As the cast stood waiting for the (late) curtain to rise, they watched as the wings became "crammed with milling crowds of the non-professionally curious" as well as scrambling stagehands and electricians.[7] The inherent absurdity of the situation was not lost on the bemused Walters, especially when the peppery Velez sprang onto a chair and let loose with a chorus of "Ah, Sweet Mystery of Life" to calm the throng.

International press reported the drama ("J. P. Donahue's London Revue Opens in Rage," screamed the *New York Herald Tribune*),[8] while the *London Times* more fairly termed *Transatlantic Rhythm* "brilliantly hollow entertainment. Among masses of elaborate scenery lurked tolerably good music hall turns, but it always seemed those concerned in these turns would be more amusing if left entirely to their native resources."[9] Such comment sparked yet another realization in Walters: no amount of decor could substitute for talent. He nevertheless won healthy applause for "The Man Who Broke the Bank at Monte Carlo" and his turn as Pierrot opposite Etting's Moon in "Finding You—Losing You." When Etting made good her threat to return to America after opening night, Ferry filled time with a Walters-Velez comedy sketch that had been banned on moral grounds by Manchester authorities. Their "America's Sweethearts" satirized a movie star couple whose vanity-driven marital problems become the responsibility of their producer. The Lord Chamberlain's office in London cleared the sequence for reinstatement pending modifications that promoted the sanctity of marriage.

Despite everyone's best efforts to keep the show afloat, the cast members found themselves sailing home on October 15. Plans for a New

York run were scrapped, and—wiser if not richer—a frustrated Walters left London without having had the grand European adventure he'd anticipated. He and John continued to the West Coast aboard the SS *California,* anticipating visits to Anaheim and gatherings of John's Hollywood friends.

The vacation was abruptly truncated, however, when Walters was summoned to *The Show Is On,* already in previews in Boston. Wunderkind Vincente Minnelli had directed and designed the revue; its stars were the broad and bawdy Beatrice Lillie and Bert Lahr. Despite their talents, something more was needed, and choreographer Alton suggested Chuck. (Columnist Lucius Beebe dryly commented, "Technological unemployment has not, it would seem from Mr. Walters' record, extended itself to the song-and-dance field.")[10]

Chuck flew from L.A. to Boston in early November. By the time the show reached Washington, he was onstage demonstrating his rapid assimilation of Alton's philosophies—in particular, the insistence that movement match character. "Bob could give you the simplest step in the world," remembers Don Liberto, "but he would say, 'Put your arms this way' and 'Put your head that way,' and you would become a character. Plus Bob was definitely fast. I don't know if he got ideas at home, at night before he came to rehearsal, or whether ideas just occurred to him. But he never seemed to hesitate. Never. He would start setting steps, and all of a sudden, something would happen, and he'd get an inspiration or maybe he'd change what he had in mind. But he didn't say, 'Let's try this.' He just knew what to do."[11]

Beyond his creativity and speed, Alton had the ability to inspire confidence. It was another lesson learned: to be a good choreographer, Walters observed, one must first be a good teacher.

Thanks to Alton's staging, Chuck proved to be a minor sensation in *The Show Is On,* especially when he and pert Mitzi Mayfair introduced the breakout hit "Little Old Lady." The otherwise modest Hoagy Carmichael and Stanley Adams tune was presented in English music hall fashion (a Minnelli conception), with Walters and Mayfair sporting gray wigs. To counterbalance the lavender and lace of the lyric, Alton cast Chuck as a spirited geriatric, performing the Suzy Q around his partner. The enormous popularity of "Little Old Lady" was evidenced in the New York Telephone Company's full-page advertisement of reduced rates for Mother's Day 1937. Its main graphic depicted a silver-haired Mayfair delightedly clutching a bouquet and smiling at Walters as he croons, "You're just like that Little Old Lady I hold dear to me."[12]

Under Alton's tutelage, Chuck had matured into a compelling performer, both technically and creatively. His success in *The Show Is On* made hot copy for theater columnists, and it gave Chuck the opportunity to verbalize his newfound ambitions:

> I have watched stage dancing now for some few years and have come to the conclusion that a clever synthesis of the various forms—tap, specialty, ballet—would prove a striking novelty. This may sound odd at first, but consider: The specialty and tap are accentuated. Ballet calls for an expression more exclusively occupied with the waist up—the arms, upper torso, and head. Then there is the modern dance which creates contradictions of movement—for instance, the arms move left as the body sways to the right. Without confusing anyone, let us assume a dancer versed in all three forms could work out routines combining them all in a startling and pleasing manner. That is the essence of what I should like to do—hope to do—for a revue next fall.[13]

It was an auspicious era for the male musical comedy dancer, with Fred Astaire's cinematic ascendancy spurring both professional opportunity and public fascination. The nimble tapper was flying high after a string of successful film musicals with frequent partner Ginger Rogers; the duo ranked among the top moneymaking stars for 1935, 1936, and 1937 in the *Motion Picture Herald* polls. Never before had a male dancer been so readily accepted as a Hollywood leading man. Walters confirmed, "Astaire was my hero. I loved the way he danced, the way he walked, his entire style." Chuck also marveled at the ingenuity of the routines Astaire created with collaborator Hermes Pan. "I remember rushing straight out of the theater to catch the midnight show of every Astaire-Rogers musical that opened. We all used to go up in the balcony so we could smoke, talk, and dream out loud of going to Hollywood. Van Johnson, Keenan Wynn, Gene Kelly, and Stanley Donen—there were quite a few of us trying to get started in those days." As youngsters, they had scarcely imagined the kind of career path Astaire would pioneer. Now it was a possibility.

Because of Walters's elegant looks, he was frequently questioned by the press about his Hollywood ambitions. He still privately gushed over M-G-M but considered it best not to make such aspirations public. "I would turn down [any] motion picture contract for some years," he declared in March 1937. "I want to remain on the legitimate stage. There are excitement and personal rewards to this work that I should not wish to part from under any circumstance."[14]

Subsequently, the *American Dancer* profiled "the boy who dances with the nonchalant ease of a Fred Astaire and can put over a song in such a way that you understand every word." Titled "One Way to Broadway . . . and No Return to Hollywood for Charles Walters!" the article in the popular magazine mused, "It is something to establish oneself on Broadway in these days of a flash of recognition, then cinema obscurity or oblivion altogether. It is something else to become Broadway's leading musical comedy juvenile with no eye toward tempting Hollywood offers. Charles Walters has done both in the short space of three years."[15] Possibly incited by Darrow's promotion, the *New York Post* confirmed that *The Show Is On*'s featured dancer had "rejected an overture from one of the major studios at present in search of juveniles who have followed the Clifton Webb–Fred Astaire tradition."[16]

Chuck's prudent decision to remain on the New York boards revealed a level of maturity rare in young performers. "I suppose it was a freak," he told yet another journalist from his Winter Garden dressing room,

> but not when the situation is closely examined. First of all, I spent my youth trying to get out of California. Secondly, I like the theater, and Broadway gave me a break. I want more time to get used to the stage boards. Besides, there is something about having a living audience that I like and feel I can do my best work for. Hollywood does need juveniles—and I am twenty-five years of age—but so does Broadway. Maybe after I've played a few more seasons, I'll change my mind, but right now I'm sticking close to the Big Stem. . . . I have prepared a series of new dance routines that are as yet untried, and if some expert opinions can be relied on, they are good Broadway material.[17]

The Show Is On played 236 exultant performances, and its closing on July 17, 1937, left Chuck free to accept his first solo engagement in New York.

His August debut at the stylish Viennese Roof, atop the St. Regis, "gave me a chance to do what I wanted, to try out the sort of steps I wanted to do—to the music I could select."[18] Liberated from the confines of a partnership and guided by his growing understanding of structure and pacing, Walters crafted a personal showcase to exploit his multifaceted personality. *Variety* cheered, "Walters is of the Astaire–Paul Draper school, reminding of both in class and style, doing smooth taps in white tie and tails. A facile performer, working neatly as well, he falls into the 'class' category, and in a svelte setting like the Viennese Roof . . . he's a natural. Besides café and stage work, Walters suggests screen possibilities."[19] Audiences agreed, swept away by Chuck's combination of devil-may-care exterior and refined grace. The St. Regis extended his freshman effort until early October.

Supper clubs such as the Viennese Roof were a magnet for 1930s celebrities who wanted to socialize and be seen. Film star Gloria Swanson, on the other hand, was there to dance. "I never jogged around the Central Park Reservoir in the early morning mists," wrote the actress. "But on plenty of nights you could find me dancing my little feet off at the St. Regis. The room might be crowded, but the floor was a breeze, [and] I went there to get high on dancing."[20]

On one fortunate occasion, Swanson was escorted by Gus Schirmer IV, a castmate of Chuck's from *New Faces of 1934*. The actress admitted, "I never knew or cared what the floor show attraction was, but this night they presented a young handsome dancer who was appearing on Broadway. . . . He was not particularly well-known yet, but I was absolutely floored by his dancing. He was the greatest male dancer I had seen since Fred Astaire."

Captivated by Walters's every move, Swanson grew furious at the upscale audience, which was "doing their usual flirting, talking, drinking, eating and rubber-necking at me." Gus and Gloria took to the floor after Chuck's final bow, but when she saw her young Astaire seated alone at a table, she stopped dancing and asked Gus to invite him to come join them at their table, "so I could apologize on behalf of the audience and tell him how thrilled—and intimidated—I had been by his dancing." After a few moments of conversation, Walters stood up and extended his hand.

"When he asked me to dance," recalled Swanson, "I was excited as I'd been at my first tea dance on Staten Island before the war. [And] when I fell into his arms, he made me feel like Irene Castle. It was eternal love after one chorus of 'Begin the Beguine.' He made me look so good, I forgot about being intimidated by his professionalism. It was fun—until the other dancers began backing off the floor, and *we* became the floor show. Now everybody was paying professional attention, as usual for the wrong reasons.

"Never mind; I had found my maestro."

Chuck made Gloria laugh, and she enthralled him with her feisty determination. Night after night, the new playmates convened and created a sensation: "We would start at the St. Regis. We would dance our little buns off. As soon as the other dancers began to recognize me—and our fun turned into a floor show—we would leave and go someplace else. Sometimes we would dance our way through four or five places in one evening." It was the onset of a lifelong friendship, a never-ending dance. More than forty years later, Swanson was still rhapsodic: "Whenever Chuck and I get back together again on a dance floor, it brings back the New York that I remember and love, as it was between the wars."

After several seasons of nonstop work, Chuck hastened back to California, both for a deserved rest and for a reunion with his partner. Darrow, ever more successful at agenting for the movies, was splitting his time between the coasts, as well as making side jaunts to Atlanta with George Cukor as they scouted potential southern talent for the forthcoming *Gone with the Wind*. "I expected to have about five or six weeks in California," said Chuck. "After ten days, I had to fly back for *Between the Devil*."[21]

"A musical triangle in two acts," the new Howard Dietz/Arthur Schwartz book show had been tailored for Britain's celebrated Jack Buchanan. Its piquant storyline of "marital pluralism" aligned an Englishman (Buchanan), his new French bride (Adele Dixon), and his not-quite-as-dead-as-expected first wife (Evelyn Laye). The racy situation—and a Dietz lyric—gave Buchanan ample opportunity to lament his lot: bigamy "has made a pig o' me," while monogamy "has made a hog o' me."

Walters's motivation for accepting *Devil* was twofold. After recent revue and supper club work, he was delighted to return to the acting role of Buchanan's private secretary. (As Freddie Hill, he would spend the better part of the comedy trying to convince his boss to choose between his wives.) Even better, Chuck would once again be in the company of Bob Alton, who teamed him with vivacious Vilma Ebsen.

It was a transitional time for Ebsen. She had just appeared in M-G-M's *Broadway Melody of 1936* with her younger brother, Buddy—her regular if towering partner. Immediately thereafter the studio dropped her option while retaining his, and Vilma departed for New York. As she put it later, "I was as close to a wreck as you can be. . . . I had lost my identity."[22]

For the pair, Alton staged "You Have Everything" and "I'm Against Rhythm," and Walters was prepared to adapt to her gangly, "eccentric" way of dancing. All went well, he recounted, until her brother "came to see one of the rehearsals. [Afterward] I asked, 'What did Buddy think?'" Rather directly, Vilma replied, "Well, he thinks you're a good dancer; it's too bad you haven't any style."[23]

That crushing appraisal was a blow to Chuck until he read the *Herald Tribune*'s assessment after the show opened on December 22: "Walters has, in emulation of the admired Fred Astaire, evolved his own style, which combines sharpness and lines from the modern with ballet and even tap."[24] He marveled, "'Where?' 'How?' 'What?!' All of a sudden people started telling me, 'Chuck, you have a very good style—we like your *style*.' Well, I had to take that home and chew on it for a week. I finally realized it [had come] by simplification. . . . It's like putting a [scripted] line into your own language [and] not just reading it the way it was written. 'Oh, so *that's* it! What I do easiest, I do best. Very interesting.' I think that's how I evolved."

To celebrate President Roosevelt's birthday week, the entire *Devil* troupe traveled to Washington, D.C., for a special performance of the show on January 28, 1938. Arthur Schwartz composed a new tune, "Command Performance," which Buchanan sang while Walters danced. According to the *Washington Post,* the evening's merits were heightened by "the exceptional abilities in song, dance, and humor of Charles Walters."[25] Chuck was especially pleased that the new number gave him the opportunity to solo once again. Just days before, he'd reflected upon his career to date as half of a duo: "Team work in dancing is very difficult—just as difficult, I should say, as collaboration in writing. Unless one partner absolutely dominates the other, each routine is pretty well-bound to be a compromise; it is neither one thing nor the other. In dancing with another, there is practically no chance for creation nor experiment."[26] He maintained a gentleman's perspective as he further rationalized, "It isn't the actor in me, either, that makes me say that the girl always gets the best of it in a dance. Connoisseurs of dancing know that this is all part of the show. But others—the casual on-lookers—are likely to regard the masculine half of the team as not an altogether necessary evil."[27]

The comments were intended as an honest statement on the plight of the male dancer, but Walters's candor instead became fodder for some of

New York's most blistering columnists. "Girls Are All Right in Certain Places, But Not in Others," read one headline (with the subhead "This Dancer Doesn't Enjoy the Way They Steal All the Attention as Partners").[28] Another offered, "Glamour Girls' Partner Prefers to Dance Alone."[29] The reports even delivered some not-so-subtle jabs at Chuck's masculinity. "Any normal male," one taunted, "would spend moments envying the duties of Charles Walters, since they include dancing with . . . Vilma Ebsen, Mitzi Mayfair, June Knight, Dorothy Fox, and Lupe Velez. Yet for Walters, such occupation is solely in the line of duty and an unenviable task."[30] The journalist then seemed to feel that some clarification was necessary, reassuring readers, "Mr. Walters is far from a woman hater."[31]

Though a fairly blatant misrepresentation of Walters's words, such cryptic editorializing could not have been lost on some metropolitan readers. The implication was clear: Broadway's rising star was a homosexual. These unflattering press reports would fuel Walters's guarded behavior around the media, as well as his future resistance toward interviews, particularly as they pertained to his personal life.

"Well, I certainly knew Chuck and John Darrow were together," offers Don Liberto. "I'd say most of the dancers did, although back then we didn't talk about such things. No, I should say, we didn't talk about such things *very much*. But they were such a striking pair, of course people noticed. And Chuck was positively beaming when John was around."[32]

In December 1937, the couple took their first apartment together—a duplex at 36 East Fortieth Street in the quiet Murray Hill section of Manhattan. Their lack of discretion was atypical. Dancer Richard D'Arcy, longtime companion to scenic designer Oliver Smith, has since pointed out the necessity at the time for same-sex couples to maintain separate addresses: "Oliver lived on Tenth Street. I lived on Tenth Street, but my address was Fifty-Seventh Street. You didn't live in the same apartment, because people would put two and two together. Some things were very undercover. . . . You didn't flaunt things like that. It was the times."[33]

More unorthodox, then, was columnist Lucius Beebe's thorough reportage of the Darrow-Walters living quarters for his *Herald Tribune* readers. "Agreeable premises," Beebe detailed in a July 1938 "Stage Asides,"

> finished with chocolate walls, plum-colored carpets, white woolly string rugs, and zebra-striped sofa pillows reminiscent of El Morocco's motif. It boasts a wide terrace in the rear where

Mr. Walters, clad in only swimming shorts, takes the sun of an afternoon. Its principal *ameublements* are books. There are shelves of them everywhere, and there seems to be a copy of *Gone with the Wind* in every room of the house. There are, too, vast stacks of periodicals. There is an amply stocked portable bar, a dining alcove where he and Mr. Darrow have dinner almost every evening, a brace of bedrooms, the customary kitchen offices, and a dressing room almost as completely stocked with clothes and masculine toilet accessories as is Mr. Walters' dressing room at the theater.[34]

Undoubtedly the well-informed could discern for themselves the exact nature of Chuck and John's domesticity. What Beebe did not mention was the couple's healthy fiscal prosperity. For the 1940 federal census, each claimed earnings above $5,000—Darrow for forty weeks of work as a theatrical agent and Walters for twenty-two as an actor. Both fabricated their ages that year—Darrow claimed thirty, although he was thirty-five, while the twenty-eight-year-old Walters maintained he was a youthful twenty-six. More telling, perhaps, was John's self-description as "head of the household," while Chuck's "relationship to household head" is rather foreshadowingly recorded as "partner."[35]

5

Broadway's "Ranking Dancing Juvenile"

Known to play down his achievements on the New York stage, Walters would later sum up his performing career in a mere eight words: "Season after season, I was young and charming." After patiently listening to Jack Buchanan's marital woes for ninety-three performances, he took his final bow in *Between the Devil* on March 12, 1938. The tepid farce had been moderately endorsed ("They're all like nice people in a nice house at a dull party," wrote critic Ira Wolfert), but after Walters left he immediately began rehearsals for one of the decade's masterworks—a musical with wings.[1]

I Married an Angel marked the third time (and third consecutive spring) that producer Dwight Deere Wiman joined forces with songwriters Richard Rodgers and Lorenz Hart and choreographer George Balanchine. Their previous *On Your Toes* (1936) and *Babes in Arms* (1937) had won unanimous audience approval, and their latest venture was set for May 1938. The score included "Spring Is Here" and "I'll Tell the Man in the Street"; Dennis King, Vivienne Segal, Walter Slezak, and ballerina Vera Zorina led the cast, with Walters and the effervescent Audrey Christie as junior lovers. Jo Mielziner contributed modish scenic design and John Hambleton the ethereal costuming; one and all were impeccably manipulated by first-time musical director Joshua Logan. In the end, *I Married an Angel* proved to be one of those rare musicals that fulfilled the promise of its participants.

Five years had passed since the Hollywood association of Walters and Lorenz Hart, and *Angel* served as a worrisome reunion, thanks to Hart's out-of-control drinking. The lyricist was, said Chuck, "a sweetheart—when sober. I'll never forget our dress rehearsal with orchestra, which went on until about three in the morning. We had people coming on, furniture going off, sets coming on . . . you can imagine the confusion and the noise. But there was snoring in the balcony so loud that we had to stop everything, and people went up to find out who was making so much noise. It was Larry, passed out."

As the title suggests, *I Married an Angel* described the nuptials of a wealthy Budapest banker whose feather-winged deity of a wife manages to offend his phony friends with her divine truthfulness. Walters, playing the role of Peter Mueller (another nimble male secretary), enjoyed working with one of ballet's most influential artists. But he also admitted, "It wasn't until years later that I appreciated who George Balanchine was. Ballet meant nothing to me at the time." Balanchine was still a decade away from co-founding the New York City Ballet, and during *Angel,* Chuck delighted in the classicist's kindly Russian humor. The two maintained a respectful relationship, Walters noted: "I was 'pure musical comedy,' so he didn't give me anything balletic."[2]

Balanchine contributed two extended sequences to the show, prompting *New York Post* critic John Mason Brown to describe the musical as "a fantasy designed for dancers."[3] Walters was exempt from the highbrow "Honeymoon Ballet" but strongly featured in the second act's raucous "At the Roxy Music Hall." A lampoon of an entire Radio City Music Hall spectacular, this blithe parody departed from the plot to deliver pure entertainment. (As Larry Hart reasoned, "You can't keep on writing about old Budapest all night.")[4] Christie opened the mini-revue by musically extolling the merits of lavish movie palaces, and later joined Segal to mock the military precision of the Rockettes in a mechanical kick line à deux. In a faux underwater ballet, Zorina and a corps de ballet kidded the clichéd girl-in-the-oyster extravaganzas. But Walters flew solo in an impersonation of the popular ventriloquist dummy Charlie McCarthy. (Edgar Bergen and his wooden sidekick were then all the rage on radio.) As seen in fragmentary, archival silent film footage, a tuxedoed and top-hatted Chuck was first discovered upon the knee of a giant Bergen cutout. He jumped down to mimic the pliable puppet for three minutes of inventive flopping, springing, and slashing though space. At the very last moment, he hurled himself back onto Bergen's knee, and the single spotlight—which had raced to keep up with the dancer—slowly faded to black as the puppet smiled up at his oversized master.

The McCarthy dance, both theatrical and bravura, was precisely the Broadway solo Walters had craved. With Balanchine's balletic assist, the spry routine was (per reviewer Robert Francis) a "bright spot" of the evening and a perfect showcase for Walters's underused *en l'air* ability.[5] John Martin, America's premier dance critic, was not fooled as to who supplied the steps: "Actually the best dancing of [*Angel*] is done by Charles Walters, quite apart from the ballets, in a solo which in all likelihood he designed for himself."[6] Walters indeed had crafted much of the number, confessing: "In evolving a dance schedule for a show like *Angel*, it is customary to allow the principals pretty much freedom in routining their own acts. Then the choreographer, who in this case [was] Balanchine, puts the finishing touches on their work, smoothing off the edges, as it were, and dovetailing the individual scenes into the continuity of the script."[7]

Memorable mishaps, of course, generally accompanied challenging solos. During one performance, Chuck missed his final leap and came crashing off Bergen's knee with an ungraceful thud. Balanchine happened to be in the audience that night and made his way backstage. "Mr. Valters," he said with a grin, "you must jump *leetle* higher."

If inventive, *I Married an Angel* incorporated a traditional musical comedy commandment: for every principal set of lovers, there must be another pair—usually funnier and younger—to second them. Walters and Christie supplied the show with its subplot. "I loved Audrey from afar," he said, "ever since [1933 when] she did *Sailor, Beware!* And to work with [her] was a real thrill."[8] Together they discovered a shared acerbic sense of fun; at times their humor was lethal and often achingly accurate. (Not to be left out, John Darrow became part of their dynamic and took Audrey as a client.) The onstage Walters-Christie chemistry was genuine. In their one extended tap sequence, "How to Win Friends and Influence People," Christie's character teaches Chuck how to save a dull party. The ensuing choreography allowed the duo to fly around the "guests," dodging the small balls the party-goers chaotically tossed around the drawing room set. Such sportiness prompted critic Robert Francis to praise their "fine number which momentarily stopped the show."[9]

The acclaim for Chuck was universal when *Angel* debuted at the Shubert on May 11, 1938, and reviewers scrambled to laud his surefootedness. "Really the best of the show," raved the *Christian Science Monitor*, "is the dancing, particularly that of Walters."[10] Brooks Atkinson dubbed him "a superior song-and-dance antic man,"[11] and hard-to-please John Anderson declared that he "dances nimbly and with increasing distinction."[12] Cheering the loudest, Lucius Beebe proclaimed Chuck "the ranking dancing juvenile of the legitimate theater. He works like the proverbial Trojan to maintain that status unimpeached."[13] And much to Chuck's delight, his boyhood idol Clifton Webb showed up after one performance to ask for *his* autograph.

Although they weren't performing together, summer 1938 brought a brief reunion for Fox and Walters. Dorothy had been cast in the political revue *Sing Out the News,* and Chuck supplied an inspired satirical staging for her appearance as the pitiable goddess of peace in "Peace and the Diplomat." Cloaked in a white sheath and carrying a palm leaf and stuffed dove, Fox was (rather literally) kicked around by five male dancers personifying various aggressive and embattled nations. *Variety* considered the number most "effective" when *News* opened at the Music Box on September 24.[14] "Peace and the Diplomat" marked Walters's first acknowledged choreographic credit on Broadway, and clearly a lively imagination was at work. While he had enjoyed devising routines for himself, working in collaboration with other dancers roused in him a feeling of completion. His appetite was whetted.

Over at the Shubert, *I Married an Angel* tallied a then-astonishing 338 performances before closing in February 1939. By then, negotiations were already in place for an extended tour that could boast much of the original cast. "It was one of those 'If she does it, I'll do it' things," remembered Walters. "We all decided that we were a happy family, and that we would all play the Chicago run—and it was a very successful, long run!" The cast also played Detroit, Washington, and Philadelphia but called it quits before committing to cross-country travel. "Vera wasn't going, Viv Segal wasn't going, so Audrey and I said that we weren't going either. I'd rather go home [to California]."[15] Chuck's role was handed to young Dan Dailey Jr., a tall, horsy hoofer newly signed by Darrow. (Dailey would drop the "Junior" as a preeminent Hollywood star of the 1940s and 1950s.)

For decades, Broadway producers adhered to the practice of out-of-town tryouts, testing new productions in front of audiences who supposedly lacked the critical acumen of New Yorkers. In the process, lackluster scenes could be rescripted; songs, dances, or performers could be replaced. Such alterations might benefit the show, but they weren't always positive for those involved. Tempers flared, and long-standing friendships could disintegrate in moments. In November 1939, Bob Alton unwittingly found himself in the midst of major out-of-town turmoil.[16]

The choreographer was in Boston, where the highly anticipated *Du Barry Was a Lady* was on the second leg of its three-city test run. Boasting the magical mix of Ethel Merman and Bert Lahr tearing through a Cole Porter score, the show might have seemed infallible, but it was hindered by an ineffectual supporting cast. Heads swiftly rolled. Phil Regan, a musically challenged Irish tenor, was replaced by Scottish baritone Ronald Graham. Tony Romano's insignificant role as Pedro was completely eliminated. A future radio performer, baby-voiced Mabel Todd, curtly left the company in Boston when her specialty with Romano was cut, and her duet with actor-dancer Johnny Barnes—"Well, Did You Evah!"—was reassigned.

Barnes, too, fell victim to Boston modifications. Merman later observed that the miscast dancer "refused to look into the soubrette's eyes as though he loved her, because he was really in love with a brunette back home. 'Help! I'm not that repulsive!' the soubrette cried. She certainly wasn't. Her name was Betty Grable."[17] At that point, the determined Grable was not yet a bona fide star, despite twenty-five movie roles in less than ten years for nine different Hollywood studios. By the late 1930s, she was contracted to 20th Century-Fox, and mogul Darryl F. Zanuck sent her east for a change of career. The twenty-one-year-old blonde stepped fearlessly into *Du Barry;* the artistic staff concluded she deserved better than Barnes, and he was shifted to a minor part.

Don Liberto, dancing in the chorus, asked producer Buddy DeSylva if he could take over as Grable's partner, but was told, "This show is very expensive, Don, and I need a name."[18] Bob Alton then surveyed the situation and made a suggestion that had played out well in the past: "How about Chuck Walters?"

In no time, the surrogate was on hand, and the role of nightclub hoofer Harry Norton underwent a reconfiguration. "Of course, I couldn't dance like the other guy," Chuck agreed. "[Barnes] was a character—used to wear a bow tie—tall, skinny, gangly." Alongside Alton, however, Waters found himself ideally positioned to study the art of doctoring a show. "I was a replacement . . . so it made it a little tough. I had to go to Boston [and] while they were rehearsing all their changes, I had to watch the show every night and do the original dialog. But after the show, Bob and Betty and I would rehearse new numbers." Creativity fought against time: Philadelphia was the only remaining stop before New York.

Alton's emerging trademark was clean, sharp routines full of fast-paced movement. Dancer Marge Champion, who worked with him several times, has since explained, "Bob was a master at what we called 'busy' choreography. He could put more steps into four or eight bars than anybody you ever met. Now *that's* wearing."[19] Wise to this, Walters spoke up during their late-night rehearsals: "Look, Bob, we've got to do this eight times a week. It's so complicated. Now, if we could simplify it, I know I would be able to do it better, and I'm sure Betty could do it better—and together *we* could do it better." Alton acquiesced, and they began discussing ways to keep the steps efficient and economic.[20] An unspoken shift in the dancer-choreographer relationship had taken place.

Du Barry soon was whipped into shape. A clever mix of present and past, the show's story line shifted between a contemporary Manhattan nightclub and the eighteenth-century court of Louis XV. Grable played chorine Alice Barton in the former, with Chuck as her café dancing partner, and Alisande to his Captain of the King's Guard during the sequences in France. If peripheral to the plot, the two were intrinsic to the production's shenanigans. They swaggered through the honky-tonk-styled "Ev'ry Day a Holiday" in the first act; Walters would kid his rambunctious costar by saying, "Betty invented the word barrelhouse." Their standout routine, however, was the second-act pleaser "Well, Did You Evah! (What a Swell Party This Is)." Assigned to the team in Boston, the song found the duo draped in powdered wigs and courtly garb as the Captain demonstrated to Alisande the unflappable manner in which "smart society" dismissed bad news. Porter's lyric gave Grable a series of preposterously unsettling situations—hurricane, avalanche, divorce, plague—each offhandedly disdained by Walters: "Well, did you evah! What a swell party this is." (Although welcomed on Broadway in *Du Barry,* the number took another seventeen years—and showcasing in Walters's film *High Society*—to achieve mass popularity.)

The revamped *Du Barry* premiered at New York's 46th Street Theater on December 6, 1939. Reception was mixed—inscrutable first-nighters barely laughed, and critics couldn't make up their minds. John Mason Brown applauded the musical as a "rowdy, boisterous, high-spirited extravaganza which stops at just this side of nothing,"[21] while Brooks Atkinson blasted, "The authors struck a dead level of Broadway obscenity that does not yield much mirth."[22] Perceived obscenity, however, sells tickets, and *Du Barry* was a gold mine. Decades later, Broadway chronicler Stanley Green put the show in historical perspective: *Du Barry* was not only the final musical offering of the year (and the decade) but also "one of the entertainment triumphs of the 1930s."[23]

Critical reservations did not extend to the cast. "Betty Grable and Charles Walters," Atkinson wrote, "dance and sing with remarkable dash."[24] Columnist Walter Winchell, however, chimed in with both compliment and pointed query: "Walters' dancing in *Du Barry* is delightful. . . . Is he married?"[25]

The back-to-back success of *Angel* and *Du Barry* left Chuck oddly unsettled, and he found himself reexamining his professional ambitions. "I was about twenty-eight and beginning to realize that I wasn't crazy about performing. I almost resented it." One unavoidable element of any stage hit is repetition, and Walters also began to feel trapped in another long-running show.

His world was brightened by the unpredictable Grable, who delighted in sending up Broadway decorum mid-performance. Her antics were still remembered seven decades later by dancer Lewis Turner: "She was very bored once the show was set. Consequently, she cut up as much as she could. She tried so hard to crack people up or to mess up, which she thought was cute."[26] Under her breath, recalled Bert Lahr, "Betty could say the filthiest things. If the audience heard [them], they'd back up the [police] wagon."[27] To Walters, his partner's "blue" remarks were more than welcome. "Betty was the dirtiest mouthed dame I've ever known," he laughed, "but on her it was adorable. Golly, we had fun."

"Betty was a Hollywood product," continues Turner, "and consequently there was very little she could do. She wasn't a dancer, she really wasn't a singer, she really wasn't an actress. But she was terribly cute, had a fantastic body, and lit up the stage when she came on. Now Chuck was a *real* professional—the ultimate *professional*! And he carried her throughout the whole show. He gave everything so that, in contrast, it evened out the performance. With him, you heard every tap that was supposed to come out of a combination. Betty, by the same token, didn't get *anything* out."[28]

If Grable lacked technique, she compensated with personality. "Believe me," said Walters, "in person she was more doll-like than on screen." The show won Betty the cover of *Life* magazine and Darryl Zanuck's renewed attention. He called her back to Fox for the splashy *Down Argen-tine Way,* and she became America's reigning pinup queen for the next decade. (Zanuck reportedly extended an invitation to her co-star as well, but Walters elected to stay the course with *Du Barry.* A year earlier he had mused to film columnist Regina Crewe, "I think the movies are great for mature artists—but not for youngsters. Time enough for Hollywood and me to get together. . . . Remember, the best dancers aren't kids.")

By midsummer 1940—and with Grable gone—the monotony got to him. "I quit," he recounted. "It wasn't that I wasn't making [good] money, but I'd just kinda had it." Chuck's final performance brought out the sur-prisingly mischievous side of the obsessively professional Lahr. The dancer expected the dialog to proceed as usual; instead, Bert greeted his first entrance with, "Oh, I hear you're leaving us." Chuck stood slack-jawed and bereft of response until Lahr laughed and offered up a sincere "Lotsa luck to ya, kid!" before continuing the show.[29]

There was another reason for Walters's departure. He knew he needed something to rekindle his dwindling desire to return to performing, and he thought he'd found it in *Pal Joey.* The George Abbott musical loomed as an unusually stellar showcase for a triple-threat male performer. There were plenty of hoofers vying for the assignment, but with Bob Alton as choreographer, Lorenz Hart as lyricist, and personal accolades for eight consecutive Broadway shows to his credit, Chuck was a front-runner. Dorothy Kilgallen used her inimitable "Voice of Broadway" column to dole out a strong recommendation for the "blue-eyed, handsome young man who looks rather like a brunette Duke of Windsor, and is a great asset to musical shows where dialogue is required of him, for he acts bet-ter than any dancer around."[30]

Author John O'Hara, however, was not satisfied. He had created the character of Joey Evans as an antihero—a self-centered, scheming dancer, quick to exchange sex and false flattery for success. In the estimation of some of the creative staff (O'Hara and composer Richard Rodgers among them), Charles Walters didn't come across as enough of a rat. Lewis Turner offers further perspective: "One should remember that most of these guys were homophobic. If they questioned the fact that Chuck Walters was possibly gay, they weren't going to give him a part where he was supposed to play a hot-shot womanizer."[31] The ax fell when Rodgers asked John Darrow if another of his clients could carry a tune.

The composer had seen Gene Kelly as Harry the Hoofer in William Saroyan's *The Time of Your Life*—a role Chuck had rejected upon learning his salary would be only $175 a week, suggesting instead "that new Kelly kid" for the part. The "Kelly kid" possessed enough voice to satisfy Rodgers and enough brash masculinity for O'Hara. *Pal Joey* was his for the taking. Chuck knew that his own unhappiness at losing the show was irrational, but he was deeply disappointed with John for supplying the competition.

There was soon a new professional distraction, though. Within days of the rejection, Dorothy Fox came through with an intriguing proposition. A year earlier she had staged the annual performance of Princeton University's Triangle Club. She was set to return in 1940, but suddenly the school's conservative trustees insisted she could not again be left alone in the all-male environment. Fox turned to Walters for help. Commuting to New Jersey, they began work in early October, once again splitting a weekly salary (this time a mere $100). Triangle Club president Robert H. Chapman kept anxious board chair John Larkin abreast of the goings-on in an October 8, 1940 letter:

> In our talk a few weeks ago, you stressed, if I remember correctly, the Trustees' opposition to our engaging [Dorothy] Fox again this year. Until four days before the date scheduled for the first chorus rehearsals, we had been unable to locate any dance director. Just at that time arose the opportunity to engage Charles Walters, recently highly praised for his performance in *Du Barry Was a Lady*. He agreed to take the position of dance director on condition that Miss Fox be allowed to work with him, since he had hitherto no experience in directing college musicals. This seemed agreeable enough to us, for Mr. Walters undertook to do most of the work on stage. Miss Fox attends all rehearsals with him, but it is Walters who creates and teaches the routines.
>
> Could you see the brilliant work which the chorus under Walters' direction is doing, you would, I'm sure, agree with me that the arrangement is highly satisfactory. They have been rehearsing five nights and have completed two-and-a-half routines already. I cannot speak too enthusiastically of the excellent quality of these routines, in conception and execution. On all sides,

we are reminded by the members of the chorus of Mr. Walters' ability in working out these dance numbers; he is greatly liked by everyone in the club—and especially by the chorus members themselves.[32]

Members of the Triangle Club (like the men of Harvard's Hasty Pudding show) prided themselves on delivering a near-professional production. New York critics were supplied tickets, Broadcast Music Inc. (BMI) published the original scores, and two-week circuit tours followed the initial Princeton performances. Eventually Chuck and Dorothy's Princeton effort visited thirteen cities, culminating in three sold-out Broadway performances at the 44th Street Theatre.

Twenty-four young men—some in drag—took the stage in *Many a Slip,* and the original musical proved to be an ideal outlet for Walters's good humor. The show spoofed Triangle Club traditions, detailing the fictitious drama faced when the young man playing their "feminine lead" is drafted. (He is secretly replaced by an actual "Gergdorf-Boodman" model, also played by a male student.) "The plot," wrote one critic, "served as something on which to hang several gay tunes and some fancy chorus work."[33]

By the time the dress rehearsal rolled around—with no less than a *Life* magazine photographer on hand—Walters felt enormous pride in his accomplishment. It was a greater challenge to persuade Darrow to journey across the Hudson River to watch a campus musical. "He wanted to [go] like he wanted to go to the moon," Chuck laughed. When finally seated in Princeton's McCarter Theatre, however, the hotshot agent was agreeably surprised. Back at their Murray Hill apartment later that evening, John turned to his partner and asked, "If you can do that with amateurs, what do you think you could do with professionals?"

Walters paused, allowing time to truly consider the question. A smile soon spread across his face. "Have a ball," he answered. "Just have a ball."[34]

6

Backstage

Dennis King was the first to give Walters the opportunity to choreograph an entire Broadway-bound musical. Their association had begun with *I Married an Angel,* and the tenor now was assembling a creative team for *She Had to Say Yes*—the quintessential vanity production. As the show's producer, principal backer, co-author, and leading man, King had enlisted commitments from ballerina Viola Essenova and songwriters Sammy Fain and Al Dubin. He convinced Walters to accept third billing in the role of Tony MacFarland and to provide dances for the chorines—drolly referenced in the playbill as "A King's Court of Queens." An almost instantaneous failure, *She Had to Say Yes* canceled its Chicago tryout when the first out-of-town performances in Philadelphia went poorly. King's musical, rhymingly retitled *Meet the Elite,* retreated to New York for repair, where it eventually became known as *Dreams Come True.* In the midst of it all (and perhaps feeling that the production's title was not its chief problem), Chuck bowed out and enjoyed spring 1941 on the West Coast with Darrow.

The decision to linger in California was primarily personal: "John and I decided to buy some property in Hollywood and build a house. We couldn't wait until [our New York] business was over, and we could rush out here."[1] The one-story residence at 1611 Marmont Avenue, located in the hills just above the famed Chateau Marmont hotel, offered an unobstructed view of downtown Los Angeles. In 1941, there was a small-town feel to the smog-free surroundings, and their West Hollywood home provided a therapeutic (though brief) refuge until Chuck's New York schedule once again kicked into overdrive.

Producer Vinton Freedley was a Broadway powerhouse. As professional partners, he and Alex A. Aarons spent the better part of the 1920s presenting some of the decade's most delightful musicals. Four of these showcased songs by George and Ira Gershwin: *Lady, Be Good* (1924), *Oh, Kay!* (1926), *Funny Face* (1927), and *Girl Crazy* (1930). Flush with success, the men built and operated the Alvin Theater, deriving its name from the first syllables of theirs. Freedley's solo producing career was launched with *Anything Goes* (1934), the first of another series of triumphs. These included two Cole Porter hits—*Red, Hot, and Blue* (1936) and *Leave It to Me* (1938)—and the Vernon Duke–John Latouche *Cabin in the Sky* (1940).

Another Freedley-Porter property, *Let's Face It,* went into pre-production in spring 1941. A retelling of *The Cradle Snatchers,* a 1925 farce about divorcees and gigolos at play, it was reconfigured by librettists Herbert and Dorothy Fields as a topical saga of three young servicemen and their innocent fling with a trio of secretly married ladies. Newcomer Danny Kaye got star billing with Nanette Fabray, Vivian Vance, and Eve Arden in support. Given such a roster, one trade paper flatly declaimed, "Most anyone in show business, if asked to go out on a limb and pick the [season's] coming favorite," would select *Let's Face It.*[2]

Bob Alton already had supplied dances for six Cole Porter originals, and Freedley again wanted him for this one. But Alton's services—thanks to Darrow—had been peddled to Hollywood for Columbia's Fred Astaire–Rita Hayworth vehicle, *You'll Never Get Rich,* and Metro's Greta Garbo comedy, *Two-Faced Woman.* As Chuck later told it, "[With Bob gone,] Freedley wanted somebody new; he didn't want any of the old hacks. [Then] Bob said, 'Chuck could do it. I'll be behind him,' although he never came [near] the theater."[3] Walters was poised to begin his professional choreographic career at the very top of Broadway's pecking order.

Chorus girl auditions began August 21, 1941, at the Imperial Theater. Sitting next to Chuck at the production table was Freedley himself, determined perhaps that any dancers under consideration be attractive and not merely technically proficient. Walters later admitted his own "major challenge [was] simply proving myself—gosh, the first time out—to Cole Porter, to Vinton Freedley ... a toughie!" Once the cast was in place, however, the eager-to-please Walters wasted no time in laying down his routines. He had mastered Alton's very definite set of rules on running a rehearsal and was prepared to put them to work:

1. Begin with something technical and definite.
2. Begin on time. Be prompt.

3. Do not let the chorus sit down.
4. Never let them make a mistake. Do not pass over a fault. Stop them in the middle of a bar if necessary and correct.
5. Polish as you go along.
6. Never seem in doubt.
7. Never let the bosses see anything unfinished. If you have only eight bars to show them, show them [that] much and no more. If you have not [that] much, get up yourself and demonstrate.[4]

Let's Face It began rehearsals on September 9. At Walters's disposal were thirty dancers; by week's end, he was expected to shave that number down to the show's allotted seventeen girls and nine boys. "But come the day," he remembered, "I was sitting in the front row of the theater, and I started getting stomach cramps...I thought I was going to die. I got through [rehearsal], got home, got a doctor, and I was having an appendix attack." Ashen and sweat-soaked, Walters was admitted to Lenox Hill Hospital to await his diagnosis. He feared as much for his position with *Let's Face It* as for his health.

Darrow did his best to suppress the story. When it did break three days later, the agent made sure that the papers announced that the choreographer was "returning to his duties tomorrow."[5] It was hoped the lie would quash rumors that Chuck been fired.

"Now here's where luck came in," Walters later acknowledged. "If I'd had a butcher [for a doctor], and he said, 'I have to operate,' I would have lost *Let's Face It*—because that takes too long. [Instead,] the doctor said, 'I am going to freeze [the appendix]. I think it's aggravated; I don't think it's ruptured or anything like that.' So he froze it."

Bed rest, however, was essential, and "Freedley called John and said, 'We cannot wait for Chuck, we've got to replace him. Tomorrow, we are going to run all the numbers that he's done, but we've got to keep going.'" The producer phoned again twenty-four hours later, determined instead to retain Walters's services: "How's Chuck? We *like* what he's done. Better yet, *Cole* likes what he's done." His job with *Let's Face It* was safe, and Walters philosophically discussed the whole incident many years later. "Oh, the 'ifs' in your life. *If* I'd had a butcher. *If* I'd lost the show. I might never have gotten another crack at a New York show, because I was fired from my first one."[6]

With speed, Walters lit into his remaining *Let's Face It* chores and continued to impress. Dancer Miriam Nelson (née Franklin) observed,

"There was nothing I can recall that suggested he was a first-time choreographer."[7] A *Friends* magazine journalist attended rehearsal and like-
wise asserted: "Seemingly made of live rubber and steel springs, Walters
is as agile mentally as physically. [He] works out the most complicated
numbers in his head."[8]

Chuck stayed open as well to any creative exchange with his performers, resulting in an atmosphere rife with exploration. Featured actress Vivian Vance, later (and forever) the unforgettable Ethel Mertz of
TV's *I Love Lucy,* described "Baby Games" as a number the choreographer
could not seem to finish.

> [Chuck] asked everybody to chip in ideas. Danny [Kaye] sug-
> gested, "Let's make a bridge of our hands, and the girls can go un-
> der while we sing, falling down, falling down." Eve went through,
> and as she stooped, the boys gave her a polite goose—[and] the
> chance to demonstrate one of those wide-eyed Eve Arden double
> takes. Next came Edith [Meiser], a tall, elegant Vassar girl, who
> responded to her touch with a look of cold hauteur. On *my* turn, I
> bent over, got my dues . . . then giggled and backed up for more!
> Laughter all around; we'd found a climax for the dance.[9]

Let's Face It had its world premiere at Boston's Colonial Theater on
October 9 and was standing room only from that point on. The *Herald*
cheered, "[The show] would be worth any customer's money just to
watch the chorus line go through Walters' dances."[10] His work additionally was lauded as "diverting," "fresh and unhackneyed," and "original
and arresting." Freedley was so confident of a hit that he invited the entire Broadway critical brigade to Boston, ensuring that the critics would
see the entire show and not miss its closing moments in a rush to file
their New York reviews.

Perhaps most important, the industry grapevine began its own buzz
about Chuck's routines. Many wondered if Walters was the heir apparent
to the Alton throne. On October 29, at the Imperial Theater, they had
their answer. New York critics bluntly labeled Chuck the season's choreographic find, and their superlatives praised his "fresh and inventive
mind," "joyous and emancipated choreography," "refreshing ingenuity,"
and "number of ways to keep [the cast] in impish motion." *Variety* rhap-
sodized the loudest, predicting, "Walters may just as well throw his own

dancing shoes away for keeps now; he's in the Bob Alton–Hermes Pan school of imaginative terp routiners."[11]

The twenty-nine-year-old Broadway choreographer could not have been more victorious.

"When [Chuck] finished our show," recalls Miriam Nelson, "he said to us, 'I'll never be able to think of another idea or step.' Of course, he thought of many more."[12] In fact, that task began instantly and continued non-stop for the next two months. Within days of the *Let's Face It* opening, Walters received an emergency call from the creators of Eddie Cantor's troubled *Banjo Eyes*. Alton had passed the assignment to assistant Charles Millang, but the poorly reviewed New Haven previews indicated that the novice wasn't up to the challenge. Walters had but a few days with the show in Boston and three weeks in Philadelphia. Finally, the December 4 New York opening was pushed to December 25 to allow for more polishing. He found Cantor "a darling" and was otherwise surrounded by friends. Director Hassard Short had staged *Between the Devil* and *Jubilee,* and the cast included Audrey Christie as a striptease artist and Chuck's "Begin the Beguine" coach, Tony De Marco.

Pretty blond newcomer Virginia Mayo, soon to make a name for herself in Hollywood, had a bit role in *Banjo Eyes.* In a November 23, 1941, letter to her aunt from Boston, she described the blend of fatigue and excitement that permeated a company while fixing a show:

> I really have been so busy, rehearsals every single minute, and shows when not rehearsing. . . . The show opened in New Haven and ran four hours—which of course was too long—so they began cutting and changing and changing some more, so that now it's entirely different from the original plot, and it is, by far, better now. Now the show runs from 8:30 P.M. to 11:15 P.M. and is shaping up beautifully. Of course, they're trying new things everyday which requires constant rehearsing. . . . We go to Philadelphia . . . for more revision of the show. . . . They certainly are working hard on it. The show is good now, but they want it to be a sensational hit.[13]

Throughout this harried doctoring, Walters continued to demonstrate his burgeoning versatility. "It is such great satisfaction," he told reporter William Hawkins, "to get a crowd of people to do what you want them to do. I never wanted to do anything else in my life but dance. Yet when I think of having danced in twelve shows in nine years, it seems almost a physical impossibility."[14]

Banjo Eyes finally opened at New York's Hollywood Theatre on Christmas night. According to *Billboard,* it had been "tinkered into something approaching good shape" thanks in part to "the dances by Walters [which] are imaginative and highly effective."[15] The choreographer, however, wasn't around to take a bow. Three days earlier, he'd been summoned back to Boston, where Dennis King's folly—now under its fourth title, *Lady Comes Across*—was once again in tryouts. Even Chuck couldn't save it, however, and the production once and for all closed out of town. Where Walters was concerned, though, it didn't matter. As 1941 came to an end, he had the satisfaction of two hit shows running on Broadway.

John Darrow had stayed just as busy in Hollywood. Despite the lack of proper licensing, he was making lucrative deals by splitting his commission with agent Leland Hayward; the latter was fully vetted with both the Actors' Equity Association and the Screen Actors Guild. Darrow finally won his own West Coast permit when the Equity council gathered for its first meeting of the new year on January 6, 1942. Thereafter, the Darrow Agency swiftly expanded into a bicoastal operation, and—just as swiftly—Chuck determined that his relationship with John would not be categorized in the same way. He flew to Los Angeles two days after receiving word about the Equity license. The *New York Times* defined the trip as "just a vacation," while asserting that Broadway's busy new choreographer "isn't Goin' Hollywood."[16]

It was wishful thinking on the paper's part. The time had come for Charles Walters and Hollywood to meet properly.

7

"You Think Like a Director"

On Sunday, December 7, 1941—while *Banjo Eyes* was improving in Philadelphia—the Japanese bombed the U.S. naval base at Pearl Harbor, Hawaii. President Franklin Delano Roosevelt went before a joint session of Congress the following day to call for a declaration of war against Japan. On December 11, Adolf Hitler declared war on the United States. The future was suddenly much more precarious for all men of draft age, and Chuck embraced the idea of remaining in California with his parents and John as long as he could.

He already had participated in a mass sign-up for duty. In October 1940, with a sense of isolationism pervading the country, celebrities provided a grand show for the New York public by lining up to receive their registration cards. On hand were comics Milton Berle and Red Skelton, movie actors Douglas Fairbanks Jr. and Gene Autry, writers Clifford Odets and William Saroyan, bandleaders Benny Goodman and Gene Krupa, and fellow dancers Paul Draper and Jack Cole. Oscar Levant, the hypochondriac pianist, took offense when the registrar commented that his complexion was "sallow." "Swarthy," Levant corrected. They compromised on "ruddy."[1]

Until called into service, Chuck would remain on the West Coast. The visiting Don Liberto remembers that, of the couple, it was Walters who enjoyed the swimming pools, but Darrow "liked to be where the action was. We'd be having drinks and he'd say, 'Well I have to run. I'm expected at Errol Flynn's house.' A real charmer, but shrewd when it came to business."[2] John had joined forces with his brother, Allan Simpson, and by the end of the first year, several of Darrow's New York clients were forging movie careers under the auspices of the Simpson-Darrow

Agency. William Eythe signed with Fox and Hurd Hatfield with M-G-M; the latter's mannequin-like face later won him the title role in *The Portrait of Dorian Gray* (1945). (Both men's rumored homosexuality, it's widely thought, contributed to the brevity of their careers.) Metro also became a temporary home for Walters's *I Married an Angel* replacement, Dan Dailey, and his co-star, Audrey Christie.

Unquestionably, Darrow's greatest success story proved to be Gene Kelly. Producer David O. Selznick had signed the Broadway star ("as an actor," remembers Kelly, "not as a dancer"), then loaned him to M-G-M.[3] Arthur Freed cast him opposite Judy Garland in his production of *For Me and My Gal* (1942), and sneak preview audiences liked the newcomer's genial Irish showmanship. Soon thereafter, Selznick sold Kelly's contract to Metro. "And then," said Gene, "I began to realize that there were some very enchanting things that were completely unexplored [in the movies]. Completely."[4]

Walters's New York reputation—or at least his contacts—quickly led to demands for his services as well. "The guy in charge of casting [at RKO]," Chuck explained, "was sleeping with a girl from a musical that I had choreographed on Broadway. She recommended me for *Sweet or Hot*," a minor military musical for rising stars Lucille Ball and Victor Mature. "The guy called Bob [Alton] to get some information on me, and they offered me the gig. . . . It's not a very impressive story."[5]

Patriotically retitled *Seven Days' Leave,* the picture featured three Walters dance ensembles, all filmed in spring 1942 and all contained within the lopsided musical's first fifteen minutes. Most successful was the boisterous "Please Won't You Leave My Girl Alone," sung in an army barracks with comic boy-boy dancing. The others—a frenetic conga and a Texas swing—were fitted to an awkward cast of character actors, including Harold Peary (best remembered for *The Great Gildersleeve*) and freckle-faced Marcy McGuire.

Chuck retreated from RKO wholly unimpressed. "At first, I hated the film medium. I thought it was all mechanical, and I couldn't wait to get back to the stage," he said.[6] A simple phone call from Gene Kelly would change all of that.

Though *For Me and My Gal* had yet to be released, Kelly was already at work on a second M-G-M musical. *Du Barry Was a Lady* came to the screen as a big-budget, Technicolor extravaganza, with Lucille Ball and Red Skelton as cinematic substitutes for Ethel Merman and Bert Lahr.

Freed produced, the dour Roy Del Ruth directed ("They called him 'Laughing Boy,'" said M-G-M dancer Eleanor Powell, "because he never smiled"), and the passé Seymour Felix oversaw the dance sequences.[7] An alumnus of many 1920s stage musicals, Felix had won a 1936 Academy Award for his opulent stagings in Metro's *The Great Ziegfeld* (one of only three Oscars ever handed out for choreography). He was well paid, in demand, and much disliked. The genial Hermes Pan didn't mince words, calling Felix "a hard-boiled, slangy type, who would shout at the girls. . . . [He looked] like a shoe salesman."[8] *Du Barry* deserved better, and Kelly called his agent to say he'd had enough.

"Where's Bob Alton?" he asked.

"Booked," Darrow replied, citing Alton's Broadway commitments to the Shubert's *Count Me In* and new *Ziegfeld Follies.*

"Well, then where's Charlie?" Gene questioned, calling Walters by a nickname that made him bristle. "I have one big number to do in this picture, and I need him."

When asked whether he'd like the job, Walters gave an "Oh, well . . . what the hell" shrug.[9]

The *Du Barry* sequence was Kelly's first major motion picture solo (with chorine backup), and the ambitious dancer considered it pivotal to his new career. Compounding the issue, the routine was set on an elegant nightclub stage and demanded an Astaire-like élan that did not come naturally to the hoofer. (Two years earlier, Kelly had floundered when making an appearance at New York's elite Rainbow Room; "[Gene] just wasn't suited for so sophisticated a [spot]," commented the venue's resident choreographer, Jack Cole.)[10] What Kelly needed now was someone like Chuck Walters for lessons in tuxedoed grace.

It had been nearly a decade since his failed screen test, but Walters was poised to crash the M-G-M gates at last. Darrow negotiated a four-week dance director deal for a flat salary of $2,000, and when later asked about his studio beginnings, Chuck would lightheartedly say, "I'll show you my first contract. It's on an interoffice memo."

In its heyday, the Metro-Goldwyn-Mayer film studio covered approximately 175 acres of Culver City real estate, and it has been likened to a small, self-sustaining city. There were cavernous soundstages, diverse rehearsal halls, well-decorated dressing rooms, floors of office suites, warehouses for props and costumes, scenery shops, and winding back lots for outdoor locations, all in addition to the studio's own fire department, commissary, barbershop, power plant, hospital, dental clinic, and water tower. A zoo maintained the trained animals; a schoolhouse staff tutored the youngsters under contract. There was even a funeral parlor just off the lot, creating an amusing (if foreboding) atmosphere as its neon sign blinked "Smith and Salsbury Mortuary" into the windows of the studio's administrative building. In a figurative sense, Metro employees could envision going from cradle to coffin virtually within the borders of this Culver City hamlet.

M-G-M had already produced some of the industry's most respected motion pictures: *Ben-Hur, Anna Christie, Dinner at Eight, Mutiny on the Bounty, A Night at the Opera, The Good Earth, Grand Hotel, The Philadelphia Story.* Here, the fading Camille yearned for her handsome Armand, a desperate Blackie Norton sifted through the rubble of San Francisco, and young Dink sobbed for the Champ. Here, the delightfully tipsy Nick and Nora Charles sleuthed, randy Andy Hardy mismanaged adolescent amours, and Dorothy Gale discovered "there's no place like home." Metro was like no other studio. A mecca for genuine talent, the entire enterprise was administered with factory-like precision by studio chieftain and master showman Louis Burt (L. B.) Mayer. Per Walters's précis, Metro-Goldwyn-Mayer was "real snob city."

"[Yet] when I started at M-G-M there wasn't a very enthusiastic feeling," he added. "With the end of the Garbos and the Harlows, everyone thought the glory days were gone." Indeed, the glamour era that had epitomized the 1930s was over. Reigning queens Norma Shearer, Jeanette MacDonald, and Joan Crawford were departing, while the popular Myrna Loy was otherwise occupied with Red Cross war duties. But Mayer and his minions counterbalanced this exodus by catering to the public's changing tastes. Studio output quickly capitalized on such down-to-earth personalities as Greer Garson, James Stewart, Spencer Tracy, and Katharine Hepburn, along with such expert youngsters as Mickey Rooney, Judy Garland, and Lana Turner.

Audiences steeped in war embraced the Metro product, from romanticized portraits of life (*Mrs. Miniver, Random Harvest*) to a series of lighthearted musicals. And if the latter genre was particularly routine, one producer aimed to move beyond mere escapism. "[Arthur] Freed was the Ziegfeld of MGM," wrote historian John Kobal, "the single most creative and controlling brain in the shaping of the American film musical as we now know it."[11] Freed had found initial career success as lyricist to composer Nacio Herb Brown. Their songs brightened M-G-M's first decade of musicals—the *Broadway Melody* series (1929, 1936, 1938), *Hollywood Revue* (1929), and *Going Hollywood* (1932). The team had hits with "You Are My Lucky Star," "Singin' in the Rain," "All I Do Is Dream of You," and "Temptation." But it was Freed's insightful contributions as (uncredited) associate producer on *The Wizard of Oz* (1939) that hinted at the revolution he was poised to launch.

Committed to making film musicals in which song and dance defined character and furthered plot, Freed surrounded himself with the finest M-G-M craftsmen and then looked to the talent pool of Broadway and Tin Pan Alley. ("For self-protection," he later explained, half jokingly.)[12] By his invitation—and through the networking of those he corralled—inspired innovators arrived in Culver City to form an unparalleled musical repertory company. Thus the "Freed Unit" was born, where ingenuity was contagious and the end product often glorious.

If Gene Kelly had been the actual delivery man, Freed would forever (and proudly) refer to Charles Walters as his own personal discovery.

"Immediately, I asked for the [*Du Barry*] script," Chuck recalled. "They said, 'What do you need a script for? You're just doing a solo staging for Kelly.' Having been in the Broadway show, I might have been curious what they [were altering]—and if Kelly was playing my part or another part." Yet it was Gene's character motivation that primarily interested Chuck. *Why* was he dancing in the first place? Such preparation, he noticed, was then uncommon in Hollywood. "I think that if I was successful as a choreographer—which allowed me to eventually become a director—it's because, as far as I know, I was the only one who insisted on reading the script beforehand. Even if I had only one number to do in a film, I needed to know who the character was, what happened in the previous scene, if there was a fade at the end of the scene or if another character interrupted it. It's because of that, I think, my numbers succeeded."

The script revealed that M-G-M's much-revised *Du Barry* cast Kelly as a poor but honest hoofer in love with an unattainable nightclub headliner (Ball). Alone with him in her dressing room, she discloses her hitherto secret affection for him—prompted by his plaintive serenade of "Do I Love You?" That Cole Porter melody also was slated to underscore Gene's subsequent dance.

Walters felt that the dressing room confession and the character's heightened emotional state should propel Kelly into the routine. Chuck cornered his producer to present his idea: "Look at the way the script has it, Arthur. The scene is played out, and then there's a dissolve to Gene's dance. What if we play it in one continuous movement? [Wouldn't] it be fun to start the number with Gene inside the dressing room and then—*pow!*—out he goes through the door, with the camera following him down the backstage hallway, through the audience, and onto the stage? This way we could slide into the number without a bump between the story and the dance." Freed remained stone-faced, leading Walters to joke thirty-eight years later: "He just *looked* at me, and I thought '*Oh Jesus,* I really bombed.'"

To the contrary, Freed was pleased and had paused only to take in his new recruit. "You know, that's the way a director thinks," he said at last. "You think like a director, Chuck. I believe you're going to be one someday." Arthur Freed was the kind of producer who didn't forget.

"The seed," said Walters, "was planted."[13]

The *Du Barry* solo came together with relative ease. Using Walters's "bridging" suggestion, the sequence begins as Kelly bounds from Ball's dressing room, circles her maid in the hallway, and struts down the corridor to enter the nightclub from the rear. Sprinting through the applauding audience, he bounces over a chair and sails onto the stage, backed by Tommy Dorsey and His Orchestra. His smooth movement is later superseded by a swingy looseness as he whizzes through clusters of synchronized chorus girls. Exuberant, masculine, and spontaneous, he's the movies' newest emblem of high-spirited optimism. After Kelly's final pose, he rushes back to Ball's dressing room to blurt, "Say it again—that you love me!" The segue back to "reality" is thus effortlessly achieved.

Freed was delighted. He rewarded Walters by assigning him the film's burlesque-tinged title number. With Lucille Ball as his star, an inspired Chuck placed her on the shoulders of a Charleston-stepping cavalier. Ball wore regal eighteenth-century couture and, with her partner's satin knee breeches protruding from under her ornate hoops, Lucy resembles nothing so much as a comic giantess—a 1920s flapper in a foot-high powdered wig. The number was another winner.

Amid such excitement came the unavoidable: Walters received his draft notice. "I had to say good-bye to everybody," he recalled, "and everything I worked ten years to get."[14] Although Freed consoled him ("M-G-M has clout"), I. H. Prinzmetal of Metro's legal department informed the producer on August 24 that Chuck was required to appear for induction. "We will not be able to get a postponement," Prinzmetal wrote. "If he passes his Army physical, he nevertheless will be permitted two weeks furlough . . . at which time he may assist us. However, I would not rely upon him and would suggest that you endeavor to hire someone else."[15]

When *Du Barry Was a Lady* commenced principal photography on September 1, 1942, Chuck was dutifully reporting for his physical. In a show of appreciation, Gene Kelly, his wife, Betsy, and twenty-six dancers had thrown a going-away party, gifting him with a fitted leather case. "It's made to meet army requirements," they joked.[16] Years after, Chuck proudly recalled their kind gesture, but added, "I was back at M-G-M the next day—I had a bad heart!"[17]

Again on the lot, Walters began intense sessions with Lucille Ball. The thirty-one-year-old star had built a small name for herself at RKO but now was working at the biggest movie studio and carrying a million-dollar musical on her shoulders. "Lucille was terrified during the weeks of rehearsal," reports biographer Kathleen Brady. "Walters was eager to prove himself and was concerned that they make each other look good, so when Lucille wailed, 'I can't sing! I can't dance!' Walters told her, 'You *can,* now stop wasting time saying you can't and get it done.'"[18] Sequestered in the rehearsal hall, the two of them established a level of trust that carried them through forty years of friendship. "At M-G-M," Ball later acknowledged, "I learned a lot of things—and learned I could *do* a lot of things— with the great help of people like Chuck Walters."[19] In the process, Lucy discovered she was not an improviser. She thrived instead when every detail was worked out in advance. Walters relished this commitment and worked vigorously on her "choreographed" slapstick, particularly for the film's Louis XV dream sequence. In rehearsal, he chased Ball around mock boudoir sets, coaching her with the rigor of an Olympic athlete.

"M-G-M didn't quite know what they had in Lucille Ball," he would comment, feeling the studio erred in limiting her to glamour queen roles. Walters saw Lucy as a vulnerable yet intelligent woman, well suited for dramatic roles, but it would take another thirty-three years—and television—before he'd have the opportunity to showcase the alternative side of Lucille Ball.

A new tension grew out of Chuck's proficiency. He was precisely the type of male dancer held in contempt by Seymour Felix, who was still

Du Barry's nominal choreographer. In the 1929 article "What About Chorus Boys?" the homely Felix declared: "I like regular fellows, real men. I detest handsome men. To a great part of the audience, they give a sickening impression. They look like collar advertisements, as if they were paid for their good looks—and no real man wants to be paid for his prettiness."[20]

As the men's rivalry grew, Ball came down squarely in Walters's camp. Her own ill feelings toward Felix dated back to her work for him as a Goldwyn Girl in the early 1930s. Gwen Seeger had danced alongside Ball in *Kid Millions* (1934) and told John Kobal:

> [Felix was] the hardest person I ever worked for; you'd go for six or seven hours without stopping. He kept himself going with coffee and aspirins, and he was just so keyed-up constantly. . . . [One day,] Felix went mad. He screamed and hollered at this kid [in the chorus] who started to pee in her pants. So [Lucy] got very angry. . . . [Felix] was a little man—about 5′ 1″, I think—and Lucille Ball, who was about 5′ 9″ or 5′ 10″, got up and walked down and put her finger in his face and scolded him. He said something to her, and she just picked him up and put him under her arm, walked off the stage and took him outside. . . . She carried him out like a suitcase![21]

Freed made his choice. Metro executive L. K. Sidney circulated a memo noting that Felix, his assistant, and his secretary "will finish Saturday Sept. 19 and go off payroll as of that date."[22] (Ironically, the deposed dance director soon journeyed to Paramount to choreograph its screen adaptation of *Let's Face It,* Walters's freshman Broadway effort.) Chuck was pressed into further service and revamped three Felix routines: "Ladies of the Bath," the "Friendship" finale, and the Ball-Skelton duet "Madame, I Love Your Crepes Suzette." His tinkering especially energized the latter, as the royally attired Lucy nibbled on a stalk of celery while simultaneously dancing the minuet with "King" Red. Their gavotte peaked when the duo hopped onto a springy double bed, allowing Skelton to bounce the reluctant Ball into his arms. Lucy recounted: "[Chuck and I] practiced for *days* on a trampoline, which made me *acutely* seasick!"[23]

Such ongoing contributions by Walters were endorsed by Roger Edens, M-G-M's supreme musical supervisor. Edens had joined the studio in 1935 and long since proved to be indispensable. The composer-arranger-lyricist was later defined by Chuck as the genre's "unsung hero who was not quite unsung but certainly not sung loud enough."[24] Edens came to Hollywood from a Broadway (and Texas) background. Cultured, friendly, and blessed with a calming southern drawl, he maintained a discerning presence in virtually every M-G-M department, over and beyond any musical assignment. Edens labored on scripts, provided casting ideas, supervised hair, makeup, and costume design, and even played substitute director on occasion. "And he was *always* excited with his work, too," remembers contract dancer Dorothy Tuttle Nitch. "So he got everyone excited."[25] Summarizing Edens's preeminence within the Freed Unit, Chuck declared: "Arthur had ideas, but Roger [provided] his taste."[26]

The dissimilar personalities of Walters and Edens complemented each other, and a professional partnership was forged that would extend for more than two decades. "I was very earthy while Roger was pretty pithy," said Chuck. "He had a 'live through elegance' attitude. I could take that elegance and make it a little more palatable."[27] Working in complete cohesion, they enjoyed a free-flowing exchange of ideas and took immense pleasure in exploring the possibilities of the cine-musical.[28]

By the time Walters finished *Du Barry*—payroll was notified to "close Charles Walters as of Saturday night, Oct. 17"[29]—Edens mentioned to the "provisional dance director" that he was in line for a full-time offer from Metro. Vinton Freedley, meanwhile, announced from the East Coast that Chuck would choreograph his next stage musical, *Jackpot*.

But Freed prevailed.

John Darrow brokered a lucrative (if standard) deal for his partner: a seven-year contract with a salary eventually topping out at $1,000 per week. Walters's hesitation about Hollywood had disappeared. He now worked exclusively for Metro-Goldwyn-Mayer.

"I didn't care if I was cleaning toilets," he said, "I wanted to work at Metro. It was not the most exciting entry, but damn it, *I got there.* It shows you what the will can do."[30]

8

Putting His *Best* *Foot Forward*

At its most basic, the phrase "Hollywood dance director" refers to the individual responsible for creating a dance or a series of dances for a particular motion picture. A popular, if simplistic, definition, it is often a wild underestimation.

Dance historian Larry Billman has ventured beyond this rudimentary description, recognizing that it was such a director's duty "to create the overarching concept for a film's musical sequences, which usually comprised the bulk of each feature's running length."[1] The best dance directors closely worked with musical arrangers, conferred with costume designers, and had influence over art directors. "As dance directors were granted greater authority over their work," Billman adds, "they found themselves filming many of these sequences as well, making them responsible for much of each picture's style, pace, movement, and character."[2]

Those who contributed to the field came to be identified by a variety of titles: *dance director, stager of musical sequences,* and later (borrowing from the world of ballet) the more significant *choreographer.* For Walters, the demarcation was clear. "I think it should be dance director—not choreographer," he said. "A choreographer does a whole creation. But in a film, you are stuck with a script, a star, a song, and you have to come up with a nice, interesting, exciting, and/or beautiful, and/or funny number. But you start with limitations. Often you have a star whom you have to make *look* like they are moving."[3] Far from being restricted by such circumstances, Chuck came to the Hollywood machine well prepared.

One can understand why Freed lobbied to keep Walters at Metro. After three years of productions, his unit had no true dance master, and staging generally had been left to the fevered imagination of director Busby

Berkeley. "He did a time step and a break!" observed dancer Sheila Ray, who appeared in several Berkeley extravaganzas. "[Buzz] was a camera man, not a dance director."[4] By signing Chuck, Freed was, in essence, acknowledging the important role dance was to play in his future musicals.

This was further underscored when the studio acquired other key choreographic talent over the next decade. With Walters and Gene Kelly already entrenched, M-G-M hired Jack Donohue, Eugene Loring, Hermes Pan, Nick Castle, Gower Champion, and Michael Kidd, as well as the then-reigning Robert Alton. These gentlemen, their assistants, and the dancers who inspired them ushered in a new era in cine-dance. They accepted some ideas from their predecessors, rejected others, and—most important—brought their individualized visions to the screen.

Du Barry wrapped on November 6, 1942, and Freed promptly handed Walters two concurrent stage-to-screen transfers: *Girl Crazy*, the Gershwin brothers' 1930 western gambol, and 1941's *Best Foot Forward*. In New York, Chuck had been the front-runner to choreograph the latter, but when the job was handed instead to Gene Kelly, he avoided seeing the show.

As both *Girl Crazy* and *Best Foot Forward* were built around academic institutions—the fictitious Cody College and Winsocki Military Institute, respectively—a call went out for dancers who looked young. Many boys arrived from nearby colleges, as others their age were being deployed overseas. (USC and UCLA permitted this unconventional "work-study," providing the young men kept up their grades.) Petite professional Caren Marsh-Doll appeared in both films and remembers her dance director as maintaining an infectious personality despite his workload: "Chuck was always smiling and seemed very happy doing what he was doing. There was something very boyish about him, like a young kid. Friendly and warm, [he was] a real sweetheart to work for and wonderful with us dancers. We just wanted to be our best for him."[5]

Girl Crazy was the first of the pictures to go into production. Ninth of the ten films in which Judy Garland and Mickey Rooney shared billing, it was the fourth and final major musical produced specifically for them by Freed. The two mega-talents had been M-G-M's money-spinning teen team for four years, establishing Freed in the process.

On November 30, Walters began all-day rehearsals (10:00 A.M. to 4:45 P.M.) for "I Got Rhythm." Called were his two young superstars and seventeen dancers—eleven girls, six boys. Edens recommended that the sequence be "rhythmic and simply staged," and Chuck took that advice.[6] He provided Judy with syncopated movement for her opening choruses and devised some subsequent cadenced cheerleading for the group. (Chorus boys to Judy: "She's got it!" Chorines to Mickey: "He's got it!" Judy and Mickey: "We've got it! *Rhythm!*") Director Berkeley, who had helmed the three preceding Rooney-Garland musicals, arrived the second week, and Walters departed to concentrate on his other Freed picture, *Best Foot Forward*. In the interim, Berkeley continued work on "Rhythm" and immediately called sixty dancers to his first rehearsal.[7]

"Lucy Ball was the star" of *Best Foot*, Chuck later asserted, "but the picture really belonged to the kids." The lightweight story involved a movie star who expects to attract some career-boosting publicity by attending a military school prom. In hopes of replicating the energy of the stage production, M-G-M brought most of the New York cast to Culver City.[8]

Future film director Stanley Donen was one of Broadway's *Best Foot* boys. He wound up in the film through his own persistence—and that of his mentor, Gene Kelly, who prevailed on Walters's graciousness. "Chuck Walters rather liked me," Donen said, "so I became his assistant on that and some of his other movies afterward."[9] Chuck remembered the situation somewhat differently, admitting that the ambitious contractee helped keep rehearsals going if he was suddenly called away. But he stressed that Donen could not be termed an assistant; dancer Jack Boyle filled that position. (A few years later, Donen looked to Walters when seeking the requisite two endorsements for Directors Guild admission; presumably Kelly supplied the other. "Have you directed anything?" Chuck questioned. "Don't you remember," Stanley chided, "I was your assistant on *Best Foot*." Walters complied but enjoyed telling *his* version of Donen's directorial genesis for years to come.)[10]

Despite *Best Foot*'s setting in an all-male school, the most promising cast members were discovered among the film's diverse female set. They included two importees from the stage show—a bruiser named Nancy Walker and a spunky blonde named June Allyson—and the velvet-voiced Gloria De Haven. Walters was charmed by the immensely capable trio.

He paired the feisty Walker with Harry James for the aggressive "Alive and Kickin'," the bandleader made nimble after much patient attention from Walters. Knockabout Nancy coaxed James into a comically awkward samba, climaxed by her fearless backward pratfall into a bass drum.

Chuck discovered that Allyson was equally fearless. "Usually the kids from the theater were very camera-conscious, *but the camera didn't bother her!*" he remarked. Taking a liking to the strong-minded blonde, he counseled her, "You've got a hell of a chance in this business. You have everything the camera wants—looks, height, style. But *honey,* you've got to do *something* about that husky voice of yours. If you have two sentences in a row, you're going to lull everybody to sleep." Years later, after Allyson became famous as "the girl with the million-dollar laryngitis," Walters could only laugh at his monumental misjudgment. "That shows how wrong a person can be," he said.[11]

"For me," Allyson later gushed, "Chuck was—besides Fred Astaire— the best dancer in the whole world. He was fantastic [and] knew exactly what to do with young people. He knew how to put them together and work with them, because he was so kind."[12]

De Haven agrees. Despite prior grooming by M-G-M, the Hollywood-born actress was unprepared for the demands of a Freed Unit musical and found relief in the pleasant demeanor of her dance director. "Chuck had a real, ingratiating personality and a wonderful sense of humor," she remembers. "On *Best Foot,* he didn't devote much serious time talking to us, because we were such babies. But compared to most choreographers— who were strictly concerned with the soundtrack and the movement—he was a very loose kind of guy."[13]

Heading up the Winsocki junior prom ensemble, the trio of Allyson, De Haven, and Walker received their shining opportunity in Walters's "The Three Bs." The lyric bemoaned the three "B" legends of classical music (Bach, Beethoven, and Brahms) and called out for more contemporary sounds: barrelhouse, boogie-woogie, and the blues. Chuck's high-energy swing session hit its peak in Allyson's vigorous glorification of the barrelhouse. Flipped and flung by the cadets, she was left standing and searching for more until Walker walked back into frame and raised Allyson's arm as if to declare her winner of the match.

Hugh Martin and Ralph Blane, the show's equally youthful songwriters, were also brought to M-G-M for the production. Walters knew them from New York, where Martin (aided by the jocular Blane) had supplied vocal arrangements for *Du Barry Was a Lady,* and The Martins (a singing quartet that consisted of Hugh, Ralph, and two girl singers) also shared billing with Chuck in Dennis King's ill-fated *Lady Comes Across.* In Hollywood, the three became solid collaborators. "I adored working with them," said Walters. "They would give me arrangements, and I would say, 'Kids, I couldn't be more grateful. This piece is staging itself. It's all right there musically.'" For "Wish I May," *Best Foot*'s newly written opener, he supplied energetic posturing for the cast. In "Three Men on a Date," he moved his cadets through a brisk campus walk. Ironically, the show's hit song, "Buckle Down Winsocki," was realized by Jack Donohue. Chuck later revealed, "It was easier to send [Jack] out onto the football field [to] do that number, while I stayed back at the studio. It was just more economic."[14]

Rehearsals sped along with amazing efficiency throughout November and December 1942. Despite a healthy, ongoing rivalry between Allyson and De Haven ("Boy!" laughed Chuck. "Would those two vie for attention!"), the fervor of the *Best Foot* "babies" made for smooth sailing.

The same could not be said for *Girl Crazy,* where Busby Berkeley had become a serious problem. The director possessed a restless talent, a caustic tongue, and an alcoholic's short temper. Accusations and inter-office memos were flying.

Garland, in particular, was upset by his callousness. "[Judy] was a very sensitive girl," Walters explained, "and Buzz treated his actors like a piece of scenery or a piece of furniture. He'd shove 'em around, move 'em around. Time meant nothing, lines meant nothing. It was just where his camera was, and where you had to be when he wanted to swoop around and slide in for a close-up. 'God *dammit!*' he'd say, 'I told you to turn on that line so I could come in!' And he'd push Judy and place her and made her feel very awkward."[15]

Acrimony spread among the ranks when cameras finally rolled on "I Got Rhythm." Berkeley's excessive concepts inflated the sequence into mammoth rodeo pageantry, and the scheduled four-day shoot telescoped to nine. "The entire M-G-M lot reeked of 'I Got Rhythm,'" said Nancy Walker. "They couldn't end it; they didn't know how to get out of it. I kept saying to Judy, 'Listen, aren't you close to the end of this?' She said, 'No, we've only done forty choruses.'"[16]

Edens called for a showdown, later telling *Sight and Sound* magazine: "Berkeley got his big ensembles and trick cameras into it again, plus a lot of girls in Western outfits with fringe skirts, and people cracking whips, firing guns . . . and cannons going off all over my arrangement and Judy's voice. Well, [he and I] shouted at each other, and I said, 'There isn't room on the lot for both of us.' But he got his way."[17]

Berkeley's triumph was temporary. On the thirteenth day of shooting, Norman Taurog—a gifted and blessedly even-tempered company director—was brought in to replace him. *Girl Crazy* was already seven days behind schedule and $97,418 over budget.

The tumult continued for Garland, as during this time she received word that the finale from her preceding picture, *Presenting Lily Mars,* had been deemed a conceptual disappointment and would need to be replaced before the film could be released.

Lily Mars was the brainchild of Joseph Pasternak, a recent defector from Universal who'd joined Metro's short list of musical producers in 1941. Known as the "Happy Hungarian," Pasternak had a thick accent, a hearty laugh, and an affinity for *gemütlichkeit* entertainment. *Lily Mars* perfectly fit that formula, recounting the tale of a stagestruck Indiana teen who becomes a Broadway star by the film's final reel. As Pasternak later recalled, however, his modest intentions for the material were compromised when "friends of the star . . . arranged to see a rough-cut [and] ran to Judy with wails of pain and distress, all aimed in my direction."[18] Louis B. Mayer suggested that Pasternak reconsider his finale.

As originally filmed, *Lily Mars* came to a questionable close with "Paging Mr. Greenback" (in Walters's estimation, "a big flag-waving thing with too many people and too little Judy").[19] Edens devised a lavish ten-minute replacement medley, built around his own composition, "Where There's Music." The routine encompassed six song standards, capped with the oft-reprised Arthur Freed–Nacio Herb Brown M-G-M anthem "Broadway Rhythm." Edens's assemblage—with Conrad Salinger's lush orchestration—begged for equally opulent staging.

"Up to this point, Judy had played mostly kids," recounted Walters, "and everybody thought it was time for a change. So they called me in." In conceiving the new finale, he grew intrigued with the idea of presenting the maturing singer in a smart Broadway-style showcase—Judy Garland as the toast of New York. What's more, the routine also proved to be a potential opportunity for Walters the entertainer. Whether or not he actively campaigned to appear as Garland's on-screen partner, he had already earned the amity of town gossip Hedda Hopper, who used her column to scold, "To me, it seems a crime that a performer like Chuck should give it up, to create and direct people who aren't nearly as good in the things that he does so beautifully."[20] The studio heeded Hopper's lament. After Chuck's casting was finalized, Sheilah Graham reported, "Judy Garland gets one of the best dancers in the country for her new finale. He was brought to Metro as a dance instructor. And then someone had the bright idea—why not let the boy do his own stuff before the camera?"[21]

Rehearsals for the new *Lily Mars* finale began smoothly on January 26, 1943. While Garland was occupied with that, the *Girl Crazy* company shot around her as long as they could, then went on temporary hiatus. Three days into the *Lily Mars* rehearsals, however, a seriously underweight Judy no longer had the strength to go on, and the rehearsals were halted.[22] When they resumed in late February, the twenty-year-old singer returned healthy and full of bounce.

"Judy *loved* to charm people," Walters said, "and just kind of 'knock 'em off their feet' with talent, with humor, with all the elements."[23] He was far from immune. The pair began to see each other so frequently outside of rehearsals that columnists hinted at a possible romance. "Favorite escort of Garland's since her separation from [husband] David Rose is Charles Walters, of MGM's dance department," reported *Screen Guide*.[24] Louella Parsons told her readers, "Judy has been seen here and there with Chuck Walters,"[25] while Graham blathered, "Judy is falling hard for the charms of Chuck Walters, her good looking dance maestro. They lunch and dine together daily."[26] (Hopper, fully aware of Chuck's relationship with John, never ran any such items.)

Decades afterward, Walters confessed that a domestic arrangement with Garland actually had been considered. "We almost got married at one point before [she wed] Vincente [Minnelli]. But I was just getting started, and she was a big star. I'd worked too long and too hard to get to Metro—on my own—and I couldn't be Mr. Judy Garland!"[27] Such marriage talk might well have been manufactured by the studio or at least encouraged, particularly with Walters due to make his screen debut opposite their young moneymaker. Prolonged bachelorhood in Hollywood, particularly for a prominent male dancer, was tolerated for only so long. The screen's most illustrious dance men, Fred Astaire and Gene Kelly, took brides (to whom they were genuinely devoted) very soon after receiving their first studio contracts. It was infinitely easier for the all-important industry publicists to promote a budding star who could hold up to public scrutiny.

Plans went ahead for Judy's transformation in the new *Lily Mars* finale. Couturier Irene designed a glamorous low-backed, sleeveless gown that complemented the upswept hair style fashioned by Sydney Guilaroff.

An expansive, glossy, multilevel set was erected, and Tommy Dorsey and His Orchestra—already on the lot for *Girl Crazy*—were engaged for backing and name value. The combined effect was that of sophistication and chic, two adjectives new to Garland's screen persona. In his staging, Walters pushed his young dance partner to her maximum, and Judy did her best to please. ("Perfection was her goal," Pasternak once observed.)[28] Aware of her limitations, however, she began to harbor misgivings, and Chuck was forced to halt a rehearsal. "Honey, we don't have much time to do this," he told her. "You're just kidding around with it. What's going on?"

"I'm not sure I can do what you want," Garland whispered. "I can't move like this."

When Lucille Ball had expressed similar self-doubt during *Du Barry*, Walters knew he could bluntly tell her to get working. With Judy, he understood that kid gloves were required. They sat down together, and in a flash of inspiration he asked, "Who is your favorite female dancer?"

Without much hesitation, she replied, "Renee De Marco."

Walters smiled, remembering how the De Marcos had taught him ballroom style when staging "Begin the Beguine" nearly a decade earlier. "All right," he announced. "From now on, whenever we rehearse, *you* are Renee De Marco." Garland looked at him with wide eyes and gave a sigh of relief.[29] "I realized," he'd later explain, "I had to create an image for her, so she could do . . . not an impersonation but [rather] get an image of someone else, instead of 'Me . . . *Judy,* trying to get up and move around.' It took her away from 'me' dancing."[30]

The new finale developed into top-flight entertainment. Edens's epic ten-minute medley was edited to a still substantial five. (Walters's solo take on "Don't Sit Under the Apple Tree" was among the deletions.) Garland's confident footwork impressed everyone, including the skilled chorines keeping time behind her. "When you're in a number with a star," recalled Dorothy Tuttle, "and you're the [trained] background dancer . . . you don't expect the star to dance the way you can. [But Judy] was just wonderful. And of course with Chuck you could do almost anything."[31]

Mayer was pleased as well by the obvious Garland-Walters chemistry—so much so that he considered Chuck for a possible artist contract. But in Walters's recollection, "Arthur [Freed] suggested that I might be more useful to them in the [dance] department." It can only be speculated as to whether concerns about his homosexuality might have undermined the studio's faith in Walters as a screen personality. Lucille Ryman Carroll, M-G-M's head of talent in the 1940s and 1950s, remembers: "The studio was very anti-gay when it came to hiring stars. We could use them in smaller parts, as writers, and in the art department, but not in major roles."[32] It also could be argued that in 1943 there was little reason for M-G-M to add another song-and-dance man to a payroll that already carried George Murphy, Gene Kelly, and, sporadically, Fred Astaire.

Filming resumed on *Girl Crazy* in mid-spring, and Freed told the studio's purported dance director to choreograph himself into the five-minute "Embraceable You" sequence simply because—in the words of Hedda Hopper—"Judy begged so hard."[33] A smitten Walters chose to present the singer as the object of everybody's affection, placing her on a pedestal of sorts—in actuality an upright piano—off which the all-male student body of Cody College pushes and spins while singing of their devotion. Walters enters and takes charge, genially wrapping Judy in his arms.

"By now, I was pretty hooked on having the script," he said, "and with that number, I'm most proud of how I was able to blend from book into the number, make the whole circle, and then blend back into the book. She's been dancing with the boys; then she hooks arms with the [specific] guy she's dating and walks outside for the next scene. So smooth."

Garland's affection for Walters was reciprocal and lifelong. More than twenty years later, radio commentator Jack Wagner surprised Judy during a 1965 phone interview by telling her that he'd appeared with her in *Girl Crazy* "in a couple of those fabulous Chuck Walters routines."

"Did you *really*?" she responded incredulously. "You were a dancer?"

"Well . . . almost," he joked. "Several of us were pushing you around on a piano during the 'Embraceable You' number, if you remember that."

"Oh, golly, yes," Garland answered. "And I was always so afraid the darn piano would tip over!"

"We all were!" laughed Wagner.

By the time of that interview, their former choreographer had long since advanced to his career as a director. Offered Wagner: "And Chuck has since become *Charles,* of course."

Judy replied warmly, "Well, he's still *Chuck* to me!"[34]

"Embraceable You" reveals just how much Walters had already discovered about filmmaking. "Nobody ever learned anything with their mouth," he said of his first years at M-G-M, "so I looked a lot and listened a lot."[35] In those days, it was standard for the stationary camera to be placed at a neutral distance, which effectively flattened movement. Chuck opted to break the trend by plotting a bold traveling shot where, in one elongated pan, the camera traveled with him and Judy as they encircled the assembly hall set. Preparation was key; the cameraman needed to keep the duo in full frame (and in focus), and the crew had to remove the cables or equipment that otherwise would come into view as the apparatus revolved in an almost 360-degree rotation. The end result was fifteen fluid seconds of visceral excitement, as well as the onset of Walters's appreciation for the physical sensations achieved by a mobile camera.

Girl Crazy wrapped after two other Walters routines were captured: the roughhouse Garland-Rooney duet "Could You Use Me?" and "Bidin' My Time," a wryly comic affair for Garland and the students around a campfire. (Chuck sprinkled the latter with novelty, allowing the guitar that Judy strummed to briefly hover mysteriously in the air, and then directing his star to break the sacred "fourth wall" by winking impishly into the camera.) When released in November 1943, *Girl Crazy* grossed in excess of $3 million—nearly triple what it cost to make—and topped all other Garland-Rooney musicals at the box office. The *Hollywood Reporter* praised: "Dance direction by Charles Walters sends Judy Garland through some of the most engaging steps she has performed for the camera."[36]

Best Foot Forward—which cost $1,161,992—had gone into theaters a few weeks earlier, tallied a healthy $2,704,000, and been hailed by the *New York Times* as a "rollicking musical film which pops with . . . the fresh spirit of youth."[37] When *Du Barry*'s figures are considered as well (cost, $1,295,543; gross, $3,496,000), it becomes obvious that the carefully primed Freed Unit entertainment was embraced by audiences everywhere.

To whet the public's appetite for *Girl Crazy*, the *Los Angeles Times* dispatched columnist Jerry Mason to interview Garland that August. He'd attended an advance screening and was particularly taken with her terpsichorean ability. "One of the things you'll enjoy most," Mason predicted, "is Judy's dancing. She looks like a Ginger Rogers or a Rita Hayworth. But not to hear Miss Garland tell it. She says: 'I am the world's Number One Dance Faker. Chuck Walters (he's Metro's dance creator and an Astaire in his own right) shows me how to do the steps. And I do them. And that's all there is to it. And it's almost as much fun as singing.'"

Mason hastened to include his own appreciation for their efforts, advising Judy and his readers, "It's almost as much fun just watching."[38]

9

A Company Man

For all the quick acceptance of his work, Walters found there was still much to learn about Metro protocol. He was particularly humbled when, during *Girl Crazy*'s protracted production, Freed delivered a blistering crash course in the collaborative spirit that guided his unit.

"As soon as I would get an inspiration," Walters recounted, "I always went *right* to Roger [Edens]. So I presented this idea, and Roger said, 'That sounds marvelous.' Arthur called me [within] a couple of hours, and said he had heard the idea. Well, I thought Roger had presented it *as his own*. Storming up to Freed's office, I went. Young, stupid, and defensive, I said, 'Mr. Freed, that idea was mine.' Well, he gave me a reading that I never forgot—and I don't to this day! Arthur said, 'Don't worry about credit. You will get credit—*due credit*. Everybody [here] knows what everybody [else] does.' Well, it went on and on, and I just shrunk and shrunk."[1]

Walters soon redeemed himself. Metro had contracted hot-tempered choreographer Jack Cole, who then sat idle until assigned George Cukor's Victorian melodrama, *Gaslight*. "They asked if I would teach Ingrid Bergman to waltz," recalled Cole, "and I said 'No.' I didn't want them to get the idea that I went around doing cleanup jobs, [or] that I was a dancing teacher. You had to set it up right away that you didn't do certain things. That was necessary . . . at places like Metro, particularly."[2] Walters voluntarily took over Bergman and *Gaslight*, receiving no credit, and Cole soon fled M-G-M for artistic autonomy at Columbia. Cole's "dancing teacher" theory was nonetheless sound, as Chuck next was asked to instruct Charles Laughton and the cast of *The Canterville Ghost* in dances authentic to sixteenth-century England. He then traveled to David O. Selznick's independent operation to fashion (without credit) the large-scale shadow waltz for *Since You Went Away*—arguably the most stunning sequence in the 172-minute home-front drama.

After these, he assisted hoofer John Bubbles when his former *Transatlantic Rhythm* castmate was in a jam: "Bubbles did a dance number [in *Cabin in the Sky*], and of course the taps weren't recorded when he shot [it]. You always put the taps in afterward. So when Bubbles was in the looping stage, he couldn't remember what the step was; they called me in to see if I could break it down and analyze his step to do his foot sounds. I never had such a challenge in my life."

Chuck Walters was fast becoming a genuine company man.

With success came some degree of attitude. Certain members of the Freed Unit elite weren't above flaunting a semi-superior air, and Walters was occasionally among the guilty. He'd frankly offer that the real reason he wanted to perform at M-G-M was "because I couldn't *stand* the way George Murphy danced." (The joke landed well with many insiders, given Murphy's growing reputation as a conservative watchdog.) At parties, Chuck would entertain with his spot-on impression of the Irish hoofer. He'd limp through an innocuous soft-shoe, sporting a squinty grin, arms out to his sides, hands flexed upward, fingers glued together. Not surprisingly, he didn't work directly with the star when he was recruited for Murphy's *Broadway Rhythm*. The bland backstager was produced by Jack Cummings (Metro's third-ranked musical maker) and significantly elevated by Walters's two contributions: "Brazilian Boogie," with siren Lena Horne, and the grouchy "Milkman, Keep Those Bottles Quiet," for Nancy Walker.

"Chuck and I were doing a number that nobody wanted to do," Walker reflected. "He said, 'We have six weeks to rehearse.' I asked, 'How long is [this number] going to last?' He replied, 'About three and a half minutes.' 'SIX WEEKS!' I yelled. 'I've been in complete Broadway shows that did it in four.'"[3]

For a quick study like Nancy, the situation seemed absurd. "We used to show up and play cards . . . it was ridiculous!" she wailed. "And the people we had working . . . Chuck was from New York. [Co-star] Ben Blue was from New York. Tommy Dorsey was an 'every-night' man, working bands here and there. And I was an 'every-night' performer. Why did we need six weeks? But that was that. That was the [M-G-M] style, and you adhered to it." Walters took the healthy time allotment in stride. "I'll rehearse all night until it is right," he said. "That to me is very important." (He had, in fact—just prior to *Broadway Rhythm*—spent fourteen days rehearsing the five-minute June Allyson specialty "I Like to Recognize the Tune" for the otherwise regrettable *Meet the People*.)

Despite Walker's later gripes, "Milkman" remains one of her liveliest big-screen appearances. She portrays a fatigued wartime welder on the night shift, heading home for "some righteous nod." In the process, she berates a dairyman (Blue) and braves a game of bottle-toss that turns into a jitterbug. As a final gag ("a kicker," Chuck called them), Walker wallops the energetic Blue over the head with a jug of "that bottled moo." "Always room for one last laugh," the choreographer maintained.

Clowning accomplished, Walters turned to subtle sex and gave the oft-stationary Lena Horne a rare opportunity to swing her hips. Hugh Martin and Ralph Blane's "Brazilian Boogie" boasted a syncopated vocal chart by Chuck's *Low and Behold* colleague Kay Thompson, new to M-G-M, and catered to the 1940s vogue for Latin American music. Walters's concepts remained fairly ambitious, and he plotted his routine with both camera operator and film editor in mind. The impressed Cummings surprised his new choreographer by allowing him to develop his directorial eye. "In those days," Chuck explained, "you would stage your number, and the [movie's] director would take it over; you didn't know what the hell he was going to do with it. I'd see them going up on a boom, and I'd think, 'What the *hell* are they going up there for?' Then when you saw your routine [on the screen], you'd think, 'Well, *that* isn't right. That's not how I constructed it.'"[4]

Entrusted with his first chance to film an entire number, Walters wondered how to cohesively move his dancers on and off the screen ("all that stuff was mechanical"). "Luckily," he said, "I finally understood that [entrances] and exits weren't necessary; you could change [camera angles] when you wanted, and make whatever you wanted disappear." A quick study, he sought guidance from others on the lot and soon gained an even greater appreciation for the creative potential of dance on-screen, marveling, "You really can do *anything*."

"Brazilian Boogie" opened with the camera swooping down to the stage and tracking sideways along a row of tapping, spat-covered feet—a shot that soon pauses to take in a feminine pair of heels. Panning upward, the camera then reveals Horne in a silky slit skirt and flaunting a bare midriff. She sings and slithers while a leggy chorus gyrates around her. Mid-number, the star is visually bordered by two vertical rows of waving gloves, positioned on either side of the frame. The climax of the number finds Horne flanked by two lanky chorus boys as her twisting torso, splayed fingers, and general abandon ignite the ensemble into full frenzy.

The sequence proved a stellar example of integration: part Latin carnival, part African primitivism, and part American boogie-woogie. Equally successful were Walters's efforts to fuse choreography, a sweeping camera, and discreet editing. When Bosley Crowther wrote a "Word on Musicals" for the *New York Times,* he grumbled about the conventional approach of current filmmakers but saluted "Brazilian Boogie" as one of the few dance sequences to "succeed" and "sustain [its] unified impulse" from beginning to end.[5]

Walters confessed he got "a crazy thrill" when shooting "Brazilian Boogie": "It was just heaven. From that moment on, I didn't want to choreograph numbers, unless I could film them also. I wanted to protect my work."

Always looking ahead, Freed had convinced M-G-M to purchase the rights to the story "5135 Kensington" in early 1942 (while *Best Foot* and *Girl Crazy* were still in pre-production). Sally Benson's account of her turn-of-the-century midwestern childhood was melodically retitled *Meet Me in St. Louis* and seemed like prime material for a nostalgic, "ginger-peachy" musical.

Many of Walters's former stage associates by now were members of Freed's expanding workforce and assigned to the film: director Vincente Minnelli (*The Show Is On*), orchestrator Conrad Salinger (*Parade, Between the Devil*), costume designer Irene Sharaff (*Parade, Jubilee, Banjo Eyes*), plus Martin, Blane, and Thompson. Completing the roster were Broadway's respected Lemuel Ayers for set design, Edens for musical adaptations, and Garland as star.

"Very seldom would I do the dances all the way through a picture," Walters recalled, but for *St. Louis,* he was on his own and initially stumped.[6] Believing Martin and Blane had written a completely original score for the film, he first agonized over "Skip to My Lou": "I couldn't let them know that I didn't know what to do with it!" Distress turned to disbelief when he offhandedly vented to his parents, "What the hell is a skip to my lou?!" Smiling at their son's desperation, they replied, "Oh, we know that song from when we were kids. It's a hundred years old." Walters would later laughingly acknowledge: "So my parents helped me choreograph the number."[7]

In a curvy web of movement, he split the sequence into three short sections—a square dance, a promenade, and a momentary variation on "London Bridge" (his old standby from *Let's Face It,* more recently used in *Girl Crazy*). He then used the scripted personalities of the cast to motivate his choreography. Brother Lon gently teases sister Esther when she sashays by with one of the tallest boys in the room. Fickle sister Rose flits from partner to partner ("I'll find another one prettier than you"). And John Truett, Esther's reticent "boy next door," attempts to join in but winds up awkwardly in the background. Rather than offer a few moments of mindless social dance, "Skip to My Lou" instead synthesized the film's central theme of family while expanding the emotions of its primary characters.

"The Trolley Song" provided its own challenge. The twenty-one-year-old Garland was noticeably dismayed at once again having been cast as a teenager, and her frustration spilled over into rehearsals. "Judy and I weren't speaking," Walters recalled. "I would set steps with the kids and then would have to go and knock on her [dressing room] door. Well, this was *ludicrous,* after the way we'd been getting along—all the good things we'd done, and the fun we had doing them. By the time we shot it, I said, 'Judy, what the *hell* was bugging you in rehearsal?' She shrugged, 'Oh, I don't know.' She couldn't remember, so it couldn't have been very important."[8]

Despite her early misgivings, Garland quickly grew to appreciate *St. Louis.* "Chuck worked very well with Judy," observed contract dancer Dorothy Raye, recalling that a good amount of amiable yet disciplined effort transpired between the two. "They got along beautifully. And I think he added some fun to her life, too, because *he* was fun—although a stickler for working when it was work time."[9]

Developing "The Trolley Song" took thought. Garland historian John Fricke explains, "This isn't just the moment where Judy sings her big song. It's 'Esther' offering her differing emotions during those three and a half minutes—from anticipation to disappointment to excitement. That's a *quantum* emotional leap, and yet it's all in the performance and the staging. Chuck and Judy worked with the plot and characters to build that sequence. Everything seems simple, but it's constant, pure storytelling—and an audience gets caught up in that."[10] (So did critics. In its original review of *St. Louis,* the *Los Angeles Examiner* unreservedly characterized "The Trolley Song" as "really one of the best-staged musical numbers ever put on the screen.")[11]

With equal care, Walters supplied other delights: a few waltz steps for "The Boy Next Door" as the teenage Esther appraises herself in a mirror, a sisterly "Under the Bamboo Tree" cakewalk for Garland and Margaret O'Brien, and a tenderly staged (but ultimately excised) "Boys and Girls Like You and Me," wherein Esther and her beau stroll—per Walters's recollection—"away from the fairground and are in a sort of bright spot from a moonbeam." At the climactic Christmas Eve ball, Garland endures three awkward partners in a round of slapstick polkas; the scene is capped by her finally realized waltz with the boy next door to the strains of "There's No Place Like Home." The film embraced an amalgam of dance forms, and when asked in later years to define his choreographic style, Walters was blunt: "Pure bastard."

"But *pure.*"

Released in November 1944, *Meet Me in St. Louis* surpassed all prior M-G-M products at the box office except *Gone with the Wind.* Walters's intelligent contributions, very often overlooked, were so subtly woven into the film's basic fabric as to be unremovable without eliminating crucial blocks of the book. "I thought of the film as a whole," he said. "Someone would suggest this or that to me, and I would respond that it wasn't possible—that it wasn't at all something the character would do."

Given the musical integration achieved on *St. Louis,* Metro's subsequent song-and-dance spectacle—and Walters's next assignment—was a thematic throwback to the early days of the talkies. M-G-M hadn't gambled on a motion picture revue since the unfinished *The March of Time* (1930). Now, with the studio poised to celebrate its twentieth-anniversary season, Freed turned to his creative team to develop a celebratory (albeit plotless) cavalcade, *Ziegfeld Follies of 1944.* Virtually every star on the lot—musical or otherwise—was at their disposal.

In several instances, "should be directed by Chuck Walters" found its way onto *Follies'* initial November 16, 1943, rundown.[12] Earmarked material included "Everywhere I Roam," a sailor-meets-pinup "dance pantomime" for Gene Kelly and Lana Turner; "Pass That Peace Pipe" for A-listers Astaire, Garland, Rooney, and others; and "The Steam Is on the Beam" for junior talents Allyson, De Haven, and hot newcomer Van

Johnson. Amid these ultimately unrealized concepts, some finalized material began filming January 24, 1944. "The *Follies*," said Walters, "was a film made of bits and pieces. Whenever a star had some time off, they would grab him or her for a number."

Chuck's first opportunity to direct on a Freed production came in June, when he helmed the unapologetically optimistic "Pied Piper" for Jimmy Durante. Walters launched the routine with a *Wizard of Oz* cinematography conceit, filming the preliminary street shots in dreary black and white and switching to Technicolor at the comic's entrance. The ebullient, gravel-voiced Durante strutted along to his own composition, "You Gotta Start Off Each Day with a Song," simultaneously energizing a throng of city dwellers.

Afterward, Chuck was immediately pulled into a second *Follies* sequence. Working with Kay Thompson, Edens had written "A Great Lady Has 'An Interview,'" in which English beauty Greer Garson would musically spoof her own celebrity as a "glamorous . . . amorous . . . *ham*-orous" screen actress. A syncopated press corps was scripted to fawn over Garson's announcement of her forthcoming "monumental biographical tribute" to Madam Gretchen Crematante, inventor of the all-important safety pin. (The Edens-Thompson satire was based, in part, on recent events. The noble 1941 biopic *Blossoms in the Dust* featured Garson's portrayal of Texas Children's Home founder Edna Gladney. That film's introductory text proclaimed, "This is the story of a Great Lady, who did Great Work." A year later, the actress won plaudits as the famed scientist in *Madam Curie,* then turned public diva in a six-minute acceptance speech when presented with the 1943 Oscar as Best Actress in *Mrs. Miniver.*)

"Once we had done the introduction," Thompson said, "everything fell into place; it was nothing but fun. Roger said, 'God, let's get Chuck up here.' So, Chuck came up, and Ralph [Blane], and we did the whole thing . . . and they just fell on the floor: 'You've got to do it just like that!' Well, I said, you have to be the reporters. So I leaned against the desk and acted it out, Roger played it, and we had a feeling we'd got it!"[13] At a "command performance" in Freed's living room, the troupe performed for Garson, while her increasingly unconvinced spouse looked on. "Her husband thought it beneath her," Walters recalled.

Dismissed but not defeated, the "performers" retreated to their car. "Well, it's perfect for Judy," said Edens. "She can imitate Kay. She'll be great."[14] It was a tall order; in the words of Gloria De Haven, Thompson was "a dynamo. Wildly talented, wildly flamboyant, and wildly wild. When she entered a room, she *entered*. She wouldn't walk in, she'd float in, and her arms would rise. She owned every place she walked into; all eyes would turn. She had that kind of command."[15] Such would be the basic "Great Lady" blueprint for Garland, who'd most recently depicted an innocent turn-of-the-century teenager.

Walters began rehearsals for "A Great Lady" on July 6. Because the war had depleted the supply of male dancers, "Metro imported twelve from New York," reported Hedda Hopper.[16] Four days were devoted to refining their agile choreography before Garland joined the all-male group. "Judy was dying to do it," Chuck said later. "She learned it in a week!"[17]

The occupational send-up lent itself to easy staging. Sixteen dark-suited pressmen are shown as they enter the home of a screen legend, dismissing other movie queens of the day in the process: "Greta," "Bette-a," "Loretta," and "The Song of Bernadette-a.'" (Referencing the last, Walters inserted a subtle jab at the inspirational 1943 Jennifer Jones film by having the dancers mime a spiritual vision, elevating eyes and hands toward the sky and then kneeling, arms wrapped around their shoulders.) The finish was a mock spiritual—lyrically invoking "Hallelujah" and "a big Amen"—as the boys undertook complicated counterpoint movement, hands clapping one rhythm while their feet tapped against the beat.

Assuming he'd be behind the camera for "A Great Lady," Walters was "extremely disappointed" to learn that Freed had given that job to Minnelli. "You can see by the way it's choreographed, I conceived the whole thing with the camera in mind," he said. "Then all of a sudden they said, 'Let Vincente film it. It's better that you get to work with Fanny Brice.' I protested that it was all ready to go, but they replied that Vincente would film it just as I had envisioned, and that we needed to advance in the project. So I didn't get 'Directed by . . .' on the screen, which I was already wishing for."

In his 1989 history of Minnelli's film career, Steve Harvey reports on "A Great Lady" and notes that "the acrobatics of Charles Walters' choreography is delightfully suave." Then, however, Harvey inaccurately assigns Minnelli full credit for the routine's fluid cinematography: "It's [his] camera work that gives the song its exhilarating momentum. Throughout the number, there is no internal cutting—the last half of the sequence is filmed in one long shot lasting three minutes, the camera swooping around Garland and the cast up to the last instant, when it tracks through a thicket of ecstatically thrust arms to a close-up of this droll Legend, simpering beguilingly above a swarm of white feathers."[18] (The passageway of outstretched hands provided a pictorial effect similar to that achieved by Walters in "Brazilian Boogie.") Chuck would receive a prominent "dance direction" acknowledgment on the sequence's opening title card. "But every shot in that routine," he maintained, "was mine."

As ordered, however, Walters reported for work with Fanny Brice, who was filming a moderately funny sketch, "The Sweepstakes Ticket," under Roy Del Ruth's direction. Chuck was asked to supply a small dancing bit wherein a winning lottery ticket could be pried—sneakily—from a rear pants pocket. He knew his task was of the "cleanup" variety, against which Jack Cole had railed. But Brice was a true show business legend and the only star in Freed's picture to have appeared in an actual *Ziegfeld Follies*. "I loved her!" Chuck recounted admiringly. "Oh God, I'd get her going, 'And then what did you do?' 'And what was he like?' Well, of course, any star loved that! And she'd talk by the hour!" Pleased by such attention, Fanny at last inquired, "Who is this boy? I like him!"[19]

The work with Brice was quickly accomplished, and Walters found himself back on "A Great Lady," assisting his dancers as the camera began to turn. "It was my first studio assignment," recounts M-G-M office-boy-turned-performer Bert May, appearing as one of the doting "gentlemen of the press." The acrobatic teenager had been staged to execute a front walkover and, after a silent one-two downbeat, offer his prerecorded line: "She's gonna win the next Academy Award." Timing was essential, yet—with cast performing, crew milling around, and filming expensively under way—the dancer recalled, "I missed the tacit *one-two* and arrived too late to mouth my line. The pianist had always followed me during rehearsal, but the tempo of the playback threw me." Walters offered reassurance, but the anxious youngster continued to make the same mistake. "At M-G-M, there was a rule," May explains, "that if a scene required a certain amount of takes, the front office had to be notified. They had to know the reason for the hold-up." In this case, it was a novice who was increasingly certain he'd be replaced. Adding to his misery, a small studio tour group had arrived to watch. Walters remained unflustered through it all, reassuring him, "You're fine, Bert. Just count *one-two*."

"I received another small reprieve," recalls May, "when one of the Technicolor cameras needed reloading. I took the opportunity to go to the playback machine with Chuck and listen. 'You'll get it,' he said. Then we started all over again. Only this time, to my great horror, everyone on the soundstage—all the grips, all the dancers, even the annoyed tour group—all hollered out at once: '*ONE-TWO!*' *Right* on the downbeat." Bert May perfectly executed his lip-synch, and the day continued.

"Not once did Chuck Walters ever make me feel that I couldn't do it," he acknowledged gratefully. It was an encouraging beginning to May's multiple decades of stage and screen work.[20]

The first cut of *Ziegfeld Follies* sneak-previewed on November 1, 1944, and ran for 173 minutes with no intermission. Audience reaction was more dazed than dazzled, and Freed began a hasty process of deletions and abridgements. (Edens could only quip, "If this keeps on, we can always release it as a short.")[21] One of the first casualties proved to be Durante's "Pied Piper," and the distressed Walters found small consolation in the fact that he salvaged the number's black and white footage for use in his ensuing musical short subject, *Spreadin' the Jam*.

At a more manageable 110 minutes, the film played a couple of road show engagements in June 1945 but was held from general distribution until the following March. It then carried the more age-appropriate title *Ziegfeld Follies of 1946*. Critical opinion of "A Great Lady" varied widely, and the satire's potency undoubtedly was diluted by the fact that all the allusions to Garson were referring to something now several years in the past. The *New York Post* groaned, "The Garland routine is flamboyantly dull," and the *Chicago Tribune* called the number "pointless [and] highly regrettable." In sharp contrast, however, the New York *Daily News* praised Garland for "[letting] her auburn hair down as far as it will go in a devastatingly funny burlesque," and the *Hollywood Reporter* cheered the loudest, calling the sequence the film's "*piece de resistance*. It is wackily and wonderfully delightful. It is sparklingly inventive in its situations."[22]

"I suppose one of the things that made those Metro musicals so alive and inventive," Walters later offered, "was that we didn't study other people's work or what was happening in the theatre, even though most of us came from the stage. . . . We'd get wild ideas and say, 'Let's do it'—and we did!"[23]

10

Good News

Metro kept its dance directors busy. Between 1944 and 1946, Walters (officially) provided steps for eight M-G-M feature films overseen by six different producers. He would later comment, "I never knew when the phone rang what they'd tell me to do next."[1] Besides supplying dances for Freed, he was asked to spruce up *Three Men in White* (1944; the thirteenth entry in the popular Dr. Kildare series), *Thrill of a Romance* (1945; an Esther Williams–Van Johnson vehicle), *Weekend at the Waldorf* (1945; an all-star *Grand Hotel* remake), and *Her Highness and the Bellboy* (1945). The last featured Walters's peculiar dream sequence for June Allyson, Robert Walker, and Santa Claus, deemed "pretentious" by the *New York Times*.[2]

In late October 1944, Chuck ventured into the short subject department to prepare the dance-infused *Spreadin' the Jam*. The studio used such one- and two-reelers to groom potential directors and test future talent—in this case Jan Clayton, the promising young Broadway star of *Carousel*. Walters followed this assignment by directing himself as a shore-leave sailor having "Fun on the Wonderful Midway" with former ballerina Frances Rafferty.[3] The relentlessly peppy sequence—offering a far-fetched look at a movie musical facing the camera—topped off *Bud Abbott and Lou Costello in Hollywood* (1945) and marked Chuck's final on-screen dancing while in his prime.

Ralph Blane penned lyrics for both *Spreadin' the Jam* and "Midway" and recognized Chuck's ambition. "[He] was doing an awful lot of choreography in those days," Blane noted, "but he had this longing to do more than just choreograph."[4]

Meanwhile, the Freed Unit's productivity was at full speed in 1945–1946. The producer failed expensively with *Yolanda and the Thief* (choreographed by Eugene Loring) but had resounding hits with *The Harvey*

Girls and *Till the Clouds Roll By* (both enlivened by Bob Alton). Walters was pleased to be assigned Freed's next gamble, a musical transformation of Eugene O'Neill's *Ah, Wilderness!* with original songs by Blane and Harry Warren. Slated to direct was Rouben Mamoulian, who already had to his credit the Broadway touchstones *Porgy and Bess* (1935) and *Oklahoma!* (1943) and such films as *Applause* (1929) and *Queen Christina* (1933). Before active pre-production could begin, however, both the director and Chuck were pressed into service to help Freed with an "all-black," Broadway-bound musical he was silently backing.

St. Louis Woman possessed an enviable talent pool, with Fayard and Harold Nicholas, Rex Ingram, Juanita Hall, and sensation-in-the-making Pearl Bailey onstage and a score by Johnny Mercer and Harold Arlen. The first New Haven preview nevertheless had been slammed as "a dull, pretentious, and boring evening of theater" by the African American paper *The Defender*.[5] Protecting his investment, Freed pulled director Lemuel Ayers and sent in Mamoulian; by Philadelphia, he'd replaced ballet choreographer Antony Tudor with Walters. The dance doctor arrived in March 1946, carrying enough clothes for six days; he would later remember his protracted stay with the show as all about the search for a clean shirt.

Although he loathed admitting it, Chuck's once limitless stamina had lessened under M-G-M's indulgences. William Hawkins profiled the choreographer for the *New York World-Telegram*, reporting that the show's round-the-clock schedule had made Walters "a very weary gentleman. After four years of dance directing in moving pictures, he is finding with a shock that the same job in the theater is a very different proposition."[6]

"Out there," Chuck explained, "you have enormous stages for rehearsals. When you stop for a rest, you can push back huge doors, and the sun comes streaming in. You have almost as much time for a single number as you have here for a whole show. And you are working with an orchestra the size of a symphony. The one thing missing [when working at a film studio] is the excitement of living performances, the tension and the contact and the reaction. Sometimes a picture may be completed for a year or more, and when you hear what audiences think of it, you have forgotten it."[7]

Walters resuscitated more than a dozen musical numbers before the once floundering *St. Louis Woman* opened in New York on March 30. It was hailed by the New York *Daily News* as "the best Negro musical in many seasons, and the best new musical of this season,"[8] and by the *Mirror* as a "fast, funny, tuneful musical [that] had first nighters blistering their palms applauding."[9] Few critics mentioned by name the Hollywood choreographer responsible for so much of the show's vigor, although the complimentary *New York Times* singled out the cast's "dancing and singing . . . [which is] at times good musical comedy. . . . There are moments of lightness. A first-act cakewalk is fine; it is graceful, fast and understands the use of a climax."[10] Walters received a runner-up Donaldson Award citation—a precursor to the respected Antoinette Perry "Tony" Award—for his choreography, although *St. Louis Woman* bowed out after only 113 performances. Freed never lost faith in the show and never stopped plotting a film of the horse jockey story, even if it meant deviating from the concept of an all-black show. "It's wanted for a white cast," Hedda Hopper informed her readers in 1946, "and Mickey Rooney."[11]

Back at Metro in June 1946, Walters began twelve weeks of dance rehearsals for *Summer Holiday* (the retitled *Ah, Wilderness!*). Director Mamoulian had written in a memo that his goal for the picture was a "musical play"—*not* musical comedy—and that O'Neill's work would "be told through the medium of dialogue, songs, dance and music. . . . Overblown [spectacle] is not the kind of musical we want to make."[12]

As a dance director who'd moved from film to film, Chuck now realized that he'd been given the great gift of four years "to watch other directors at work, [which is] something you can't very well do when you turn director yourself. It's generally considered bad form, [as] most directors don't welcome other directors on their sets." Walters had a monumental teacher in Mamoulian, who was noted for his unique ability to synthesize all the elements of cinema. "On stage," Mamoulian told John Kobal in 1968, "you have only one action—that of the actors. On screen, you have three: 1) the action of the actors, 2) the action of the camera, 3) the action of the editing. All three should be rhythmically integrated. Add music, and you have one cohesive whole to which you can apply Michelangelo's definition of a perfect sculpture: Roll it down the hill, and nothing will break off."[13] (In time, two properties Freed once envisioned for Mamoulian—*The Belle of New York* and *Jumbo*—would be realized by Walters.)

Summer Holiday was in its third month of filming when word came that Winifred Walter had died on September 7, 1946. Her only child briefly traveled to Anaheim for the private funeral and then quickly returned to work at Metro. There is no record of Winifred's reaction to

Chuck's success, but as she deeply appreciated music, it is reasonable to think that she was proud of her influence. Unfortunately, she passed just before her son's definitive career came into focus. (Joe Walter eventually would remarry, remaining in Anaheim with his new wife, Amelia.)

The Freed-Mamoulian musical wrapped in mid-October and wound up with a hefty price tag of $2,258,235. Its rarified approach, however, failed to entertain preview audiences. As a result, M-G-M heavily re-edited certain numbers and completely dropped others—including an Omar Khayyám sequence fashioned by Walters for Mickey Rooney and Gloria De Haven. "The few who have seen the Persian fantasy," notes Freed biographer Hugh Fordin, "speak of it with delight and regret that it never was used."[14] *Summer Holiday* stayed on the shelf for eighteen months before finally being released in April 1948. At a truncated ninety-two minutes, the movie was a critical and commercial failure.

"I laid out all the numbers on [that] picture," admitted Chuck. "It was a very frustrating time. Maybe I had been spoilt in getting a *taste* of directing."

Freed empathized, but this was not a new situation. He later divulged that he had "had a hell of a time" getting the studio behind Minnelli for his first directorial assignment in 1942. "One of the biggest criticisms of the business," he explained, "was that they wouldn't give young people a chance. Everything had to be [an old reliable like] Robert Z. Leonard and so forth; there was a 'patent' on who was a director."[15] Freed, however, stayed determined to break this tradition.

Good News had opened on Broadway in September 1927, and audiences delighted in being led to their seats by ushers wearing collegiate jerseys. The pit band entered through the rear of the 46th Street Theater, leading cheers as they marched down the aisle and prepared to play. The subsequent, tuneful evening celebrated the joys of youth.

M-G-M grabbed movie rights to the Buddy De Sylva–Lew Brown–Ray Henderson musical and captured much of that fun in its 1930 release. The film's young cast jubilantly pounded out "The Varsity Drag" and reminded post–Black Tuesday America that "The Best Things in Life Are Free." Nine years later, Freed seriously considered *Good News* as the Garland-Rooney follow-up to his smash *Babes in Arms,* but it took another seven to get the vintage property locked into Metro's production roster—now for the sunny team of Van Johnson and June Allyson.[16] Renewed enthusiasm quite possibly stemmed from the recent success (artistic if not financial) of Broadway's *Billion Dollar Baby,* another melodic, wry representation of the Roaring Twenties. Freed enlisted that show's star dancer, Joan McCracken, and its clever librettists, Betty Comden and Adolph Green, for his own flapper entertainment.

When Walters heard *Good News* was in the offing, he found it difficult to conceal his enthusiasm. "It was like somebody put a firecracker under me," he said, recalling the amateur variation he had steered at Anaheim High. "And right there I gave [Arthur] a private audition." (Years later, Walters merrily remembered his shameless lobbying: "Arthur couldn't help but give it to me after *that.*")

"You know, Chuck," the producer responded, "I think this might be a good picture for you. You should direct *Good News.*"

If the debuting director harbored any apprehensions, they had to be short-lived. *Good News* was allotted only eighteen days to rehearse and fifty-five to shoot. Freed sent a memo to studio executive J. G. Mayer on January 27, 1947, saying, "As you probably know, Chuck Walters has been assigned as the Director of this picture. Would you kindly arrange for Chuck to have a director's office where he will have the necessary space for a secretary and etc. We want to move as fast as we can on the preparation for the picture, and the above would help a great deal."[17] To further assist, Freed surrounded his freshman with experienced talent and friends. Edens was made associate producer and told to "stay close." Also retained were vocal arranger Kay Thompson, editor Albert Akst, and cinematographer Charles Schoenbaum (with whom Walters had worked on *Summer Holiday* and the Abbott and Costello picture). Of ultimate significance was the appointment of Al Jennings; this friendly, detail-oriented assistant director would eventually tally eleven Walters pictures over the next thirteen years.

The two associates with whom the director felt little rapport were Comden and Green. "We didn't get along too well," Walters noted with a shrug. "They were very superior, [and] I was 'novice Charlie' on my first picture. By the time they did their stuff, it was in Roger's hands. I had very little contact with them."[18]

Regardless of their demeanor, the first-time Hollywood librettists delivered a snappy script that would be best propelled by a director-choreographer who understood rhythm. Their faintly revised story line was set in "the year of 'flaming youth,' when a girl was a flapper, and a boy was a sheik." At fictional Tait College, the student body fears football hero Tommy Marlowe (Johnson) won't pass his French exam and retain his eligibility to play in the big game. The athlete is further distracted by Pat McClellan, a gold-digging transfer from the Black Briar Finishing School (De Haven), and Connie Lane, a sensible student librarian who coincidentally happens to tutor French (Allyson).

On January 31, 1947, Walters spent his first day monitoring tests of potential supporting cast members. Baby-faced Ray McDonald, a gifted tapper with a six-year history at the studio, landed the part of Bobby, the bench-warming runt of the Tait team. Making her film debut, Joan McCracken unseated the previously approved Betty Garrett and won the plum role of Babe Doolittle, Bobby's pushy paramour. The production then hit a snag when Johnson proved unavailable, and Mickey Rooney—scarcely the quarterback type—came and went as his replacement. The role of Tommy Marlowe finally passed to an equally miscast Peter Lawford. To his merit, the British actor worked hard to Americanize his speech. "[And] when I'd slip," Lawford remembered, "Chuck would nudge me and urge, 'Cut the Back Bay stuff.'"[19] Walters also devoted time to improving Lawford's very limited musical abilities. (Upon seeing the finished film, Lawford's boyhood dance teacher, Muriel O'Brien, declared: "I kept watching him [perform] and thought, *Oh, my God!* Anybody who could teach that boy to sing and dance in time has got to be a genius.")[20]

Rehearsals for *Good News* began on February 12, with Allyson determined to establish herself in a Freed musical. Wary of her neophyte leader, she corralled her producer and said, "I love Chuck. I truly do. But do you think he's ready to direct a whole picture?" After a particularly stretched silence, Freed replied, "You must remember, June . . . *somebody* had to give you your start." To her credit, Allyson soon adjusted, and later she acknowledged, "Chuck knew exactly what he wanted, and he knew exactly how to get you to do it."[21] His abilities, however, didn't stop Gloria De Haven from abandoning her unsympathetic role. The *Hollywood Reporter* announced that the young actress had been put on suspension after "differences over the script."[22] Her part was given to De Haven doppelganger Patricia Marshall, another untried Broadway transfer whom Chuck had to make camera ready.

Good News remains significant in that Walters also staged eight of the film's ten musical sequences, thus making him the first of Freed's "new boys" to both direct and choreograph a picture. The presence of Bob Alton, hired for production numbers, brought an even more familial feeling to the set, and Alton's devotion to his former protégé impelled him to create two of the most explosive dance routines in M-G-M history: "The Varsity Drag" and "Pass That Peace Pipe" (finally slotted here after being abandoned during *Ziegfeld Follies* pre-production). Proclaimed Alton, "I have exactly six minutes in which to raise the customer out of his seat. If I cannot do it, I am no good."[23]

Historian Ethan Mordden would praise the Freed-Walters *Good News* some forty years later, complimenting its retention of

> a goodly amount of the original score (more, in fact, than the 1930 film did), cunningly rewriting or expanding [it] to help nudge the story along. "Lucky in Love," for instance, an up-tempo ballad duet in the stage show, becomes an ensemble number on a sorority-house porch. All the principals chime in, each with characteristic lyrics and business, McCracken dodging one swain and teasing another, Marshall shooting Lawford down with the French word "*incorrigible*"—thus setting up some plot development when Allyson coaches Lawford in French. And *that* yields a new number written by Freedians Edens, Comden, and Green, "The French Lesson." We see the Unit ingeniously at work, respecting its source while improving it according to new standards of composition.[24]

Besides these sequences, Walters brought spirit to the film's title song, set on the steps of Tait College, and the brisk "Be a Ladies Man," in which Lawford and his fellow frat brothers instruct McDonald in the manly art of swagger. He also staged the ultimately deleted "An Easier Way" (Comden-Green-Edens), which pitted Allyson's theories on the pursuit of a male against Marshall's. As set by Walters, June's pantomime ridiculed the man-snaring techniques of famous historical females. Had the routine made the final cut, it would have played as a feminine counterpoint to Lawford and McDonald's testosterone-driven "Ladies Man."

Edens continued as an untiring aide. "Roger actually took over production," Walters gratefully acknowledged. "His contributions were tremendous, [working] with Comden and Green on dialog, writing 'The

French Lesson,' pushing the period to keep it as '20s as possible: just *tremendous* contributions."[25]

Jennings felt similarly, feeling that Freed's contributions in this instance were perfunctory. "Roger was the producer on *Good News*. He really had things to say and things that he liked; yet if Chuck would want [anything done] a little bit differently, why, Roger would listen to him. They worked well together.... [T]hey *always* worked well together."[26] In one such instance, Walters remembered, "we were rehearsing 'Ladies Man' with a piano, and I asked, 'Rog, can you give me an eight bar filler?' He said, 'Sure, kid!' Then I asked, 'Hey, why don't we just let it keep going?' He *immediately* understood. 'That's great!' he replied. Roger then gave it a big sound [so Lawford and McDonald could dive] over the fence" for a big finish.[27]

Filming commenced March 10, 1947. Fearful, yet wanting to make a favorable impression, Walters asked if he could begin with a musical sequence. "It was the only thing I was familiar with. Nobody realized that I hadn't even directed a dialog test." He chose the title song, wrapping it up ahead of schedule, and then watched with mounting anxiety as technicians wheeled away the pre-recording playback machine. He ruefully recalled, "I thought, 'There goes my only friend in the world.'" Jennings looked on as the tenderfoot "came unglued a little bit."[28] Also present were Alton and Lela Simone, a pragmatic member of the Music Department, who also noticed the tension. "Chuck almost collapsed," she remembered. The concerned Alton pulled her aside and quietly asked, "Do you believe Chuck will make a good director?"

"How could he be?" she replied dismissively. "All he ever reads is *House and Garden*."

Salvation came in the form of Freed's personal assistant, Bill Ryan, who took the overwrought Walters aside and told him, "Chuck, the toughest part about being a director is *getting* a picture to direct. I want you to go make a list of everybody working on this picture—the producer, the cinematographer, his crew ... all the way down to the guy making the coffee. Then put yourself at the bottom of that list, and you'll find you're gonna have to work your ass off to *find* something to do! Remember: everybody wants to do their job. *Just let them do it.* They know a hell of a lot more about it than you do. And don't be afraid to ask questions; they'll love it. They want to help."

It was brilliant advice and allowed Walters to regain faith in his instincts. "A week later," confirmed Jennings, "Chuck was very competent."[29]

Filming dance had been easy; he had always cut on movement. Filming dialog, he realized, was similar; the words were his steps, and all he had to do was keep them flowing. "Having been a dancer," Chuck later disclosed, "my fear was in making people *too* busy. To see characters buzzing around all over the place, for no reason, just irritates me. My job was to keep it all fluid. And honest."

Walters further discovered that the direction of actors was a derivation of instructing dancers—and that he was capable of both. A contemporary journalist observed him in action and commented admiringly, "It was a show within a show. In scenes between the stars . . . he would play June's part with Peter to show her how he believed the scene should be portrayed. Then [he] would play Peter's part with June while Lawford looked on. In turn, he would act out the roles of Patricia Marshall . . . and Joan McCracken. It certainly was a more strenuous type of directing than Hollywood is used to."[30]

When *Good News* wrapped on May 23, the production was eight days ahead of schedule and under budget by $135,270.[31] Chuck found himself in the good graces of M-G-M's moneymen, and he resolved to stay there.

The film went through two months of post-production, during which Walters joined Darrow for an eighteen-day Hawaiian holiday.[32] The men returned for the sneak preview on July 18 at Inglewood's Loyola Theatre, and Chuck—for the first time—saw in the credits of a feature film "Directed by Charles Walters." He had arrived. This was confirmed by the comment cards submitted by the audience on their way out of the theater: out of 281 opinions, 114 found the production "good," while another 90 rated it "excellent."[33] Freed knew he had a winner and convinced M-G-M to hold it for December release as the Radio City Music Hall Christmas attraction. He expressed his more personal gratitude in a letter:

Dear Chuck,

Now that we have had a preview, and that the audience has corroborated our good opinion of *Good News,* I would like to congratulate you on your direction of the picture. You are entitled to be very proud of your first venture in this field, in handling of people, the charm and good taste you projected. I hope this will be the start of a wonderful career. I am really very proud of you.

Fondest regards, Arthur[34]

Edens offered similar encouragement. On the day of the preview, he scribbled on the front page of the director's script: "Dear Chuck—'Good News' Hopefully, gratefully, and affectionately—Roger." The inscription spurred a new Walters tradition: he thereafter archived all shooting scripts, embellishing them with on-set photographs, humorous annotations, and key documents. Such scrapbooks remained cherished souvenirs.

Good News found an appreciative audience, even if some critics carped about the old-fashioned plotline and substandard singing of much of the cast. *Collier's* named it "Picture of the Month" and "Musical of the Year": "a youthful, tuneful, joyous shot in the arm in the form of the gayest, fastest-paced film ever brightened by Technicolor's magic."[35] The *Hollywood Reporter* called Walters's direction "intelligent and showmanly. He made the most of the rich, abundant material he was handed, keeping the pace moving and showing a clear over-all conception of the book, music, and dancers."[36] Best of all, *Variety* declared: "Producer Freed and [associate] Edens can puff out their chests over this one. They were smart—and fortunate—to secure the services of Walters, who knows how to fit a tune and a production number into a plot without any dallying around."[37]

The film grossed more than $2,956,000—or, in Chuck's dry summation, "*Good News* made nothing but money!" Such success led to increased media attention for Walters; in one instance, the *Milwaukee Journal* pegged him as "M-G-M's Cinderella director." This feminizing moniker was conjured by Metro's publicity wizards, and it was a distant cry from the past promotion of William "Wild Bill" Wellman, Victor Fleming, or W. S. "Woody" Van Dyke, whose hard drinking and profligate womanizing had garnered estimations of masculinity that at times eclipsed their directorial achievements.[38] The *Journal,* however, meant no offense with the nickname and was most taken by the thirty-six-year-old and his eagerness: "When you first meet Chuck Walters, you feel that a young chap with such a pleasing, boyish personality and appearance belongs in front of the camera rather than behind it."

"But, no, he is now in the spot, he will tell you, where he always hoped he would land."

11

A Swell Couple

"Freed was a hero-worshipper of talent," wrote lyricist Alan Jay Lerner, "and if you were one of the fortunate ones whom he respected, his loyalty knew no bounds."[1] That being true, nothing prepared Walters for his second directorial assignment from Arthur.

The producer had been focused for much of 1947 on *The Pirate,* a plush Caribbean musical fantasy starring Judy Garland and Gene Kelly. Despite Kay Thompson's manic vocal arrangements, the rushes seemed stylistically imaginative, and Freed planned to immediately re-team Garland and Kelly for *Easter Parade.* They would be joined by *Pirate* director Vincente Minnelli, choreographer Alton, writers Frances Goodrich and Albert Hackett, and cameraman Harry Stradling. Expectations were high for *Easter Parade,* which was being conceptualized around Irving Berlin's prolific songbook.

Unfortunately, Garland's participation in *The Pirate* was marred by weeks of absenteeism as marital strife, the pressures of first-time motherhood (with baby Liza), and overmedication collided. After completing *The Pirate* in July 1947, the twenty-five-year-old singer made "a quiet, unpublicized attempt at suicide," reports biographer John Fricke, and was sent away to two psychiatric treatment facilities.[2]

On September 18, Freed reassigned *Easter Parade.* "Judy and Vincente were on the complete outs," he later recounted. "They could hardly finish *The Pirate* together. I couldn't put Vincente on it. So I said: 'Chuck, I'm going to give you *Easter Parade.*' Chuck said: 'Do you think I can do it?' I said: 'Of course you can.'"[3] It was a bold move on the producer's part, as *Good News* was still three months from general release. Remembering that chain of events, Walters deprecatingly acknowledged that he "got *Easter Parade . . . not* because of my great talent" but because of the turmoil surrounding *The Pirate.* "Arthur told me he was going to give me the film. I almost cried. It was a big film with a fat budget, and instead of June Allyson, I had Judy Garland and Gene Kelly. It's a little like passing one day to the next from the Bronx to the Palace Theatre."

The new director started attending dance rehearsals, already under way. Kelly kidded him about making it to the major leagues, while the refreshed Garland seized the moment. "Look, Buster," she joked, "you're in the big time now. You're not doing a little college musical here. I'm no June Allyson, you know. Don't get cute with me—none of that batting-the-eyelids bit, or the fluffing of the hair routine for me, buddy!" ("Oh, Judy loved to growl," he later laughed, "loved to *pretend*.")[4] Chuck played along with her charade, responding with a mock bow.

Berlin, however, was not joking when he voiced his opposition to Walters's assignment. The songwriter had been a vital participant in pre-production and anticipated a generous percentage of the film's eventual profits, so he was not happy to learn that a former Broadway dancer was in charge. Freed remembered that "Irving came to me and said: 'I'm going to discuss it with Mr. Mayer.' I said: 'Irving, go ahead.'" Berlin returned to Arthur's office the next day, and Freed baited him, "So you're the producer now?" Berlin muttered, "Forget it" and went home to New York. "When he came back about four or five weeks later, we ran [some] stuff for him. [Irving] said: 'You were right.'"[5]

Walters hit another major snag as soon as he read the Goodrich-Hackett script. "It was terrible, it was *heavy*." The plot centered on Don Hewes (Kelly), an egomaniacal vaudeville dancer whose partner, Nadine Hale (a role slated for Cyd Charisse), deserts him in favor of a Ziegfeld contract. The vengeful Hewes vows he can teach any girl to replace her, and randomly selects Hannah Brown (Garland) out of a café chorus line. (Don: "I think you'll do." Hannah [incredulously]: "You think I'll do *what*?") Further complications arise from the unrequited affection of Hannah for Don, Don for Nadine, Nadine for Don's pal Jonathon Harrow III (Peter Lawford), and Harrow for Hannah.

At its core, the story was a *Pygmalion* variant in which the scenarists opted to continually berate their Galatea. "Gene's character [verbally] beat the shit out of [Judy]," Walters explained. The callous tone was scarcely softened when Lawford's character finally confronted Kelly: "You self-satisfied, self-centered, self-sufficient, arrogant little squirt ... you're so wrapped up in yourself. You've been snapping the whip over that girl as if she were a trained seal. She's a human being!"[6] Walters took additional exception to the manner in which Garland's character was crafted: despite a stream of snide put-downs from Hewes, her Hannah remained enamored. "The script completely martyred her, and it was neither refined nor pleasant," he observed.

The director turned to his stars for assistance, telling them, "Listen, I have no clout. I'm lucky to get the goddamn picture. But let me tell you something—it stinks. And the audience is going to hate you both. They're particularly going to hate you, Gene, for what you're doing to this poor girl. Don't forget, Judy always gets the sympathy in her movies." Over lunch, the trio charted a plan of action, and a long-distance call was placed to Freed, who was in New York on business. "The phone was in the room where we rehearsed," Walters recounted. "I fed Judy and Gene the lines. I thought my concerns should come from them, so my name was never mentioned. [Arthur] wouldn't have liked that."

The ploy worked. Freed also took Walters's subsequent suggestion that young scenarist Sidney Sheldon collaborate with him to soften the dialog and make a joyous musical comedy of the property. Key scenes involving Garland, Lawford, and Kelly were given a more upbeat tone. Setups for Berlin's tunes were revamped as well, and Garland would no longer sing her rueful "Better Luck Next Time" to Lawford. Her reprise of "It Only Happens When I Dance with You" now ended with Hewes realizing he loves Hannah, rather than (as first scripted) with him flying into a rage as he recalls his former partner's selfishness.

Everyone agreed that the brighter—and tighter—story line made a better frame for Berlin's optimistic tunes. (Indeed, in 1949, *Easter Parade* would win Sheldon, Goodrich, and Hackett the Writers Guild of America Award for Best Written American Musical.) Sheldon felt mutual admiration for his director: "I loved Chuck. I found him to be *very* enthusiastic, which is important for a writer and for a director. He was creative, came up with ideas for scenes, and he was just wonderful."[7]

Easter Parade leaped another hurdle when popular tapper Ann Miller made her M-G-M bow to replace the injured Cyd Charisse. Miller herself was still recovering from an unfortunate combination of fall, back injury, and miscarriage, but she silently suffered for the prize role of Nadine: "I really just killed myself trying to be good."[8] There was an additional perk in the arresting good looks of her director. "I just thought Chuck was one of the cutest people I ever met on that lot," she confessed in a 1996 interview, "and Judy did, too. We gave him a pretty bad time, because we were [both] carrying on, laughing and giggling and talking with him."[9] In turn, Miller endeared herself to Walters, who found the dancer "kind of kookie. A darling . . . but just kind of a kookie darling."

Dance duties were once again split. Alton developed eleven numbers and Walters nine, including his torchy "Mr. Monotony"—a key solo for Garland, who was costumed in tuxedo jacket, hose, and fedora, devoid of any June Allyson–like cuteness. He also staged "A Couple of Swells," arguably the film's high point. In that number, developed as a baggy-pants encore to Judy and Gene's "Be a Clown" from *The Pirate,* the duo was presented in raggedy-tramp attire, deriding the aristocratic set.[10] Using Berlin's lyric to dictate the staging, the tramps mimic a sailboat when they "sail up the avenue," turn up their noses at "the city's smells," and show some ankle as they confess to looking "cute" when they're "dressed in shorts." Chuck also supplied the introductory portion of "I Love a Piano" but noted that Alton "took it from [apartment to stage] with a key change and did the full vaudeville montage. . . . That's how in-sync we were in our thinking."

The property was beginning to coalesce when a final, major catastrophe occurred. On October 12, Gene Kelly spent his day off playing ball in his backyard and wound up on crutches. "This is the plot of a movie," cried Sidney Sheldon. "This doesn't really happen!"[11] Two days after Kelly's ankle fracture, Fred Astaire agreed to take the role. The eminent hoofer had retired in 1945 after completing Irving Berlin's *Blue Skies* ("I had some plans that my wife and I were going to go live in the country," he said) but soon grew restive.[12] Persuaded by the chance to appear opposite Garland—and a flat $150,000 fee—the forty-eight-year-old Astaire was keen to return to work, if a bit trepidatious. "I wondered if it was safe for me to kick forcibly without having a leg leave the body!" he recalled later.[13]

"I couldn't contain my joy," said Walters. "[Astaire] was my hero, my idol. I could not get over the fact that I was going to work with him. I will never forget the moment when, while we were trying out wardrobe, Fred approached me—in that elegant way that only he has—and asked me what I thought of [his] jacket and vest. I said, 'You're kidding. *You're* asking *me*?' He was clearly delighted."

Sheldon's lightened script needed little alteration for its new leading man, with Chuck admitting, "It was even better for Fred than it was for Gene." The same could be said for the score: Berlin's music had graced four Astaire movies and provided him his signature song, "Top Hat, White Tie, and Tails." That classy film image, however, was a bit at odds with *Easter Parade*'s Kelly-styled dances. "If you look very closely," said Chuck, "you'll see that the numbers don't really fit Fred." The exception was "Swells," with its mock elegance and threadbare tailoring. "Astaire and Garland as a couple of deadbeats, for God's sake!" said Walters. "All I had to do was stand back and let it happen."

Ordinarily, Astaire insisted upon lengthy rehearsal periods for his dances—and still worried about their effect. Chuck had to tread lightly when suggesting a new step: "Well, Fred, what have we got to lose by trying? If you don't like it when you see it in the rushes, we'll redo it." Despite such tact, "never would [Fred say] 'Oh! That sounds great! Let's get in there and do it!' [Never] any enthusiasm. So [I'd] kind of say [to myself], 'Please, God, I hope I'm right.'" The director's awe, however, never diminished. "Fred's complaining about anything and everything [was a kind of] defense mechanism," Walters observed, and watching him rehearse epitomized "exciting because . . . well, *hell*, you were working with the best."

Principal photography ran from late November 1947 to mid-February 1948, and his *Good News* experience gave Walters the confidence to take risks. A quietly emotional Garland-Lawford restaurant scene easily could have slowed the film's pace, but Chuck approached the intimate tête-à-tête with voyeuristic imagination. As he described it:

> I started with a general set, so you could see the restaurant while their conversation was still an exchange of pleasantries. When their conversation became serious, I asked the cameramen if they could move the camera very slowly. They answered that we could advance as slowly as I wanted. So we approached very, very slowly, and I had given the directions so that Pete, who at first was leaning back against his chair, would lean forward a bit, and then lean all the way forward across the table. We ended up with a shot of just their two heads. In other words, as the conversation got more interesting, we gently advanced, rather than changing shots, which can be abrupt for the audience and ruin the scene's charm. It's like when someone tells you a story, you have a tendency to lean forward as the story becomes more and more interesting.

By eliminating typical action-reaction shots and maintaining the scene's spatial unity for a single four-minute take, Walters provided Garland the opportunity to create something special and uninterrupted.

During her first months of *Easter Parade* rehearsal and filming, Garland also was called to re-shoot a dozen portions of *The Pirate.* The extreme Minnelli and/or Thompson approach to some numbers had played poorly in previews, necessitating major changes. Her demanding schedule reached a zenith in December: for *Easter Parade,* she filmed "Swells" on December 3–4, "I Love a Piano" and "Snookey Ookums" on December 5, "Ragtime Violin" on December 6, "Everybody's Doin' It" and its attendant scene on December 8, the "Michael's rehearsal hall" scene on December 9, and "Michigan" on December 10. The next day, she returned to the Minnelli company to rehearse a new arrangement of *The Pirate*'s "Mack the Black," which she pre-recorded on December 15 and filmed—in Alton's revised staging—December 16–18. On the nineteenth, she returned to Astaire to rehearse "When the Midnight Choo-Choo Leaves for Alabam'," which they committed to film on the twentieth.

Despite that calendar, Garland's spirits remained high. "I never had any problems with Judy," Chuck maintained. "Really I didn't." Working opposite Astaire kept her on her toes: "She was pretty excited." She was also pleased to be part of the film's creative process. When the scenario called for a sleepless Hannah, up pacing the floor till dawn, Garland opted for realism: "She wanted to play it with her hair all stringy and no make-up," explained Walters. "The studio was aghast," and executives reprimanded the director for his unflattering presentation of one of their biggest assets.[14] "That was a big deal in those days," Chuck continued, "because stars had to look pretty at all times—whether they were going to sleep, or in the middle of the night, or particularly early in the morning. But we insisted," and Garland au naturel brought a refreshing alternative to the artifice of the M-G-M musical.[15]

Walters would be dressed down again, and remembers being "almost yanked off the picture by Arthur," while filming the Lawford-Garland "A Fella with an Umbrella." For the number, the crew laid tarp over four city blocks on one of the back lots, running piping underneath to create the necessary rain shower. "[Freed] came on the set: *'I hear Judy Garland is WET!* Where *is* she?' And there she [was] wrapped up in a blanket." Garland recognized the producer's fury and leaped to Chuck's defense. "Arthur," she said in exasperation, "how the *hell* do you expect me to do this scene if I don't get wet?!" Grateful for her devotion, Walters later confessed: "She was fighting [the] battle, because I didn't have the clout. But, oh, Arthur was red in the face."[16]

Filming concluded with the celebratory title song on Metro's re-creation of New York's Fifth Avenue. Not content to simply follow the stars with his smooth-moving camera, Walters added two plot points to their stroll. After Don hands the glowing Hannah an engagement ring, she ribs him for his early attempts to turn her into a sophisticate by art-fully posing for rotogravure photographers. It was the same kind of amusing kicker that concluded so many Walters's dance sequences.

Despite Kelly's injury and Minnelli's competing attempts to remedy *The Pirate,* Walters brought in *Easter Parade* a week ahead of schedule and $191,280 under its $2,503,654 budget. The film's only casualty was Judy's sedate "Mr. Monotony," and Berlin later admitted, "Arthur and I were sorry to see it go because we both liked it."[17]

The film opened in June 1948 to unanimous praise. "Charles Walters directed, and such entertainment has seldom been seen and certainly not heard before in this splendid guise," went the admiring review in *McCall's.*[18] The *Hollywood Reporter* raved: "Walters' direction could only appear so effortless because of painstaking effort to make every line and every turn of the fragile plot as feathery light as an Astaire dance step."[19] Howard Barnes at the *New York Herald Tribune* praised Walters for smartly avoiding "pretentious flourishes,"[20] while Chet Skreen of the *Tacoma Times* went even further: "Under Walters' direction, [*Easter Parade*] manages a direct and simple approach that is altogether unique among picture musicals."[21] At the end of the year, *Look* selected the film as one of the screen's "top achievements for 1948," aligning it with Laurence Olivier's *Hamlet,* Howard Hawks's *Red River,* Victor Fleming's *Joan of Arc,* and John Huston's *Treasure of the Sierra Madre.*[22]

Astaire considered *Easter Parade* "a lucky break for me just when I wanted it. My comeback had been completed."[23] (Bing Crosby was a bit less understated when he wrote to Fred, "For a guy who had retired os-tensibly, your comeback represents the greatest since Satchel Paige.")[24] Mature and in command, Astaire continued to dance on screens big and small for another thirty years. The film also sent Garland's star to new heights, and the *Hollywood Reporter* openly declared her "the screen's first lady of tempo and tunes." Wrote Garland's biographer Christopher Finch, "It was apparent to everyone that *Easter Parade* was going to be a winner. They had rediscovered the 'real' Judy and began to plan for her future."[25]

Best of all, with earnings in excess of $6,803,000, *Easter Parade* was M-G-M's top-grossing picture in an otherwise troubled fiscal year. That success aligned with Chuck's personal philosophy: he would always contend that people liked to be entertained—and were willing to pay for their pleasure.

12

Fred and Ginger

During this period, Walters's home life remained tranquil. John Darrow's client roster continued to grow and now included such future stars as Gwen Verdon and Gene Nelson. The agent also expanded into real estate, having begun purchasing land around Malibu in 1944. Lured by the spread of its undeveloped shoreline, John convinced Chuck to relocate from Santa Monica (their brief homestead after the war) to a sizable stretch of beach at 22506 Malibu Road in 1948. The bungalow-style house they built faced the Pacific and provided sophisticated, bohemian living quarters befitting a top talent agent and rising Hollywood director. One entered from the rear into a vast living room boasting a fireplace and a bar near glass patio doors. A deck with a green and white striped awning was a comfortable outdoor adjunct. The oversized upper balcony—dubbed "the lookout"—jutted from the loft bedroom and provided the best ocean view.

Their Saturday nights in Malibu were devoted to poker games, while Sundays were kept casual. The occasional party was absent the customary get-up-and-perform rule that dominated so many Hollywood social gatherings. Such showing off, one must assume, was not welcome. "I partook of the Hollywood social scene for a while," said Chuck, "but I found it just as much work as working, and I'd be tired the next day. And it was pretty much the same bullshit. If you'd been to one party, you'd been to all of them."

Easter Parade was still in mid-production when Freed began to plan a Garland-Astaire-Walters-Alton follow up. With the working title *You Made Me Love You,* the new project teamed Ira Gershwin and Harry Warren for its songs and brought back *Good News* scenarists Comden and Green for an original screenplay. Their script, delivered in March

1948, celebrated fictional Josh and Dinah Barkley, a husband-and-wife musical comedy team who split when she rebuffs her spouse's incessant instruction and goes solo as a dramatic actress. Edens, acting as associate producer, appropriately retitled the property *The Barkleys of Broadway*, and if *Easter Parade* was *Pygmalion*, Josh and Dinah could be equated with Svengali and Trilby—Fred once more teacher and leader and Judy posited as pupil and follower.

Walters dove in. Pleased to once again glamorize Garland, he worked with Irene Gibbons on concepts for Dinah's modern gowns, inspired in one instance by Gertrude Lawrence's fashions for *Lady in the Dark*. He also cast redheaded Gale Robbins (a new Darrow client) in the choice role of Shirleen May, Dinah Barkley's overly ambitious understudy.

Astaire began rehearsing a month before pre-production officially commenced. During his short-lived retirement, he admitted to being "full of ideas and ambition, but [with] no picture to do." Now he had his opportunity. From mid-May through mid-June, he locked himself away for a seven-hour workday, six days a week. "Dancing," he explained "is a sweat job."[1] On June 14, his longtime collaborator Hermes Pan reported to M-G-M to assist, and they began to develop the ambitious "Shoes with Wings On," in which a shoe shop owner is besieged by an animated fleet of footwear.[2]

Garland also joined *Barkleys* on June 14, rehearsing full days with Alton and Astaire during her first week but switching to an afternoon-only schedule by the second. Assistant director Jennings, who had watched the star at work for seven years, observed that she simply didn't require that much preparation. "Judy was great. I swear to God, they would rehearse these numbers and work on 'em and work on 'em and work on 'em. Judy'd come in—or wouldn't come in or couldn't come in or didn't feel like coming in. [They'd] finally get to the point where [they were] ready to shoot . . . and she'd come in for a day or a couple of hours or something, and, goddamn, she'd do 'em. She'd *do* 'em! It was amazing how she could do that."[3]

Over the next month, however, Garland's attendance grew more sporadic. On July 19, M-G-M placed her on suspension and cut off her salary. It was the first time such an action had been taken against the actress. "They didn't even give me the courtesy of a call or a meeting or a discussion. They sent me a telegram," she later disclosed.[4] Concurrently, the Astaire "Shoes" routine went before the cameras, and daily production reports show that the film's setbacks continued. On July 16, "Astaire cut his hand on a broom while rehearsing"; on July 17, "Astaire called to say that his front pivot tooth had broken and was doubtful it could be fixed in time for shooting on Monday"; on July 22, "Astaire hit his right knee against the counter during a take on 'Shoes.'"[5]

Overtures were swiftly made to Ginger Rogers as Garland's replacement. "Would you object to appearing opposite Astaire again?" they asked. Those poorly chosen words set off a small firestorm. "What kind of question is that!?" Rogers hollered back. "I was irritated at the manner in which I was asked," she later wrote. "How ungracious to assume I *wouldn't* want to work with Fred. We had parted as friends and maintained a cordial, if distant, relationship. I think it's ridiculous for anyone to corner me in such a way! I *never* felt that way about it."[6] Regardless, Rogers accepted M-G-M's offer—at a salary reportedly twice Garland's.

"There is an element of luck in all pictures," Walters later reflected, "as there can be the lack of luck. The fortunate thing, just as Fred was so much righter for *Easter Parade* than Gene, also Ginger was so much righter for *The Barkleys of Broadway*. The Barkleys were a famous acting team in New York, and Judy was just a little immature for it." (Rogers was eleven years Garland's senior.) Even so, the swiftness of the changeover produced mixed feelings. He was "devastated" because of Judy and her problems, "but on the other I was delighted because of Ginger. . . . I'll never forget [her first] day. Fred was rehearsing 'Shoes'; Ginger came down the aisle, up onto the stage, and when they embraced, I started to cry—because of the reunion and the years of adoration and worship of the Astaire-Rogers pictures. I just broke down. I couldn't believe I would be directing them."[7]

To movie audiences of 1948, the Astaire-Rogers partnership was fondly remembered, if consigned to a romantic cinema of yesteryear. The duo had chosen to go their separate ways after completing RKO's *The Story of Vernon and Irene Castle* (1939), and Rogers both broadened her career and hit the bull's-eye one year later, winning a Best Actress Oscar for *Kitty Foyle*. Given this history, the Garland-Astaire *Barkleys* script seemed tailor-made for Fred and Ginger and played out like a not-too-subtle parody of their former partnership and parting. Walters conceded that its cynical edge was at odds with their earlier lighthearted farces, but he decided the best way to approach the film was from the standpoint of "Whatever happened to Astaire and Rogers? Well, they've been on Broadway," he imagined, "big stars in New York all this time." He aimed to make *Barkleys* a mature epilogue to their legendary on-screen romance.

Astaire described his re-teaming with Rogers in the most pleasant of terms: "Our rehearsals brought forth a new set of gags and jokes, and we had fun working with Chuck. There were a slew of dance numbers with which we hoped to top our past performances."[8] Others on the production, including Hermes Pan, remembered there was less euphoria, as Fred believed they were trying to evoke something that couldn't be recaptured. Walters came to a similar realization: "It came as quite a shock to find out that Mr. Astaire was not too keen about Miss Rogers. . . . They got along well, [but] Fred complained about her incessantly. . . . He would say, for example, that he couldn't stand a woman who was taller than he was. . . . [Fred could be] a real nag."

Most of Ginger's dramatic scenes—plus a pair of musical interludes—would shoot in August and conclude the next month. This allowed her more time to master Alton's elaborate "show-within-a-show" presentations, scheduled to go before the cameras in early October. Ginger "did an *awful* lot of rehearsing," Walters conceded, but admits she was "not really a dancer. She moves well." He guided her through his own stagings of "A Weekend in the Country" and the relaxed "You'd Be So Hard to Replace" (and would appreciate the comic irony of steering his fashion-setting idols through a concise pas de deux in which they were dressed in bathrobes).

The Gershwin-Warren songs proved a more difficult challenge. Rogers's vocal talents contrasted significantly with Garland's abilities, and when the latter left *Barkleys,* so did much of her music. Dropped from the script were "Natchez on the Mississip'" (a blues solo), "The Courtin' of Elmer and Ella" (a hillbilly routine), "Poetry in Motion" (a comic ballet), and "These Days" (the picture's opener). Such elimination troubled Walters, who believed a reduced score might well lead to a mediocre musical.

There was, however, welcome encouragement in Hedda Hopper's nationwide plug. A week prior to the onset of principal photography, she hailed the return of Hollywood's classic dance team and then queried, "I wonder if they all know how lucky they are having Charles Walters."[9] On August 9, when cameras began to roll, it appeared that everyone did.

Even co-star Oscar Levant, world-class musician and self-proclaimed neurotic, remained uncommonly excited. His role as sharp-tongued sidekick Ezra Millar was a distant cry from the humorous, devoted cohorts (embodied by Edward Everett Horton and Eric Blore) who had popped up in prior Fred and Ginger pictures. As Adolph Green observed, however, "Freed would have cast Oscar Levant as Huckleberry Finn if he thought he could get away with it."[10] From Walters's viewpoint, Freed's admiration led him to do "a really unpardonable thing." On set, and with Levant in earshot, the producer announced, "Now, Chuck, don't forget that Oscar is a very funny man. I want him to feel free to do anything he wants." Flabbergasted, the director later declaimed, "One does not say such things to an actor—and certainly not to a weirdo comic like Oscar Levant! He is capable of doing just anything, [like] putting his finger up his nose in the middle of a scene if he feels like it." Judiciously, Walters found ways to praise Levant while keeping the musician's impulses in check. "You know, Oscar," he would compliment him, "that's really very, very funny *for you,* but it's just not quite right for the scene as a whole. You do understand, right?" In the end, Freed's faith in Levant's talent proved warranted: at each *Barkleys* preview, the acerbic pianist received the highest audience approval ratings, surpassing even those for Fred and Ginger.

Unfortunately, Walters's longtime association with Alton now required special handling as well. "We were at a point where you could tell both Bob and I were a little uptight," he noted.[11] The choreographer had achieved his own directorial credit, helming the mildly diverting Red Skelton comedy *Merton of the Movies* (1947); after that, however, his directing career sputtered. This left Alton noticeably frustrated when assigned (yet again) as Walters's second-in-command—a simple case of the disciple surpassing the master. Chuck affirmed, "It was a bit evil of Arthur to keep Bob and me in this uncomfortable dance. It was almost like a baiting. Why didn't [he] get someone else? Arthur knew that I came to Metro in the first place because Bob wasn't available."[12] Squaring off, the men agreed to give each other complete privacy and (friendship mostly intact) were quick to tease if one of them broke the promise.

"Excuse me, *Mister* Alton," the director would grandly kid, "*I* am still filming this scene. *You* may enter when I am quite through."

"Oh, Mr. Walters," Alton would gush, giving as good as he got, "the Academy will be *so* pleased."

One consequence of their schism is the noticeable lack of musical integration, customarily the duo's hallmark. Virtually every Alton number is inserted sans any attempt to bridge story and song until the "Manhattan Downbeat" finale. That routine begins with Walters's bright preliminary movement for Fred and Ginger in their penthouse suite; the emotion of their dancing finally, effortlessly propels them into Alton's splashy onstage finish.

After obliging so many bruisable egos, Chuck's own self-esteem was shaken when Freed told him that another director should film Rogers's recitation of the French national anthem, "La Marseillaise." The sequence was an essential plot point, demonstrating Dinah Barkley's acting capability in portraying Sarah Bernhardt. Ginger, however, steadfastly refused a substitute. "For her to have that much confidence in me," Walters later said, "really made me want to work that much harder." He methodically placed his camera at a low angle, allowing the grand theatrical set to loom ominously around her and bring out the vulnerability of both Bernhardt and Barkley. Chuck "thought it worked all right," but several critics later disagreed. A Montreal paper reported: "Laugh of the week is given the French Canadians [by] Metro's *Barkleys* when Rogers wades through her interp of the 'Marseillaise.' The embarrassed silence which greets her opening lines soon turns to loud yucks."[13]

The director had a chance to repay Rogers's kindness when Judy Garland arrived unannounced on the *Barkleys* set. As the playful presence of the first Dinah lingered longer than the second Dinah could handle, Walters was asked to take action. His peacekeeping efforts went awry, however, and word spread. "I didn't deliver any ultimatum for Judy to leave my set," Ginger explained to columnist Harrison Carroll. "I was having a tough time with a difficult scene. I couldn't seem to get it right. Chuck came to me and asked if it was going to bother me to have another actress on the set. I admitted it would. If I had known Judy better, I would have explained the trouble myself. Chuck *did* know her, so he talked to her. There certainly was nothing personal about it. I am very sorry if she was offended."[14] (Reportedly, Astaire arrived just as Walters was leading an upset Judy off the soundstage, and Fred sympathetically asked, "What are they doing to that poor kid?")[15]

October was given over to Alton's sequences, including the kilted "My One and Only Highland Fling" and the "Swing Trot" opener, seen under the film's opening titles. Edens conceived the then-novel idea of marrying credits and initial action, which Walters wholeheartedly supported. "I don't like to tease," he said. "I prefer to be honest, to give the public what they're waiting for—in this case Astaire and Rogers, from the opening credits on."

Barkleys wrapped at the end of that month ($87,000 under budget), and despite all his initial anticipation, Walters was now rather disappointed. "I only wish it was a better picture," he (much later) confided to film journalist John Cutts. Enumerating the flaws, he said, "I liked neither the music nor the dance sequences"; the script was "hit or miss," the score "routine." Describing Fred and Ginger's Scottish "Fling," he cringed: "Too cute by far." The only element that excited the director was the team's "They Can't Take That Away from Me," an interpolated song by George and Ira Gershwin and staged by Alton. "That one took my breath away," he said. "It had a nostalgic effect on me."

Glendale's Alexander Theater previewed *Barkleys* on December 16, 1948. Metro brass and contract players turned out en masse, eager to see Astaire and Rogers on-screen again; Chuck attended with John. Mayer reportedly loved the film, afterward inviting Comden and Green to his private dining room. The preview, however, was more pleasant than victorious, and surviving comment cards from an Inglewood screening five days later were uncommonly blunt. "Do not take so many close-ups of Miss Rogers. Wrinkles, you know," went one. "If Fred just wouldn't sing," remarked another. Freed saved one card for his files. It came from a male in the eighteen-to-thirty age range who vehemently wrote: "I DO NOT LIKE MUSICALS. I DID NOT ENJOY IT."[16]

The professional critics were more easygoing. When *Barkleys* opened in May 1949, *Variety* deemed it "an ace dance fest," though noting the movie lacked "the one popular ingredient that would have guaranteed socko business in any situation. The songs are ordinary."[17] The sometimes caustic Richard L. Coe of the *Washington Post* called the picture "a model of excellence. The pace is sparkling, and if the year brings a better musical, it will have to be pretty elegant."[18] Perhaps summing up public sentiment, Bosley Crowther at the *New York Times* offered up this valentine: "Age cannot wither the enchantment of Ginger and Fred."[19] His was the prevailing reaction; the film grossed more than $5,500,000 against production costs of $2,318,000.

If *Barkleys* failed to meet Walters's expectations, he'd nonetheless made a grand impression on Rogers. "Working with you dear Chuck is something wonderful," she cabled after finishing the project. "Thanks for being such a real live angel."[20]

As the decade drew to a close, the type of "enchantment" Crowther wrote of was on a slow decline, thanks to many changes in postwar Hollywood. Motion pictures that once boasted glamour or escapism were giving way to frank noir naturalism. Televisions had begun to proliferate in homes across the nation, and audiences relaxed in their living rooms for their entertainment. A May 4, 1948, Supreme Court ruling decreed the divestiture of studio-owned theater chains, eventually eliminating guaranteed distribution channels. Compounding these events, the House Un-American Activities Committee (HUAC) began mindlessly investigating members of the film industry who were suspected of communist leanings. Beliefs clashed as the atmosphere turned distrustful.

Life on the M-G-M lot suffered an additional dramatic change. "Although . . . still regarded as the industry's No. 1 company," historian John Douglas Eames reported, Metro "was in fact running behind Paramount, Warner Bros., and 20th Century-Fox in both gross income and profits. Worse, its customary domination of Academy Awards and Ten Best lists had vanished."[21] M-G-M's 1948 financial statement showed earnings at their lowest since the bleak year of 1933. Such a slide would have been unimaginable only a few years earlier and occurred just as Walters was coming into his own.

Yet the problem was not him. Between December 1947 and May 1949, Walters and the Freed Unit provided three all-out winners in *Good News, Easter Parade,* and *The Barkleys of Broadway.* Their combined grosses surpassed $15,180,000 and largely underwrote the expenditures of the entire M-G-M factory.

13

Metro-Goldwyn-*Schary*

1949 marked Metro-Goldwyn-Mayer's twenty-fifth year of filmmaking. To hype its "Silver Jubilee," the studio threw a lavish luncheon on soundstage A for exhibitors, executives, and the media. Heralded as arriving royalty, contract players (plus one well-behaved collie) were announced by George Murphy as they entered and then assembled—primarily alphabetically—at dining tables on a tiered stage: Gable next to Gardner, Lansbury next to Lanza, Hepburn next to Horne. Behind all the pomp and white linen, however, was a movie company in uncertain transition.

M-G-M's parent company in New York, Loew's Inc., had demanded economic reform, and Mayer complied by appointing Dore Schary as the new vice president in charge of production. Arriving on July 15, 1948, the ambitious forty-two-year-old had had a career that encompassed scenarist, B-movie unit producer at Metro, producer at Selznick International, and production chief at troubled RKO. He vowed to make efficiency the new order in his return to M-G-M, boldly promising sixty-seven new pictures for the 1949–1950 season—an increase of forty-three films over the preceding year.

Schary's approach more rankled than appeased many at the studio (eventually including Mayer himself). "The big change for me," said Walters, "was that Schary and I couldn't stand each other." The new production chief belonged to a Hollywood clique some would disparage as "the elite." "You didn't hang out with people like that," offered Metro star Esther Williams, "you bore their scrutiny."[1] Chuck attended one of Schary's mighty dinner parties, but not as an invited guest. "He was *summoned*," said Williams, and was told to bring with him the day's rushes—a highly unethical request. "The last people you would invite to see dailies would be a group of industry-wise colleagues, particularly when they were a bit drunk and raucous," she continued.

Chuck arrived with his rushes . . . in cans under his arm and [was] told to wait in the entry hall until the eminent folk in the dining room had completed their gourmet repast. He listened as they nibbled their dinner with considerable gaiety. Some had a little too much champagne, and there was a lot of joking, with everybody talking just a little too loud. Finally, they filed out of the dining room with the ice in their fresh drinks clinking. They headed for Schary's luxuriously appointed projection room with the deep-cushioned chairs. Schary gave a curt nod, and Chuck was commanded to hand over his cans of film to the projectionist. Then he had to sit off to the side like an outsider or one of the help and have his work . . . shown as after-dinner entertainment.[2]

It was a humiliating experience. For the next seven years, Walters strove to keep his relationship with Schary professional—but at arm's length.

"Schary was the antithesis of Mayer," said rising star Arlene Dahl, "and the retrenchment at M-G-M during that period was quite noticeable."[3] Lengthy rehearsal periods were put to rest. Expensive properties that had languished in file cabinets were dusted off. Even routine contract renegotiations took on heightened unpleasantness.

This was something Walters was to experience in winter 1948, with his original contract set to expire. "Although Arthur had made me a director," he later recounted, "the studio hadn't rewritten my contract. My first three pictures . . . were all done under the old [one]—they got a choreographer *and* a director for the same price . . . something that appealed to [M-G-M] very much." Compounding matters, Freed was baiting Walters with the colossal Broadway hit *Annie Get Your Gun* to star Garland—provided Chuck signed his new agreement. "Go in and negotiate, for God's sake!" Chuck urged Darrow, and then (always a company man) obligingly adjourned to the set of the Clark Gable–Loretta Young film *Key to the City* to stage the balloon-clad Marilyn Maxwell in a small nightclub routine. Despite such ongoing cooperation from Walters and his track record, the agent got nowhere. "The end result was pitiful," Chuck recalled, "like a dollar raise," and the revised agreement also stipulated that he could be assigned as a choreographer should he refuse to direct. The new contract was rightly rejected. "Let 'em sweat," John proposed.

Walters later said of the double-dealing atmosphere: "Intrigue positively thrived at M-G-M in those days, but I never thought a battle between my manager and the accounts people would come between me
and *Annie* and Judy. I believed Arthur and I had an agreement." With
negotiations stalled, however, film editor Albert Akst (Freed's brother-
in-law) innocently let slip that another director had been signed to *Annie*. Storming the producer's office, Walters demanded, "What's all this I
hear about Buzz Berkeley? I thought *Annie* was mine." Freed casually
looked up from his paperwork and said, "Well, you got greedy. You didn't
sign the contract, so you don't get the picture." Chuck was unprepared
for the sudden coldness in Freed's tone. "That broke my heart," he later
acknowledged, and the drive home to Malibu was spent in a daze. "I
went off to the beach to sulk," said Walters, "and Judy started the picture
with her nemesis."[4]

Some compensation arrived in the form of an old friend. A dozen
years earlier, when Gloria Swanson and Chuck had danced across the
supper club parquets of New York City, she was still a bona fide stage and
screen star. Her celebrity thereafter declined, but by early 1949 Swanson
was back in Hollywood and poised to play the stellar role of Norma
Desmond in Billy Wilder's *Sunset Boulevard*. She took over the Walters-
Darrow guest room, and the trio enjoyed a reunion at the beach.[5] Anticipating a strenuous shoot, the ever-disciplined fifty-year-old actress
launched a series of rigid physical workouts on the sand while simultaneously planning her own homecoming celebration. Pen in hand and
tongue in cheek, Swanson drafted an invitation:

> Having hired the Muscle-Beach performers* (*including Mr.
> America of '49, girls!) to put me in shape after a long lay-off, I am
> inviting a few friends to visit one of our work-outs. . . . Due to the
> locale, this Nostalgic Spectacle will start promptly at 3:30 P.M. Early
> cocktails and supper. Sunday, March 27th. Place: The home of
> Charles Walters**
> (**God Bless Chuck for being so sweet!)
>
> Gloria Swanson

The actress's "few friends" read like a resplendent *Who's Who* of
Hollywood: director Wilder, Mary Pickford (an earlier Wilder consideration as Desmond) and husband Buddy Rogers, Hedda Hopper and

Cecil B. DeMille (both of whom made *Sunset* cameos), Clifton Webb (Walters's boyhood idol) and mom Mabelle, William Haines and partner Jimmy Shields, George Cukor, Sam Goldwyn, Louella Parsons, Frances Marion, Cole Porter, Edith Head, Fanny Brice, and Ethel Barrymore. William Powell, Ronald Colman, and Robert Montgomery were among the few M-G-M invitees.

It was a pleasant foreshadowing of things to come. When *Sunset Boulevard* opened in summer 1950, Swanson threw a spectacular post-premiere victory bash, where she and Walters celebrated by taking over the dance floor with a high-stepping Charleston. The attendees were dazzled, and for the first time, the elated pair didn't care who was watching.

Chuck's days with Gloria at Malibu were ended by news from Metro, where *Annie Get Your Gun* was floundering. Berkeley had been quick to cause catastrophe for leading man Howard Keel. On the second day of principal photography, the director's repeated demands for speed, issued through his bullhorn, had caused Keel's horse to topple, breaking the actor's ankle. Off the set, Keel would slowly recover; on the set, Garland would not. "They shot around me for six weeks," recalled Keel, "and Judy just fell apart. . . . [S]he was exhausted."[6] Assistant director Al Jennings also remembers the unrelenting schedule and Garland's inability to face Berkeley's dictates: "We shot Judy with Alton. We shot Judy with Peter Balbush, a second unit director. But every time we tried to get Judy and Buzz together, Judy would go home ill."[7]

When star and director did align, the dynamic was tense and disappointing. "Buzz started treating her without care, brutally ordering her around all the time," recounted Walters. "She was having none of that. 'You do this—like *this*. You do that—like *that*.' He was such a brute with her; there was never any diplomacy. So under that sort of handling, she soon fell apart. She'd come in, do a few days, then quit and go home."[8]

"I was a very tired and very distressed woman," Judy explained later. "Now, I think [Buzz is] a wonderful director. I think he did a fine job with the earlier pictures. But psychologically, Buzz represented all the years of Benzedrine to work as hard as we worked [to] just exhaustion. . . . And to tell you the truth, he was in a very bad mental state himself doing *Annie*."[9]

Freed at last had to admit his director "had no conception of what the picture was about." After eighteen expensive days of filming, Berkeley was fired on May 3. (Garland was absent that day.) "I got an urgent call from Arthur to come in and look at the *Annie* footage," said Walters, whose new contract was now in place, guaranteeing $1,500 a week, with no dance director allusions. "I went, and my God, it was horrible. Judy had never been worse. She couldn't decide whether she was Mary Martin, Ethel Merman, Martha Raye, or herself. She didn't know who the hell she was." Given Garland's lack of one-on-one direction, Walters sympathized with her plight, but he remained contemptuous of his rival. "Nothing Buzz shot was usable. He had been very theatrical in shooting the whole thing—like a play. Everyone would come out of the wings, they'd say their lines [and] then back away 'upstage' for their exits. It was such a waste."[10]

With an already incurred cost of $1,742,775 and very little to show for it, Freed asked Walters to take over production. "Okay," replied the director, "but the first thing I must do is have a long talk with Judy." A lunch was set up in Chuck's office so that he could discuss character and story, but Judy confessed, "I don't have the energy or the *nerve* anymore." After a three-hour pep talk, Garland finally agreed to stay the course.

On May 7, *Annie*'s new director began restaging "Doin' What Comes Natur'lly," Judy's all-important opening number (filmed earlier by choreographer Alton). Much of her success as Oakley, he recognized, would rest on viewers' immediate identification with—and affection for—the character's optimism. He spent five hours devising a sharper, funnier routine, assisted by Garland "dance-in" Betty O'Kelly and the four child actors portraying Annie's siblings. The following day, Judy joined the group to preview the new number.

Filming resumed May 10, and Walters was scheduled to shoot the pickup dialogue that followed Alton's elaborate "I'm an Indian Too." The day instead evolved into a series of mistakes and misunderstandings. Garland was two hours late, written reprimands were prematurely delivered, and after much miscommunication, *Annie Get Your Gun* was closed by Mayer's order at 2:10 P.M. At month's end, the troubled star entered Boston's Peter Bent Brigham Hospital to rid herself of her dependency on amphetamines and barbiturates. *Annie* contract dancer Norman Borine later spoke for many of her co-workers when he said, "We all believed Judy would never again pass beneath the M-G-M arch she'd figuratively helped to build."[11]

The removal of a star of Garland's stature from a high-profile production provided a field day for the press. "I knew I was in for a public beating," Judy later said, "and I got a hell of one."[12] Louella Parsons equated her with a spoiled child. The *Los Angeles Times* quoted a Metro executive: "Under the strained economic circumstances . . . anything of this character that adds materially to the cost of a picture . . . will henceforth call for drastic action."[13] Only Thomas Brady of the *New York Times* offered a sympathetic view. "The studio, usually indulgent to its errant actors, apparently decided to abandon paternalism in favor of severity. Miss Garland was selected as the ultimate example of corporate rigor."[14]

Among those considered to play Annie: June Allyson (a popular choice), Betty Garrett (Schary's choice), Betty Grable (Walters's choice), and ultimate victor Betty Hutton (Freed's choice). "It's a nice challenge," Chuck told Arthur, "trying to make Hutton legit for once. You know, cutting down that chewing-up-the-scenery and tearing-down-the-curtains routine of hers." Hutton would come to Metro after completing *Let's Dance* at Paramount with Fred Astaire. So "Arthur told me to head for the hills for six weeks or so," Walters remembered. "Down to the beach I go." Then on June 6, while enjoying a quiet breakfast in Malibu, he read in Hedda Hopper's column: "When *Annie Get Your Gun* reaches the sound stage with Hutton, George Sidney will be the director." Shocked, Chuck immediately reached for the phone. "Oh, well, you know Hedda!" Freed hedged. "She has to print *something*!" But Walters sensed trouble was afoot and contacted the gossip columnist directly. "You didn't know?" Hopper sighed. "I'm so sorry, but it's true. It's George's picture. I got the scoop from L.B. himself."

Admittedly "crushed" by his second unceremonious removal from *Annie,* the director knew instantly how events had played out.[15] The "Sidney Steamroller" was a known quantity at Metro—and he had been flattened by it. The son of studio vice president Louis K. Sidney, George Sidney had started at M-G-M at age seventeen. He rose from messenger to office boy to screen test director, directing his first feature in 1941; he later married Metro's drama coach Lillian Burns, one of Mayer's closest adjuncts. That sealed the deal. "If Georgie wanted something," said Walters, "or Lillian wanted it for Georgie, that was it!" *Annie Get Your Gun* was their goal. "They wanted a possible Academy vehicle for Georgie. They even snowed Bob Alton into not having his proper credit [on *Annie*], so it could be *all* George. At that time it had to be a solo directorial credit to qualify for nomination; a 'Dance Director' credit would kill his chances."[16]

John Darrow stepped in to do just that. On behalf of Alton, the agent wrote Freed on December 5, 1949: "This request, coming from a director with the professional stature of Mr. Sidney, is not understandable. If it is contended Alton needed assistance in the staging of said numbers, we were not aware of it; and should that be the contention, it is surprising, considering Alton's long career of successful activities in this line."[17] Freed made sure Alton received his proper credit, and though there would be no Academy Award nomination for Sidney, his *Annie Get Your Gun* would become one of the top-grossing pictures of 1950.

Chuck only had to wait until mid-June for his next assignment, but he was dismayed when the script arrived. *Summer Stock* was in every sense a "barnyard entertainment" in which theatricals who want to "put on a show" overrun the property of a girl farmer. The project first had been announced for Garland, Gene Kelly, and producer Joe Pasternak in December 1948. June Allyson then was mentioned in place of Garland in February 1949, with Gloria De Haven as her sister.[18] On June 14—just a month after the Garland-*Annie* fracas—Louella Parsons broke the remarkable news that Judy was being reinstated. Because of his strong rapport with the actress, Walters was assigned to direct.

He had plenty to say when story conferences began. In a private memo to Schary dated September 12, 1949, Walters stressed that while he did not "want to go over [Pasternak's] head . . . Joe seems so excited and enthused over the whole venture that it is very difficult to approach him with the major faults I find in his 'baby.'" He then went on to enumerate those problems:

> First of all, the story is trite and obvious and has no deviation from the straight, formularized pattern which I feel we have seen under the shroud of other titles too many times.
>
> Second, it's a shame to waste the talents of Judy Garland in a straight ingénue role. She is a female Charlie Chaplin for my dough, who can make you laugh and cry simultaneously—the perfect "patsy" who, nine reels later, fits Prince Charming's glass slipper.
>
> Third, *Summer Stock* is a great title and the actual working of a stock company—the roughing it, physical labor of painting

scenery, making, borrowing, or begging costumes and props—has never been, to my knowledge, depicted in its true form. I have outlined a story that not only would give full value to our title *Summer Stock* but be an ideal characterization for Judy; that of a stage-struck farm girl, who joins the local stock company, only to become the Patsy who paints, and hauls scenery, props, etc.; and gets, momentarily, no nearer the stage than the moving of scenery and working the act curtain. I would like to give you this story outline in full.

Fourth, if we must use the present story, we need a Sid Sheldon or Freddie Finklehoffe to make the scenes, dialogue, and situations interesting, amusing, and believable; and make a few detours off that beaten-up beaten path.[19]

Schary could not be convinced, and the picture geared up under a cloud of apprehension. Chuck later said of the experience, "*Summer Stock* was my first ulcer."

14

Get Happy

"I was miscast," Gene Kelly maintained in a 1974 *Films Illustrated* profile. "[*Summer Stock*] was a revamp of one of Judy's films with Mickey
Rooney. It needed a teenager, and I was pushing forty at the time."[1] While
willing to put aside those concerns so as to assist Garland during this
troubled period, Kelly couldn't hide his displeasure with the feeble script,
adding, "[Chuck] had the sophistication and the grace to realize that
what he was working on was a piece of crap."[2]

Summer Stock doled out the "unknown-saves-the-show" fable that
was a cornerstone of the Hollywood musical. Dependable Jane Falbury
(Garland) is struggling to keep her Connecticut farm operating, while her
erratic, wannabe-actress sister Abigail (Gloria De Haven) is in New York.
She returns with a struggling theatrical company, their director Joe Ross
(Kelly), and his assistant Herb (Phil Silvers). Amid rehearsals for a show
in the barn, Abigail decamps with the leading man; Jane and Joe are
pressed into service as replacements, and—of course—fall in love.

Triteness aside, Walters strove to make *Summer Stock* an honest de-
piction of rural theater, conveying the backstage chaos, the amateur temperament, and the curious mix of fear and anticipation that beset opening
night. The slight story at least explored the need for self-fulfillment, particularly in Garland's character, and her evolution from subservience to
star attraction provided the film's emotional core. In Kelly's Joe, Chuck
essentially found a portrait of himself: a director-choreographer who
balances egos and could (and would) throw on a costume in order to make
sure the curtain went up.

"When you start a picture," Walters said, "and the bets around the
lot are two-to-one that [it] will never be finished, it's disconcerting and
discouraging." Rehearsals nevertheless began the first week of October.
Harry Warren and Mack Gordon delivered much of their agreeable

119

score, while Kelly and co-choreographer Nick Castle laid out dance routines. On October 13 Garland pre-recorded two songs: "If You Feel Like Singing, Sing" and "(Howdy Neighbor) Happy Harvest"; her voice was steady and robust. Unfortunately, that big sound emanated from a four-foot-eleven-inch woman with a similarly hearty figure, and studio executives were immediately concerned about the additional poundage Garland had brought back from her Boston recuperation. "We tried to make her look as thin as possible," remembered costumer Walter Plunkett, "but we weren't miracle workers and we didn't succeed."[3]

Complicating matters, Betty Hutton had by now arrived at M-G-M. *Annie Get Your Gun* resumed filming on October 10, with Hutton bedecked in costumes designed for Garland. "It was like a bad dream that I thought I had put away," Judy later said of her return to medication for both slimming and bolstering.[4] After missing six days in the first twenty of pre-production, she was sent an official warning on October 31; Garland sensibly requested a release from *Summer Stock* and her Metro contract. Mayer reportedly talked her out of both.

"Judy needed more reassurance than anyone I've ever known," said Walters, "professionally mainly, but even as a person." Recognizing that her lack of self-confidence was inseparably linked to her misconceptions about her appearance, he would barrage her with daily compliments: "Judy, you look adorable today." "Oh, those shoes are marvelous." "Baby, that dress is darling." "I love your hair, honey." Flattery, he insisted, "was food to her."[5]

Principal photography began November 21, 1949. Schary sent Walters a note of encouragement: "I know how hard you [have] worked on *Summer Stock,* and I appreciate your sincere and unselfish interest in it."[6] Attempting amends, Freed wrote a memo of support as well, saying, "I know that you will do a fine job and that you will add your inventiveness and good taste to *Summer Stock* and make it a distinctive picture as you always do. We miss you here in the Unit and are all rooting and waiting for you to come back."[7]

Walters began with the film's opening musical number, "If You Feel Like Singing, Sing." His crane shot panned across Falbury Farm, the camera navigating exterior foliage and plunging through a bedroom window to discover Judy caroling in the shower. It was the perfect manifestation of the character's inner vivacity; regardless of her outward conformity, she is happily uninhibited in private.

The picture was off to a promising start, but there remained mounting pressure on Garland to deliver. "I was late," she admitted. "I've been unpunctual all my life—and there were fights over that. I hate fights. I can't stand ill-feeling. I was wobbly and unsure and desperately trying to prove, not to the world but to myself, that I was making good as a person."[8] As autumn dragged into winter, Judy's attendance became ever more unpredictable, but Walters understood. "She couldn't help herself. [There was] just too much turmoil inside. She just had to get away from everything and everybody."[9] Pasternak, however, was noted for his on-time delivery of moneymakers and became increasingly anxious. "Not showing up for work," he'd point out, "is quite a serious matter. . . . All sorts of things, running to vast expense [and] complicated arrangements—this is what a [carefully prepared] shooting schedule involves."[10]

Veteran costumer Plunkett, who had watched Garland grow up on the M-G-M lot, observed: "[Judy] was paranoid about her inability to work and she felt she was letting Gene and Chuck down terribly. And the more she tried to pull herself together, the more hysterical she became. It was heartbreaking to see."[11]

The bad days were somehow endured, and the director always hoped for the best. ("I can't say enough about Charles Walters and his patience," stressed Pasternak.)[12] When set to film her "Happy Harvest" tractor ride through the San Fernando Valley, Garland announced she wasn't feeling well enough to face the camera. "Hey, Judy," Chuck encouraged her, "come listen to your playback for a minute." Assistant director Al Jennings recalled, "Well, she did. The music started, [and Judy] said, 'Gee, that's great.' . . . She got on the tractor—and we did it! She had been on her way home, very ill, but she stood there and did that number. The funny part was that something went wrong with the playback, and I was furious. And Judy was calming *me* down! She said, 'They'll get it. Don't worry.'"[13]

On another day, Walters's desire to mollycoddle his star was nil. "Well, if you'll wait until I finish my coffee," he declared after she had said she was leaving, "I'll go with you. Because I feel as much like making you act as you feel like acting." True to form, Garland sensed his displeasure and was overcome with concern: "Oh, no, Chuck. *We've got to.* . . . [C]an't we get the crew? . . . [W]hat am I supposed to wear?"

Young Carleton Carpenter, playing an eager theatrical intern in one of his first M-G-M appearances, remembers that Garland wasn't the only *Summer Stock* star whose insecurities burdened the director. "Mr. Kelly had a thing about my height," said Carpenter, whose six-foot-three-inch frame towered over the diminutive dancer. "He was very peculiar with me . . . but always with a smile on his face. First he'd come to me: 'Is that where you're going to be, Carp?' And I'd say, 'Yes, Mr. Kelly.' He'd then go [speak with] Chuck: 'I think Carp ought to be over there.' So he'd always be moving away from me."[14] Walters remained tolerant of Kelly's re-blocking but was less amused when the dancer's own inflexibility resulted in a near-altercation with the film's choreographer. As Jennings observed, Kelly and Nick Castle "never quite jibed. Gene was proud of Gene . . . and Castle was a little hot-headed, too. They got into a little kind of a thing. . . . I thought they were about to come to fisticuffs. I stepped between them and said, 'You two little boys!' I really let them have it."[15]

As overseer of all this unrest, Chuck later said his *Summer Stock* experience was often "absolute torture."

Miracles of adjustment were made to the schedule. "Make sure to get Phil Silvers in every shot," Walters scribbled in his script.[16] When the comic pled his colossal fear of heights, the director climbed a tree to demonstrate how safe it was. Actor Eddie Bracken, who played Garland's anemic fiancé, remembered that the day-to-day stress never seemed to tire Chuck but that he "was hard to reach as a buddy, because [he] was so busy. . . . a workaholic. He was always thinking of things to direct and do, and when he'd come to talk to you, he would be very gentle."[17]

Downtime was spent developing witty visuals, even for mere insert shots. At one point the chorus dancers are shown as they stretch in the barnyard among wandering chickens. Character actress Marjorie Main (playing Garland's no-nonsense cook) completes the incongruous picture as she lumbers across the makeshift rehearsal space with a mooing cow. It was a deliciously unforced sight gag. "That was a lot of fun," remembers dancer Dorothy Tuttle, "but the sets were very hot, [and] the animals were rather odoriferous. . . . [W]e were very happy when we had that over."[18] Acknowledging the pleasure of the work despite the odds, the crew, before breaking for the winter holiday, presented their selfless director with a large card that good-naturedly ribbed: "Chuck, your mule train wishes you a very merry Xmas."[19]

Summer Stock's production was the antithesis of Schary's newly implemented fast track. "It went along inch by inch," Chuck recalled.[20] The rushes, however, were solidly entertaining. "How *dare* this look like a happy picture!" he'd marvel. Kelly never flagged in his help, leading Walters to freely compliment him: "He'd placate [Judy] and hold her hand, [asking,] 'Anything I can do today?'" Such real-life tenderness translated nicely on-screen, and historian John Cutts found the result "an entirely unselfish performance" from the sometimes self-amplified actor.[21]

Walters took full advantage of this gentility for the Garland-Kelly "You Wonderful You" sequence. As described by historian Douglas McVay, the episode

> begins magically as Judy moves across the deserted, atmospheric stage and into a spotlight where she stands, taut, nervous yet exalted . . . and then Kelly slowly moves to stand beside her in a second spotlight. Their simple costumes, dark-hued, almost "practice dress," have the effect of stripping them of the roles they are playing in the film and . . . [they] come together before us to make an explicit statement about their joint enslavement by their musical comedy profession. The statement is first verbal (in Kelly's speech about the lure of show business and Garland's reactions), then musical (in the song and dance which acts as illustration of the magic about which they have just been speaking).[22]

Walters filmed the lengthy sequence (dialog, number, and kiss) in three extended shots, with the entire dance powerfully captured in one. "Normally," he said, "when I do a really long take, it's because what's happening seems really interesting to me, and I don't see the point in cutting it. It's not because I'm looking for a certain visual effect."

Equally effective is Garland's "Friendly Star," sung as she agonizes over her recent kiss from Kelly. Judy begins in the farmhouse foyer, turns out the light, and—singing throughout—eventually exits to the porch, gazing at the night sky. Instead of the customary cutaway shot, Walters's traveling camera pulls away from Garland so that the audience (but not the singer) discovers the listening Kelly. The camera then pans back to Judy, resting at an oblique angle for her poignant conclusion.

"Friendly Star" exemplified the director's approach to the staging of ballads. As historian Gerald Mast observed, for Walters "space is centripetal, not moving outward from the performer into space but moving inward from the edges of the frame toward the performer. . . . When [his camera] moves, it keeps the performer as the fixed foot of a compass, traveling around him or her, attracted to the performance as if magnetized or hypnotized."[23] Typical for Walters and Garland, there was also irreverence amid the artistry. Chuck confessed, "I was on the [camera] boom just above her head, and we were moving in for a giant close-up. Judy looked up with those giant liquid eyes of hers, and it was the most fantastic shot in the world. 'Cut,' I yelled. 'Will someone please hand me a towel. I've just cum!' Now that might be thought indelicate, but Judy loved that sort of foolishness. 'C'mon what's next?' she'd ask."[24]

Topping all other difficulties, Walters suddenly found himself accused of unacceptable behavior with his leading lady. Studio spies were lurking everywhere, keeping watchful tabs on Garland and eager to report any assumed transgressions. "We had a little saloon café just off the lot, and Judy would say, 'Let's go over to the [so-nicknamed] Retake Room,'" recounted Chuck.

[Once there] she said, "Now, look, Buster, I'm going to have a beer. I'm going to have a beer if you want me to work this afternoon." I said, "Sure, honey, have a beer, as long as you eat and get back to work." I'd have a martini, and she'd have a beer.

Then one day, I'm called *from lunch* to Mr. Mayer's office. The first thing that throws you is the double-doors. I open the door, and there's a door, and I open this door and—*boom!*— there you are in this room; I can't tell you how enormous. Now the *entire* upper echelon is lined up along one wall, and at the far end of the room at this gigantic desk is Mr. Mayer. So he gets up from the desk and says, "I don't know you personally, Mr. Walters, but I feel it is important I speak to you. It has come to my attention that you are encouraging Judy Garland's drinking." Well, of course, I got myself together and said, "Mr. Mayer, if you want Judy to work in the afternoon, she's going to have a beer, come hell or high water or she's 'heading for the hills,' as she very pointedly puts it to me. Now, which do you want? She doesn't have a beer and heads for the hills or has a beer and comes back to work?"

> That's when I met Mr. Mayer. I'd been there eight years, and *this* was my introduction to him.[25]

Photography neared completion in late January 1950, with Walters running "on nothing but coffee and cigarettes." Some of the dancers were leaving for other assignments, and a premature wrap party was organized. (The *Summer Stock* chorus employed stellar talent, including Kelly's future wife Jeanne Coyne, protégé Jimmy Thompson, and soon-to-be Broadway favorite Carol Haney.) Walters was deeply touched by the crew's farewell gift of an attractive travel clock.

What remained to be shot was the picture's show-within-a-show finale, comprising reprises of the film's earlier songs. This concept was discarded at the last minute in favor of new material from music director Saul Chaplin, whose gifts would eventually lift such pictures as *An American in Paris, Seven Brides for Seven Brothers, West Side Story,* and *The Sound of Music.* Chaplin furnished two original tunes, the elegant "All for You" (with Gene, Judy, and chorus in evening clothes) and the hayseed star duet "Heavenly Music" (to be performed in overalls and oversized rubber feet, with overwrought dogs). When Garland opted out of playing hillbilly, Phil Silvers filled in.

Judy's work on *Summer Stock* was deemed complete in early February—after two and a half months of filming—and she headed to Santa Barbara to rest. Meanwhile, Walters oversaw editing of the picture, and it soon became obvious that a Garland payoff was missing. "She was the star, but she never had a star turn in the final show," he pointed out. Judy solved the problem herself, as he recalled, telling him, "I'll give you a week. I want Harold Arlen's 'Get Happy,' and I want to wear the costume from the 'Mr. Monotony' number cut from *Easter Parade.* And I want [you] to do it." The director admitted the request seemed "a nice little challenge," and he was pleasantly stunned when "she returned two weeks later, thin as a string."

"Get Happy," a quasi-spiritual from 1930, had been famously introduced by Ruth Etting as the first act finale of *Ruth Selwyn's 9:15 Revue.* Thought Chuck, "What the *hell* am I gonna do with it? What does it say? What does it mean?" His answers to those questions proved iconic: a spare, sophisticated staging with Garland as a cool jazz vamp and accompanied by eight equally smooth male dancers.

"Chuck came into rehearsal knowing what he wanted," recalls enlisted dancer John Angelo. "He showed us our part—and *he* did Judy's part." Time was of the essence, but that didn't daunt Walters. Angelo continues, "I would describe Chuck as soft but strong. Often he was camp! He'd say to us guys, 'Oh, c'mon *girls,* let's get it together.'"[26] They had three days to set, and, per Walters, Judy rehearsed for one. "Chuck was what I call an 'ape-er,'" said Angelo. "He could 'ape' anyone. So when Judy would come in, she'd say, 'Chuck, would you mind running through it with the boys,' and he'd do it—and you thought he *was* Judy Garland! He did everything."

To prepare his star for "Get Happy," Walters gave Judy the mental image of Lena Horne. "This got her away from 'me dancing,'" he explained, "and she 'felt' Lena: so cool!—snap!—push the hat! It worked beautifully."[27]

Garland pre-recorded the number on March 15. By contrast, Kelly and Silvers pre-recorded "Heavenly Music" on March 6 and filmed the following week, which belies decades of later claims that "Get Happy" was completed months after *Summer Stock* wrapped. Carpenter returned to watch "Get Happy" go before the cameras, he recalled, and "after that . . . I had to go back and do a lead-in for Kelly's newspaper dance, so [he and Judy] had equal time on screen."[28] (Gene's bravura squeaky-board solo kept production open until mid-April.)

The three-minute "Get Happy" was earmarked for a two-day shoot, and a trim Judy took obvious delight in the crew's whistles as she came onto the soundstage. After her first takes, however, Walters told her she seemed too tentative, and the discouraged Garland retreated to her dressing room. Her fearful director followed. "I hated to say it that way," he ventured, "but . . . it was your first crack at it." Judy remained silent, prompting Chuck to return to the set, kicking himself: "Me and my big mouth!" Garland soon re-emerged, heading straight for her critic. Hands on her hips, she quipped, "You know, Chuck, if you had any *class,* you would *use* that travel clock the crew gave you."[29] It was a classic Garland non sequitur. "All right, fellas!" she announced. "Let's do this."

In essence an afterthought, "Get Happy" was swiftly accomplished and found a definitive interpretation. Walters requested but did not receive screen credit, yet in retrospect the sequence became such a classic template for M-G-M musicals that the credit spoke for itself.[30]

Despite the holdups, *Summer Stock* was completed in fifty days at a cost of $2,024,848, just $43,000 over budget. The additional costs were primarily incurred by the film's added finale sequences and Kelly's news-paper dance—none of which figured into Pasternak's original estimates. When released in August 1950, the movie was dubbed "delightful sum-mer entertainment" by the *Hollywood Reporter*.[31] "Walters' direction is light, airy, and full of fun. He makes the rural locale count for beguiling humor, and his approach to characterizations is in the best musical com-edy manner."

The musical played to capacity at New York's Capitol Theater and recorded 70,608 admissions over Labor Day weekend—the best business the theater had experienced for that holiday period since 1946. Future American playwright Edward Albee, then twenty-two, was among the crowds, and fifteen years later he would write: "When Garland finished singing ['Get Happy'], the audience watching the film was breathless for a moment and then, to a person, burst into sustained applause. . . . Noth-ing has instructed and gratified me more than the time she convinced a bunch of afternoon movie watchers that a strip of celluloid was the real thing."[32] Such reports were a particular validation for Garland. "When Judy gives of herself," Chuck once told journalist Erskine Johnson with-out hesitation, "there's some of her blood on the film."[33]

The troubled production ("a blur," in Walters's later memory) remains one of the director's most personal movies. His shrewd modification of the backstage musical blueprint and his graceful ability to balance and contrast emotions in song and dance would encourage critic McVay to conclude, "If [Minnelli's] *The Band Wagon* is the definitive Hollywood musical about 'putting on a show,' then *Summer Stock* must rank as runner-up. Yet in the 'You Wonderful You' duologue and the bouquet-presentation scene [on opening night], it strikes more loving and touch-ing show business chords than anything in the *Band Wagon* script."[34]

Summer Stock routinely has been dismissed as the fallback film Gar-land made after losing *Annie Get Your Gun*—and as Kelly's outmoded musical sandwiched between the innovative *On the Town* and *An Amer-ican in Paris*. Against those pictures, the simple rural love story of Jane Falbury and Joe Ross indeed pales in import and size. But, under Wal-ters's eloquent care, it unquestionably conquers in heart.

15

"A Dear Dame"

If it can no longer be proved, it's certainly possible that Charles Walters's first encounter with L. B. Mayer happened—as he claimed—eight years after he joined M-G-M. It was no secret that the conservative studio head had a checkered history with his gay or bisexual-identified staff, but "Mayer's homophobia gave way to the higher needs of business, money, and stockholders," reflects Fox producer David Brown.[1]

Openly gay writer Arthur Laurents, who came to Hollywood in the late 1940s and eventually worked as an M-G-M scriptwriter, remembers the industry as more hypocritical than blasé. "Hollywood only cares about image. If you projected the right image, they didn't care what the truth was. They were very practical. . . . So long as they could use you, all they cared about was appearance. But everyone knew what the truth was. You could be gay and still be a big success, if you kept up the right image."[2] Producer Sid Luft (Judy Garland's third husband and longtime manager) believes Walters did just that. "The studio moguls were homophobic, but Chuck had a very deep voice which seemed to make them feel better," he says. "An exceptionally good-looking man, he was allowed to go forward at the studio because of his talent and his manly appearance. The moguls had a fear of men who swished."[3]

Even so, there weren't many homosexuals at the top of Hollywood's creative ladder who were brazen enough to build a home with their partners, particularly during the overmonitored HUAC era. "But Chuck didn't alter his life one iota," adds Luft. "He lived with another man . . . as in a marriage. They owned property together and lived well." Fully aware that M-G-M employed several gay men in various capacities, Luft distinguishes Walters as one of the few to truly hold an important place at the prestigious movie factory. "Roger [Edens] was well liked, too, although he didn't have the power with the studio that Chuck [ultimately] did."[4]

Gene Kelly was still tearing up newspapers with his feet when Freed invited Walters back to the unit, sending him the script for *Royal Wedding*. Alan J. Lerner's original story paired Fred Astaire with rising star Vera-Ellen as a brother-sister team, invited to perform in London during festivities attendant to the marriage of Queen Elizabeth II. Officially assigned to the project as of May 1, Chuck oversaw rehearsals, offered casting suggestions (Peter Lawford and Keenan Wynn), and discussed wardrobe with designer Helen Rose. Casting switched in pre-production, with June Allyson taking the lead—and the director was privy to rising gossip, as he noted: "Everyone was thinking, 'June is getting fat.'"[5] The company soon learned she was pregnant. Pressed for a replacement, Freed contacted Judy Garland.

Walters was stunned. "I went to Arthur shaking. Tears running, I said, 'Arthur, I'm sorry, I just can't.' He said, 'Chuck, don't worry.' So they called me 'sick.'"[6] On May 23, Garland arrived for her first day of work on *Royal Wedding,* and on May 25 the *Los Angeles Times* reported that "Walters needs a rest because of a decisive loss of weight."[7] (Stanley Donen replaced him.) "I felt no animosity toward [Judy]," the director explained later, "but I just couldn't face a repeat of the *Summer Stock* experience. Judy could not help herself when she was behaving badly—and when she was feeling good, you would never have met anyone wittier, sharper, [or] better company. And bright as a penny. But those good days now were getting fewer and further between."[8]

Typical of Garland's genuine concern for those closest to her, she phoned the following morning. "Oh, Chuck, I just heard about your condition from Arthur. I'll be right over." An hour later Judy was at the beach—blindly unaware that she was the motivation for his withdrawal. Of the paradox, Walters later laughed, "Judy kept coming to my house *to make me well* so that I could do the picture."[9] He kept up the ruse with a list of phony maladies, many of which Garland had spoken of to her director in the past. "Oh, yes," she would commiserate, "I know how *that* feels." When Judy's maid dropped off a suitcase and announced Judy's intention to move in, Chuck finally balked. Freed suggested he leave town, but Walters instead chose to hide out at Roger Edens's home in Pacific Palisades. The subterfuge might have worked had they thought to inform Bob Alton (another Palisades resident). But he was clueless when a worried Garland phoned in search of her missing friend. The choreographer then unwittingly told her, "I don't know what's happened, darling, but I've just discovered it's Chuck's car that's been parked in front of my house for the last two days, and you know I'm only a block from the cliff." With Garland thinking the worst, Walters had no choice but to rematerialize.[10]

Pre-production shifted into high gear, but Judy never made it to filming. Freed had made a brusque comment about her appearance, triggering Garland to cancel a next-day rehearsal, and M-G-M once again suspended her. At her Brentwood home, the distraught Garland broke a drinking glass and ineffectually jabbed at her neck. Immediate headlines followed, and friends rallied. When Hugh Martin visited the convalescent, he mentioned his own run-ins with Freed. Garland readily sympathized: "Arthur affects people in different ways." Then she dryly added, "*I* cut my throat."[11]

Jane Powell went into *Royal Wedding,* and three months later, by mutual consent, Garland and M-G-M parted company after sixteen years. Her release put several future projects in peril, including Freed's planned Technicolor remake of *Show Boat.* Walters returned in July to screen-test singer Peggy Lee for Garland's role of Julie, but the part of the troubled riverboat chanteuse ultimately would be cast with a vocally dubbed Ava Gardner.

As a comparatively new contract director, Chuck was expected to accept any script he was assigned. He made it a personal pledge, however, to take on only those projects to which he "could add something." *Three Guys Named Mike* was a light Sidney Sheldon comedy that romanticized commercial air travel, and (despite his acute dislike of flying) Walters "was thrilled to get it." The screenplay recounted, if loosely, the real-life adventures of plucky American Airlines stewardess Ethel "Pug" Wells and emphasized her escapades with a trio of suitors, each named Mike.[12] "The story was episodic," admitted Walters, and he applied a choreographer's logic to Sheldon's work. "Each scene could be like a dance number, with a beginning, a middle, and an end. If one [sequence] was quite agitated, the next could be calm—like in a musical revue, only with drama instead."

Three Guys was overseen with "great enthusiasm" by producer Armand Deutsch. "I would bring up a scene to him and read it," said Sheldon,

In performance, Anaheim High School assembly, 1929. Per the original yearbook caption: "Chuck Walters scored decidedly with his dancing and was insistently called back for encores." Courtesy Anaheim Historical Society.

WALTERS, CHARLES
Musical Comedy '30; Drama Club '29, '30, President '30; Spanish Club '29, '30, President '30; Junior Play '30; Christmas Program '29.

Senior class yearbook, 1930. At eighteen, Walters pioneered Anaheim High School's first musical comedy production, a thinly designed mounting of the popular *Good News*. Courtesy Anaheim Historical Society.

NEW FACES

FULTON THEATRE

Program cover for Broadway's *New Faces of 1934*. Leonard Sillman is center, with Imogene Coca to his right, Henry Fonda above Coca, and Walters at the end of the second row. Photograph in author's collection.

Broadway's "new face" confirms Sillman's estimation of the young Walters as "square." Courtesy Leonard Sillman Collection, Howard Gottlieb Archival Research Center.

Fox and Walters publicity photos for the 1935 Club Versailles engagement. Both photographs in author's collection.

Fox and Walters in their deleted number from Paramount's *The Big Broadcast of 1936* (1935). Photograph in author's collection.

Walters and June Knight prepare for "Begin the Beguine," *Jubilee* (1935). Photograph in author's collection.

John Darrow, Walters's longtime companion, circa 1934. Photograph in author's collection.

Robert Alton rehearses Vilma Ebsen and Walters in *Between the Devil* (1937). Photograph in author's collection.

Walters and Ebsen onstage in *Between the Devil* (1937). Photograph in author's collection.

Walters and Audrey Christie in *I Married an Angel* (1938). Photograph in author's collection.

Walters confers with Cole Porter, *Let's Face It* rehearsal (1941). Photograph in author's collection.

"Do I Love You?": Gene Kelly and ensemble in the first number choreographed by Walters at M-G-M, *Du Barry Was a Lady* (filmed 1942). Photograph in author's collection.

(*Left*) Walters rehearses Lucille Ball on a trampoline for *Du Barry*'s "Madame, I Love Your Crepes Suzette" (1942). Photograph courtesy John Florea/Time & Life Pictures/Getty Images.

(*Below*) Walters makes his film debut, partnering the maturing Judy Garland in the finale of *Presenting Lily Mars* (1943). Courtesy David Price Collection.

"Gotta dance!" Garland and Walters, "Broadway Rhythm," *Presenting Lily Mars* (1943). Courtesy John Fricke Collection.

Walters gets Lena Horne "hep to step" for "Brazilian Boogie," *Broadway Rhythm* (1944). Photograph in author's collection.

(*Left*) Stepping out: Garland and Walters on a date at the Mocambo (1943). Courtesy John Fricke Collection.

(*Below*) Walters coaches Ingrid Bergman on the set of *Gaslight* (1944). Photograph in author's collection.

(*Above*) Peter Lawford, Patricia Marshall, June Allyson, Joan McCracken, and Ray McDonald—the principal cast of *Good News* (1947), Walters's debut as a feature film director. Photograph in author's collection. (*Below*) On the set of *Easter Parade* (1947), Walters and script clerk Les Martinson take obvious delight as Garland shares a tale. Courtesy John Fricke Collection.

(*Above*) Walters rehearses his idol Fred Astaire for a petulant moment on the terrace, *The Barkleys of Broadway* (1948). Courtesy Scott Roberts Collection.

(*Right*) Producer, star, and director: Arthur Freed, Ginger Rogers, and Walters on the "Swing Trot" set for *The Barkleys of Broadway* (1948). Courtesy Charles Walters Collection, Cinema-Television Library, USC.

(*Right*) Enjoying the view from the lookout of the Walters/Darrow Malibu beach home, April 1949. Courtesy Gloria Swanson Inc. and the Harry Ransom Humanities Research Center.

(*Left*) Hitting the pool in Palm Springs, April 1949. Courtesy Gloria Swanson Inc. and the Harry Ransom Humanities Research Center.

One of many happy moments with lifelong friend Gloria Swanson, Palm Springs, April 1949. Courtesy Gloria Swanson Inc. and the Harry Ransom Humanities Research Center.

(*Above*) Director and muse: Garland's "Get Happy" goes before the cameras, *Summer Stock* (1950). Courtesy John Fricke Collection. (*Below*) Walters's first non-musical, *Three Guys Named Mike*, with Jane Wyman at his left hand (July 1950). Courtesy Charles Walters Collection, Cinema-Television Library, USC.

Happiness prevails on the set of *Texas Carnival* (1951): Walters with Red Skelton (*above*) and Esther Williams (*below*). Photographs in author's collection.

(*Above*) Showing Garland her "Get Happy" steps at a Los Angeles rehearsal hall in preparation for *Judy at the Palace*, 1951. Courtesy Fred McFadden Collection. (*Below*) Back to Broadway: Walters partners Garland for "A Couple of Swells" at the Palace, October 16, 1951. Courtesy Fred McFadden Collection.

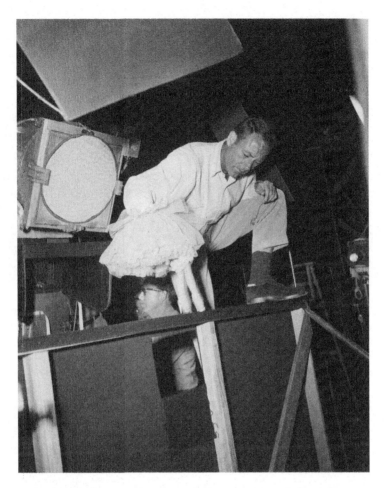

Letting his fingers do the dancing: Walters participates as the legs of puppet Marguerite in "Hi-Lili, Hi-Lo," *Lili* (March 1952). Courtesy Charles Walters Collection, Cinema-Television Library, USC.

Lili: (*above*) Walters, Leslie Caron, Zsa Zsa Gabor, and Jean-Pierre Aumont film "The Adoration Ballet"; the director appears as the dancing double for the movement-challenged actor. Courtesy Charles Walters Collection, Cinema-Television Library, USC; (*below*) Caron, second from left, with her compatriots in the "Ballet of Paul and the Puppets" (1952). Photograph in author's collection.

Easy to Love: (*above*) Wearing an eye patch after a minor on-set accident, the shirtless Walters provides inspiration for Tony Martin; (*below*) Esther Williams with her self-confessed favorite director (1953). Both photographs courtesy Charles Walters Collection, Cinema-Television Library, USC.

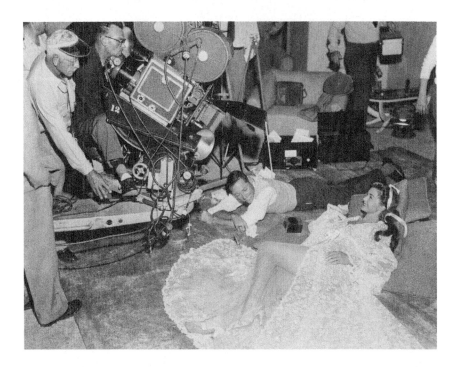

Rehearsing for the opening sequence of *Torch Song* (1953), in which Walters returned to the screen at Joan Crawford's request. Photograph in author's collection.

(*Left*) Producer Henry Berman, Walters, the ever camera-ready Crawford, and Dore Schary on the *Torch Song* set (April 1953). Courtesy Charles Walters Collection, Cinema-Television Library, USC.

(*Right*) Director and date at the Hollywood premiere of *Rear Window* (1954). Photograph in author's collection.

A fireside chat with Cinderella (Leslie Caron), *The Glass Slipper* (1955).
Photograph in author's collection.

With Caron on crypt, Walters shows the somber approach he desires from actor Michael
Wilding in the climactic "Tehara Ballet," *The Glass Slipper* (1955). Courtesy Charles
Walters Collection, Cinema-Television Library, USC.

Welcoming Bing Crosby to Chuck Walters Presents, the director's Palm Springs menswear shop, circa 1956. Courtesy Palm Springs Historical Society. All Rights Reserved.

Flanked by Frank Sinatra and Desi Arnaz, Walters celebrates at a Palm Springs party in his honor, circa 1956. Courtesy Palm Springs Historical Society. All Rights Reserved.

Suggestions for Debbie Reynolds in *The Tender Trap* (1955). Photograph in author's collection.

Walters demonstrates playful posturing for an amused Grace Kelly, *High Society* (1956). Photograph in author's collection.

(*Above*) Assembling "Well, Did You Evah?": Sinatra, Walters, music supervisor Saul Chaplin, and Crosby; *High Society* (1956). Courtesy Charles Walters Collection, Cinema-Television Library, USC. (*Below*) Staging "Now You Has Jazz" with Crosby and Louis Armstrong. Courtesy Charles Walters Collection, Cinema-Television Library, USC.

(*Above*) Sinatra and Grace Kelly are guided through a *High Society* dance rehearsal (1956). Courtesy Cinema-Television Library, USC.

(*Right*) Chatting with Louis Armstrong, *High Society* (1956). Courtesy Cinema-Television Library, USC.

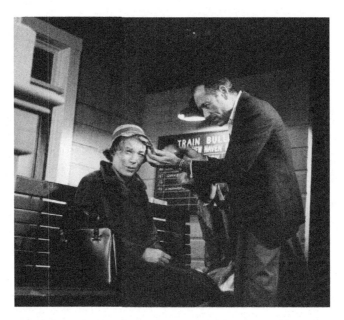

Walters segues to the new generation of Hollywood stars and provides the wet look for Shirley MacLaine in *Ask Any Girl* (1959). Courtesy Charles Walters Collection, Cinema-Television Library, USC.

The actor looks on as Walters "plays" David Niven opposite Doris Day, *Please Don't Eat the Daisies* (1960). Courtesy Charles Walters Collection, Cinema-Television Library, USC.

(*Left*) On location in Palm Springs: Walters prepares Shirley MacLaine for the ultimately deleted dream sequence of *Two Loves* (1961). Courtesy Charles Walters Collection, Cinema-Television Library, USC. (*Right*) Two of Metro's preeminent music men on the back lot for *Billy Rose's Jumbo*: Walters and partner in perfection Roger Edens (1962). Courtesy Charles Walters Collection, Cinema-Television Library, USC.

(*Right*) An agile Walters—at fifty—clowns at the "circus school" established for *Jumbo*. Edens (at left) brandishes an issue of *Variety* (1962). Courtesy Charles Walters Collection, Cinema-Television Library, USC.

(*Left*) Walters explains concepts for a *Jumbo* aerial sequence to producer Joe Pasternak (1962). Courtesy Charles Walters Collection, Cinema-Television Library, USC. (*Right*). Director and star finally see eye to eye: an *Unsinkable Molly Brown* conference (1964). Photograph in author's collection.

Walters welcomes family to the set of *Molly Brown* (1964): his stepmother, his father, and his partner Jimie Morrissey. Courtesy Jimie Morrissey Collection.

"Colorado, My Home": The Molly Brown crew, Walters (standing center, in white pants), and singing star Harve Presnell (upper right) camp it up. Photograph in author's collection.

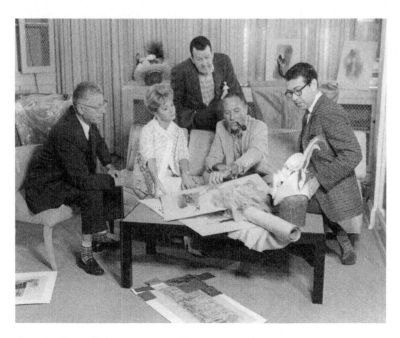

Shooting the Molly Brown costume featurette: producer Lawrence Weingarten, Reynolds, Edens, Walters, and designer Morton Haack (1964). Photograph in author's collection.

Walters poses for the Metro
publicity machine near the end of
his twenty-two-year studio tenure.
Photograph in author's collection.

In Tokyo for Columbia's *Walk, Don't Run* (1966), Walters crouches to
counsel Jim Hutton, Samantha Eggar, John Standing, and Cary Grant.
Photograph in author's collection.

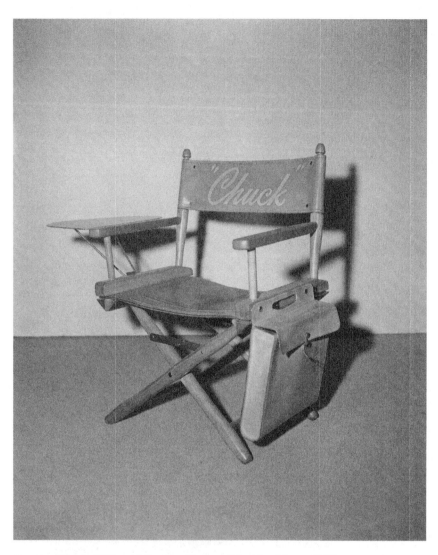

Courtesy Charles Walters Collection, Cinema-Television Library, USC.

"and he would literally jump up and down."[13] Deutsch later insisted he "had more fun making [*Three Guys*] than any picture I ever produced. Most pictures are a terrible chore to produce; problems exist every day. For some reason, this one was just a piece of cake."[14] Wells herself took special delight at being asked to appear for a one-line cameo. "When I arrived on the set for the first day's shooting," she recalls, "I found they had given me a dressing room. There were flowers in it, with a card from Chuck Walters. The card read: 'All stars get flowers on opening day—Happy new star to you!' Well, I burst into tears."[15]

Though rumored for both Lana Turner and her antithesis June Allyson, the film's starring role went to Oscar winner Jane Wyman, on loan from Warner Bros. "Jane had come [over] with complete director approval written into her contract," said Chuck. "But there were no problems, we sort of clicked from the start." Comedically adept, the actress was ably supported by her three Mikes: Van Johnson, Barry Sullivan, and Howard Keel (the last a replacement for Robert Walker).

Walters began shooting on July 26, and the cheerleading Deutsch never wavered in support of his director. "Certainly the preparation has been hectic and hurried," Deutsch acknowledged. "In spite of this, however, it's been a lot of fun, and I know that even though the picture will be brutally hard work, there will be some fun in that too—and a lot of satisfaction."[16] (Elsewhere occupied with *Royal Wedding* and aware of Walters's antipathy to air travel, Edens telegraphed: "Happy landing on this one but next time, *why not try the train*?!")[17] Filming on the black and white feature lasted less than a month, with Walters getting efficient—if not textured—work from cameraman Paul C. Vogel. Their tight production schedule benefited from the advance creation of "navigation charts" that plotted the moves of camera, lights, and actors within the cramped confines of actual airplanes.

"Those directors who shoot a scene from every angle imaginable do so because they don't really know what they want," Chuck said. "If you know what you want, why not shoot it that way? The set isn't going anywhere; if you find out later that you need something else, you can always come back. What's more, it's boring to do the same thing over and over again." Such a premeditated approach allowed for both speed on the set and control over editing. "I 'shoot-cut,'" he'd say. "That way, if I want a certain scene to take place a certain way, I only shoot it that way, and then they can't do anything about it."[18] In the editing room, department head Margaret Booth had no problems; she sent word that Chuck's footage was "darling" and full of "bounce."[19]

Many critics disagreed. *Three Guys* was released in March 1951, and Bosley Crowther evidenced an odd hostility toward what he termed a "contrived cloudland confection" and "an oppressively bird-brained little romance."[20] He seemed inordinately perturbed by the film's seeming promotion of American Airlines—an objection echoed by other reviewers. (Wells, on the other hand, was given one hundred shares of American Airlines stock in appreciation for the exposure.) Despite such cavils, *Three Guys* found a reasonably responsive public, earned an estimated $1.7 million, and inspired plans for a sequel in which a trio of like-named airline hostesses would fall for the same man.[21] Though *Three Girls Named Mary* never made it to the screen, Walters remained "fairly proud" of his first non-musical, anticipating further such pictures and noting how much less work they were than full-scale song-and-dance projects. As the decade progressed, Chuck's comedies became an indispensable addition to M-G-M's lineup, as well as a boon to its ledgers.

M-G-M's proudest boast during its heyday was an unprecedented roster of superstar personalities. "Louis B. Mayer could take a take a person off the street and make them a star if he wanted to," stated Hollywood publicist Jim Mahoney. "There isn't anybody in this business who can make a star, not anymore. [But] Mayer could."[22] Of all the mogul's creations, none proved a more unexpected phenomenon than national swimming champion Esther Williams.

She was signed by Metro in 1941, and the studio's coaches and marketing department coalesced to make her a sort of all-American aquatic girl next door. The public was fascinated by her lovely face and figure, her skill in the water, and her wry sense of fun, all of which were captured by the camera. (One critic keenly observed that Esther even swam with tongue-in-cheek.) Walters later defined her as "a dear dame . . . the only actress I know who became one, really, in spite of herself. But she made a big effort to learn, and she made progress from film to film." In early winter 1950, the two were given their first opportunity to work together in what was provisionally titled *The Carnival Story*.

"Chuck Walters gets the job of directing," Hedda Hopper reported on December 8, 1950, "and what a list of stars he'll have—Esther Williams, Red Skelton, Howard Keel, and Ann Miller."[23] Unfortunately, the stars had little with which to work. Producer Jack Cummings's endeavor was saddled with four bland songs by Harry Warren and Dorothy Fields and a slender screenplay by Dorothy Kingsley. Her scenario built on a case of mistaken identity, with down-and-out sideshow team Cornie Quinell (Skelton) and Debbie Telford (Williams) erroneously thought to be a cattle baron and his sister. Ranch hand Slim Shelby (Keel) knows they're imposters but plays along in order to get close to Debbie, while sheriff's daughter Sunshine Jackson (Miller) is smitten with Cornie. His intoxication during a chuck wagon race is all the plot could corral for a big finish.

Several years later, Kingsley rationalized the script's flaws, sweetly blaming the film's director for failing to capture her perceived sense of comedy. "Chuck was very good," she said, "[but] I used to think he sometimes didn't get enough close-ups." She went on:

> There was a funny scene in . . . *Texas Carnival*. Red Skelton was posing as someone else, a big time millionaire, who gets into this poker game where they're using jellybeans as poker chips. He keeps eating his, and they think, "Oh, my God, five thousand [dollars] means nothing to this guy. . . ." Afterwards, when he finds out how much he ate, he nearly dies. They ask him, "How are you going to make it up?" and he says, "If I could get a stomach pump, I know where I could locate $10,000!" I probably shouldn't say this about poor Chuck, but he wasn't in close enough on Red to get the full effect. It played, but Chuck used to get a little tired of taking close-ups, I think. Today, you know, they're practically in their tonsils in all the pictures.[24]

Esther, on the other hand, found Walters's guidance supportive. Visiting columnist Erskine Johnson noticed it was "the film's director . . . who's put M-G-M's prize mermaid in such a happy mood."[25] While filming on location at the Beverly Wilshire Hotel's swimming pool, the actress unguardedly told Johnson: "He's the first director who has ever helped me with my acting. It's a whole new world. We rehearse, and then I do it in one take. Working with him is like going to drama school. It's wonderful."[26]

Filming ran from early February until late March, and Williams was admittedly "distracted about everything." She had given birth—six weeks early—to her second child the previous October, and the baby was plagued with colic. "Bleary-eyed, I was on the set every morning at 6:30, on time, ready for hair, makeup, and a 'swim.'"[27] She was sustained by the ribald sense of humor she shared with Chuck, and neither ever forgot her three-word summation of the film's sexy underwater fantasy sequence. Using a process shot, Esther "swam" into Keel's hotel room and thoughts, floating and wiggling in midair in a billowing negligee that took on the appearance of a white puddle. A smirking Williams labeled the scene "Howard's wet dream."

Skelton further amplified the on-set merriment, and while Chuck knew the value of a happy set, he soon discovered that his star's genius for improvisational comedy was a liability to the production schedule. Remembered Keel,

> Red was terribly, terribly funny. [He] was doing a scene with Keenan Wynn; I [arrived] at lunchtime and said, "How ya doing?" Keenan said, "Forget it, you're not gonna work today." "What do you mean?"—because I was supposed to work right after lunch. He said they "can't get anything in the camera. . . . Red is so funny that everybody's breakin' up." "Well, I gotta see this." So I . . . went down [as they were] getting ready for a take. And Red started. He hadn't been at it twenty seconds, and I was on the floor—just roaring out loud. Finally, about three o'clock, they threw everybody off the set except the camera operator and Chuck.[28]

Despite such hilarity, Walters later admitted *Texas Carnival* "never really came alive." The scant seventy-six-minute feature was further burdened by flat cinematography by Robert Planck, clumsy editing by Adrienne Fazan, and dances both staged and filmed in lackluster fashion by Hermes Pan. Reviews were kind but varied. *Variety* considered the direction "particularly outstanding,"[29] while Philips K. Scheuer said in a softly patronizing review, "Walters . . . has a knack for sophisticated corn like this."[30] At the *Daily News,* Dorothy Masters predicted that "despite the marquee bait of Williams and Skelton, Metro won't find a big market. . . . Sophisticates won't buy its slapstick. Musical comedy devotees will be disappointed in the tunes. [And] a lot of folk who ordinarily like their humor broad are going to object to having it come out of the liquor bottle."[31] There were even censorship problems, although Metro was long practiced at stringently following the directives of the Production Code Administration. (The studio specifically had been warned that "none of the bathing suits shown should be of the so-called tie-on, or diaper style.")[32] Even so, when *Texas Carnival* played Maryland, the local censor excised the line "If you strike her tail, then you've struck water" from Skelton's opening song. The film's final shot of Keel embracing a dripping, swimsuit-clad Williams was deleted entirely in Erie, Pennsylvania. Notwithstanding—or perhaps because of—such prudish objections, *Carnival* netted more than $700,000.

M-G-M's publicity wizards found a special angle by which to hype the picture, trumpeting the payoff Metro had realized in making film directors of their choreographers, including Donohue, Alton, Donen, and Kelly. In the process, they acknowledged that Walters "is probably the busiest of the lot."[33] Chuck took the recognition in stride, commenting, "I can only speak from experience when I say that, if I hadn't once shown dancers how to lift up their feet, I might have found it tougher to show Esther how to swim in and out of camera range on cue, or to guide Red in maintaining pace through one of his comedy routines.

"Timing and pace," he added, "are important in any film, whether it be comedy or drama. And how better to learn the fundamentals of these two show business ingredients than by dancing?"[34]

16

Playing the Palace

The Academy of Motion Picture Arts and Sciences held its annual ceremony at the RKO Pantages Theater on March 29, 1951. Noticeably,
M-G-M received its only major award in the honorary Oscar presented
to Louis B. Mayer. It was hollow recognition. Hailed by the Academy as
a studio executive who "always believed in the policy of 'the greater risk
for the greater return,'" Mayer resigned from Metro just three turbulent
months later, defeated by the parent company's support of Dore Schary.
"[It was] the beginning of the end," reflected dancer Cyd Charisse.
"[Schary] was the biggest mistake they ever made."[1] As Mayer biographer Scott Eyman relates: "Schary considered himself a David Selznick
protégé, telling people that everything he knew about movies he had
learned from Selznick. When the compliment was relayed to Selznick, he
snorted and said, 'He never finished the course.'"[2]

Schary's speedily made, socially conscious pictures had long been at
odds with Mayer's generously budgeted, family-friendly approach to
filmmaking. But even Schary was hard pressed to dismiss musicals
(which Mayer championed), given that much of M-G-M's profit and es-
teem continued to be derived from such entertainment. Though long a
"Mayer man," Arthur Freed was thus safe in ignoring the political shift,
and he offered some calculated words to Philip K. Scheuer of the *Los
Angeles Times:* "I examine each story on its own merits. It doesn't matter
whether it has a message or no message. The first rule is: Don't bore the
audience."[3] Unfortunately, the producer's next venture with Walters
would largely do just that.

Modifying Broadway for mass audiences had become a Freed Unit
specialty. Between 1939 and 1951, nearly half of their movies originated
in one way or another on the Great White Way. True to their instincts,
Freed and company took liberties with New York's rarified 1944 dance

novelty *On the Town* and added a Cole Porter score to the sophisticated 1942 Lunt-Fontanne comedy *The Pirate.* "You can't make your show a bible," Freed claimed. "Otherwise you're not making a motion picture."[4] Occasionally he dusted off antiquities with uncontested success: George M. Cohan's 1922 charmer *Little Nellie Kelly,* and of course 1927's *Good News.* But no other movie producer in the 1950s would go as far back as Freed when putting before the cameras the 1897 comic opera *The Belle of New York.* "That picture," Walters later groaned, "was a duty. Arthur was stuck with the property, and they'd paid a lot of money for it."

In addition to an initial 1943 purchase price of $45,000, the property also carried the cost of writers' salaries across eight years of attempts to overhaul the original book.[5] Freed first saw it as a Rodgers and Hammerstein musical for Garland and Astaire, with Rouben Mamoulian directing. At one point in its lengthy evolution, *Belle* was even considered as Walters's first directorial assignment. "If it had been," he laughed, "I think my career would have been much shorter." Final scenarists Robert O'Brien and Irving Elinson shifted the story to 1910, and the picture's romance linked playboy Charlie Hill with chaste Angela Collins, welfare worker for the Daughters of Right (a rather loosely reimagined Salvation Army). Freed would later deny he had been influenced by the enormous success of *Guys and Dolls,* with its "bad boy and missionary girl" plot, yet even though *Belle*'s scripting preceded production of that 1950 Broadway show, the timing of his realization of *Belle* is suspicious.

The entire premise of the film rested on the clichéd notion that "love makes you feel you are walking on air." Employing trick photography, the leads were to be wafted above Manhattan at several plot points in the picture—a concept that would scarcely resonate with movie-going audiences of 1952. (At a *Belle* sneak preview, one woman was overheard commenting to her friend: "Well! How silly can you get?")[6]

Up-and-coming dance team Marge and Gower Champion were briefly announced as stars, until Freed coerced a reticent Astaire to step in. (If only somewhat kidding, Astaire later wrote, "I had avoided [*Belle*] back in 1946 by retiring.")[7] Vera-Ellen, with whom he'd recently danced in *Three Little Words,* was cast opposite him—an assignment that sealed the fate of the film for its director. "I couldn't stand Vera-Ellen," Walters freely admitted. "Yes, technically she knew how to dance, but I yawn as I say so."[8]

Hoping to bring humor to the mix, Chuck pushed M-G-M to cast Mae West against type as Astaire's pious Aunt Letty, a society matron.

"But the studio fluffed it," he said; they couldn't or wouldn't meet her price. Selected instead was Marjorie ("Ma Kettle") Main, also playing out of her own customary "down home" image. Supporting roles went to two of Walters's favorites, Gale Robbins as a gold-digger and Keenan Wynn as Astaire's lawyer and confidant. It was, per Wynn, typical type-casting: "I usually appeared as a vacuous friend-of-the-hero-to-whom-things-happen."[9]

Alton took his expected post as choreographer and began rehearsing Astaire and Vera-Ellen an astonishing three months before *Belle* commenced principal photography. When it did, on June 18, 1951, he filmed Astaire's "Seeing's Believing," which gave the airborne hoofer a chance to tap along the top of the famous Washington Square arch. Jack Martin Smith of the Art Department, however, failed to deliver the goods for a seamless superimposition of images, and Astaire sadly admitted, "Dancing on air [was] one trick . . . we had hoped would prove effective . . . and that, above all, failed to register."[10]

Walters then took the reins, with Edens acting as associate producer. Freed stayed noticeably preoccupied with the concurrent *Singin' in the Rain,* which lucratively exploited his own songbook. As a result, *Belle* became—in the words of unit regular Lela Simone—"a picture that was not given attention. There were no conferences; there were no set meetings, nothing. It just sort of wandered along."[11]

"Not that we didn't try," Walters later said in the film's defense. Copious edits were penciled into his script. New dialogue arrived daily. Under such duress, Astaire's habitual moaning only increased. "Fred was never happy," said Chuck. "I'd be amazed at the lightness, the gaiety in a scene. Then I would say, 'Cut,' and his face would drop, the shoulders would drop, and he'd say, 'Oh, it's terrible. I can't stand it. I hate it.' It was a waste of time trying to convince him it was fine." Working with Vera-Ellen was no more enjoyable. "I would talk to her about a scene, and she'd be doing pliés. That's the kind of concentration you got." Given the meager response from his stars—and with no choreographic duties to enliven him—Walters grew weary of *Belle.* He took to chain-smoking and later confessed that the job "was like putting a gun to your head every day."

The dour atmosphere briefly lifted in early September when Astaire's pseudo-biographical "I Wanna Be a Dancin' Man" went before the camera. Chuck's intentionally modest aspirations gave the number a nostalgic, charming simplicity. Freed, however, was not pleased. "He didn't like the [small casino] set," Astaire remembered. "He didn't like the way I was dressed . . . as a bartender. So he made us do the whole thing over again."[12] A slick version was reshot by Alton a few weeks later, and the dancer, now in a spotless white suit, executed the exact same steps on an expansive soundstage. Such changes—augmented by state-of-the-art lighting, an initially silhouetted Astaire, and a 1950s sophistication—must have convinced viewers that Webber's Casino was the most avant-garde beer garden in Victorian New York.

After ninety-nine days of rehearsal and fifty-four days of photography, *Belle* closed production on October 17, having cost $2,606,644 (including $81,500 for retakes). Vera-Ellen embarked on a thirteen-city publicity junket to launch the film in March 1952 but scarcely influenced the critics. Archer Winsten of the *New York Post* considered *Belle* "drowsily elegant,"[13] while Otis L. Guernsey Jr. of the *New York Herald Tribune* defined it "as unsubstantial as the head on a nickel beer."[14] The film lost just over $600,000 in its initial release, but even Astaire found compensation beyond his disappointment: "I was on *Belle* for eight months, beating my brains out. And all I got out of it was . . . a fortune."[15]

Walters's "drowsily elegant" picture eventually attracted a small but loyal following. In 1975, essayist Douglas McVay praised *Belle* as "near perfection . . . [an] intricate fusion of the iconographic, the terpsichorean, and the choreographic. Of all Hollywood musicals, [it remains] the most depressingly underrated and neglected by both critics and public. . . . [F]or some inexplicable, irrational and infuriating cause, fantasy-musicals have always run the risk of being accused by reviewers of sentimentality and whimsicality."[16] Chuck, however, accepted no such rationale. When another writer admitted similar affection, the director could only marvel, "Why you think so highly of it baffles me."

Regrettably, *The Belle of New York* was the last feature that Walters (fully) directed for Freed, and he later spoke quite candidly of it as "the least favorite" film of his career. "The initial idea was good—that, when someone's in love, it's as though they're flying through the atmosphere. But that didn't work for Astaire, because can he *really* be in love?

"And with Vera-Ellen, it became absolutely ridiculous."

It's important to note that some of Chuck's disinterest in *Belle* stemmed from his preoccupation with a much more appealing project. It had been less than a year since Judy Garland departed M-G-M, classified as unemployable by the entertainment industry. The twenty-eight-year-old had some immediate radio success (including a broadcast version of *Easter Parade* with Astaire) and triumphed in a four-week engagement at the London Palladium and subsequent British Isles tour. Returning to New York in August 1951, she had new manager Sid Luft at her side. It was his idea to book Judy into Broadway's famed Palace Theater in a revival of "two-a-day" vaudeville. Chuck took Sid's long-distance call from the St. Regis Hotel and instantly agreed to stage the show.

"Oh, there were unlimited possibilities," Walters later enthused. "That very night, I called Roger and said, 'It's so exciting, because Judy has such a wealth of material—*you* have such a wealth of material. Let's give them more than just a movie star doing a personal appearance.' Well, Roger grabbed on to it!"[17] Eagerly the two began devising an evening of song and dance intended to cap Garland's comeback.

"We headed back to Los Angeles as fast as you could travel with a person who didn't fly," said Luft, referencing Judy's preference for trains rather than airplanes.[18] Walters invited them to Malibu, where he and Edens pitched ideas. The production would include both the best of her film repertoire and an homage to great vaudevillians. She would be backed by a male chorus line, billed as "Judy's Eight Boy Friends." The men would dance with her, as well as provide filler while she changed costumes. "Get Happy" was programmed ("Of course we had to," Chuck said), and its chic style was to be contrasted by the ensuing low comedy of "A Couple of Swells." Garland's signature song would without question be the finale, and it was Roger's inspiration to put Judy on the edge of the stage in her tattered tramp attire to plaintively offer "Over the Rainbow." At that, according to Chuck, "well, we all fell down!"[19]

"Initially Chuck wasn't available," recalled Luft, as the director was stuck in the middle of *The Belle of New York*. "But he, like Judy, 'had to go to Broadway.' He wouldn't allow anybody else to take his place. Chuck said, 'You'll never open this show without me.'"[20] In a private meeting with Freed, Walters requested a sabbatical from *Belle,* and though it was highly uncommon for such an expensive production to purposely halt mid-shoot, the appeal was granted. *Belle* was closed for eight days, from August 17 to 26.

The Garland show immediately began rehearsals in Los Angeles at the Nico Charisse dance studio on La Cienega Boulevard, and included in the eight male dancers was the dynamic Bert May. He'd never forgotten

Walters's earlier kindness during *Ziegfeld Follies*. "I would compare Chuck to Alfred Hitchcock," says May. "By that, I mean he would come in with everything prepared in his head. He could visualize the whole thing. He would give one group their steps, then go to another group and do the same. It came out so easily, but it was all prepared beforehand in his head."[21]

Walters and Edens worked toward making certain Judy's act would never falter in its hold on an audience. "Roger told stories in music form," Chuck affirmed, and at the Palace Theater, the story they told together was that of Judy Garland.[22]

Two full-throttle Edens originals were combined for the opening: "Call the Papers" and "On the Town" (the latter written with Comden and Green for the 1949 M-G-M movie of the same name). Walters supplied a "surprise" entrance for his star by having the Boy Friends stop short in their dancing and "accidentally" reveal a crouching Garland sneaking across upstage. "Judy caught with her pants down," Chuck laughed. "They'll love it." As Garland's recent travails with weight gain would be familiar to virtually everyone, Edens supplied a self-deprecating musical salutation: "It's lovely seeing you / But the first thing I must do / Is give an interview to the press / To tell them of the struggling / Of the long and ceaseless juggling / Every time I get into this dress!" The special material— with a press conference conceit not unlike that of "A Great Lady"— culminated as Judy linked arms with the boy dancers and swiftly box-stepped toward the front of the stage.

In early October, Walters, Garland, and the company traveled east. (Edens remained behind, acting as *Belle*'s substitute director for its re-takes.) New York City was abuzz. Tickets were in demand despite a top price of $4.80, and even those close to the star had difficulty scoring seats for the opening. Hugh Martin phoned Judy for help, and she countered, "I have a better idea. Why don't you sit on the stage with me and play piano?" Five vaudeville-styled acts—including British comic Max Bygraves—were booked by Luft for act one; all of act two would belong to Judy. Given their bond, Chuck agreed to perform "A Couple of Swells" with her on opening night (replacing Bygraves). His decision, however, came with some trepidation: "I hadn't been on the stage for ten years, and the Palace meant something to me."

Rehearsals in New York were held in a small rented studio, as the Palace was being renovated for their show. After work, the star and director took a quiet evening stroll down Broadway, where they suddenly were brought up short. The Palace frontage was aglow, and in giant letters the three-story marquee proclaimed: "In Person Judy Garland & All Star Show." An adjacent portrait of Judy smiled down onto Time Square. After all the publicized upheavals and personal humiliation of the preceding years, Garland stood in amazement.

Chuck, with tears in his eyes, softly whispered to her, "Honey, you are such a star."[23]

"The impact of opening night hadn't hit us yet," Walters would recount of Tuesday, October 16, 1951.

> We were at the Plaza, having a steak sandwich and martinis; we were both a little uptight so we just picked at the steak. And I had to go on that night . . . so that was an excuse for another martini! Anyway, we got a cab, and when we got to the little pie-wedge traffic island at Broadway and Seventh [Avenue]—all we saw were people jammed on the pie. The cabby said, "I don't think we can get any farther, they have the street blocked off." I asked him what was happening. "Judy Garland's openin' tonight, and them's the fans out there waitin'," he replied.
> It was like somebody punched us in the gut.[24]

There it was, both glorious and absurd: Judy Garland caught in a traffic jam of her own making and unable to get to her own opening. On foot, they headed to the Forty-Seventh Street stage door.

The mob scene out front only grew, and the throng pushed forward to glimpse the celebrities as they walked the red carpet into the theater. There was a barrage of flashbulbs for everyone from Irving Berlin, Billy Rose, and Lee Shubert to vaudeville legends Jimmy Durante and Sophie Tucker. Gloria Swanson arrived at intermission, perhaps tipped off by Chuck that she needn't bother to get there sooner.

By act two, audience anticipation was palpable. As Walters had anticipated, Garland's "surprise" entrance bred hysteria. The tiny chanteuse finally had to shout it down herself, and then—in the eyewitness account of critic Robert Sylvester—"went on to do one of the most fantastic one-hour solo performances in theatrical history."[25] Between numbers, Garland wiped away perspiration ("It isn't very ladylike, but it's

very necessary") and confessionally removed her shoes ("They hurt!").
The crowd whooped and howled at her informality.

Walters remained in the wings throughout, cheering her on. "She
loved being yelled at from off stage," he explained. "Loved it if you'd yell,
'Yeah, that's it! Wow! Go girl!' That stimulated her."[26] Their "Swells" duet
inspired "roars of approval" from the 1,740-seat house.[27] Then Garland effortlessly shifted emotion to offer the evening's undisputed highlight. Describing her "Over the Rainbow," Clifton Fadiman later wrote, "We forgot
who she was, and indeed who we were ourselves. . . . She had no 'glamour,'
only magic. . . . When she breathed the last phrases . . . and cried out [the]
universal, unanswerable query, 'Why can't I?,' it was as though the bewil-
dered hearts of all the people in the world had moved quietly together and
become one, shaking in Judy's throat, and there breaking."[28]

The curtain calls brought a ten-minute tumult that even the Palace,
in all its rich history, had never before witnessed. Tucker wiped away
tears; Durante hollered a continuous stream of bravos. Audience member Fred McFadden, who saw the show multiple times, remembers the
crowd's sheer astonishment: "We simply could not believe so much music could come out of one person."[29]

The pandemonium continued backstage. Recalled Walters with pride:

After the show, Judy was getting dressed in a lovely evening gown
to go to a big party. Someone mentioned to us that the people
were still standing out on the [Seventh Avenue traffic] pie. Judy
said, "I don't believe it. What do they want?" "They just want to
see you," somebody explained. "Well . . . ," she said, "I'm going
out the front door instead of the stage exit. If they want to see
me, *they're going to see me.*" The Palace lobby was filled, as was
the pie. As we walked through this sea of humanity—[there was]
not a word! She's getting into the limousine and says, "What is
this? Nobody's saying anything." They had given her a silent
tribute . . . I can't tell that without choking up.[30]

Critics were equally enraptured and scrambled for ways to describe Garland's spell, crediting in the process the two men who crafted her triumph. *Variety* boasted, "Edens' special material is virtually a musical
biography . . . literate and showmanly," and acknowledged, "A nice intra-
trade courtesy is Metro's loan-out not only of Edens to its former star but

also Walters who did a capital staging job. . . . [T]he routining [is] in the big league manner, as befits a big league motion picture director."[31] Ed Sullivan called the performance "a masterpiece of showmanship," parenthetically adding, "Thanks to Chuck Walters."[32]

Post-production duties on *Belle* awaited in Culver City. As a result, columnist Earl Blackwell of Celebrity Service announced a Walters going-away party to be held several days after the Palace opening. "Everybody who could beg an invitation, or crash the gate," crowded the Pen and Pencil restaurant on East Forty-Fifth Street.[33] Hollywood was represented by Van Johnson, Ginger Rogers, Rosalind Russell, Ann Sothern, and Robert Preston. In anticipation of an impromptu Garland performance, proprietor John Bruno littered the wall behind the club's piano with posters and photos tracing Chuck's film and theater successes. "Though weary from her two performances earlier that day," columnist Lloyd Sloan observed, "Judy got her second (or third) wind, giving out with songs until the wee hours."[34]

Walters would continue his creative partnership with Garland into the 1960s. He supplied another riveting entrance for her 1956 return to the Palace, where a pinspot suddenly illuminated the singer's face against a sea of black backdrop. Two years later, he stripped away all vaudeville trappings for her one-woman Cocoanut Grove concertizing and her stint at Chicago's Orchestra Hall. *Variety* saluted such "happy simplicity."[35]

Sensation-seeking journalists and biographers would later press Chuck for personal stories about his association with the often-troubled star, especially after Judy's premature death in 1969. Though candid in acknowledging the challenges, Walters remained resolute in his praise. Her genuineness, he insisted, was the key to her unparalleled appeal. "People would cry when she'd sit [at] the footlights . . . and do 'Rainbow,'" he told. "All she was doing was sweating, and she was out of breath. *But* she made it work for her. She used her theatrics, knowing that the gimmick was good—she's sweating and she's out of breath. So make it work. It's not a lie. It's still the truth. And I think what endeared her to audiences was that they felt the honesty."[36]

17

Hi-Lili, Hi-Lo

In spring 1952, Metro screenwriter and Malibu neighbor Helen Deutsch arrived at Walters's beach house with script in hand. She sought his opinion on her simply titled *Lili.* ("To tell the truth," recalled Chuck, "I was more impressed by Helen Deutsch than I was by the script as it was at that point.") She had based *Lili,* a coming-of-age tale, on Paul Gallico's short story "The Man Who Hated People," first published in the *Saturday Evening Post* on October 28, 1950. If not completely sold on the script, Walters considered Deutsch's work refreshingly mature and told her it could make for an interesting picture if they resisted typical musical grandiosity.

There followed a brief repetition—sans the final resolution—of the *Annie Get Your Gun* situation. Chuck was summoned to a private meeting with producer Edwin Knopf, who received the director "in his library *and* in his bathrobe." Knopf announced that Lillian Burns, again campaigning for director-husband George Sidney, had warned him against assigning Walters to *Lili:* "Lillian told me that when anyone watches your films, they can see you have no heart." Chuck squarely met the accusation, telling him, "Well, Eddie, if you can tell me how much heart one can put into an Esther Williams film, then maybe I would know how to reply to that remark. 'Oh, Esther, honey, put a little more heart in that backstroke. . . .'"[1] (Having circumvented the Sidney Steamroller, Walters later commented with a grin: "Eddie still ended up giving me the film.")

Lili's fragile story line followed its orphaned sixteen-year-old title character through her adventures with a traveling carnival in France. She is attracted to Marcus the Magnificent, a handsome (though secretly married) magician, and blindly unaware of the devotion of crippled puppeteer Paul, who can only express his feelings for her through his diverse characters: Carrot Top, Golo the Giant, Marguerite, and Reynardo the Fox.

The principal parts were dark by Metro standards: a suicidal heroine, an implied adulterer, and—as "hero"—an alcoholic, self-pitying war victim. There was even a sexual predator in the form of a boorish shopkeeper. With the Production Code Administration's seal of approval still an industry necessity, Schary paid close attention to the censors' preliminary objections.[2] In Paul's jealous abuse of Lili, "the slap should be completely out of frame"; the shopkeeper's attempted molestation should be "handled with great care." They declared that Marcus "seems to be pretty much on the promiscuous side," to the extent that his "biting into a peach seems symbolic and troublesome." With delicacy, Deutsch began to shave her more suggestive content.

M-G-M lothario Fernando Lamas was the Marcus front-runner, until the studio announced it would cast an unthreatening actor "along the lines of Michael Wilding."[3] Handsome Jean-Pierre Aumont ultimately took the role, while lanky Mel Ferrer was borrowed from RKO to play Paul. (The actor had some prior dance training and could create multiple voices for his puppets.) Likable Kurt Kasznar was selected in support as manager Jacquot, with Hungarian sexpot Zsa Zsa Gabor playing Rosalie, the magician's assistant and wife. Walters admitted that the former Miss Hungary of 1936 "was the biggest name in the cast [but] not worth two cents as an actress. We needed a miracle to make her work with music." Still, he remained amused by the lofty air Zsa Zsa brought to the set.

The picture, however, really belonged to young ballerina Leslie Caron. The twenty-year-old contract player had impressively debuted in Metro's *An American in Paris* a year earlier and coveted the title role in *Lili.* "When I got the part," she said, "to me, the world had opened. This was exactly what I could do, and I threw myself into it with a passion."[4] To help with characterization, the French dancer remembered her own anxieties from a childhood spent in war-torn chaos.

> I was playing this poor little orphan who had no fun in life—coming straight from the war—[who] had lost her parents, was completely bereft and lost. I was . . . very concentrated on this character, all the more so because I had suffered very much the same thing. I was in France during the German Occupation with all sorts of dangers and privations. [It] had been a very painful

and difficult moment in my life. When I was given the part of Lili, it seemed that I was the one who could express the despair of that little girl who had lost everything. I arrived on the set like this little soldier with blinders on. I was absolutely ready. . . .

What I found in Chuck was somebody who understood that emotion of the orphan—the *desolate* orphan. He had a sense of pathos. He understood melancholy. He understood innocence and childishness. And he allowed me and helped me [to] release all those qualities.

From the beginning, Walters admired his leading lady's total commitment: "She *became* Lili while we were shooting the film. She was Lili when she arrived in the morning, and she still was Lili when she left at night." Caron would later laugh when hearing this comment, saying, "Oh, Chuck was impressed by my dedication, but he thought, 'My God, she's a bit of a bore.' When the book portion of the film was finished, suddenly I started clowning around with everybody, and Chuck said, 'Hey, this is a new person.' I said, 'Chuck, this is the real me.' I had to keep concentrated on the *malheur* of Lili."

As a classically trained dancer, Caron instinctively brought a specific physicality to her characterization. It was a concept furthered by concurrent studies with the Stanislavsky-trained coach George Shdanoff (her choice over Lillian Burns). As she explains, "It's part of the building of the character to discover where 'the center' is, the way the character moves, the speed at which she or he moves. Lili's center was in the knees. Once you have that, the brain functions slow, and everything goes together." Caron allowed her body to relax only when Lili was speaking with the puppets; "Chuck," she said, "understood my structuring of the character through this physical awkwardness." *Lili*'s director was nonetheless disturbed when his young gamine emerged "all dolled up" from her first visit to the hair and makeup departments. Determined to keep his central character simple, he shook his head and told her, "Oh, honey, this won't do. Lili has *gone Metro!*"

"Everything had to stop," Caron recalls, and

I figured I had a few things to say to the big boss. I asked for a car and was driven up [to the executives' building]. I . . . went to the top office, got to his secretary, and said, "Can I see Mr. Dore

Schary, please?" Finally the door opened and Dore Schary—like God Almighty—opened his arms. "Darling, what can I do for you?" I was all worked up; I was in tears. "Mr. Schary, I know you think I should be more glamorous. But this little character, there's absolutely no way she knows what glamour is. She doesn't even know where to buy powder."

In a typical display of Schary's attitude toward musical movies, Caron remembers, "He said, 'Remind me . . . what film are you making?'"

Lili went before the cameras on March 10, 1952, with a modest $1,216,960 budget. It was Walters's first go-round with the Knopf unit, and even after ten years at the studio, his boyish anonymity remained somewhat intact. "On that first day," Caron relates, "Chuck caught two old grips talking to each other. One of them said to the other, 'Who's the director on this one?' The second one answered, 'Well, I don't know who the director is, but we have this kid here today.'"

Walters held fast to one credo: create a picture of true sentiment rather than sentimentality. "I knew enough by then to avoid platitudes. But *Lili* was so delicate and so light—mixing fantasy and reality. I had full confidence in what we were doing, [and] that we were doing it as it had to be done. But I hadn't the slightest idea whether or not the public would bite." Walters balanced the saccharine by injecting moments of playfulness, and Caron recalls that her director had "terrific fun" while staging Lili's clumsy attempts at waiting tables. The scene required well-timed choreography, and as a punch line, he instructed the hapless girl to grab the apron strings of a more seasoned worker to lead her through the crowded café. "That is something he really adored," says Caron, "the clowning . . . sort of Charlie Chaplinesque. *That* is Chuck."

Walters's balancing touch is even more apparent in the pivotal introduction of both the puppets and the film's theme song. Lili's suicide attempt is interrupted by Ferrer's wooden characters, led by vigilant Carrot Top, and her melancholia subsides when he asks her to sing. "I remember 'Hi-Lili, Hi-Lo,'" Lili admits, and more excitedly adds, "I used to sing it with my father." She begins the number (with Chuck's own puppeteering simultaneously manipulating the legs of ballerina Marguerite), and her harmonizing with Carrot Top quickly draws a crowd of beguiled spectators. The orphan is soon central to Paul's act.

Lili's gentle tone would also be created through its color palette. Trying to avoid the usual garish aesthetic of Technicolor, Walters sought the more muted hues he had seen in films coming from England. Tests were undertaken, and as he explained, "I tried everything—[and] even sent some negative to England to process. Finally, I found out that the English color was from the atmosphere. It was from the air itself."[5] M-G-M's Technicolor processing department offered to "bleed the color," and upon seeing their efforts, Walters leaped from his seat. "That's it!" he blurted out. "That's the softness we need." From that point on, the lab was ordered to bleed all footage, infusing the visual with a dreamlike quality.

Less easily solved was the colorful challenge provided by the agitating leading man. "Mel was difficult," remembers Caron, "a sensitive person but very difficult. [He] had been a director—he had directed this theater somewhere down south—and so Mel saw himself as a director. [Now] Chuck wasn't imposing. He wasn't one to say, 'Do this . . . do that . . . go here . . . go there.' He was very easygoing, and Mel started taking advantage of that and taking over. Very soon Chuck couldn't stand this anymore and said, 'Coffee everybody . . . over there. I will call you back.' He got into his trailer with Mel, and you could hear them shouting at each other. Mel came out of there very sheepish and respectful, and that was the end of his directing."[6]

Offering a more self-inflated account, Schary later insisted that his own diplomacy brought an end to the melee: "Helen Deutsch found herself involved in the imbroglio, and not being a totally calm woman, she added to the rumpus. The producer, his hands full with the fracas, came to me quite often, and after a few visits to the set, we were able to calm the troubled waters."[7] Deutsch undoubtedly would disagree, feeling that Knopf's insensitivity only added to the ill feelings. "During the short time I was around," the writer insisted, "I had to listen to Eddie's constant destruction of Chuck."

Ironically, all this egomaniacal energy was expended over a picture in which corporate Metro had little interest. "The higher-ups believed in it less and less," Walters said, shrugging. "Schary hardly even said hello to me; he had his entourage and only bothered with serious films. It was clear that everyone just pissed on the very idea of *Lili*, and that no one cared to respect the spirit of the film."

It took less than a month to complete the book scenes, and—for the first time since signing his 1949 director's contract—Chuck next assumed all choreographic duties as well. Each of the picture's two dream sequences was allotted twelve days to rehearse and five days to shoot, and each was termed "a ballet," even though Walters and assistant Dorothy Jarnac decided there would be no pointe shoes and no technically demanding steps. (Dance historian Martin Gottfried would sardonically comment that "ballet" was "a loosely used word" in 1950s Hollywood: "It served for any long dance. It could be jazz dancing, it could be acrobatics or toe work. But as long as it lasted more than three minutes and had no singing, it was a ballet.")[8]

"The Adoration Ballet" was fashioned first. In Lili's femme fatale daydream, she seduces Marcus away from Rosalie, and M-G-M fancied a reprise of the Oscar-winning ostentations found in the recent Minnelli-Kelly triumph *An American in Paris.* Deutsch herself envisioned Caron in a pale pink chiffon dress enjoying "a dance promenade in the deserted carnival. The background is to be an idealized version of the carnival square, [spotlessly] clean, with no people—a sort of spacious fairy land."[9] Walters, however, wholeheartedly disagreed. "The first of Lili's dream ballets was supposed to be pure Metro," he recounted, "all pink and glittering. But this girl is not going to dream that way. She dreams simply of being a good waitress and of replacing Zsa Zsa in the heart of the magician she [loves]. I wouldn't let them clean the floor for the scene; I even added cigarette butts and used napkins. They almost forced me to re-do [it] because the floor was dirty! It wasn't in *the Metro style.*"

Another obstacle remained. "Aumont was like a piece of wood," said Chuck. As an expeditious alternative, the director donned a blond wig and stepped into the actor's tuxedo as his dancing double. He was seen from behind or in long shot, lending grace and masculine panache; it may have been the only time in Hollywood history that a director-choreographer doubled for a leading man.

The ten-minute "Ballet of Paul and the Puppets" brought filming to a close, as it did the plot itself. Lili has defiantly left the carnival, but once on the road she dreams herself into a dance with life-sized incarnations of Carrot Top, Marguerite, Reynardo, and Golo (played respectively by Arthur Mendez, Dorothy Jarnac, Dick Lerner, and Frank Radcliff). In the process, each of them dissolves into Paul himself. The puppeteer, initially skittish, is gradually less angry and no longer lame;

each successive dance with him allows the girl to comprehend his long-veiled affection for her and her own love for him. At ballet's end, they embrace—suddenly adrift in Lili's imagination—and Walters's camera soars skyward, looking down on (and adding momentum to) the joyous dance of the exultant Lili. When the music quiets, the couple walk forward, hand in hand.

It was Chuck's hope that the ballet would both clarify and resolve the preceding seventy-five minutes of longing and uncertainty. As he put it, "I was particularly proud of the ballets, which seemed to say many things very quickly." *Lili* wrapped in late April 1952.

The director enjoyed a quick ten-day respite in New York before returning to Metro to prepare another Esther Williams musical. On arrival, Walters was horrified to be told by Keenan Wynn that *Lili* had been shown to a group of visiting Loew's executives. "While I had resisted [their] intrusion," Schary said in an attempt to justify his action, "the question was whether or not they would place the picture into a release spot and date."[10] *Lili* had been projected in its unfinished state—"no music track, color imbalanced, sound not corrected, the picture still interspersed with blank film reading 'Dissolve' . . . It did not impress. At the conclusion, there was a silence. Not a pregnant one. Just plain, rotten, quiet, chilly silence." *Lili*—with but one song and its romantic story told through puppets—was deemed an art-house picture, a disdainful classification at M-G-M. The defensive Deutsch let rip with a stream of curse words directed toward the roomful of executives, and the disillusioned Knopf reached out to Arthur Freed, only to be told: "Chuck has ruined Leslie. There's *nothing* you can do with this film. Don't waste your time tinkering with it. Leave it alone." (Walters later shared a drink with Freed, and the producer casually remarked, "Oh, incidentally Eddie asked me to run *Lili* with him, and you know what I told him? I told him, 'Don't touch it. Don't touch a thing.'" Chuck knew precisely what had been said, but he let it slide. He rationalized that Freed hadn't exactly lied; "he just read the line differently!")[11]

The problem of distributing *Lili* was resolved by one man. Harry Brandt was the president of the Independent Theater Owners of America, visiting Los Angeles to scout pictures for his movie houses in New York City. Though warning him that *Lili* was still unfinished, Schary said, "Harry, I have a film to show you." Brandt was charmed and agreed to play the picture at one of his primary Manhattan theaters, provided he was given exclusivity. "No one else can play *Lili* until I am through with my run," he stated, "regardless of how long this might be." (The Trans-Lux at Fifty-Second and Lexington had a cozy 578-seat capacity; by comparison, Loew's most modest New York theater, the Astor, was nearly double that size.) Relieved, Schary accepted Brandt's terms, and the studio finished *Lili* for a sneak preview.

Admittedly, Walters was "scared to death" at seeing the film with an audience. Throughout his years in Hollywood he "had heard about these previews where there's no one left by the fourth reel—and they just turn off the projector. That had even happened with a really big film, [*Desire Me*] with Greer Garson, directed by George Cukor. I feared the worst [and filled] a thermos with martinis before leaving for the theater." To his great relief, however, the picture played beautifully. "The public laughed at the right spots, fell silent at the right spots, and applauded at the right spots," he recalled. Yet no one at M-G-M would believe the glorious survey cards submitted by that audience: "[Executives] were asking if I hadn't somehow filled the room with my own friends." A second preview was immediately arranged, and the cards "had even better things to say. Suddenly *everyone* was very proud of the film."

M-G-M went so far as to throw a celebratory party, and Walters watched in disbelief as Schary and Deutsch danced around Roger Edens at the piano, singing "Hi-Lili, Hi-Lo." They were joined by other studio executives, while Chuck hid his bemusement. "It was amazing to watch those shits climb on the bandwagon," he observed wryly.

Lili premiered at the Trans-Lux 52 on March 10, 1953, and was an astounding success. *Cue* magazine was typical in its rave: "*Lili* is an adult's delight as well as a child's pleasure. It is a simple, tender, irresistible and nostalgically enchanting fable . . . a movie romp, a Technicolored cinematic symphony in dazzling sight and sweet sound—a picture overflowing with rich, poetic visual and aural rhythms, with imagination, gentleness, kindness, and understanding—but most of all with great beauty."[12]

M-G-M announced its own invitational Hollywood premiere for Tuesday, March 17, at the Vogue Theater, but all further exhibition was prohibited by its agreement with Brandt. As *Lili* continued to pack the Trans-Lux, Schary confessed, "M-G-M finally paid a tidy sum to get Harry to allow them to run the film in Europe, then bring it into the States. . . .

But [we couldn't show it around] New York until Harry finished the run."[13] *Lili* eventually exited the Trans-Lux on December 22, 1953, after ten victorious months of exclusive box office.

When finally able to launch the picture, M-G-M promotionally promised, "You'll fall in love with *Lili.*" Special cross-country handling and premieres were planned. By June, the film had opened in Philadelphia, Boston, Pittsburgh, Kansas City, Seattle, Portland, and Washington, D.C., and the praise only mounted. Richard L. Coe of the *Washington Post* reported that "Deutsch and especially director Walters have spun things out so gently, cut their sequences so wisely, that you'll be happy throughout and for some hours thereafter. . . . More than anything else, it has taste."[14] *Lili* also achieved international acclaim, playing that spring to an ovation at the Cannes Film Festival. "Dearest Chuck, You won your first prize with *Lili!*" wrote Caron on a postcard. "The title of the prize was 'International Prize for the Most Entertaining Picture, with Special Mention for the Charm of the Interpretation.' I hope you will get many more."[15]

At year's end, *Lili* appeared on virtually every Ten Best list. It ranked fifth with the critics at *Films in Review,* and in an echo of their original critique they re-proclaimed the film "an example of something quite rare: the *effective* utilization of synthetic subject matter. . . . *Lili* is so well-acted, mounted, and photographed, and is so skillfully sentimental, that we are charmed, and forget the tricks and enjoy the illusions."[16] In effect, the Screen Directors Guild of America concurred when announcing its Best Directors of 1953: Walters was cited in the particularly distinguished company of George Stevens (*Shane*), Fred Zinnemann (*From Here to Eternity*), Billy Wilder (*Stalag 17*), and William Wyler (*Roman Holiday*). The crowning moment arrived when those same five names were listed as Oscar nominees at the twenty-sixth annual Academy Awards. Compounding the glory, *Lili*—the film that had almost been shelved—was announced in five other categories as well: Best Actress (Caron), Best Screenplay (Deutsch), Best Music (Score of a Dramatic or Comedy Picture; Bronislau Kaper), Best Color Art Direction, and Best Color Cinematography.[17] Chuck realized that winning the award in his category would be a long shot, and indeed, only Kaper took home an Oscar for *Lili* on March 25, 1954. (Caron would later receive the Best Foreign Actress prize at the British Academy Awards.) Still, the nomination strengthened Walters's standing at M-G-M. It had been two years since Metro had posted a Best Director nominee, and it would be another two years until the next.

In 1961, *Lili* was reimagined as a Broadway musical. *Carnival* starred Anna Maria Alberghetti and Jerry Orbach, with direction and choreography by former M-G-M dancer Gower Champion. In preparation for the show, Gower's wife and longtime partner, Marge Champion, remembers that her husband "looked at the movie *Lili* quite a lot."[18] *Carnival* was a major hit, and Freed—once so unimpressed by *Lili*—immediately acquired movie rights with the (ultimately unfulfilled) hopes of filming it in 1963.

By the time the stage show opened, Walters had long considered the material his personal property. He did see Champion's musical and could only reflect, "I suppose it's like going back to a house you've sold, and you hate the way the new occupants have furnished it. You think, 'They don't deserve to live here.'"[19]

18 .

"A Masterpiece of Modern Moisture"

In the early 1950s, Esther Williams's pictures were among the very few foolproof box office draws, and Walters managed to direct two of them in the eleven months between the completion of *Lili* and that film's New York debut. The first was tentatively (if aptly) titled *Everybody Swims* but more positively realized as *Dangerous When Wet*.

"Chuck and I had a good rapport from . . . *Texas Carnival*," said Williams, "so I looked forward to this one."[1] Both star and director were encouraged by an amusingly folksy Dorothy Kingsley screenplay that cast the swimmer as Katy Higgins, eldest daughter in a family of health-conscious dairy farmers. To fund a new milking machine, the Higginses team up with promoter Windy Webbe, who sponsors their travel to England so the family can participate in a competitive English Channel swim. In the process, Katy meets French playboy André Lanet, who wastes no time in wooing the farmer's daughter.

Walters and new producer George Wells (co-author of *Texas Carnival*) incisively cast the picture with veteran actors William Demarest and Charlotte Greenwood as Ma and Pa Higgins, replacing the intended George Murphy and Una Merkel. Barbara Whiting (younger sister of singer Margaret) and Donna Corcoran played Williams's siblings, Jack Carson was a comically inflated Windy, and shapely Denise Darcel completed the troupe as Gigi Mignon. Metro publicity later capitalized on what was termed Darcel's *oh-là-là*, but Greenwood remained a more quotable presence. At fifty-nine, the much-adored comedienne joked that appearing with Williams bordered on the ridiculous: "When we got in the water together, I felt like an old scow beside a torpedo."[2]

Walters, who had been unable to cast Fernando Lamas as Marcus in *Lili,* made him the first choice for the role of André. The actor possessed smoldering good looks, a lean muscularity, and (like Williams) a playful awareness of his ample physical attributes. He could also carry a tune. Lamas nevertheless heartily resisted the assignment. When he first arrived at the studio in 1950, he'd informed M-G-M's publicity department of his athletic achievements in boxing and rugby while purposely neglecting an even more salient credit: he was South American and Pan-American swimming champion. "If I tell them that," he reasoned, "I'm going to do nothing but movies with that swimming girl."[3] After reading the *Dangerous* script, Lamas scoffed at the character he'd been asked to play: "He has champagne; he has vineyards, and all that is very nice. He's got a marvelous chateau and a yacht. But nothing happens to [him]." Williams herself had come to realize that leading men had comparatively little to do in her vehicles. She requested that his role be expanded, and she promised him several songs. Lamas took the part.

Walters noticed the instantaneous attraction between the Latin actor and "that swimming girl" as soon as rehearsals began. Initially at least, the duo maintained their professionalism, and Esther was soon surprised by Fernando's skill in the water. "There is a whole sequence in which I invite her to [swim at] my chateau and I'm on the make," the actor recounted.

Chuck was directing, and . . . I still hadn't opened my mouth to the fact that I had won many competitions internationally in the water. Chuck is saying, "Don't worry about a thing. We're going to rehearse it. It's a chase, a very simple jump in the pool, and you chase her. Then, when she realizes you can take her, you begin to swim a couple of things together. You kiss each other underwater, and that's it. Don't worry about a thing. . . . [Esther will pretend] she's going fast, but she won't. She's going to make it look good." I said, "All right."

So now we rehearse. Chuck said, "Well, Esther, you go in first, and then Fernando, you go in after her and try to catch her." She went in, and I did seven strokes and passed her. She stopped me and said, *"What the hell was that?"* Generally, she always looked back to see who was drowning.

Thanks to a rich Johnny Mercer–Arthur Schwartz score, *Dangerous* was more musical comedy than aquacade spectacle, and Walters (assisted by co-choreographer Billy Daniel) provided staging for half a dozen numbers. Filming began with the unapologetically cheery "I Got Out of Bed on the Right Side" in early August 1952. Walters's initial camera pan shows the Higgins farm, where livestock coexists with barbells and exercise equipment, in early morning. One by one, the hearty clan bursts through their front door to vigorously march, sing—and swim.

Once again, Chuck infused the simplest of numbers with light comedy. At the conclusion of Lamas's love ballad, "In My Wildest Dreams," Walters had the actor rest his head in Esther's lap and appraisingly gaze upward. Self-protectively, she crosses her arms over her ample bosom, well-aware of—and feigning indifference to—the playboy's obvious tactic. The song then was reprised in the film's expertly animated underwater dream sequence, where Esther swims with M-G-M cartoon mascots Tom and Jerry, and Lamas is comically reconfigured as a grabby octopus who's all arms.

"Ain't Nature Grand" provided another typical Walters highlight, encompassing the entire principal cast in song-and-dance activities true to their characters: Williams and Lamas harmonized as they changed into their bathing suits, Whiting flirted with a collection of clean-shaven beaus, Darcel cuddled up to the apathetic Carson, and Demarest and Greenwood reflected on growing old while swinging Tarzan style from a tree limb. The venerable comedienne then segued into a welcome solo turn, complete with her signature high kicks.

Katy's harrowing trek across the English Channel made for a legitimately suspenseful finale. That sequence, Lamas later remarked, didn't play into Walters's strengths, so the director wisely opted to call in assistance. "It's funny," the actor explained, "if you pay attention, suddenly it's like two different movies. Because the whole beginning of the movie had that slick, wonderful quality that Chuck had—everything moved . . . the people moved. Then the swimming of the Channel begins, and it's like a documentary. That was [filmed by] Andrew Marton." (The picture's uncredited second-unit director, Marton would helm larger-scale action sequences for Metro's *Ben-Hur* in 1958 and Fox's *Cleopatra* in 1963.)

Dangerous When Wet wrapped in mid-October 1952 and impressed many critics as a welcome improvement over the studio's usual aquatic fare. The *Chicago Daily Tribune* happily reported, "The popular Esther Williams has finally been given a palatable, down-to-earth, and quite believable script. [It's] refreshingly funny . . . an unusually pleasing and lively musical."[4] Chuck could also boast, "For the expenditure invested, it was the biggest money-maker of any Esther Williams film. That's a nice satisfaction for a company man."[5]

Earlier that year, Esther had been named "the number one female star in fifty states" by the Hollywood Foreign Press Association, this largely on the strength of *Million Dollar Mermaid,* a winter 1952–1953 smash across the country. *Dangerous When Wet* followed it into theaters in June 1953, but by then Metro had already finished another Walters-Williams vehicle.

Easy to Love was originally conceived as a John Houseman–produced drama for Lana Turner. It became instead a frothy Joe Pasternak musical about the overworked star attraction of a Florida water show. Having appeared in seventeen feature films in less than a decade, Williams was perfect casting. Walters agreed to direct, though he admitted, "[Our story line] was corny; we knew it." The frail script offered an uneasy to love quadrangle in which callow nightclub crooner (Tony Martin) and sincere but beefy swimmer (Johnny Bromfield) pursue Esther, who secretly pines for her no-nonsense boss (Van Johnson).

Williams's box office was so solid that M-G-M agreed to location shooting for most of the film's exteriors. Cast and crew were flown to Cypress Gardens in Winter Haven, Florida, which provided the expansive Lake Eloise for an epic aquatic show. (In keeping with popular phraseology, M-G-M would promote the sequence as "The Sensational Water-Ski Ballet.") Chuck, however, had no real fondness for staging extravaganzas—aquatic or otherwise—and assigned the sequence to the past master of cinematic pageantry, Busby Berkeley.

"We had him fly down to Florida," Walters recollected, "to do all the second unit work. I [arrived] on location while Buzz was in the middle of a number. There he was, bullhorn in hand and playback blazing away, surrounded by motorboats, swimmers, water skiers, and helicopters. I was introduced to everybody, and I heard one of the swimmers whisper, 'Jesus, if this guy's the director, who's that ham we've been working for?'"

Unfortunately, Berkeley brought along his customary disregard for actors. "Busby was both a showman and a show-off," insisted Esther.

When filming *Easy to Love*'s water-ski escapade, she said, "he liked to load the camera-boat with friends so that everyone could appreciate his marvelous creativity."[6] It didn't occur to Berkeley that the extra weight would slow his boat, and a frightening collision was barely averted when the quick-thinking star dove to get out of the way. "But Busby still didn't get it. He was yelling at me as I headed for the beach. 'Esther, come back! Why did you ruin the shot?'"

In total contrast, Walters's concern for his actors was paramount. According to Tony Martin, "Chuck would come up and say, 'Do you like your lines? Are you pleased? We can change them. If you feel uncomfortable about anything, please let me know.' A very, very nice man, Charles Walters—[he] put everybody at ease, which was wonderful."[7]

Such on-set calmness was further tested when Esther announced she was going to have a baby. "Poor Joe Pasternak," she said. "This would be the third picture I did for him when I was pregnant."[8] Upon hearing the news, the producer barked in his Hungarian accent, "God damn it . . . if you don't tell that husband of yours to knock it off, he'll be barred from the lot." Esther replied, "Joe, it doesn't happen on the lot!"[9]

Assistant director Ridgeway Callow rescheduled bathing suit and athletic sequences for the initial weeks of photography, and Chuck spent his first day staging Williams's swim to the title song (as crooned by Martin). The playful poolside rehearsal made such an impression on Walters's chauffeur, Pete, that the driver asked if he could bring some friends to the set to meet him. "Well, he brought them over," the director recounted, "and said, 'This is Chuck Walters. He is Esther Williams' swimming instructor.' Well, I looked at Esther, and I looked at Pete, and I thought, 'Oh my God, he's serious!' I let it lay."[10]

The unit returned to Culver City, where attention stayed focused on Martin's musical moments. "We had great numbers in that picture," the singer said in 1997, crediting their success to "wonderful Charles [who] had a taste about how to stage [them]. He could have been a great musical star himself. He just knew what to do . . . and he did it *well*." The lilting if pallid "Did'ja Ever" enabled the tuxedoed Martin to sing to young ladies he'd plucked from a nightclub audience. Walters endearingly contrasted this idea with the later "That's What a Rainy Day Is For," in which Martin musically romanced Florida's adoring geriatric set.

Martin also was pleased by frequent on-set visits from his stunning new bride, M-G-M dancer Cyd Charisse. Chuck, in turn, made the most of her recurring presence: when one scene called for an anonymous nightclub dance team, he asked the leggy Charisse to step out with him. As the camera filmed them from the waist down, no one was ever the wiser, and the fleeting sequence of four agile legs doing the cha-cha remained their little inside joke.

Equally inside (if less private) was the film's surprise ending, including an unexpected walk-on from Charisse and a humorous "walk-off" with her real-life husband. "That [ending] was impromptu," recalled Martin. "It was arranged by the studio without my knowledge. All of a sudden, Cyd appears. . . . [I]t was cute as could be," and undoubtedly a delight to 1953 moviegoers.

Coming in under its estimated $1.6 million budget by $48,410, *Easy to Love* finished principal photography on April 20. M-G-M showcased the film as its Christmas 1953 release, and Richard L. Coe reported, "Well, kids, Mr. Berkeley has not lost his gargantuan touch. . . . As for the rest of the musical, it's slight but light, thanks, I suppose, to Charles Walters, who manages to put satirical moments into whatever Pasternak production he touches."[11] *Variety* went further by labeling the silly, sexy picture "a masterpiece of modern moisture."[12]

It was during *Easy to Love* filming that *Lili* was released to its rapturous critical praise. "[Esther] was swimming in her tank," Walters recalled, "and I was alongside, reading them aloud. They said things like 'poetic' . . . 'a lasting joy.' And Esther was so touched, she started crying."[13]

"Chuck, I can't keep asking for you," she told him. "I can't hold you back. What are you doing around here with this wet woman, when you can make films like that and get reviews like these?"

Still, they wanted to continue as collaborators—just with better material. Over meals in the studio commissary, Walters, Williams, and writer Leo Pogostin huddled together, devising a scenario. The trio then handed the scoop straight to Hedda Hopper. "Esther already has a picture set for after the birth of her third child," her readers read on March 7, 1953. "Titled *Athena,* it's about five beautiful sisters whose lives are ruled or ruined by astrology and numerology. Esther will play an ugly duckling, and that clever chap, Chuck Walters, will direct the picture."[14]

When Williams returned from maternity leave, however, she learned their plans had been thwarted. "*Athena* is already shooting—with Jane Powell," Walters told her. "They took out the swimming sequences and made them singing scenes." Infuriated by what she perceived as studio treachery, Esther went directly to Schary. "You knew I had written it with Chuck and Leo," she fumed. "You saw our names on it." Schary dismissed her perceived dramatics with a curt "We have a studio to run" attitude. The box office champion knew then her tenure at M-G-M was near its end.[15] She would make only one more Metro musical, George Sidney's overblown *Jupiter's Daughter,* and when filming finished, her only good-bye was exchanged with the guard at the gate.

Later, however, Esther Williams could claim one lasting souvenir of M-G-M when she (more or less) tamed her "ridiculously handsome" *Dangerous When Wet* playmate Fernando Lamas, marrying him in 1969.

19

"Two-Faced Woman"

Few Hollywood celebrities ever played the role of movie star with greater conviction than Joan Crawford. Stardom was the intense, all-consuming commitment she gratefully (if at times ungracefully) courted and culti-vated. "I want so *desperately* to be liked," she said in 1965.[1] Of such un-bending ambition, Walters once commented: "I believe if you want something badly enough, you'll get it. But look out for what you want, because you're apt to be stuck with it. I think Joan wanted to be a movie star so badly that she was completely stuck and enveloped in that."[2]

Crawford's journey began in 1925 when M-G-M groomed the San Antonio–born hopeful, then named Lucille LeSueur, into a gutsy glam-our star. After eighteen years of (often) playing the shopgirl who comes out on top, her popular appeal had begun to wane, and Mayer "sug-gested" that she and the studio part company. The intrepid Joan de-camped for Warner Bros., where—in a triumph of will over adversity—she received a 1945 Best Actress Oscar for her first non-Metro performance, in *Mildred Pierce*. The win was the very essence of the Joan Crawford story. Seven years and several subsequent hits later, Joan was a free agent, and an unexpected invitation took her back to her alma mater. "[Execu-tive] Benny Thau, one of the gentlemen at MGM who thought me all washed up ten years before, sent me a script strictly undercover," she re-called.[3] The small musical melodrama piqued Crawford's interest despite its stale title, *Why Should I Cry?* "When I got as far as page forty-five, I picked up the phone and said, 'When do we start?'"[4]

The property, retitled *Torch Song*, told the cautionary tale of Jenny Stewart, an egocentric musical theater star who falls for her blind re-hearsal pianist, Tye Graham. Crawford delighted in the meaty role but had one stipulation: "I'd seen Chuck Walters' delightful *Lili*, and if I were to achieve *Torch Song*, I felt he was the director for me."[5] The actress

162

placed the phone call herself, but Chuck initially dismissed it as a prank. "Oh, sure honey," he mocked, "and *I'm* Cary Grant."

"No, darling," she firmly corrected, "this *is* Joan Crawford."[6]

"She asked if she could bring over dinner and a bottle of vodka," recalled Chuck, "and come read me the script. I replied that I *had* a bottle of vodka, that I was actually in the *middle* of dinner, but that—of course—if she really *wanted* to make the trip out to my place . . . I still wondered if it wasn't a joke!"

Joan arrived in Malibu with "a magnum of champagne." When she began to read aloud, her audience of one was not impressed. "To tell the truth," Walters said, "I found [the script] a little dumb. She was supposed to play a tap dancer, and one of the first shots was supposed to be a close-up of the tap shoes as she's getting into a taxi. I said—to myself—that, at her age, Joan Crawford should not be prancing around in tap shoes."

Crawford was determined to prevail. She went to the star of *Easy to Love*, admitted her "mad, mad crush" on Walters, and requested, "Esther, please let me have your director."[7] Williams would reflect, "It sounded to me like she wanted to make it with him a lot more than she wanted him to direct the movie, but that was Chuck's problem, not mine!" Although Metro had promised him a vacation (as he put it, "I *was* tired, I had just finished the two pictures with Esther"), Louella Parsons announced in March 1953 that Walters had accepted the assignment.

It was the onset of major hype for the star and her return to Culver City. On her first day, a large banner was draped over the studio's front entry proclaiming, "Welcome back, Joan!" She was incessantly photographed as she walked a red carpet from the gate to the star dressing rooms. By coincidence, many of M-G-M's top-line actresses were in between pictures then, which allowed Crawford to combine dressing rooms A and C into one palatial suite. Once filming commenced, she did not return to her Brentwood home until *Torch Song* was finished. "This way," Joan rationalized, "when we'd stop shooting at six, I could see the rushes, go back to my dressing room, talk over the next day's scenes with Chuck and the cast. We'd eat peanut butter and crackers, have a drink, and talk."[8] Crawford had found a way to once again play Metro movie queen, twenty-four hours a day.

Ever-prying columnist Walter Winchell would soon publicly hint at the actress's affection for her hand-picked director: "Joan Crawford's latest grin-maker is director Charles Walters."[9] Indeed, as production geared up, their after-hours meetings did become more frequent. On one occasion she traveled all the way out to Malibu just to ask which jewels she should wear in the picture. On another evening Walters trekked to Brentwood at her request and found her coiffed and fully made up but still in her housecoat. Drinks were served, after which she opened the robe to reveal her naked forty-eight-year-old figure. (Chuck would later rhetorically ask journalist Barry Norman, "Well, I mean—at a time like that—*where* do you look?!")[10] In her defense, he also maintained that "there was absolutely nothing sexual in what she did. It was purely professional. This was our first film together, and what she was saying was, 'Okay, you'd better see what you've got to work with.' She simply wanted to show me the equipment."[11]

On the eve of filming, Crawford took great pleasure in presenting the director with a potted rubber tree; hanging from its flat, thick leaves were a cashmere sweater, a stopwatch, vitamin pills, and other items Joan felt he would need for endurance. There were also a dozen lamb chops wrapped in cellophane, as she considered Chuck's rail-thin frame in need of nourishment.[12]

Torch Song "meant much more than just a triumphant homecoming" to Crawford.[13] It was the opportunity to prove herself in a musical drama. "There were moments," she confessed, "when I thought I had bitten off more than I could chew." This was made clear when she valiantly attempted to record her movie ballad, "Follow Me." Through numerous unsuccessful takes, Joan respectfully addressed music director and composer Adolph Deutsch as "sir" and apologized for her vocal shortcomings. Frustrated, she finally instructed the recording engineer, "Just keep going until I get it right!"[14] No amount of Crawford determination could produce a usable track, however, and singer India Adams was brought in to dub the vocals.

This actually allowed Joan more time to practice her choreography. It had been Walters's idea to begin *Torch Song* in dance. "Let's not tease the audience," he had suggested. "Let's get a dancing Joan Crawford right out front." Budget constraints were such that Chuck was forced to use the three-year-old orchestra recording of "You're All the World to Me" from *Royal Wedding* for the introductory sequence. He cast boyishly handsome contract dancer Marc Wilder as Crawford's nervous partner, Ralph Ellis, but the resolute star had other ideas. "Oh, Chuck," she would press, "I'm so comfortable when I'm rehearsing with you. Would you consider doing the routine with me in the film?"

"If you'll feel better," he reluctantly agreed, well aware that the actress hadn't danced on-screen in decades, and her Charleston notoriety was long past. (Walters made amends to young Wilder a year later by featuring him as Debbie Reynolds's dancing partner in *The Tender Trap*.)

Thirteen-year-old Christina Crawford, Joan's adopted daughter, visited the set and observed that her mother "really had to depend on Chuck to make her look good. . . . The problem was [that] she had great legs but a middle-aged body."[15] Crawford additionally requested that close friend William Haines "come to the studio and watch my rehearsals." As an actor, Haines had been Metro's golden boy in the 1920s, relinquishing his film career to live in an open relationship with Jimmy Shields and pursue their interior design business. "I was so worried," Joan told Hedda Hopper. "I needed [Billy] as a friend who would give me an honest opinion and no wisecracking. Well, he watched me work. I was sweaty and messy, and Billy seemed to be biting his lips to keep from laughing."[16] Haines waited until she finished with Walters, then quipped, "Only God or a good-looking man could get your legs up that high."

With a shooting schedule of only twenty-four days, filming began on April 27. Walters was ready at 10:00 A.M., costumed in his chorus boy ensemble of gray slacks, black dress shirt, and top hat ("My hair was getting a little thin at the time; that was the reason for the top hat"). He was quietly approached by assistant director Al Jennings with a less than encouraging message: "Joan's in costume, but wants to see you alone in her dressing room."

From her makeup table, Crawford gravely whispered, "Chuck, I cannot get out of this chair."[17]

"Honey, you're gonna be great," he reassured her, politely closing the door. "The routine is down pat. We're lit. We're ready to go."

"I know this is a terrible thing to ask, but would you be upset if I have a little vodka?"

"Baby, *anything* that's going to relax you is fine. Have a little slug if it's gonna help."

"Well, you have to have one with me." Together they toasted Joan Crawford's return to the M-G-M cameras, and Walters later admitted it took about three drinks to shore up her confidence. ("We came out of the dressing room a *hair* high—but relaxed and comfortable.")

Joan, on the other hand, would retell the episode with an air of romance: "Chuck took me by the hand, led me out onto the stage, and we started the first dance number. His is a touch, a delicacy I've never seen in anyone else."[18]

Torch Song's first day of shooting ended with a carefully orchestrated commencement party. Schary arrived full of smiles, and Joan playfully fed cake to her director. At a precisely timed moment, she majestically swept off the soundstage, expressing profound gratitude to cast and crew. In her suite of dressing rooms that night she wrote each of them a personal thank-you card.

"When you make a Crawford picture," Walters explained, "you've got to go all the way. *She's* the picture, and she dominates. I remember stealing ideas from her personal life to fit the character. For instance, we had a bedroom scene where she draws the curtains—first the drapes, then under the drapes, then the blackout material. Three layers of curtains in one bedroom! Well, that idea came from Joan's own room. That's the way she lives—like someone out of her own movies." In the film's party scene, Walters introduced another conceit. "I thought, 'What kind of party would Joan Crawford give?' Then it came to me—all men, with nary another woman in sight!"

Though *Torch Song* would be constructed as a one-woman tour de force, Crawford was ably supported. Noted Broadway thespian Marjorie Rambeau played the parasitic but proud mother with such aplomb that she later received an Academy Award nomination as Best Supporting Actress. Harry Morgan (of future *M*A*S*H* fame) offered a skillfully underplayed turn as a patient stage director, and accomplished choreographer Eugene Loring made a rare on-screen appearance as a diplomatic dance director after Hermes Pan proved unavailable. If his cast had one ineffectual member, Walters would admit, it was Michael Wilding. "He was playing a blind pianist, and we had to tape his words across the keyboard," he said. "He didn't know his lines, he didn't know anything!"[19]

Wilding's autobiography some thirty years later would include the actor's claim that he didn't remember Walters's name, as well as a sour report on *Torch Song* proceedings:

"How does one simulate blindness?" I asked the director the day before shooting began. [He] gave me a blank look and said, "Don't ask me. Just play it by ear." I learned what I was in for the first morning [when Crawford] walked onto the set. She was an hour late, and the harassed director did not even get round to

introducing us before I found myself in front of the cameras doing our first scene together, which called for me to wrap the lady
in my arms and kiss her passionately. When the director called
"Cut!," I turned to her with a friendly smile, remarking, "That's
the first time I have ever kissed a lady without being introduced."
In reply, Crawford turned her back to me, walked off the set, and
went into a huddle with the director, leaving me standing there
like some forgotten extra. The whispered conference over, the
director strode over to me and said solemnly, "Miss Crawford
says could you please move your shoulder a shade to the right, as
you were blocking her profile."[20]

Dialog scenes were finished by May 23, and rehearsals began for
"Two-Faced Woman"—the picture's intended musical high point. Chuck
had six days to mold Joan Crawford into the song-and-dance legend she
was portraying, and the number would prove to be one of the few re-
sounding failures in Walters's career. Metro's cost-cutting didn't help;
the song title had long been associated with a 1941 George Cukor–Greta
Garbo disaster, and the tune itself was a 1932 Arthur Schwartz–Howard
Dietz original, revived for but then cut from the 1953 film *The Band
Wagon*. "I was stuck with a track that had been orchestrated to go with
[*Band Wagon* choreographer] Michael Kidd's dance," said Walters, "and
I was doing a totally different number. I had to stage everything to the
rhythms that had already been recorded. But M-G-M saved an awful lot
of money that way."[21]

Nothing about the sequence worked. The slow-moving staging placed
Crawford on an impressionistic Harlem nightclub set, where she was
manhandled and denigrated, respectively, by the male and female chorus members. Designer Helen Rose added greater indignity by smother-
ing the star in a garishly sequined peacock-blue gown whose diaphanous
tulle skirt was slit to accentuate Joan's legs. Preposterously, Crawford
and cast were slathered in mulatto-toned pancake makeup, and the projected exotic effect was both muddy and ludicrous. The leading lady,
however, took the high road and told visiting columnist Harrison Carroll, "I was so proud. I hadn't a sore muscle on this picture until I started
this slow number. In the old days, a number like this would have taken
several weeks to film. We are trying to do it in six days. . . . I never had a
better time in my life!"[22]

On June 2, Walters brought the minor musical to a close at a final cost of well below $1 million. Executive producer Charles Schnee wrote: "Chuck, I just want to say I think the end you came up with for *Torch Song* is just great. Would you please do me a favor? Would you just once let me find you wrong about something on this picture?"[23] With speed, *Torch Song* was edited, scored, and readied for a June 28 preview at the Picwood Theater in West Los Angeles—just three months and a day after the "*hair* high" star and director first sauntered onto the set.

Two hundred and thirty-four audience reaction cards were handed out that evening; 196 rated Crawford as excellent, and 199 said they would recommend the picture to a friend. So convincing was Joan's lip-synching that some were unaware she had been dubbed: "Why hasn't Joan Crawford sung before? She has a sensational voice." (Others were not so fooled: "Why a singing and dancing picture with an actress who can't sing and dance?") Some were impressed by the star's figure ("Joan Crawford doesn't have to worry about Marilyn Monroe"), and many were impressed with her performance: "Was dubious at first about this type of role for Miss Crawford, but I was completely won over. I am convinced she can play any part." There were random statements that must have mystified, such as "Miss Crawford seems to be under-acting," and others that must have delighted, including "More pictures like this will kill TV." *Torch Song* was either hailed or panned, especially when it came to the dance sequences. One rather knowledgeable observer (possibly John Darrow, who was present) reflected upon the ill-fated Garbo film and candidly offered: "*Two-Faced Woman* almost wrecked [George] Cukor; it's liable to do the same for fair-haired Chuck. Did love his Fred Astaire bit. More Walters, less Crawford."[24]

The film was released in October, and critical response was surprisingly good. "We need Miss Crawford always before our eyes," endorsed the *Saturday Review,* "a need which in *Torch Song* she isn't reluctant to satisfy. All the scenes are her scenes, and every moment tends to be magnificent."[25] Otis Guernsey Jr., in the *New York Herald Tribune,* wrote that Crawford delivered a "vivid and irritable, volcanic and feminine [performance]. Here is Joan Crawford all over the screen, in command, in love, and in color, a real movie star in what amounts to a carefully produced one-woman show."[26] Finding fault, the *New Yorker* sweetly booed: "Crawford ... proves she is still a handsomely configured lady. ... She doesn't prove, however, that a plot about a Broadway star and a blind pianist can excite anything more than a faint droop in spirit."[27]

Twenty-five years after the fact, Walters confessed that Crawford's iron will had inadvertently sabotaged *Torch Song*. "I've worked with actresses like Judy Garland and Shirley MacLaine," he said, "and I always figured I could get the best performance from them if I knew them better than they knew themselves. It worked with Judy and Shirley but not with Joan. . . . [T]he façade never dropped."[28]

Over the next two decades, however, they remained loyal friends, and Joan's autographed photo was one of the few Chuck kept on display at the Malibu house. "[Once] I had a birthday in New York," he reflected later.

> Joan couldn't attend, but we were coming back on the train the next day. She was recently married to Alfred Steele. [Joan] said, "Well, Chuck, let's have dinner together." Steele came into the dining car with the jewel case *and* the liquor case—she didn't trust the booze on the train. "Chuck, what do you want?" "Oh, just scotch and soda." So she fixes the drink down [under the table], and we're talking and sipping. The ice had melted, but I still hear jingling. She said, "Oh, come on . . . come on, drink up. We've got a long way to go . . . all the way to California." Well, I got down to the bottom [of the glass]—and there were *ruby* cufflinks and studs.[29]

Their final meeting came when a Crawford tribute was staged in Newport Beach in 1976. Sensing she might be lonely afterward, Walters sent a note saying to phone if she wanted to have a drink. As he recounted,

> She did call, and when we were out on the [hotel] balcony overlooking the bay, I said, "Joan, there was the big tribute downstairs—all the friends [in attendance]. And now you're going to bed alone. Doesn't it bother you?" She said, "No. No, it doesn't. Don't ask me why, but it doesn't. My life is very full, and it's busy. I guess that's what I want." It seemed so empty. It was almost as though Joan Crawford was trying to escape sitting down with Lucille LeSueur and saying, "*Honey, where are we, really? And what do we want?*"[30]

She kept busy enough not to face it.

20

Cinderella Stories

On June 29, 1953, the ever-loyal Gloria Swanson wrote to Chuck Walters, "I wish you had a public relations man, because it seems crazy that there is so little mention of all the good things you have done. As a matter of fact, I think I am going to sic some magazine and newspaper people on your trail, so don't start turning your already up-turned nose on them."[1]

The auteur theory of filmmaking was then in its infancy, and it would be decades before the general public began referencing motion pictures by the names of their directors rather than their stars. But the presence of a self-promotional filmmaker wasn't foreign to the trade by the 1950s. Ezra Goodman, an often scathing industry journalist, noted in 1961 that William Wyler kept "a high-powered press agent on his personal payroll for more than twenty years." He continued, "George Stevens is astute at public relations. . . . He had three different sets of publicity experts working for him on *Giant* and *The Diary of Anne Frank*. . . . Director John Huston is a colorful character whose peccadillos have been extensively documented in print. . . . Billy Wilder, the Peck's bad boy of directors, is witty and highly quotable. . . . None of these directors has any real on-screen individuality or identity," Goodman concludes, "although each has plenty of off-screen press agentry."[2] (These were oddly dismissive words for the directors of, respectively, *The Best Years of Our Lives*, *A Place in the Sun*, *The African Queen*, and *Some Like It Hot*.)

Chuck remained averse to self-inflation and, as Swanson predicted, begged off the media spotlight she was pushing. His salary was now a respectable $1,750 a week; M-G-M was happy. Why tempt fate?

His fate, however, took an unexpected turn when, by November 1953, Walters once again found himself working on a Broadway musical. *By the Beautiful Sea* seemed like an exciting prospect, staffed as it was by an exemplary creative team: Herbert and Dorothy Fields (book), Arthur Schwartz (music), and Dorothy Fields (lyrics). Their charm-heavy story and songs celebrated the residents of a Coney Island boardinghouse during the vaudeville era, and budding theatrical producers Robert Fryer and Lawrence Carr looked to Hollywood for their director.

Chuck found little with which to argue, especially their choice of a leading lady: the beloved Shirley Booth had just won a Best Actress Academy Award for *Come Back, Little Sheba* and—ten days later—a Leading Actress Tony for *The Time of the Cuckoo*. Popular Wilbur Evans, with international credits in opera, operetta, and musicals, was to play opposite her. (Given this assemblage of distinguished talent, Fryer and Carr were praised in advance by the press for stirring up "one of the most exciting events of the season.")[3]

M-G-M's Sigmund Romberg musical biography, *Deep in My Heart,* was reassigned to an uninspired Stanley Donen, and Walters received a five-month leave from Culver City. Gloria Swanson, still with her eye on promoting Chuck, threw a kickoff celebration for *By the Beautiful Sea* on December 20 in New York, and rehearsals began a couple of weeks later.

At first all was well. "Chuck and I worked together very nicely," recalls choreographer Donald Saddler. "We would talk about things; [later] the company would come in, and he would set certain things . . . and I would *embroider* with the rest."[4] Above all, Walters respected the tacit rule that, as the show's director, he was not to interfere with the choreography.

"The problem on that show," contends Saddler, "was Arthur Schwartz," whose past reputation as a Broadway and Hollywood producer somehow enabled him to take control of many aspects of the production. After viewing a dance routine led by former ballerina Maria Karnilova and the energetic Peter Gennaro, he voiced his disapproval. "The number," Saddler recounts, "took place on a Coney Island fun house set, designed to look like a giant clown face. As the chorus girls entered the mouth, a surprise burst of wind blew up their skirts." All the chorines shrieked and tried to protect their modesty—and Schwartz objected: "I want those other girls to keep their skirts *up*. I want to *see*."

"Yes, Arthur," Walters cautioned, "but this is a Shirley Booth show . . . and she just won the Academy Award . . . *and* it's supposed to be 1907. We just can't have the chorus girls showing off their panties." The conflict was a sign of things to come.

On February 11, *Beautiful Sea* headed to New Haven, where a bluesy Genevieve Pitot musical arrangement thrilled the company ("Brava, Pitot!" they cheered) but didn't sit well with Schwartz. He strode down the aisle of the theater and proclaimed, "By the time we get back to New York, every note of music that woman has written will be out of the show." A hush came over the rehearsal. Pitot's credentials were impeccable, and Walters took Schwartz aside to emphasize that her dance arrangements of the composer's tunes had been constructed with reverence. "[Remember] when we did *Between the Devil*," the songwriter countered, "they took my song and played it over and over and over again. And it worked." Angry and frustrated, Chuck went to Fryer and Carr to plead, "What the hell?! Can't we at least do one performance to see the audience's reaction to Genevieve's arrangements?"

"Sorry, Chuck," Fryer replied uncomfortably, "but Arthur has ordered them out, so they're out."

As Saddler observed, "Suddenly, it was a very different show."

Beautiful Sea saw its first audience on February 16, 1954, and the New Haven reviews were polite. Several critics rightly remarked the show lacked a second act. *Variety* didn't mention Walters by name but referenced one of his hallmarks when they noted that the "staging is credible in regard to smooth blending of song and story."[5] With a bullying Schwartz calling the shots, Chuck had to admit the show no longer represented his vision, and he informed Fryer and Carr that he was withdrawing. (He then phoned his date for the Broadway premiere, cheekily telling Joan Crawford: "I think we should plan on doing something else that evening.")

"I believe Chuck's feelings were, 'Who needs all this? I can go back to M-G-M, where I'll be listened to,'" reflects Saddler.[6] Certainly, as early as February 9, Metro was heralding his upcoming re-teaming with Leslie Caron, and Fryer and Carr issued an "official" statement on February 28 that actually cited a Metro movie commitment as the reason for their director's departure. Quick to fan the rumor mill, one paper stated Walters "didn't see eye-to-eye with the show's authors,"[7] while the *New York Times* claimed he "reluctantly . . . decided to relinquish the directorial reins" because of *Beautiful Sea*'s delayed New York opening.[8] (Jo Mielziner's sets had grown so big that instead of opening at the St. James, the Booth musical had to wait until *Me and Juliet* vacated the larger Majestic.) There was a tinge of truth to all three rationalizations.

Joshua Logan (a viable replacement) saw *Beautiful Sea* when it traveled to Boston, but he took a fast train out of town. By the time tryouts finished in Philadelphia, Walters was gone, as were Saddler, Pitot, Karnilova, and Gennaro. The eviscerated show limped into New York, where local press wondered if Charles Walters or Donald Saddler would have their names in the Broadway program.

"No!" said Saddler many decades later. "Absolutely not. We didn't want it!"[9]

Beautiful Sea opened on April 8, 1954, with choreography by Helen Tamiris and direction attributed to Marshall Jamison. (The latter was a Logan assistant whose sole Broadway credit was the 1953 revival of *On Borrowed Time*.) Unfavorably reviewed for its script, the musical ran for a scant seven months on its advance sale and Booth's appeal. It was Charles Walters's last official contribution to the Broadway stage, and the director forever after held a soft spot for the material. In 1959, he announced that his "dream project" would be a screen version of *By the Beautiful Sea*, wanting Judy Garland and Bing Crosby as his stars.[10]

If American audiences of the 1950s favored any particular storybook heroine, Cinderella undoubtedly was it. Walt Disney told her rags-to-royalty tale in animation at the onset of the decade; it concluded with the filming of Jerry Lewis in the gender-switching *Cinderfella*. In between, Judy Garland portrayed the maltreated lass on a 1951 *Hallmark Playhouse* radio broadcast, and in 1957, 115 million television viewers watched the Richard Rodgers–Oscar Hammerstein II presentation starring Julie Andrews. (Disney then capitalized on their success with a reissue of his cartoon.) To this catalog, *Lili* scenarist Helen Deutsch added her own variation with her elegantly titled *The Glass Slipper*.[11]

Deutsch took the legend out of its storybook frame—eliminating the pumpkin that became a carriage and mice that became horses—yet never wanted her audience "to close the door on the possibility that the tale *could* be make believe."[12] M-G-M saw Deutsch's quirky screenplay as its desired successor to *Lili* and gave producer Edwin Knopf a budget of nearly $2 million. In a humorous echo of his early publicity as "M-G-M's Cinderella director," Chuck was put in charge . . . or so he thought.

Deutsch delivered her first complete version of *Slipper* on February 15 (Walters was still in New Haven) and subsequently received "pages and pages of wildly unrelated notes for revision" from Knopf. "[The success of] *Lili* made a different man of him," said the writer, emphasizing how the producer's ego had grown as he fabricated stories about all the "trouble he had re-cutting" that picture. "Memories are so short."

The director returned to Metro in early March, joined the writer for a working week in Palm Springs, and was shown Knopf's maddening directives. "Cinderella doesn't own a mirror," the producer had decided, "her coach to the ball should be hired for only three hours," and "the sisters should not eat for three days to squeeze into their ball gowns." In Deutsch's recollection, Walters offered her "the best piece of advice. . . . He said to ignore the notes and hope Eddie would forget them, and that he [Chuck] thought they were incredible and idiotic." He also promised to be on her side "if it came to a showdown." On March 17, Helen typed an eight-page response to Knopf, which included her suggestion that

> where we are in basic disagreement, it might be a good idea to try the ideas out on Chuck. I was very much impressed with his reactions to the ballets, weren't you? My own feeling is that the ball sequence is potentially the best sequence in the picture . . . and that it will give Chuck great opportunity for comedy and invention. A long time ago, after *Lili,* when Chuck and I met in New York, we got to talking about scripts in general, and I said to him then that if I ever wrote another script for him, I would leave big hunks wide open for his imagination and improvisation and invention, for that is when he functions best.

Slipper's final screenplay was okayed by Knopf by month's end. There followed—in Deutsch's words—"a minor discussion" about the producer's missing interpolations. "I turned to Chuck, he backed me up, and then Eddie (to save face) said the script was now so good that he wouldn't insist on the changes. The truth was that Chuck and I made no changes, other than to put back some things from my rough draft—which Eddie had changed or cut—and to elaborate [on] some stage business and one or two other minor odds and ends. [For example] Chuck liked the ball [scene], so we broke it down into more shots [and] extended descriptions [that were] already there."

When Schary wrote to Deutsch about Knopf's sound contributions, she heatedly typed: "To date, only Chuck has contributed, for he has understood the characters and the concept, and has backed me up in an unequal and dispiriting struggle!" A cautious Deutsch then reconsidered the note, and it went unsent.

Lili had made Leslie Caron America's favorite waif. She was perfect *Glass Slipper* casting, bringing both defensiveness and defenselessness to Ella—nicknamed "Cinder-Ella" by the locals because of her sooty appearance. When crafting her brusque portrayal, the actress found an unexpected inspiration: "I had just seen *On the Waterfront*. The film and Marlon Brando made quite an impression upon me, [so] I played Ella as if I was Brando."[13]

Co-starring opposite her as Prince Charles was *Torch Song*'s discontented Michael Wilding. (The Essex-born actor would joke about such typecasting, "I've played enough Earls to fill the House of Lords.")[14] Elsa Lancaster appeared as Ella's cruel stepmom, the Widow Sonder, with beauties Amanda Blake and Lisa Daniels as the vainglorious stepsisters Birdina and Serafina. Knopf had insisted upon Eva and Zsa Zsa Gabor for the roles of the stepsisters, but Deutsch objected that they were "all wrong. Also, too old."[15] Second only to Caron in terms of charisma was Estelle Winwood, a fifty-year veteran of stage and screen who wafted in and out as Ella's flighty godmother. The character's fey aphorisms brought a welcome level of whimsy to the proceedings, as did her reiteration of words and phrases she savored, including *windowsill, elbow,* and *pickle relish* ("That one has a nice snap to it!"). Such a mix of humor and fantasy played directly into Walters's sensibilities and drove his enthusiasm for Deutsch's fractured fairy tale. As Caron put it, "There was a bit of childhood left in Chuck."[16]

Filming started May 11 on M-G-M's Lot Two, where "Copperfield Street" had served as a quasi-European background for countless films since first constructed for Cukor's 1935 adaptation of the Dickens classic. From the onset, Knopf maintained a strong and disheartening presence. Both he (and Metro) now conceptualized Caron as a glamorous film star, and their tampering would lead the *New Yorker* to later describe her Cinderella as "a combination of elf, tomboy, and sweater girl."[17] In addition, the producer brought in ballet impresario Roland Petit to create epic en pointe dream sequences. Walters could only shake his head and remark, "Since [Eddie] had felt robbed in *Lili*—deprived of his big luxurious ballets—he was going to have them this time around."

Petit had mentored Caron since her teens and brought his Ballet de Paris to M-G-M to perform three extended dream ballets with her. (Two of these were set in a crypt and eventually were edited into a single macabre routine in which Ella melodramatically dies without the love of her prince.) "I think [these sequences] spoiled, even killed the film," Walters later said, "because we went from a simple Cinderella story to Petit's grand classical ballets. [They] squashed the plot."[18] Caron disagrees and finds Petit's first effort "very, very successful." "The Son of the Cook in the Palace of the 'Dook'" was spritely fantasy, and "the idea was so amusing. Poor little Ella cannot dream of the salons and the reception rooms. All she knows well is the kitchen. So the ballet takes place *in* the kitchen. I think that's absolutely fabulous—so witty."[19]

Wilding, however, was once again miserable. When he first reported to work, he thought he was just there "to meet Miss Caron and possibly to discuss the script with Chuck. Instead, as I walked in the door, someone tossed a pair of tights my way and told me to get ready to limber up."[20] According to Caron, "Michael was an angel, a pet—he tried to get me to get him fired! He took me to lunch at the commissary and said, 'You know I can't dance. Why don't you put your foot down and say, "I don't want this Michael Wilding"?' I said, 'I can't do that, Michael. I won't do that.'"[21]

In the end, Wilding (aided by Metro publicity writers) graciously credited Petit as "clever . . . fiendishly clever. He'd show me just what was to be done."[22] Walters, however, recalled Petit's indifference at having to coach a film actor. "Michael [was] a charming man [with] four left feet," said the director. "When we got to the part where Michael had to do something, Roland unmistakably turned his back and went to sit down somewhere, and it was I who had to try and get him to do a couple of steps—or at least give the impression that that's what he was doing."[23] (Dancing double Oleg Tupine was employed for Wilding's long shots, as Chuck was unwilling to stand in on this film as he had for Jean-Pierre Aumont in *Lili*.)

Despite filming overruns on both ballets, production closed—under budget by $9,146—on July 31, 1954. A December test audience genuinely enjoyed the rather unusual fairy tale. "If Metro would make more pictures of this quality," one reaction card commented, "once more they would be the top studio."[24] Before the second preview, however, Knopf inexplicably recut moments that had already proven delightful, and Walters was forced to argue that Caron now came off as sullen in her first throne room daydream—and that the exit of Winwood's character at the picture's conclusion was no longer the "solo curtain call" he had staged. His January 10, 1955, memo to Schary maintained, "The biggest and most familiar point in the original Cinderella legend is the trying on of the glass slipper. Yet in the film, the entire thing is dissipated much too quickly, so that the audience seems cheated. The film does not even use the phrase 'glass slipper.'"[25] He also requested an orchestral swell in the underscoring to provide the necessary "happily-ever-after" tag to the production.

Slipper had become "too top heavy by far," the director worried, but this inflated Cinderella, done in Eastmancolor and Perspecta stereo, seemed to be just what M-G-M fancied. That March, the feature was booked into Radio City Music Hall as accompaniment to the emporium's annual Easter pageant. The notices were mixed: *Films in Review* concurred with Walters and summarized, "Virtuosity supplants charm."[26] The *Morning Globe* agreed with both of them and ridiculed the movie, saying, "*Slipper* is a movie drenched in charm. Charm oozes out of every foot of it, pours out of every frame, spills over from every sequence and situation."[27] Yet the *Hollywood Reporter* was enchanted: "A romance that contains no magic, except the magic of perfectly told entertainment. Walters has coordinated many perfect elements into a perfect picture."[28]

Regardless, the public stayed away, which meant a considerable financial disappointment for M-G-M. Walters was usually sensitive to the box office take of his pictures, but this time he didn't much care. *Slipper*'s fiscal loss vindicated what he already knew: sincere storytelling beat arty pretension every time.

Chuck would never again work for Eddie Knopf. Later that year, the producer released his Restoration-era yarn, *The King's Thief*, to terrible notices and poor box office. (Knopf's son Christopher penned the screenplay.) Gleefully, Walters sent Deutsch the *Hollywood Reporter* critique of the film; his accompanying note offered, "Thought you might get a smug laugh out of this." He had underlined one sentence of the review: "But for some reason this film fails to get the uniform charm and atmosphere that make most of Edwin H. Knopf's productions such delightful experiences in the theatre." Alongside this, Walters scribbled a sardonic "REALLY??"[29]

Even as *Slipper* was being edited, the director and writer had begun another collaboration. Based on the graphic best-selling memoir of Broadway and Hollywood entertainer Lillian Roth, *I'll Cry Tomorrow* chronicled the singer's bright career in the 1920s and her eventual dissolution in a haze of alcohol.[30]

Many major stars were interested in the property (Jane Russell, Ann Blyth, and Shelley Winters among them), but Walters and Deutsch were firm. They fancied M-G-M's sunny sweetheart, June Allyson. "I wanted to start with this innocent façade," Chuck explained, "and have the fears gradually eat at her. I personally know how tough June can be, and she could have kicked the hell out of that part. With that gravel voice and getting drunk—I think she would have gotten an Academy Award."[31] Metro's preferred Roth, however, was Susan Hayward.

"Hayward had played a drunk [before] in *Smash-Up* and had gotten an Academy Award nomination," Walters said. "She'd played a singer before in *With a Song in My Heart*. Now she wanted to play a drunken singer; I said, 'I've seen this already.'"

But the studio was set in its casting. "Helen and Chuck went to work on *I'll Cry Tomorrow* for June," reported columnist Mike Connolly, who co-authored the Roth memoir, "blissfully unaware that it was Susan who had brought the book to Dore Schary . . . and that it was Susan who had told him this was for her!"[32] The 20th Century-Fox actress owed M-G-M a picture and had the say on what part she would play. Publicly, Walters repudiated her casting—"not suitable," he told the *New York Times*[33]—which triggered a forceful confrontation in his office. Chuck remained resolute, as did the studio. "Helen couldn't manage to work on the script with Susan Hayward in mind. So we both abandoned the picture." Metro responded in typical fashion, immediately placing Walters on suspension.

A flabbergasted Louella Parsons reviewed the situation in her column: "Seldom have as fine a writer as Helen Deutsch and as good a director as Charles Walters walked out on a picture after a disagreement about the star."[34] She next sought an "exclusive" from Hayward's camp, and the gossip maven was told the actress had "gone fishing."

Privately, Deutsch explained what she dubbed "the Susan Hayward nonsense" and defended their actions. "Chuck and I had nothing to do with it, although for a few hours we were pretty scared, expecting to be called murderers!" she pointed out. "What you read in the papers about our walk out was, of course, not true. Chuck did walk out because he disapproved of casting. I walked out because of what he [Chuck] told me Hayward had said about the script, and about the utterly ridiculous revisions she was going to ask for in order to make the role more suitable for herself."[35]

Walters eventually would shrug off all the absurdity with a joke. "Susan knew I didn't want her . . . [and that] I never really believed her too much on screen," he said later. "[But] the scene she played with me in my office was one hell of a scene. They should have gotten *that* on film!"

21

In *High Society*

Walters retreated to Malibu to wait out the suspension. Given his studio loyalty and penchant for work (five films and one Broadway show between 1952 and 1954), such idleness was unsettling. His stress was further compounded by the situation at 22506 Malibu Road, where home life with John had splintered. Their once-devoted relationship now fluctuated between adoring and abrasive, with the latter playing out even in public. "Darrow always wanted to be the center of attention over Chuck," remembered their friend Alan Cahan. "I'd have dinner with them, and Chuck would say something, and Darrow would say, 'Oh, what do you know, you faggot?' I don't know how Chuck put up with it."[1]

Walters, at forty-three, had matured into a Hollywood success independent of his domineering partner, while Darrow's prominence as a top agent was on the wane. His most significant achievement in the early 1950s had been in establishing a screen career for boxer Scott Brady. "John wanted everything to be his way," recalls Jimie Morrissey, who'd soon begin his own relationship with Chuck. "He had a necklace he liked to wear, a fancy one with turquoise, and he'd say, 'I'm the big chief.'"[2]

The fracture was further enhanced by all-too-frequent imbibing, as alcohol had become the predominant vice across Walters and Darrow's two-decade union. The pair purchased the Windham liquor store only a few yards from their house as an investment, and their living room bar stayed commensurately well stocked. "I think Chuck started drinking with owning the store," remembers Morrissey.[3] "A lot of liquor was flowing in and out. But Chuck was never a mean drunk." The same could not always be said of Darrow, and the couple had reached a point where their personal relationship was no longer mutually nourishing. "I don't know what the deal was with money when Chuck got out," adds Morrissey, "but I'm sure he didn't get what he should have from John." Walters did, however, retain the Malibu home, Darrow continued to professionally represent him—and there remained a bond of friendship and shared experience that was indissoluble.

In an ironic mingling of life with art, Chuck's next project was all about a self-absorbed, swaggering theatrical agent—a sort of heterosexual John Darrow. Metro summoned him back in early June 1955 to helm *The Tender Trap,* although he "hated the play, which the studio sent me to see in Chicago. But the screenplay that came out of it [from *Casablanca* writer Julius Epstein] was damn good, so I accepted." Taking the film also meant an end to his three-month suspension: "I wanted to get *that* over with!"

A three-act Max Shulman and Robert Paul Smith "verbal comedy" from the 1953–1954 Broadway season, *The Tender Trap* centered on Charlie Reader, a New York talent agent and happy bachelor, who represents self-confident actress Julie Giles. His bachelorhood then is threatened by the advances of both his client and Sylvia Crewes, a violinist from the NBC-TV orchestra. When Charlie's boyhood buddy Joe McCall—eleven years a husband—pays an unexpected visit, the playboy begins to reevaluate his swinging lifestyle, while Joe, in turn, is tempted to put an end to his marriage vows.

"A *lousy* play," said Walters, "but the [movie's] cast fitted perfectly": Frank Sinatra as womanizer Charlie, Debbie Reynolds as confident Julie, and David Wayne as tempted Joe. Dore Schary fought the employment of Oscar-winner Celeste Holm as Sylvia ("Dore hated Celeste," said Chuck) but was overruled by producer Larry Weingarten.[4] Another casting victory for the director came when he secured a brief tap solo for longtime dance assistant Jack Boyle in an audition sequence. (When Wayne's character asks if the dancer is any good, Sinatra dryly retorts, "He can't be—he's not one of our clients.")

Tender Trap, claustrophobic and static onstage, proved a brain-teaser to cinematize. "It was very difficult to do," the director explained, "being so talky and taking place almost entirely in one apartment. There was always someone ringing the doorbell, and I wondered how in the hell am I going to make [them] open the door in a new and interesting way?" As a result, Walters sought "different spots to play out each scene. . . . For example, the day we filmed the [lengthy] scene in the bathroom, where Frank is shaving and talking to David Wayne at the same time, I knew we needed something to shake the scene up, at least a little. So I asked someone to bring us a shower curtain. That was all we needed, because I could make [Frank] hang his bathrobe on the door, then pull the curtain and [say his lines as he pretends to shower]; the shower noises could be added in afterwards. [The scene] was a little better after that."[5]

Achieving any sense of intimacy became all the more difficult when M-G-M insisted the picture be shot in CinemaScope, one of several wide-screen technologies developed in the 1950s to compete with television. Though grand for atmospheric westerns, mammoth musicals, and biblical epics, it was inconsistent with straightforward storytelling. Walters neatly sidestepped the issue by utilizing the sprawling expanse for the opening and closing of the picture: "I knew the film needed a frame—the show would be in the middle." An early concept—in which a plane flew from right to left at the opening and from left to right at the finale—was dismissed by the director. ("That *wasn't* very interesting," was his judgment.) Inspiration hit late one night when Walters realized that, despite the non-musical property, he had a musical cast and "I had to use that somehow." When the Sammy Cahn–James Van Heusen title song was delivered, Chuck "decided we could have Frank sing it at the beginning and the others sing it at the end. It was really fun to do."

Walters minimalistically composed Sinatra's prelude, positioning the singer in an extreme long shot—barely visible against a CinemaScope-wide, sky blue backdrop. As the lyric suggests, he remains "a spot, just a dot on the map." The casually suited Sinatra slowly advances toward the stationary camera. His croon is playful, his walk is nonchalant, and his hat is tilted at the same rakish angle that Chuck had given Garland years earlier for "Mr. Monotony" and "Get Happy." When Sinatra strolls into medium-shot range, the camera then travels with him for the final verse; the overall aesthetic was elegant, yet disarmingly simple. (Film historian Alain Masson later described it as an intelligent "interplay of free movement and clearly built shooting.")[6] Lyricist Cahn was of the opinion that Walters's concept proved "to be one of the all-time most successful main titles for a movie."[7] Arguably this remains the sequence that best captures the singer's warm and easygoing manner on film. New York University film professor Dana Polan offers, "That's the Sinatra we [the audience] know of as the light entertainer, the figure that hasn't a care in the world. And the film then will be about how he has to start to have cares in the world."[8]

"I'm still up to my 'Trap' in 'Tender Ass,'"[9] Chuck wrote to Helen Deutsch on July 21, "but glad to report it's all going well and quite funny."

The film's only minor setbacks were occasioned by the somewhat disgruntled leading man. As Walters described it, "Frank had agreed to do [*Trap*] on an old commitment, so he was sour. Apparently the money the studio paid him was under the old agreement, too."[10] (Presumably the director was referring to an aborted 1952 movie version of *St. Louis Woman*.)

The singer's indifference put some strain on an otherwise undemanding shoot. Reynolds recalls, "I think it was Mondays that he didn't want to work. So that day he'd just come in [and sit]."[11] She adds, "He [also] didn't like shooting a scene a lot. He would try to get it in the first take, which is always better in comedy anyway." To accommodate, the overall production schedule was "Sinatra-fied"—that is, a scene was rehearsed and then immediately committed to film. "But," Reynolds confirms, "he didn't have the hard-and-fast rule that has been ascribed to him—insisting that a scene be shot once and printed, even if it was bad."[12] Said Walters with a smile, "I could usually snow Frank into two or three takes. After that, his patience gives."

The actor may have been a challenge at times, but as the director would freely admit, "Give me a son-of-a-bitch *with talent*. When Sinatra learned his lines and did his scenes, he was excellent. He was a hell of a performer." Shedding the contrived puppy-dog persona with which M-G-M had saddled him in the 1940s, Sinatra now had come into his own, persuasive in dramatic roles and able to play comedy with boyish cheekiness. In one witty episode, he and Reynolds come to a coital impasse when their petting becomes too intense. "I'm afraid your idea of necking and my idea of necking are a little far apart," she scolds, and suggests instead "quiet time" watching television. "Oh goody," he mocks, "and perhaps later we can go in the kitchen and make some fudge!" Walters contributed his own personal imprint by programming the TV with a sequence from his *Easy to Love*—a sensual Busby Berkeley water pas de deux featuring Esther Williams and Johnny Bromfield. Sinatra and Reynolds sit in silent bewilderment as the slippery, on-screen ecstasy reminds them of what they could be enjoying. For a finish, Chuck "choreographed" Debbie's limpid slide into Frank's entwining arms. "They were funny and romantic," said daughter Nancy Sinatra. "They should have made more movies together."[13]

In all, filming took just twenty-four days, from late June to late July 1955, and *Tender Trap* cost $37,490 less than its estimated $1.2 million budget. "Chuck seemed to handle all the problems," Reynolds maintains, "because he knew how to get along with stars like Frank. He [could deal with] their eccentricities—their 'demands,' if you want to put it that way. But Chuck ultimately got his way. . . . The schedule went off on time. The movie came in on time. The studio was really happy with him, because they wanted a director who could bring films in on time . . . and on budget."[14]

Released the following November, the picture did big business across the country. "Walters' direction pinpoints the characters well," declared the *Los Angeles Times*,[15] while in New York, Bosley Crowther defined the Radio City Music Hall attraction as "a vastly beguiling entertainment" with "smooth and lively" direction.[16] "I don't think it's a *great* film," says Reynolds, "but it's charming and lighthearted, and that's all it's meant to be. It was just supposed to be light comedy—and Chuck was great at comedy. His timing was wonderful, being a former dancer and choreographer."[17]

Years later, when watching the film on television, Walters regretted not going far enough in the film's messy, morning-after party scene. "I gave a Christmas Eve party once," he stated, "and the next day I found a high-heeled shoe on the bar. If only I had thought of putting a damn high-heeled shoe in the film, amongst the ashtrays and the empty glasses. That would have been so eloquent!"

At the same time *The Tender Trap* was coming together, Sol C. Siegel arrived at M-G-M from 20th Century-Fox—the first independent producer to join the studio under Dore Schary's regime. (A dignified man skilled at corporate hardball, Siegel would succeed Schary as head of production within three years.) He cannily reviewed Metro's holdings and chose to musicalize a past classic. It was a brave selection: Philip Barry's *The Philadelphia Story* first had been a glossy stage comedy and then a faultless 1940 George Cukor picture, the latter top-lined by Katharine Hepburn, Cary Grant, and James Stewart. Siegel's pet project was sophisticatedly retitled *High Society*.

Walters admitted to only a vague recollection of the Cukor film, "and then what I mostly remembered was the excellent couple that Grant and Hepburn made together." Siegel sought similar first-class casting with—at the top of his roster—the ultimately unavailable Elizabeth Taylor and (among others) Howard Keel. Eventually, the producer even bettered that wish list, corralling a historic assemblage of talent: music legends Bing Crosby, Frank Sinatra, and Louis Armstrong, appearing together for the first time and augmented by M-G-M's decorous Grace Kelly.

The task of reimagining Barry's masterwork as a musical comedy fell to John Patrick, author of Broadway's successful *The Teahouse of the August Moon*. Keeping his twists to a minimum, Patrick maintained the core plot: socialite Tracy Samantha Lord (Kelly) is about to take a stuffy second husband (John Lund), but her plan is complicated by the surprise return of first spouse C. K. Dexter Haven (Crosby) and a probing journalist and photographer (Sinatra and Holm). In Patrick's major alteration and contribution, the story shifted from Pennsylvania to Rhode Island; Crosby's character became a successful pop composer, and Louis Armstrong and his band were imported as themselves to play at the Newport Jazz Festival.

It was a serendipitous alliance. Some historians claim that American jazz music began "when the trumpet of Louis Armstrong met the voice of Bing Crosby."[18] Sinatra, twelve years his junior, was heir apparent to the Crosby throne, emotionally extending Bing's intimate style of singing. ("He was," said Sinatra, "the father of my career, the idol of my youth.")[19] During the 1940s, their friendly faux rivalry amusingly played out on their first radio appearance together on Bing's Kraft show:

FRANK: Bing, I came here tonight because you can do me a big favor.
BING: You know me, anything—just ask.
FRANK: *Retire!*

The announcement that Crosby, Sinatra, and Armstrong were to appear together in a motion picture was more than significant. It was an anticipated milestone in music history.

Potential apart, it took three months for Sinatra to commit to the project. When he did, the singer had one suggestion: "For my money the only guy to direct this picture is Chuck Walters." Siegel took the cue as a command, but common sense was a factor as well. "Sol and I got along very well," Walters reflected. "We got down to him saying, 'Who do you want to choreograph the picture?' I said, 'It's my bag, it's exactly up my alley.' It was the kind of thing I feel I do best and love to do, because the numbers were integrated into the story. Siegel was apparently thinking, 'Oh, well, that saves my cash register, two jobs for the price of one.' So I did the choreography." (Studio records indicate the director received $71,500 for his contributions.) Having this kind of complete control over *High Society* was "very satisfying" for Chuck, who noted, "That's when you are very appreciative of your dancing background."

Equal satisfaction came from piloting his powerhouse cast. In Kelly, Walters had an undeniably lovely leading lady, but her gracious appeal was entirely dissimilar to the individuality of Katharine Hepburn. He spent considerable time helping Grace tap into the defenseless interior of Barry's icy socialite. The actress acknowledged, "I tried to find the point where [Tracy's] haughtiness was a cover for insecurity, and for the pain she felt over her father's thoughtless behavior."[20] (A minor plot point saw patriarch Seth Lord embroiled in an affair with a New York dancer.) As Alain Masson would later articulate, the key difference between Hepburn and Kelly "lies in the fact that Hepburn—though she may lose her composed image—always seems to master the game, at least intellectually, [whereas] Kelly sometimes is really at a loss."[21]

Her male co-stars, nonetheless, didn't bother to analyze; they patently adored her. A doting Sinatra called her "Gracie" and poured on the charm, leading Chuck to privately refer to them as "Beauty and the Beast." Crosby, victorious beau in the *High Society* love triangle, called Grace "kind, considerate, and friendly with everyone."[22]

"The Old Groaner," now fifty-two, had his own vested interest in the picture's success. Along with Siegel and Loew's, Inc., Bing Crosby Productions was one-third of the *High Society* corporate force, and he took to learning his material with the enthusiasm of a newcomer. "It was a pleasure to be in the picture," he stressed. "Chuck's a very fine director with great taste and sophistication. It was just a breeze, really."[23] Walters was his equal in praise: "Bing [was] the most darling man I ever worked with. The nicest man. Calling him professional is almost wrong, his demeanor was so simplistic. He was so honest; he'd say, 'Whatever you want, Chuck.'"[24]

High Society was clearly a "prestige" musical-in-the-making, the likes of which only Arthur Freed still assembled on a semi-regular basis at M-G-M. This fact became all the more clear when Cole Porter signed on to write the songs. Not since *The Pirate* (1948) had the legendary tunesmith written a full score for a motion picture. It was to be the fourth and final Walters-Porter alliance (following *Jubilee, Du Barry Was a Lady,* and *Let's Face It*), and the arrival of each new Porter composition was an event. Chuck remembered, "When Cole would get a number, Sol Siegel, [music director] Saul Chaplin, and I would go to Brentwood to Porter's [home] for luncheon. . . . [M]enus at each place. Very, very formal. A glass of wine before. A glass of wine with. All very proper. Then, while we had a demitasse, Cole would go to the piano and play his new song. Cole says, 'This is the number I think would be nice for Bing and Mr. Armstrong. *And now you has jazz jazz jazz jazz jazz jazz.*' *One* note and *one* finger. And I'm thinking, 'What is this? Cole has blown it out the back!' Sol is saying, 'Oh, yes, Cole, yes.' I looked over at Saul, questioning . . . but it worked."

The song "worked" because Porter's groundwork was then fine-tuned by genuine jazz artists in team with the brilliant Chaplin. "Now You Has Jazz" was given two-hour rehearsals every afternoon for a week. "They were the equivalent of jam sessions based on the tune," explained Chaplin. "I tried to get Louis to say the Italian *arrivederci,* but what came out was *averaduci.* [Of course,] coming from him, it sounded right."[25] Walters attended most afternoon jams and later worked exclusively with Bing, supplying arm gestures and body movement to help sell the song during filming.

From October through December 1955, Cole delivered "Little One" and "I Love You, Samantha" for Bing, "Mind if I Make Love to You" and "You're Sensational" for Frank, and the catchy "Who Wants to Be a Millionaire" for Sinatra and Holm (cleverly staged among an array of impractical but ultra-expensive wedding gifts). *High Society*'s biggest hit, however, came in the Crosby-Kelly ballad "True Love." Practically a lullaby, the song required simple direction, and critic Douglas McVay later praised Walters's "talent for musical naturalism," adding, "This sequence (significantly not present in *The Philadelphia Story*), in which the newly-married couple quietly and blissfully duet . . . on board their yacht of that name, invests the love between Tracy and her former husband with a sense of physical truth, and thus makes their movements towards reconciliation in the rest of the film equally credible. . . . [The duet] emerges as one of the most persuasive illustrations of the power of song (or dance) to convey sexual passion and affection more intensely than any exchange of spoken words or fervent embraces can do."[26]

Holm recalled: "[Grace] had a very dear contralto—lovely and totally appropriate. She made no effort to sound like a professional singer. On the day she was to [record] with Bing, we all hung about to hear them."[27] After receiving his disc from the session, Porter wrote to Metro conductor Johnny Green, "I can't tell you how surprised I am at the singing of Miss Grace Kelly."[28] The public was in agreement, and sales of the "True Love" single earned Kelly her first and only gold record. "My brother," she later said, "once made a very unbrotherly remark by saying that he thought my voice on a golden record was one of the 'modern miracles.' But I was very delighted about it."[29] "True Love" later won a Best Song Oscar nomination, and M-G-M joined with Porter's press agent to lobby hard for a win. When Doris Day's chart-topping "Que Sera, Sera" took home the prize, the agent received a succinct cable of defeat from Porter that read: "Whatever will be, will be."[30]

Dreaming up staging possibilities for "Jazz," "Millionaire," and "True Love" proved unproblematic, yet Chuck ran adrift with "You're Sensational," a seduction song for Sinatra to woo Kelly. "I couldn't think what to do," he admitted. "[Then] I woke up in the middle of the night and thought, 'Just a minute. [Frank and Grace are] getting an awful lot of money, individually and collectively. I'm going to make *them* do the work.'" The next day he showed up for rehearsal with a simple directive: "Go with it, dears." When his stars became too artificial in their actions, he offered one final piece of advice: "Play it like a scene." With that, the performers acted—and aced—the Porter lyric, with Sinatra, lustful and lost, melded to Kelly's mute response. Her radiant mix of yearning and uncertainty enchanted Walters, who said, "I thought she was marvelous."

"There was only one song that Cole didn't manage to furnish us," he continued, "and it was *the* song everyone was going to be waiting for"— the much heralded first on-screen vocalizing between Crosby and Sinatra. Porter tried but repeatedly came up empty, and Chaplin later wrote, "One of the reasons he was having difficulty was that the scene indicated for the song made no story point. It was inserted [only] so that Bing and Frank could do a number together. [They're] both at an elegant Newport party, [and] they happen to wander into an empty room that had a bar. There's nothing particularly funny about that. Yet a song for Bing and Frank was a must."[31]

"It was getting late," offered Chuck, "and actually we were into shooting the picture. We were all thinking, 'What are we going to *do?*' Saul came up with a [vintage Porter] song, went to Cole with it, and Cole said, 'I think it's perfect.' [Then] Sol, Solly Chaplin, and I had a meeting, and Chaplin said, 'Chuck, this is what we are going to use for Sinatra and Crosby. It might sound familiar.' He showed me the lead sheet, and it was 'Well, Did You Evah (What a Swell Party This Is),' which Betty Grable and I had introduced in *Du Barry Was a Lady*. . . . The past can come back and haunt you sometimes." (At Porter's urging, Chaplin altered the original lyric as necessary.) The director felt no pang in relinquishing "his" number to the two stars: "It was a great song [and] a fun switch to make it fit Crosby and Sinatra . . . [and] the easiest thing to shoot. One day of camera rehearsal and one day of shooting. [But] it was tough to stage because Frank had a bug about coming to rehearsals. So I staged it with Bing, with [me] doubling for Sinatra. Bing is a hell of a worker—if you put in a call for 8:30, he's there at 8:00. When Frank saw us go through it, he loved it." Given its mode of creation, there is more than a little Charles Walters in the performance Sinatra committed to film.

Additionally, the suggestive lyric, masterful arrangement, and jocular delivery ensured that "Well, Did Ya Evah?" would be an audience pleaser, deserving of an encore. "Towards the end of the number, I did a fairly audacious thing," said Walters. "When they exited, I simply let the camera [roll]," focused on the empty library. Then without warning, the duo burst back into their safe haven, made a beeline for the bar, tossed back one final drink and offered one final chorus. It was a unique example of a stage convention working neatly on the screen. During the film's first sneak preview, the audience broke into spontaneous applause at what they assumed was the song's finish. Then Frank and Bing rushed back onto the screen for another drink and another verse; by the time the pair made their arm-in-arm final exit—bellowing, "What a swellegant, elegant party this is!"—the crowd was cheering.

High Society's musical moments fell into place, yet Walters regretted his inability to fully develop a character—and story line—for Louis Armstrong. Even playing himself, the famed trumpeter deserved better than what he was being asked to do. Armstrong initially was cast as a sort of Cupid for Crosby and Kelly, his instrument in lieu of bow and arrow. Porter's lyric to the film's opening calypso hints at this, referencing Satchmo's vow to "toot his trumpet" to bring the couple back together. When it became clear that the screenplay wouldn't continue the Cupid concept, Walters added some Armstrong action on the sly: "You see it a little when [Louis is] playing . . . 'Samantha,' which Crosby hears and starts to sing himself, and which [Kelly] in turn hears from her room. I wanted to flesh out this idea—and Louis' character—but *they* insisted, saying it wasn't worth the trouble."[32] Walters's comment offers no further specifics as to which corporate entities "they" might have been in this instance, but he continued, "I think they were wrong because we needed a stronger hook to justify the transformation of *The Philadelphia Story* into a musical." Even without additional scripting, however, Armstrong remains a strong connective thread. His humor, bafflement, and charisma give undeniable shape and tone to *High Society*.

Sol Siegel, eager to exploit his heralded "Cast of the Year," regularly invited visitors to the set. As Hedda and Louella haggled for exclusives, Walters's sound stage became a thoroughfare for journalists, each working a different angle: "Bing and Louis—the jazz greats," "Frank and Bing sing together for the first time," "Grace makes her musical debut." Enough journalism was being generated that Porter felt left out; he wired agent Irving "Swifty" Lazar, "Everyone else connected with [the picture] gets almost daily publicity, including Sol Siegel. Maybe you have some method by which this could be solved?"[33] But Porter's return to Hollywood couldn't compete with the human interest story that trumped all others when Kelly announced her plans to wed Prince Rainier III. The overriding press question became, "Will or won't she continue to make movies after becoming a princess to the ruling sovereign of Monaco?"

Curiosity peaked when the prince and his father, the Duke of Valentinois, arrived in Culver City. Company-conscious Schary went into overdrive to persuade them that Monaco royalty and Metro royalty weren't mutually exclusive. As Holm recalls, things did not go according to plan. "[Grace] invited me to lunch," she begins, along with the royals, Schary, and Chuck, "who had a tendency to be enchantingly obscene."[34] The luncheon was given in the paneled executive dining room, which at M-G-M was considered a bit of a joke; it only seated eight. "So we were all sitting at the table, and I can't imagine who would have been dumb enough to have said, 'How big is Monaco?' But somebody did. Well, there was a pause, and I think the Prince gave him the area in feet. Dore laughed and said, 'Why, that's not even as big as our back lot.' Now *that* was just bad manners!" An awkward, uncomfortable silence came over the luncheon, until Holm smartly stuck a fork in her steak and propelled it across the table. "While everybody was busy getting straightened out over that," she concludes, "I changed the subject. Nobody knew that I'd done that on purpose."[35]

With nearly double the budget of Walters's recent Esther Williams musicals and a shooting schedule twice as long, *High Society* began filming on January 18 and closed on March 6, 1956. Throughout, the production had had a feeling of being a miracle. "It was one of the most enjoyable experiences," Kelly later said. "We had such fun."[36] Johnny Green agreed: "You talk about one big happy family, that's what it was."[37] Even Chaplin, with his lists of past and future cinematic blockbusters, would unhesitatingly proclaim, "Of all the films I've been associated with, *High Society* was the most pleasant."[38]

Kelly became Her Serene Highness the Princess of Monaco on April 19, impeccably gowned by *High Society* designer Helen Rose. The press dubbed the event "The Wedding of the Century." Even M-G-M couldn't buy such publicity, although the August 1 world premiere at the RKO Pantages Theater in Los Angeles was carefully orchestrated pandemonium. Shouting street crowds were showered by flower petals, and the floral display was a convenient distraction from the fact that none of the film's stars were in attendance. (Crosby was relaxing at his ranch, Sinatra and Holm were in New York, and Kelly was away playing princess.) To compensate, George Murphy presented Porter with a civic citation, Bob Hope kidded Crosby's no-show, and Walters's former stars Ann Miller and Debbie Reynolds represented the home studio. Ever recalcitrant, Chuck later admitted, "I wasn't going to go to the premiere either, [until] my dear friend Earl Blackwell of Celebrity Service phoned Ginger Rogers and told her to call me. She told me to get my tuxedo out of mothballs, get a limousine, and come pick her up. And I enjoyed it. I was like a kid in a bathtub: it was hell to get me in, but once you did, I didn't want to get out."[39]

After the premiere, Walters was besieged by back-patters at Romanoff's but finally had to approach Porter for his opinion. "Cole, you haven't said a word. Are you pleased?" he asked. Believing they were past such formalities, Porter sighed, "Oh Chuck, don't tell me I have to. . . ." Three days later, Walters received "a very formal note of thank-you":

> *This is a typed record of my congratulations to you for your great job on* High Society.
>
> > *All my best, dear Chuck.*
> > *Cole*[40]

For posterity, Walters tacked Porter's cool missive into his shooting script, along with dozens of on-set snapshots of the company. There was a further addition when Crosby died in 1977; Chuck clipped the crooner's obit, circling this: "But his favorite movie, he once said, was *High Society*, which he made in 1956."[41] Such acclamation was the greatest review.

Summarizing the joyous production, a poem of reflection (presumably penned by Walters himself) was typed on the first page of the director's script:

"High Society"
This was a
picture of music,
rehearse and
shoot. More
music, more
rehearse and
then more
shoot. But
then—we
also had
publicity,
both oral,
written and
photographed;
we had visitors,
and then more
visitors, and
more publicity.
Was there
ever before
such a sucha?
Besides a real "Prince"
yet, who
stole our
beaut-ee-ful
girl.[42]

22

Branching Out

High Society was M-G-M's biggest moneymaker of 1956 and ranked number five at the box office in *Variety*'s annual industry roundup.[1] The reviews had been complimentary if conditional. "Lacks the brittle wit of Barry's original," opined the *New York Herald Tribune,* "[but] on the whole . . . an entertaining film."[2] Nevertheless, it would be six more years before another Walters musical came to the screen. The times and their music were changing.

"*Everybody* turned their heads away from musicals," insists actress Jane Powell. "It wasn't always Dore Schary's decision. He had to answer to New York. [Loew's president] Nick Schenck came around a little bit, not that often. But the telephone lines went every day."[3] Those telephone lines, presumably, were abuzz with directives on what kind of films to make—and decisions about personnel, which resulted in an exodus from M-G-M. "There is always anxiety when people are losing their jobs," continues Powell, "and when Schary was there, people were losing their jobs. Everything was changing, and everything had to be changed. That was the attitude. . . . [P]eople wondered if they were going to be next."

Perhaps few were surprised when Schary himself was given his walking papers. After eight years of uneven performance, proffering A-list movie stars in mediocre B-grade pictures, the studio chief was removed in November 1956, leaving behind a much-depreciated empire. He later boasted that under his leadership, "the average cost of [a Metro] film [went] from about $2,200,000 to $1,400,000."[4] By comparison, *High Society* had been given a healthy $2,400,000 budget, and audiences responded to the tune of $5,782,000 in its first release alone.

Firing Schary had been Joseph Vogel's first order of business when he replaced Schenck as Loew's president. In his place, long-standing Metro executive Benny Thau was left to administer studio operations until Sol Siegel took on those duties two years later. Siegel's rule, which lasted from 1958 to 1962, helped bring about a short-lived resurrection—so much so that the lavishly mounted *Gigi* and *Ben-Hur* won Best Picture Oscars in 1959 and 1960. (The two titles amassed eighteen other Academy Awards as well.) Given the expert care Walters provided Siegel's initiation picture at M-G-M, he remained a personal favorite of the new boss and proudly asserted that after the changeover "they really listened to me." He had no anxiety about losing his job.

Chuck, by this time, had leased a modest Hollywood apartment, and its proximity to the studio made for easy early-morning commutes. After weekday work at Metro, he would adjourn to 969½ North Doheny Drive, eat dinner in his study, and prepare for the next day. "Chuck really didn't go out," states Jimie Morrissey. "He was working most of the time. When he wasn't working, he went to the beach—or to Palm Springs," which is where his relationship with Morrissey began.[5]

Roughly one hundred miles southeast of Los Angeles, the desert town of Palm Springs was a favored destination for those in the film industry—and for gay men. The promise of tranquility and privacy were key enticements. Many homes and hotels were walled in (a symbolic match for the partition Walters discreetly created around his private life), and consequently "the Springs" became an ideal setting in which Chuck could cut loose and enjoy the rewards of success. One frequent visitor recalls watching with delight as the director—an eternal sun worshiper—took to the pool to perform an impromptu water ballet, joking, "Look, I'm Esther Williams." Similarly, columnist Mike Connolly recalls Chuck doing "a pretty good 'take off'" on Garland singing "Zing! Went the Strings of My Heart" while at a Pasternak dinner party in the Springs.[6]

Walters decided to build a Springs home in the Las Palmas neighborhood in late 1954—a one-story residence with four bedrooms and three baths—and he invited Fox set designer Paul Fox to decorate the interior. "The Palm Springs house is *finally* finished,"[7] Chuck wrote to Helen Deutsch on July 21, 1955, as he prepared for his first relaxing weekend at what he christened "Casa Contenta." That easygoing name was soon emblazoned on a large welcome sign in the front garden.

Palm Springs, however, was not just a place for leisure. Perhaps prompted by Gloria Swanson's entry into the world of fashion (her "Swanson Originals" were quite popular in the 1950s), Walters took the salary he had earned on *The Tender Trap* and launched his own clothing line at Chuck Walters Presents on North Palm Canyon Drive. This elegant men's store specialized in resort wear and gentlemen's accessories and was well situated in the front of the popular Desert Inn Hotel. Chuck adorned the walls with large photographs of famous friends—Garland, Ball, Lawford, and Astaire among them.

He had held an interest in men's fashion for years, having designed functional workwear for his own personal wardrobe—a solution to the irritation he felt when his shirttails pulled out of his slacks during dance rehearsals. (His remedy was a waist-length shirt that didn't require tucking.) This creativity evolved into an extensive line of casual wear for the shop. "He designed great pants for the beach," says Morrissey. "They were seamless and so good-looking; just one button and a zipper—and they didn't wrinkle. He had them in all colors."[8] Mike Connolly attended the store's February 1956 preview party and reported, "Walters is offering for sale a hand-woven Siamese shirt with solid gold nuggets for buttons and cufflinks for $250. No takers yet." Friendly jibes aside, Chuck Walters Presents was touted by friends and handsomely received by the public. The successful haberdashery eventually moved to the Del Mar Hotel in 1961 before closing later that decade.

In addition to an entrepreneurial outlet, Palm Springs also provided Walters with a new companion. Morrissey remembers, "Manuel Alvarez, the shop's co-manager, was a close friend of mine. One day at the store he said, 'I'm giving a party in my room tonight. You should come.' Well, there was one picture on a shelf that had always caught my eye. I said, 'Who's that? He's good-looking.' Manuel said, 'That's Chuck Walters, the movie director. He owns this place. He'll be at the party.'" That evening, Jimie locked eyes with the man in the photograph, and although Chuck was twenty years his senior, they exchanged genuine compliments. As Morrissey puts it, "That was that." Their caring if casual romance continued for the next five years.

"The first restaurant Chuck took me to was Romanoffs in Beverly Hills, and he invited Mr. Romanoff over to the table to introduce me—and perhaps impress me," Morrissey recalls. Quite quickly, the young newcomer met others in Walters's circle, and one thing that was instantly apparent was John Darrow's ongoing hold over his former partner. "John didn't like Chuck to have a boyfriend. He preferred him to have a one-night stand. He kind of controlled him." Darrow's objections were a tad hypocritical, as he had already begun his own relationship with clean-cut new client Jonathan Gilmore. (The actor—who later married three times—maintains, "Darrow was very good to me, very influential in my life."[9] Although a frequent guest at the Malibu house, Gilmore never met Walters; more tellingly, he never heard John mention him.)

It had been three years since the high-water mark of *Lili,* and Metro continued to benefit from Walters's rising reputation. In thirty-six months, he had given the studio two lucrative aqua-musicals (*Dangerous When Wet, Easy to Love*), a soap opera with music (*Torch Song*), a fairy tale with a twist (*The Glass Slipper*), a smart comedy (*The Tender Trap*), and a runaway smash (*High Society*). It was an eclectic collection, but the director was the first to admit they all had a common denominator: he'd been tagged "a woman's director."

"We'd get typecast," Chuck would say, "just as actors were typecast." Throughout the 1950s, the studio continued to align his name with those of its female stars: "Walters to direct Ava Gardner in *The Paris Story*" or "Debbie Reynolds will be guided by Walters in *The Reluctant Debutante*." Though usually amenable, the director resisted some of the possibilities. He was particularly vehement about Metro's proposed musical version of Eugene O'Neill's *Anna Christie,* largely because he disapproved of their implausible choice for leading lady: Doris Day. ("I think Chuck and the others are crazy," Helen Deutsch expressed to Schary. "I finally saw a couple of Doris Day films. She is absolutely perfect for the role of Anna.")[10] The property eventually moved to Broadway, calibrated for the multifaceted Gwen Verdon as *New Girl in Town.*

Walters, with calculation, next accepted *Don't Go Near the Water.* "I didn't really want to make that movie," he admitted. "It was a [military comedy] about sailors, which I found boring. But my agent wanted me to avoid getting a reputation like Cukor's—to be the kind of director who only did movies for women or musicals. So I decided to do it."

Based on William Brinkley's best-seller, *Don't Go Near the Water* harked back to World War II and a group of bored sailors working in naval relations on a combat-free South Pacific island. The property was produced by Lawrence Weingarten, who'd overseen *The Tender Trap,* but apart from old friend Keenan Wynn (in his M-G-M swan song), Walters was set to guide a new generation of actors: Earl Holliman, Russ Tamblyn, Jeff Richards (identified in the director's personal script as "Yummy

Jeffie"), Fred Clark, Anne Francis, Eva Gabor, and Gia Scala. The last re-placed Anna Kashfi, who withdrew due to illness several weeks into film-ing. Although Ernest Borgnine had been considered, Glenn Ford won the leading role of soft-spoken Lt. Max Siegel.

A two-day read-through of the heavily subplotted script launched production and provided the director an opportunity to formulate an overview of the completed movie. "The way it's arranged in episodes is a curious effect," he said, "but [this] allowed us to introduce a new charac-ter or a new situation at any time. When Mickey Shaughnessy comes in [at midpoint], for example, we're really ready for something new." Shaugh-nessy portrayed Farragut Jones, a brawny seaman selected to represent the "ideal navy man" at public events despite his penchant for a certain obscenity (drowned out by a soundtrack boat horn). "His sequence is one of my favorites out of all my films. We had a lot of trouble finding the right noise to cover up the dirty word—in fact, he said 'stinking' and not 'fucking'—but finally someone came upon this marvelously ugly sound effect." The director was also proud of the explosive climax he devised for the first love scene between Holliman and Francis, "where you know that he is very excited. . . . [And] cannon-fire *could* make people think of an orgasm. It was pretty daring for the time but, after all, it *was* a war scene, and that's *what* cannons do."

Filming began March 4 and lasted thirty-four days. The New York opening on November 14 proved victorious, and the picture's box of-fice—$4.5 million in North American rentals alone—won Walters a second-place Exhibitor Laurel Award for Top Comedy of 1957. The pub-lic's enthusiasm was matched by critics' cheers. "It's rowdy, clever, per-fectly cast, and hilarious," praised Mae Tinee at the *Chicago Daily Tribune,* "a combination of many forms of humor—sly wit, scathing parody, deftly handled ribaldry, and a bit of just plain old slapstick, all presented at a smooth, sparkling pace."[11] *Variety* was similarly admiring: "Walters' direction is paced at full throttle and organized remarkably well, considering the numerous separate little adventures tucked into the overall smooth continuity."[12]

On page two of Walters's script, the following preamble was later typed: "The end results look effortless, no? . . . In retrospect, there was much fun, yes—teamwork (in spades)—some strife (but the Navy is quite familiar with strife)—a bit of gnashing of teeth—scratching of brows—Oh, you know . . . But, if not, bear with me while I turn back the clock, then you'll soon be convinced (maybe) that one should never, never GO NEAR THE WATER."[13]

A brief lull in Chuck's Hollywood schedule was broken by sad news on June 12, when Robert Alton died from a kidney ailment at age fifty-five. It was a shattering development for many who'd worked with the veteran choreographer—especially his one-time Broadway and Hollywood protégé. Though there had been some friction during their work at M-G-M, Alton had provided Walters with outstanding career opportunities, a priceless theatrical education, and the all-important lesson that superior staging, coupled with vital dancing, could enliven and excite an audience.

"When I have a dance to do," Alton once quietly reflected, "I study the script, listen to the music, and then go away and dream."[14]

"I was told that I was not an *auteur* director," Walters said in 1980. "John Darrow, my manager, said this many years ago, that I was not an *auteur*—I was a company director. And I thought, 'Gee, I guess I am.'"[15] The studio, he recognized, was the *auteur,* and if there was any doubt that film production at M-G-M (particularly on a musical) was a group effort, his next project would confirm that fact.

Gigi, a costly Freed-Minnelli production based on the Colette novella, planned to wrap its three-month shooting schedule in Culver City in October 1957. (The M-G-M soundstages were thriftily employed to complete work that hadn't been accomplished during approximately ten weeks of location filming in France.) Among the remaining sequences was "The Night They Invented Champagne," an Alan Jay Lerner–Frederick Loewe song intended for young Gigi, Grandmamma, and playboy Gaston (played by Leslie Caron, Hermione Gingold, and Louis Jourdan, respectively). The intimate number required staging that reflected the trio's growing excitement over an imminent trip to the seaside. "We needed ideas," recalls Caron, "and direction for movement."[16] Walters agreed to provide this as "a family favor" for Freed, and the *Los Angeles Times* announced that the unbilled director had been "lured into acting as Caron's choreographer."[17]

"It was a short thing," cinematographer Joseph Ruttenberg said of the routine, "but it required a lot of rehearsal, because none of the people were dancers, except Leslie."[18] Walters worked with the actors for four full days, determining how each would stay in character while in the midst of song. Jourdan enacted the gracious host, Gingold became the giddy girl she once was, and Caron effusively started to can-can—the mischievous Gigi obviously intrigued by the "naughty" dance. All three mimicked the sound of popping champagne corks, and a gusty polka made the most of the room's limited parameters. The result was nonstop ebullience, and once Walters completed rehearsals, Minnelli committed the scene to film. (The latter's biographer, Mark Griffin, has keenly observed that Vincente "graced [*Gigi*] with a stately elegance, but it was Walters who added a welcome ingredient: energy. Throughout the film, the principals often perform their songs while seated. In a refreshing change of pace, Walters gets everyone up on their feet and moving.")[19] Freed was genuinely appreciative and wrote: "Dear Chuck: It was so nice of you to help us on the sequence in *Gigi*. It really turned out fine. It was good to be with you again. As ever, Arthur."[20]

Completed by month's end, *Gigi* was "sneaked" twice to mixed results, and Lerner and Loewe immediately requested $300,000 worth of retakes. When the Metro hierarchy refused, the composer and lyricist bluntly offered to buy the film outright for $3 million. Stunned (and nonplussed) by the bluff, the executives approved the additional expenditure, and a nine-day schedule of retakes was set for February 10–20, 1958. With both Minnelli and Ruttenberg in Europe filming *The Reluctant Debutante,* Freed placed the *Gigi* revisions squarely on the shoulders of Walters and cinematographer Ray June. "Arthur had given me the opportunity to be a director in the first place," said Chuck. "It was flattering to be asked."

This wasn't the first time a substitute director had been called in to complete a Minnelli picture. Donen provided finishing touches and retakes on *Kismet* (1955), and Cukor added to *Lust for Life* (1956). For *Gigi,* Freed "dragged Chuck in," recalled sound advisor Lela Simone, "not [for] grandiose things, but small things. . . . I mean, they were in a panic. Absolute panic. It had to be done. . . . He smoothed all the rough edges in the picture."[21] The film's leading lady remembers Walters's contributions differently. "History has now inflated his participation beyond the truth," Caron feels. "Much as I loved Chuck, I have to insist that the rumor is wildly exaggerated."[22] Tales that Walters reshot much of the film are indeed inaccurate. "I often had a beginning and an end [of a sequence]," he recounted, "and I had to film the middle and tie it to the rest."[23] This does not, however, diminish his participation.[24]

The retooling of Jourdan's final "Soliloquy" began on day one, and the director admitted, "It was murder trying to have Louis make exits in Paris and match it with shots taken on Metro's Lot 2." The following morning, *Gigi*'s culminating proposal scene was tackled once more. Six takes were required to soften Gingold's final "thank heaven" blessing before Walters considered her reading heartfelt enough to end the picture. After lunch, cast and crew moved back to Lot 2 to lay out the exterior action for Caron's solo, "The Parisians," but nothing was filmed due to weather. There followed another all-day reshoot of Jourdan's "Soliloquy."

"She Is Not Thinking of Me" was initially photographed within the plush confines of Maxim's in Paris—a number "sung" in Gaston's head to reveal his mounting distrust of his mistress (Eva Gabor). "The [Minnelli-directed] dailies looked beautiful," recalled Lerner. "There was only one disturbing omission: there were no close-ups of Louis singing. And how can an audience know a song is being sung in someone's head if one cannot see the head?"[25] A reconstituted (albeit less ostentatious) Maxim's was assembled at M-G-M, and Walters spent hours on February 14 staging Jourdan and showing Gabor how to animatedly primp, twitter, and flirt. Recognizing the need for a final kicker, Chuck instructed Louis to subdue Eva by dumping wine into her cleavage. "You can't do that," cried Freed. "It's crude." Lerner convinced Freed otherwise, prompting the director to later wryly comment: "Sometimes it's good to break away from parents."

Chuck's second week of retakes included the addition of movement to the opening of "The Parisians" and further work on "Soliloquy." He completed the picture on February 20, re-filming Gaston and Gigi's first scene together, as well as the comical finish to Caron's "Parisians" as the aggravated schoolgirl pulled her hat down over her face, crossed her arms, and slouched on a park bench. ("Innocent plagiarism," says Caron of that moment, having appropriated her final pose from Rex Harrison at the conclusion of *My Fair Lady*.)[26]

Memories of those involved in Walters's retakes would prove faulty over time. Caron doesn't fully recall redoing "The Parisians"; her recollections remain frozen on Minnelli's original waterside direction and his excitement at finally getting cooperation from the swans swimming behind her. (No swans appear in the final print, however, which suggests a retake.) Lerner's memories were equally hazy, and he erroneously insisted that Chuck filmed the duet between Gingold and Maurice Chevalier, "I Remember It Well." The Frenchman, however, did not participate in the marathon February revisions, and Walters insists that he and the *boulevardier* never met. The director himself later clarified aspects of the "Soliloquy" reshoot, noting that "they finally went back to Minnelli's original"—with its background of upstaging swans—despite all the time Chuck spent enlivening Jourdan's footage. Yet Walters's contributions to *Gigi* are significant. He staged and filmed the majority of two key numbers, one of which introduces the title character, while the other adds necessary appeal to the droning male protagonist. He provided subtextual characterization and choreography for "The Night They Invented Champagne" and also directed and filmed the central couple's initial conversation and climactic reconciliation.

With Chuck's warming enhancements and other editing and underscoring implementations, *Gigi* was previewed once again. "The reaction of the audience dramatically changed from appreciation to affection," acknowledges Lerner. "The studio still passed out those demented cards in the lobby, but it was not necessary to read them. We had all been a part of their spontaneous involvement. We had seen them with tears in their eyes at the moment there should have been tears in their eyes. And we heard their applause at the end." Per Walters: "Lerner and Loewe wanted to send a flowered horseshoe to say 'Thank You,' but they were afraid it would get back to Vincente."

At the thirty-first annual Academy Awards ceremony, *Gigi* won an unprecedented nine Oscars—ten if one counts a special honor for Chevalier. A triumphant Minnelli, later considered one of M-G-M's greatest *auteurs,* made his way to the podium to receive the statuette for Best Director of 1958. What he thought of the picture's final cut has never been recorded, but when he accepted the Oscar, he said it was "about the proudest moment of my life."[27] Walters remained silent on the matter for almost two decades. Around the lot, however, it was no secret that a distance existed between the two directors long before *Gigi.* Chuck would later explain the difference in their approach—and compensation: "Vincente paints with people, and lets himself get carried away, and avoids worrying about the budget. So even though he was a great director and had lots of success, they paid him less, and gave him a bonus afterwards—if the budget had been respected. Since it never was, he never got that bonus."[28]

By 1961, they were the only veteran M-G-M directors who remained under contract. "But," Chuck liked to add, "I was better paid."

23

A Virgin and a Housewife

Although proving he could tackle a wider variety of assignments with *Don't Go Near the Water,* Walters returned to familiar "woman's director" territory for his next two projects. *Ask Any Girl* starred Shirley MacLaine, and *Please Don't Eat the Daisies* top-billed Doris Day, with both comedies benefiting from the playful approach of producer Joe Pasternak. The happy Hungarian was now working independently through his own Euterpe Corporation—which utilized M-G-M distribution channels—and he cast both women opposite refined British actor David Niven, then at the height of his film stardom. ("David was witty," said MacLaine, "and an excellent technician in both comedy and drama. He never missed his marks, was always in his light, was letter-perfect in his lines, but he never looked me in the eye. . . . Years later, when I saw his performance in *Separate Tables,* I was ashamed I hadn't recognized the depth he was capable of as an actor.")[1]

Adapted from a Winifred Wolfe novel, *Ask Any Girl* followed the adventures of naive Meg Wheeler (MacLaine) as she struggles with the wolves of New York City. Surrounding her are stuffy boss Miles Doughton (Niven), his playboy brother (Gig Young), hormonal executive Rod Taylor, lecherous employer Jim Backus, and chirpy friends Elizabeth Frasier and Dody Heath. Unremittingly sexist by contemporary standards, the film has been stamped (if not completely dismissed) as an archetypical 1950s "women's picture." MacLaine bristles at the notion. "The term 'women's picture' never really came up in Hollywood until the middle of the '70s, when women were being redefined in our culture as a result of the success of the women's movement. Until then, pictures about women's lives starring Joan Crawford, Lana Turner, and Bette Davis were pictures for everybody. . . . If pictures with women are termed 'women's pictures,'" MacLaine counters, "why are pictures with men just 'pictures'?"[2]

Sans any analysis, Walters enjoyed getting to know this bright, youthful eccentric. She had made seven movies in four years, demonstrating an impressive versatility. Best of all, the camera loved her. Director and star—both former Broadway gypsies—bonded at once, and he adored her free use of expletives, particularly "shit." ("Boy, I really dig that word, don't I?" she wrote him once.)[3] Chuck let Shirley set the pace of the film, a decision that showcased her unspoiled spirit and curiosity.

The forty-three-day production—yet another classified by its director as "fun"—filmed from December 1, 1958, through January 19, 1959, and Walters again demonstrated his command of the genre:

> You try to throw the comedy over your shoulder, [and] let it take care of itself. You start from the insight in the scene and, after that, see where the jokes naturally come in. It's a good general rule that if a scene itself *isn't* funny, you can't make it funny with stage business or overplaying. In the lunch counter scene, for example, the three girls [MacLaine, Frasier, and Heath] had read their lines at home, and they came in ready to do it all up with little sighs and winks. But I told them to forget they were playing comedy. All they had to do was play the scene—it's the scene that's funny.[4]

Both stars experienced career high points during the *Ask Any Girl* shoot. On set, Niven received word of the New York Film Critics Circle Award for his 1958 performance in *Separate Tables* ("Shirley let out one of her traffic-stopping shrieks," the actor related).[5] MacLaine joined him as an Academy Award nominee soon thereafter. Niven then won Best Actor for *Tables* on April 6, 1959, which—along with MacLaine's recognition (if not an Oscar) for *Some Came Running*—made them the favorite screen team of the moment. This was borne out a few weeks later when *Girl* "achieved the highest rating ever given an M-G-M film at a New York sneak preview. . . . [A] capacity audience roared approval. . . . 99.4 percent of the audience highly recommended the film."[6] Booked into Radio City Music Hall that May, the comedy did capacity business and earned almost half a million dollars in its first three weeks.

The critics were as pleased as the bookkeepers. "Ask any girl (or fellow) about *Ask Any Girl*," declared Philip Scheuer in the *Los Angeles Times,* "and the answer is almost sure to be a rousing 'Yes!' This new MGM comedy . . . has been put together by experts."[7] In the *San Francisco News,*

Emelia Hodel identified the key expert: "That the movie has a shine and sparkle of sophistication is the work of Walters, one of Filmville's top comedy directors. He knows just how far to go with a gag or double entendre to keep them in good taste and still give them the slant of burlesque. . . . [W]e bow to the team of Pasternak and Walters."[8] (In turn, the jubilant team immediately announced forthcoming projects: comedies *Please Don't Eat the Daisies, Where the Boys Are,* and *The Courtship of Eddie's Father;* a biopic of World War I–era singer Elsie Janis for MacLaine; and the drama *Unholy Spring.* Eventually, only the first of these was directed by Walters.)

Ask Any Girl earned $3,475,000 against a $1,140,000 budget and was the first genuine hit for Pasternak's Euterpe.[9] Chuck escorted his boyfriend and Debbie Reynolds to the Hollywood premiere—Jimie's first exposure to the hoopla of a big studio event. "It was at the Egyptian," Morrissey remembers. "We pulled up in Debbie's car, and there were klieg lights everywhere. The place was *filled* with people; I thought it was more like the Oscars."[10] On the strength of the film's unqualified reception, the men continued on "to a party at Joe Pasternak's house. He lived in Bel Air, and it was the kind of sprawling house that reminded you of those mansions in *Gone with the Wind.* Pasternak's wife was very pretty, and when we arrived, she was standing outside greeting her guests. Everybody was telling her how much they loved the film and how much money it was going to make. As we got out of the car and walked toward that enormous house, she threw open her arms and cried out, 'Oh, thank you, Chuck . . . *you've saved Tara!*'"

By then, Walters was already deep into pre-production on *Please Don't Eat the Daisies,* an immediate pleasure thanks to scenarist Isobel Lennart. "She had a nearby house in Malibu," remembers Morrissey, "right down Paradise Cove. She was so sweet and fun" that Chuck gave her the affectionate nickname "Maw."[11]

Lennart had a long and complicated history at M-G-M. She had been fired from the mailroom in 1934 after attempting to organize a union. Two years later, she returned as a script girl and ultimately wrote screenplays for a couple of dozen films, including such Pasternak confections as *Anchors Aweigh* (1945) and *Holiday in Mexico* (1946). Her female characterizations were much like the lady herself: self-reliant, self-possessed, and armed with a good sense of humor. When HUAC emerged on the scene in the early 1950s, Lennart fought against "naming names" but ultimately caved to the pressure; it was a decision she regretted all her life. Pasternak, however, hired her to write *Skirts Ahoy!* (1952), *Love Me or Leave Me* (1954), and—in 1958—*Please Don't Eat the Daisies,* based on Jean Kerr's popular, fictionalized account of married life with *New York Herald Tribune* theater critic Walter Kerr. "Isobel did very good work on that script," Walters commented, "especially starting from a novel that wasn't terribly cinematic." In Lennart's adaptation, Columbia University drama professor Lawrence Mackay (played by Niven) trades academia for an elite newspaper position as a Broadway theater critic, quickly alienating both his best friend, who is a theatrical producer, and a Broadway leading lady. Mackay's devoted wife (Doris Day) simultaneously relocates their household, including four mischievous sons and a cowardly sheepdog, from an uptown Manhattan apartment to a decaying suburban home.

Although there was enough backstage flavor to keep Walters engaged, he sensed he wasn't the perfect director for the movie. "I'm a bachelor," he acknowledged, "and I wondered if I was going to be able to do a good scene with the 'typical' family." He was also nervous about working with Day, of whom he "was not a fan." Lennart's sweet-and-sassy characterization, however, assuaged any trepidation. "My God," he admitted after reading the screenplay, "this *is* Doris Day."[12] The actress felt much the same way: "All my life, I just wanted to be married and have children and the big dog (or six) and the big house. That's what [*Daisies*] was, with everything going crazy in it. So it was the perfect film for me. I adored it."[13]

Walters and Pasternak once again gathered superlative supporting players: Patsy Kelly as a wisecracking maid, Jack Weston as an agreeably ambitious cab driver and wannabe playwright, Margaret Lindsay as a condescending actress, Richard Hayden as Mackay's fussy impresario cohort, and—in a piece of inspired casting—doting and daffy Spring Byington as Day's mother. Chuck was even able to employ Cole Porter's longtime lover, Joe Corbin, as a callow pianist who makes a pass at Doris while (not surprisingly) playing Porter's "Easy to Love" and "I Concentrate on You."

Betty Grable was everyone's first choice for the plum role of Deborah Vaughn, the film's musical comedy temptress. Over luncheon with the star, Walters explained his plans for a Grable-esque, sequins-and-feathers production number intended for the movie's show-within-the-plot, *Mlle. Fantan.* (The theater's neon marquee of a woman wiggling her derrière paid sly homage to Grable's legendary World War II pinup photo.) Grable reportedly loved everything she was hearing, until Chuck mentioned the early August start date. "Oh, but sweetie," she demurred, "that's when Santa Anita opens." Walters would later sigh, "With Betty, horse racing came first."

The striking and comedically adept Janis Paige arrived in her stead. Though a veteran of diverse film roles, Paige won her real stardom on Broadway in the Jerome Robbins–Bob Fosse hit *The Pajama Game* (1953) and was therefore grateful her *Daisies* director had his roots in musical comedy. "Chuck was an actor's director and a good musical director," she said. "He could break down any scene. He could do with an acting scene what a good acting director would do. But he could also turn around and know what to do with musicals. So you had the combination—one of the few. And a gentle man."[14]

Near the end of pre-production, Pasternak arranged a July "company picnic" so that the adult actors could meet the four juveniles who would play the Mackay boys: Charles Herbert, Flip Mark, Baby Gellert, and future *My Three Sons* co-star Stanley Livingston. Walters, unused to working with youngsters, tacitly studied the boys at play, and later incorporated their impulsive antics into his direction: "In this way, I was able to get them to project as children—not child actors."[15]

"He'd pull us aside and give us direction," Stanley Livingston recounts,

like how to fill a paper bag full of water. "Now you fold it like *this* and hold it *this* way." Or "Now you skip into the scene like *this*." Everything was rehearsed, all those bits of business. They had to be; as soon as you pull that trigger on the camera, it costs you money. Chuck was pretty patient, and so were we. Life on a movie set can be tedious, but we were professional children actors. I think the older cast members were asked to keep us occupied while the crew set up a scene. Jack Weston was the sweetest man; he always joined us between takes, wrestling and stuff. Doris would play horseshoes, and Spring Byington was teaching us how to play poker. It was a very good experience . . . and I've been on some film sets where it wasn't, where the director was . . . well, a screamer. Henry Hathaway directing *How the West Was Won*—now *he* was a screamer.[16]

Chuck launched *Daisies* on August 3 with an all-day rehearsal for the film's opening apartment sequence. In it, the Mackay boys—armed with

Walters's choreographed "bits of business"—relentlessly drive their mother to distraction while she attempts to prepare for an evening out. ("Just once in my life I'd like to get dressed without an audience," she sighs.) The following day, the director received a note from his star: "If all the days on *Daisies* are as nice as the first one, I hope it never ends. Love, Doris."[17]

Walters's reservations about working with Day were quickly put to rest. "To know her is to love her," he would say, "and I loved working with her." Pasternak had already starred the popular singer in his dramatic *Love Me or Leave Me* and recognized that, "for all her effervescence and apparent *joie de vivre*, I sometimes have the feeling Doris is busting inside. Sure, Doris is a wonderful, wholesome girl, but she *is* complex, and she *does* have uncertainties about herself. That's what makes her such a great performer. Simple girls can't act."[18]

Her casting, however, meant a side helping of manager-husband Marty Melcher, who negotiated himself into all of Day's deals. He took a fee for her services, expected co-producer status, and constantly sent memos with his opinions of scenes and songs—even when they didn't involve his wife. (In the film's cocktail party sequence, Paige confronts Niven about a published critique on the appearance of her "fanny" and asks if he is "flexible enough" to change his mind. She then turns and saunters away, and he admits, "I was wrong." Melcher viewed the rushes and pontificated: "I must admit, in all honesty, if I were the critic, I wouldn't change [my mind]. It may be the angle of the camera, but she looks like a lady with a very large problem.")[19] Despite such unwarranted interference, Walters invited the Melchers to the beach, and not too long after they took a nearby rental. "So what happens?" Hedda Hopper reported. "They're rehearsing scenes for *Daisies* on the sands of Malibu."[20]

Pasternak approved a budget of nearly $2 million, as well as his director's request for some location filming in New York (agreeing to the latter, laughed Chuck, "as if he was doing me an *enormous* favor"). Lennart remained in Malibu, writing two potential Walters productions: *Restless Night*, a romantic comedy for Niven, and *Two for the Seesaw*, an adaptation of the Broadway play for MacLaine. She nonetheless sent her long-distance support—in verse—to Manhattan.

Dear dear *dear* Chuck:
> When the problems of our Daisy
> Begin to drive you somewhat crazy.

Do not weep and wail and mope
Or cry to Heaven, "I'm a dope!"
There are ways, if you ain't lazy
To escape from any maze-y (Oy!)
First you take a sidelong look
At any chapter in this book.
If your hand's still not on throttle,
Take a gulp from outta the bottle.
Then if you still feel all alone
Just pick up the telephone.
Give a yell for dear old Maw
She'll climb off her new "Seesaw."
She'll chop outta the mean old scripp
Whatever's made her nice boy flip!

Love + kisses, Maw [21]

Thanks to its theatrical milieu, *Daises* evolved into a semi-musical, and four songs were slotted—three for Day's character and one for Paige's Vaughn. Doris reprised her Oscar-winning "Whatever Will Be, Will Be" from *The Man Who Knew Too Much* (1956); the licensing fee added $5,000 to the budget. She also ukuleled her way through the movie's title song by Joe Lubin and performed the coy "Any Way the Wind Blows" in a scene set in a community theater rehearsal. When the film was released, Melcher mercilessly pushed the last of these tunes on disc jockeys.

Paige was handed Josef Myrow's flashy "(I Think) It's Here to Stay." Written with Grable in mind—Myrow penned several of her scores at Fox—the intentionally tacky star-with-chorus showcase was allotted two weeks to rehearse, pre-record, and film. "It would have been so perfect to do a bad number with Betty," said Walters, "because you can take any of her [movie] numbers and say, 'She can't sing, she can't dance, but she looks great!' With anybody else you say, *How do you do a bad number?* So that's why we finally eliminated [Paige's] number. We could have done just a straight Betty Grable number, and it would have been fine. [We] could have torn it apart. That's all the critics did anyway."

Filming wrapped on October 7, and Chuck immediately left for Europe with Roger Edens to scout circus talent for a much-anticipated production of *Jumbo*. The enjoyment of the trip abroad (Walters's first on an M-G-M expense account) was heightened a few days before Christmas when Pasternak cabled him at Rome's Hotel Excelsior: "*Daisies* previewed New York. Withstood severe snowstorm. Got excellent reaction. Booked Music Hall for Easter. Have fun. Love, Joe."[22] On Chuck's return, he viewed the finished film and admitted, "I really like the scene with the mother-in-law at the Plaza; they don't have anywhere to go, so they go [into] the bathroom. Niven sits on the edge of the shower, and she sits down across from him. I think it was pretty funny to see Spring Byington, all pretty with her little hat, and then you realize she's sitting on the toilet seat."

Please Don't Eat the Daisies was M-G-M's big spring offering for 1960. "It truly had a cast that would appeal to every age group," Livingston remembers. "I'm not surprised it became a hit. It's clever. It's in the writing."[23] The notices, however, were mixed, and several key reviewers took personal offense at the perceived ridicule of a theater critic. "So completely preposterous," bellowed Bosley Crowther,[24] while Philip K. Scheuer declaimed, "Improbable . . . any resemblance between Lawrence Mackay and any drama critic I ever heard of is purely co-incidental."[25] The *Hollywood Reporter* thought differently and applauded, "Pasternak, Walters, and Miss Lennart have collaborated to create a bright, clean film, sparkling with all the attributes of comedy."[26] (*Daisies* had enough popular appeal to warrant an afterlife as a weekly family sitcom on NBC-TV from 1965 to 1967.)

The film itself brought in $5.38 million—M-G-M's biggest box-office success for 1960 after the enduring *Ben-Hur* and the Elizabeth Taylor–Eddie Fisher *BUtterfield-8*—which scored on the heat of the stars' illicit off-camera love affair.

In a more personal achievement, Walters placed third on the industry's list of the top moneymaking directors of the 1959–1960 season. (Minnelli was seventh, Sidney ninth, and Cukor tenth.)[27] At nearly fifty years old, Chuck was at the very top of his game.

24

Spoiled Spinster

"At M-G-M, we worked on a lot of pictures that we didn't take credit for," Gene Kelly once explained. "Chuck always seemed to be in line if somebody broke a leg, or went away, or whatever. They'd call on Chuck, and he'd finish a [film]. He did a lot of that."[1] In April 1960, with *Daisies* a smash, Metro asked the obliging Walters to assist in yet another cleanup job that wouldn't have as successful an outcome as *Gigi*.

The studio had engaged director Anthony Mann to resuscitate the 1931 Best Picture, *Cimarron,* in the hopes that it would continue the return-to-epic formula that *Ben-Hur* (1959) had lucratively initiated. *Cimarron's* preview in spring 1960, however, proved a disaster, and Hedda Hopper reported, "Metro decided added scenes were necessary. They had to fly [actress] Maria Schell over from Munich, Anne Baxter from Australia, and get a new director, Chuck Walters, to finish it."[2] (On his recent European sojourn, Chuck had discussed with Schell the possibility of doing a movie about modern dance pioneer Isadora Duncan.) All the efforts were fruitless; even with Walters's additions, Mann's stodgy *Cimarron* remained an expensive misfire and lost over $3.6 million.[3]

The western genre, Chuck joked, "wasn't *really* my thing. One of the first scenes I did was with 'the bad guys.' I remember the prop guy came to ask where I wanted them to tie up the horses. I answered that I didn't have the slightest idea, and they'd do better to ask the horses."[4]

He was assigned another salvage job when the provocatively titled *Go Naked in the World* was shelved after its first preview. Gina Lollobrigida was a beautiful but unintelligible star, and it was—in Walters's own words—a "horrible" film. "I redid the beginning," he recalled, "and [then] Gina said she'd be willing to work for free if they let me redo the whole film!"[5] Producer Aaron Rosenberg, eager for more fixes, pitched his plan for re-shooting to *Naked* co-star Anthony Franciosa. "Aaron began to explain, with great care, that M-G-M wanted to redo all of Lollobrigida's close-ups," recalled Franciosa's then-wife, actress Shelley Winters, "and that he needed Tony on set to feed her the lines and cues. . . . Chuck, wonderful at directing women, would be brought in to work with her. Tony seemed to understand everything Aaron was saying."[6]

On the first morning of retakes, however, Winters was frantically paged to the studio. "By the time I got [there]," she recounted, "I was shaking. Chuck and Aaron met me at the front of the stage door. I knew Chuck from my musical comedy days. . . . He was a very beloved director to all the actors who had ever worked with him. . . . Chuck's lip was bleeding, and his right eye was turning purple and yellow. A car from the M-G-M hospital arrived, and he said, 'Shelley, don't be upset. I'm going to the hospital now. I'll be back on my set after lunch.'"

Rosenberg was left to explain the events of the morning. After Lollobrigida's first retake, the crew began to disassemble the makeshift set, and Franciosa suddenly hissed, "Wait! Don't I get to improve *my* work?" Chuck kidded, "Listen, I'm just a guest here," but his face was the nearest target for the actor's immediate frustration. Winters went to comfort her husband, who was "shaking and wet" in his small dressing room. "Tony was trying to treat the whole morning as a joke, but when he took a good look at Chuck . . . in the light, he walked away from the set for a moment." The repentant Franciosa returned "and, in tears, apologized profusely."

"Needless to say," adds Jimie Morrissey, "when Chuck came home that night he was quite upset. I had a scotch and soda waiting."[7] The director wanted to keep the matter private but couldn't conceal his bruised face. "Chuck always turned everything into comedy," says Leslie Caron, vividly remembering the black eye. "Everybody at the studio asked him how he got that, and each time he invented a new story. When I asked, he said, 'I happened to tell an M-G-M executive that I didn't like *Ben-Hur*.'"[8]

For all its subsequent failure, *Go Naked in the World* was representative of the "new" Hollywood film. American moviegoers had begun to abandon the dictates of the much-weakened Production Code; M-G-M's biggest star in 1960 was Elizabeth Taylor, with her scandal-prone personal life and racy recent hits, *Cat on a Hot Tin Roof, BUtterfield 8,* and

Suddenly, Last Summer. (Of the last, producer Sam Spiegel purportedly quipped, "A dash of incest, rape, sodomy, and cannibalism never hurt at the box office.") The loosened censorship helps explain *The Spinster,* arguably the most puzzling film assignment of Walters's career.

Based on Sylvia Ashton-Warner's novel, *The Spinster* was scripted by Ben Maddow (who had been blacklisted by HUAC) and described the plight of a Pennsylvania woman who traveled to the backcountry of New Zealand as a teacher. Maddow's explicit sexual approach had less to do with Ashton-Warner's courageous heroine than with a triangular relationship between a virginal educator, a neurotic male co-worker, and an unhappily married school inspector. Themes of adultery, pedophilia, teenage pregnancy, and suicide caught the attention of the Production Code office, which quickly submitted three pages of objections. "Whore" needed to be changed to "tart"; a reference to menstruation needed to be omitted; the line "She was sore, very sore" needed to be replaced with "She was tired." There was additional concern that an umbrella and umbrella stand had the "possibility of a phallic interpretation."[9] Filming nonetheless commenced without a Code-approved script.

Production head Sol Siegel gave Walters the job of directing, confident he would "capture all the values of the script," and recent M-G-M arrival Julian Blaustein was announced as producer.[10] By late August 1960, they had assembled their principal cast: Shirley MacLaine as the virginal Anna, *BUtterfield 8*'s Lawrence Harvey as the abusive Paul, and *Ben-Hur*'s Jack Hawkins in the sympathetic role of Superintendent Abercrombie. Chuck took immediate action and called off a planned New Zealand location shoot after screening advance second unit footage that "didn't seem too interesting. I didn't see how we could justify the enormous expense to go and film there." Production 1770 instead was completed on a Culver City soundstage, dressed (as *Time* magazine would eventually sneer) with the "artsy-craftsy exotica of Trader Vic's."[11]

On October 14, "on the eve of battle," Siegel offered Walters his encouragement. "I again say you're a wonderful guy," he wrote. "You've taken enormous responsibility off my hands with a minimum of trouble; I may never forgive you for this. Good luck—God bless you."[12] Despite such well-wishes, filming was both hurried and tense. The director brooded over the script, fought for rehearsal time, and attempted to placate two stars who truly could not bear each other. MacLaine, in particular, found

Harvey "insensitive and pompous."[13] Although principal photography was slated to run through mid-December, there was additional pressure from the fact that Harvey was due at Paramount on November 19 to begin Tennessee Williams's *Summer and Smoke*. "This is absolutely murderous," Walters complained to visiting reporter Murray Schumach. "We've got to do all our key scenes in one bunch. Every day and every moment is a climactic scene. I have never done anything like this before, and I *never* want to do anything like this again. There is not enough time for anything, least of all for rehearsal, which is particularly important in this sort of rush situation."[14] Harvey agreed, protesting the far-from-ideal conditions to Schumach—after which, the reporter noted, "Miss MacLaine uttered a derisive, one-word rebuttal."[15]

Siegel stayed involved, voicing concern over MacLaine's deglamorization and Harvey's too-forceful performance. Yet when a half hour of *The Spinster* was screened for him in early November, the studio chief (troubled by bad reports from several other big-budget productions) decided he "couldn't be happier."[16]

Walters planned to begin *The Spinster* with a psychological dream "prologue," so that audiences "would understand and be interested" in the complexities of MacLaine's character.

It's a sequence that came to me partially in a dream, and that we filmed in the desert near Palm Springs. You see Shirley running in the sand, barefoot and hair windblown, wearing a robe under which one can imagine her to be naked. She finds a dead rabbit in some thorns and starts to tenderly cradle it. You hear— and begin to see in the distance—a motorcycle coming in her direction. Excited by the arrival of the motorcycle, she drops the rabbit. She grabs the biker, who lets her do it, and leads him to a nearby cave. From behind, we see her rip off the robe, then pull the man on top of her, and then pull a dirty tarp over them both. At that moment, we hear the noise of rocks falling and, little by little, the sound of the rocks transforms itself into the sound of an alarm clock ringing. A trembling hand shuts off the alarm, then nervously takes a cigarette, leaves the frame and then returns to grab the matches; we follow the hand this time, and we see that it's Shirley sitting up in bed, who has just had this dream.

Later, when we meet the man from the dream—Laurence Harvey—we discover that he's the opposite of this passive object she'd dreamed of. He's aggressive and rebellious, the "when do we fuck?" type. And she's very afraid of him and his advances. But we understand from the dream that she's a frustrated woman, torn between contradictory feelings about her sexuality.[17]

The sexually charged sequence was a reminder of just how fast adult themes were overtaking Hollywood. ("I remember a love scene in *Ask Any Girl*," said MacLaine, "that was impossible to stage because I couldn't do it with one of my feet on the floor"—then a Code requirement).[18] Siegel thought the raw dream footage "should cut up into a very exciting, provocative sequence. [But] unless you want both of us arrested, you had better get me a protective cut on Shirley and Larry in the pit. Keep up the good work."[19]

By December 8, Siegel had had a change of opinion. He watched the edited nocturnal adventure in context with most of the film and told producer Blaustein:

I have the utmost confidence in Chuck because of his creative ability and his extraordinary talent, but I would be remiss in not pointing out that this dream sequence has thrown me for a loop every time I have run it. I must tell you that Chuck and I have a very good relationship, and I have found him to be not only a fine creative talent but someone who understands the overall meaning of the film. . . .

Chuck has done a wonderful job in holding on to the characters and making them work within the confines of this unusual story. However, his sensitivity cannot blind us to the fact that film is film, and the dream sequence does *bother the hell out of me*. It is bizarre, unusual, and frankly if this picture opened after the dream sequence [set] in New York City, I would believe it—but I would not believe it in New Zealand. . . . Let's bear in mind that Chuck had very little time for preparation, and I am sure that he would be the first to recognize the fact [of] what it is good or bad [for the film].[20]

Siegel had the erotica removed and then kept a more vigilant eye on the proceedings. He listened when Walters argued for a scene wherein MacLaine's character stopped defending her virginity. Per Chuck:

> I said to myself that I was going to hate this woman if she didn't at least *try* to give herself to [Harvey]. So finally she decided to give in to his advances.
>
> She goes into her dimly-lit bedroom and, during a close-up of her face, we understand she is completely undressing, taking off her shoes, her stockings, her bra, and the sound is pretty suggestive. The close-up follows her while she walks to her dresser and, from behind, we see her lean over to look for something in a drawer. Finally, she takes out the black robe she was wearing in the dream and slips it over her shoulders, leaves the room and stands motionless in front of Harvey. He screams that she's acting like a lamb being taken to slaughter, that no one is that intent on depriving her of her *precious* virginity, and then he leaves— and she crumples to the floor.

Like MacLaine's wild dream, "they didn't dare keep that scene either," Walters sniffed. "Instead, they made me film a version where she '*can't*.' 'I *can't*,' she cries, 'I want to but . . . I just *can't*.' The first version was so much more interesting: that she tries and he mocks her."

The Spinster opened in May 1961 with a Production Code seal and the new title *Two Loves*. (A laughable alternative, *I'll Save My Love*, had been considered and rejected.) Critical reaction was primarily negative. "Spoiled Spinster" was the headline on *Time*'s pan.[21] "Outright Hollywood trash," offered *Newsday*.[22] And the movie was "so bad cinematically, and so reprehensible sociologically," said *Films in Review*, that "Walters should have declined this assignment."[23] Audiences stayed away, and more than fifty years later, MacLaine told *Daily Variety*, "I should have done *Breakfast at Tiffany's*. I did *Two Loves* instead, which I think was horrible."[24] The film's dispirited director concurred, stating in 1972, "I have bad things to say about the film as it stands now because—in fact—it was sort of castrated."

Yet Walters's professional future remained unusually secure, especially for that era. He'd signed a new five-year contact with Metro in March 1961 and was one of the few directors of any stature in Hollywood then working under such a long-term agreement. And his prospects for happiness under Metro's current regime seemed better than good. Loew's president Joseph Vogel had emphatically announced that M-G-M was once again going to make movies for a "family audience"—a demographic then dominated by product from the Walt Disney Studios.

Nothing could have pleased Chuck more. Two years earlier, he'd confessed to *Variety* a deep desire to return to song-and-dance entertainment: "What I'm pitching for is . . . one of the old-fashioned musicals . . . something with all the kicks of a circus, but with concentration on the story." He was referencing a looming pachyderm picture, and so eager was he to begin *Jumbo* that MacLaine wrote him to offer her own brand of encouragement: "Here's hoping you don't have to shovel elephant shit."[25]

25

"What Elephant?"

In 1935, *Jumbo* provided a flashy, final hurrah for New York's Hippodrome—a venue so expansive that it occupied the entire city block of Sixth Avenue between Forty-Third and Forty-Fourth Streets. Producer Billy Rose instructed designer Albert Johnson to decimate the theater's cavernous interior and place a new stage in the center, creating the illusion of a circus ring. The minimal book, in which two rival circus proprietors coped with an unanticipated romance between their offspring, was supplied by Ben Hecht and Charles MacArthur. In the role of a press agent for the big top, Jimmy Durante made his first entrance atop an elephant; bandleader Paul Whiteman had it somewhat easier and galloped in on a horse. The real star of the evening, however, was an oversize elephant named Big Rosie, who amply filled the title role. George Abbott directed, John Murray Anderson mounted the circus sequences, and the whole extravaganza was graced by an elegant Rodgers and Hart score. Despite the spectacle, and such eventual standards as "My Romance," "The Most Beautiful Girl in the World," and "Little Girl Blue," *Jumbo* ran for only five months (after rehearsing for six).

M-G-M paid a respectable $100,000 for the musical's screen rights in 1943, and Arthur Freed initially planned to co-star Garland and Rooney with Wallace Beery and Frank Morgan. Later in the decade, Garland (or Kathryn Grayson) was to be paired with Frank Sinatra, with Roger Edens as associate producer and Rouben Mamoulian as director. (In 1947, *Jumbo* was also discussed internally as a possible directorial bow for Chuck but was supplanted by the ready-to-go *Good News*.) Stanley Donen came to the property in 1952—with Red Skelton, Debbie Reynolds, and Donald O'Connor as his players—but it went no further than pre-production.

Walters began tackling the musical as the realization of a long-held dream. He enthusiastically requested three ideal co-workers: producer

Joe Pasternak ("because I could control him"), scenarist Sidney Sheldon ("Who better?"), and Edens (brought back to M-G-M after working independently elsewhere).[1] It was the "glory days" all over again as Chuck and Roger effortlessly slipped back into their earlier camaraderie. On their 1960 post-*Daisies* European "vacation," they searched Denmark, Italy, and England for distinctive circus acts, and after Walters filmed *Two Loves,* the talent search began anew in spring 1961.

"[Roger and I] used New York as our base," he remembered. "We saw the Ringling show at Madison Square Garden, the Clyde Beatty show in Ohio, [and] looked at more [performers] in Philadelphia and Hartford."[2] At New Jersey's Palisades Amusement Park, they found a good high-wire act, then moved on to Chicago and Toronto. "Supplementing this, for two months before the picture started, we held auditions for circus acts on the M-G-M back lot every Tuesday afternoon under the direction of our circus coordinator, Alexander Dobritch."[3] All the effort paid off, especially when the Beatty outfit supplied an elephant named Sydney to play the gentle Jumbo, as well as two of her 7,500-pound girlfriends, Hattie and Anna-May, to serve as doubles. This led Chuck to gleefully herald them as "performers with thirty years of experience between them!"[4]

Publicity about *Jumbo* began early. Two years before cameras turned, the excited director promised *New York Times* readers, "You won't have to be a circus buff to like this picture as I plan it. This will be a sweet love story, a sort of Romeo and Juliet in a circus tent."[5] His young Juliet was cast with *Daisies* matriarch Doris Day; she would play opposite handsome Irish actor Stephen Boyd, while Jimmy Durante coupled with the outrageous Martha Raye as the plot's senior lovers. "Sidney Sheldon and I started from scratch," said Walters at the time, "and did the screenplay together, more or less with our actors in mind."[6] Their new story line involved the family-owned Wonder Circus, circa 1910, where bareback rider Kitty Wonder (Day) has fallen in love with Sam Rawlins (Boyd), a newly hired laborer. To Kitty's dismay, Sam is eventually revealed as the son of a more prosperous circus owner with designs on their debt-ridden establishment and star attraction, Jumbo. "Our story," enthused Walters, "divides easily into three sections—we call them acts—and it's a yarn about rebuilding a sick circus. Our big number, 'Little Girl Blue,' goes on just before the second act intermission; then we have an upbeat third act."[7]

The director's passion was contagious. "Chuck was just in his element making that film," recalled Day. "He loved every minute of it, and we all felt that excitement."[8] Given her fondness for animals, the actress also enjoyed her pachyderm co-star. When they met, "it was love at first sight. I checked into M-G-M two months before the picture actually began . . . to get acquainted with Syd. One look, and I knew we'd be pals. . . . Needless to say, a lot of peanuts passed between us."[9] Day had further reason to exult. Like Walters, she hadn't made a musical in half a decade, and six Rodgers and Hart tunes were prepared for her return to the genre. (Edens augmented four songs from the stage score with two additional gems from their catalog: "This Can't Be Love" and "Why Can't I?")

In Martha Raye, *Jumbo* had another superb female vocalist, though Walters had to fight for her casting. "She was the only actress who could have played that role," he defended, "and she did a really good job." Raye, the real-life daughter of Irish carnival performers Reed & Hooper, had not made a film since Charles Chaplin's 1947 misstep, *Monsieur Verdoux.* For her return to the screen, she had the added guidance of her attentive *Jumbo* director. As assistant director William Shanks told an on-set reporter: "Martha Raye has always been a broad comedienne of the baggy-pants school. I think she is unhappy unless she can amuse the crew. It makes her feel secure in what she is doing, but it isn't necessarily good for the picture. . . . [S]he has to be a character rather than a mugger. Chuck's main problem is to keep her within the characterization, to cut her down a bit, and for this she is going to thank him. She'll think of herself as an actress, and when she sees the picture, she'll realize he's made a whole new career for her."[10]

Said Raye to the reporter: "If I told you what I think of [Chuck], you'd throw up. It would be—well, icky. And I'm a very icky girl. He acts everything out, shows you just what to do, and he's understanding. He appreciates it when you do things well. That's what actors like."[11]

Boyd also benefited from his director's experience. The chiseled brunette had established himself in drama, most notably as Messala in *Ben-Hur.* Though slated to play Marc Antony opposite Elizabeth Taylor in the much-delayed *Cleopatra,* he welcomed the circus musical instead. "I'll try anything once," he said, smirking, "like any good Irishman."[12] Walters later admitted that Boyd "tried very hard, but he just wasn't right," and his vocals were eventually dubbed. (Interestingly, the director's initial choice had been the Welshman who eventually filled Boyd's role in *Cleopatra.* "I had wanted [Richard] Burton. Almost got him too, but something in Egypt with Liz came up!")[13] Boyd's presence—on camera and off—was somewhat redeemed by his sense of humor. On one occasion, the actor was to drive a farm wagon drawn by a spirited horse, and Chuck asked, "Can you come around that curve a little faster?" Boyd responded with a question: "Didn't you see *Ben-Hur*?"[14]

Although the enormity of Cinerama was briefly considered, *Jumbo* was lavished instead with Panavision, Metrocolor, and a $5.3 million budget. Multiple acres of the Culver City back lot became sprawling circus terrain, and the studio liberally leased props used in Walt Disney's unpopular *Babes in Toyland* (1961). These included diverse circus wagons, a steam calliope, and a chariot for Day to ride while being pulled by a brigade of horses, each augmented with white wings. Knowing the jumbo-sized musical rested heavily on his shoulders, Walters joked, "I guess I am walking a sort of tightrope. It may be that I am walking a plank!"[15]

His goal, however, was to match the original stage spectacular. The large-scale circus sequences were developed early, "and there were sketches for each. I said: 'Someone has to film these really well. Why not get the biggest specialist? Why not get Buzz Berkeley?' They replied: 'We can't, Chuck. He's too old, he drinks too much, he has already cost us too much money in the past, and this film is expensive enough as it is.' But I insisted that it wouldn't cost us anything to give him a try, and that everything was so well-organized and sketched out that he couldn't follow his inspiration and lead us way off base—even if he wanted to."[16]

Day, however, was not willing to join the ranks of those Berkeley had humiliated. "My agreement with Doris," said Walters, "was that if she was in a scene, I'd shoot it: [sequences] like 'Over and Over Again' and 'This Can't Be Love.' Buzz would do all the pre-shooting work, like getting the wagons in place, but when the cameras rolled, it was all mine."

Day's "Over and Over Again" launched principal photography in late January 1962, and the number's jaw-dropping climatic shot brought Walters specific satisfaction. His personally selected circus talent performed in harmonized motion everywhere under the big top, while Day's double spun on a rope high above the center ring. "There was a lot of using doubles in this circus story," he later confessed, but skilled lighting and editing kept up a grand illusion.[17] To maintain such magic—and blend as seamlessly as possible with their doubles—*Jumbo*'s four stars attended multiple weeks of "circus school" at M-G-M to learn the basics of trapeze technique.

Yet Chuck didn't expect more of them than he demanded of himself. Visiting *Cosmopolitan* columnist Jon Whitcomb, who was to write a profile of the "self-effacing young director . . . about whom surprisingly little has been printed," arrived to find *Jumbo*'s fifty-year-old captain happily preparing to demonstrate aerial maneuvers. "Mr. Walters," reported Whitcomb, "began proceedings by leaping nimbly onto a trapeze and showing the stars how he wanted them to swing. When the bar was moving in its maximum sweep, with rhythm matched to sound-track music, he dropped backwards to a knee hold, then to a toe hold, then onto the mattress. Mr. Boyd had trouble following suit. In his first few tries, he lost his toe grip and landed on the mattress headfirst. This broke up the crew, and Boyd laughed the loudest." (Durante, meanwhile, "climbed up on his trapeze, muttering, 'As a baby, I couldn't *afford* a swing!'")[18]

Given their early professional history and friendship, Chuck found genuine gratification in presenting Hart's work to a new generation. (The lyricist had died in 1943.) Hart's melancholy stanzas for "Little Girl Blue" had been an uncontested highlight of the original stage show, with the Hippodrome awash in indigo light. In the movie, the ballad played out after the Wonders lost Jumbo and their circus, and historian Douglas McVay later described Walters's "elaborate, subtle, visually striking treatment":

> His handling of the number begins with a long-shot of Miss Day walking slowly, sadly away from the camera. She pulls back the circus big-top flaps, and enters the marquee, her figure seen against a patch of blue outside, so that the image signals the title of the song which she now starts to render. As she strolls in long and medium shots, the camera tracking in keeping with her measured pace, we hear her commence the ballad on the soundtrack but her lips stay closed, so that the effect is that of a pensive "interior monologue." . . . The camera moves behind her shoulder as she seats herself in the deserted circus ring—and only then, as the lens tracks from left to right in close-shot past her face, do her lips open in song.
>
> The next stage of the sequence has her walking into the middle of the ring, away from her seat and the camera, into medium-long shot—and suddenly striking an exuberant, legs-astride, arms-apart pose in a spotlight (the spotlight being scarlet, her costume mauve, and blue spot-machine lights circling the marquee backcloths), upon the lines in the lyric's bridge-passage. . . . Then the camera travels in to a close-shot of her, face once again

forlorn, the gay spotlights and colors fading and vanishing, the previous gloomy hues returning, as the lyric changes. . . . Miss Day also enters, at one point, abruptly at the left of the frame, into medium close-shot, her sudden surging entry accentuating the urgent desperation of the lyric.

And the scene finishes as she once more strolls away from us into a medium long-shot, her rendition of the ballad concluding on a wistful "dying fall" echoed in the orchestral finale, the muted musical ending matched by the lonely, distant isolation of the singer.[19]

Not since Garland's "Friendly Star" in *Summer Stock* more than a decade earlier had Walters displayed such inspired camera framing for a female solo. "[Doris] didn't come to us," he later explained, "we had to go to her." In the sequence, which remained a personal favorite of his, the camera entered the scene as a concerned friend to the on-screen character, but ultimately was left behind when the character wandered away from any attempt at consolation.

The concluding moments of *Jumbo*'s plot showed Durante, Day, and Raye—bereft of circus and elephant—reduced to the level of a three-person fakir and carnival act. Out of the blue, a reformed Boyd returns their beloved pachyderm, and the five of them work to reestablish their prominence as a circus troupe. "There was to be more of an ending after the Wonder Circus split up," admitted Walters, "[with all of them] on their behind. Then Roger wrote 'Sawdust, Spangles, and Dreams,' and I said, 'We can't tell any more story after this. *This* has to be the end of the picture."[20] His staging for the finale nonetheless went to an extreme: circus pizzazz collided with slapstick as the four stars donned clown white for a garish, bloated eleven-minute divertissement.

Friday, May 1, 1962, marked the final day of principal photography for Durante, Raye, and Boyd (who all finished atop a mechanical horse while reprising "This Can't Be Love"). Day remained another week to film "Little Girl Blue." After eighty-four days of production, however, Walters faced his most difficult farewell with the departure of Sydney: "Fifty years old and a grand old gal; we all cried when she finished her role and returned to the circus."[21]

Out of reverence for the stage show's pugnacious (and litigious) original producer, the film was formally titled *Billy Rose's Jumbo* and given its first sneak preview just two weeks later, on May 23. Chuck could not attend, but Sheldon cabled:

> I can't tell you what an exciting experience last night was. When I first got there, there was such a wave of optimism and enthusiasm that it made me nervous. People in Hollywood these days are supposed to be cynical about the pictures they have worked on. All I can tell you is that when the evening was over, I joined them all on Cloud 9. It is a lovely feather in Hollywood's cap.[22]

Momentum, hype, and additional press previews continued through the autumn as a promotional campaign trumpeted "Jump for joy, it's Jumbo!" Walters was named "Personality of the Week," and the *Los Angeles Times* exclaimed: "With the Oscar Awards coming up shortly, Hollywood shop-talk has it that quiet and modest director Walters will be in the running for his inspired handling of M-G-M's musical, *Billy Rose's Jumbo*. Producer Pasternak showed a rough cut to some of the industry's toppers, and the unanimous reaction is that it's one of the best musicals ever put together at the Culver City studio. . . . Chuck is one of the most highly respected and highly-prized craftsmen in the movie world. We hope he gets his Oscar. He deserves it."[23]

Buoyed by such legitimate fervor, *Jumbo* opened at Radio City Music Hall to accompany the annual Christmas spectacular, and *Variety* was quick to predict "a sockeroo $165,000 for opening week."[24] *Time* raved, "Director Walters . . . skillfully mingles cinemagic and circus-pocus, and he almost always gets the best out of his players."[25] More thoughtfully, the *Saturday Review* offered: "To reproduce any kind of stage production on celluloid is purely journeyman's work, a matter of picking the pieces and pasting them together. True adaptation, on the other hand, calls for imagination, finesse, and creativity. Perhaps that is why it is so rare. It is, therefore, a special pleasure to be able to report that *Billy Rose's Jumbo* fully meets the above specifications."[26]

The occasional critical jeer ("alarmingly dated," opined the *New Yorker*)[27] didn't stop the musical from scoring January's Box Office Blue Ribbon Award from the National Screen Council, a "Picture of the Month" award from *Seventeen,* and the "Gold Medal Movie of the Month" from *Photoplay* in February. But just as quickly as the 1962 holiday season came and went, so did *Jumbo*'s audience. The hoopla disappeared. Oscar talk stopped. Ticket sales evaporated. One year later, in January 1964, *Variety* reported the picture's total anticipated domestic rentals as only $2,750,000—a major financial loss.

One may wonder why. Film musicals based on Broadway were back in fashion; 1961–1962 saw the winning releases of *West Side Story, The Music Man,* and *Gypsy.* All of these, however, were comparatively recent New York hot tickets, and as Bosley Crowther yawned, "*Jumbo* is hitting the screen about 25 years late."[28] Pasternak reflected on the picture in 1985 and conceded, "We were getting older while audiences were getting younger. I loved *Jumbo;* I thought Charlie Walters did a great job. But Doris wasn't a kid—she actually came to me complaining her *cameraman* was getting too old!"[29]

Whatever the reasons, the film's failure hurt deeply. It implied that the director had lost touch with the *zeitgeist*—and it was Walters's second consecutive feature to lose money.

26

Ain't Down Yet

Months before his circus film bottomed out at the box office, Walters was nationally congratulated by Hedda Hopper, who told her readers, "[He] won't have time to enjoy his jumbo-sized success. He's already set for *The Unsinkable Molly Brown*."[1]

There was, however, no true surge of excitement over the prospect, as there wasn't much of a musical to entice. "Roger and I were in New York looking at circus acts," he recounted. "*Molly Brown* was playing on Broadway, so I said, 'Let's go. I hear the studio is hot for it.' Well, it was very disappointing. There were certain attractive things—a good rags-to-riches story—but the sum total was way off. When we got back to the coast, the first thing we heard [at M-G-M] was, 'We've bought *Molly Brown,* and we want you to do it.'"

The show originally premiered on November 3, 1960, as songwriter Meredith Willson's follow-up to his Tony Award–winning *The Music Man*. Produced by the Theater Guild and directed by none other than Dore Schary, *Molly* starred Tammy Grimes, who had a unique voice. She played a fictionalized (but real-life) backwoods dreamer who strikes it rich, survives the *Titanic* disaster, and triumphs over community snobbery in Denver. Strapping Harve Presnell debuted as her patient husband, Leadville Johnny Brown, and the crowd-pleasing vehicle ran for a profitable 532 performances.

M-G-M first announced Pasternak as producer, but another studio shake-up deposed Sol Siegel, and new chieftain-of-the-moment Robert Weitman handed *Molly* to Lawrence Weingarten (*The Tender Trap, Don't Go Near the Water*). "Poor Larry had never done a musical," said Walters, who was quick to insist that Edens be retained as associate producer.

Lili scenarist Helen Deutsch worked to make the property filmic and initially offered nine pages of "Character Analysis and General Notes" about the title character, a social climber. "Molly," she wrote, "is a woman in error. She pursues a false ideal. It should be made clear that she has been in error, or else we shall be saying that her petty ambitions and her lamentable treatment of Johnny are okay with us. . . . On stage, this weakness in Molly's character is obscured by fast pace, noise, music, and the performance of Tammy Grimes. On the screen, it will be disturbingly apparent."[2]

Walters, in turn, felt Shirley MacLaine ("who *is* Molly Brown!") would be the ideal actress for the part, bringing some sympathy to the character, and Robert Goulet ("who then was the hottest thing around") was everyone's choice for the sweet-tempered Johnny. A screen test proved the baritone could play bumpkin, and Metro offered him a package deal that included both *Molly* and Arthur Freed's forthcoming *Carnival*. "Then," reported Weingarten, "came the stunning news from the Board of Directors that we could not use him if we could not get the rights to his [soundtrack] recordings."[3] Goulet was under contract to Columbia Records, and the label unbendingly refused to consider such a proposal—even in the face of Weingarten's admission that *Molly* possessed "anything but a best-selling score . . . [not even] the greatest singer in the world could sell records of [it]."

MacLaine's participation proved to be another insurmountable obstacle. Weingarten later stated that a verbal deal had been struck, but "when it came time to finalize the agreement, we found out that Hal Wallis had a contract with her that preempted ours. . . . Unless she did the picture *he* wanted her to do, he would not release her for *Molly*."[4] Neither Shirley nor Chuck could have been more disappointed, and when Deutsch heard about such "new Hollywood" maneuverings, she wearily admitted, "I find that more and more I am intrigued with independent productions and low-budget films."[5] Replacement rumors flourished. Doris Day and Shirley Jones were briefly considered, and Judy Garland wanted the role, as she had earlier planned to do *Molly* on the London stage as a presage to the movie. Waiting not so quietly in the wings, however, was Debbie Reynolds. The pint-sized star with fifteen years of moviemaking credits had seen the New York show and identified with the determined Molly: "I started campaigning for it as soon as I got back to California."[6] Reynolds's agent nevertheless received a response from Weingarten that said, "Debbie's not the right type." Only when MacLaine was prematurely announced in the press did Reynolds grudgingly give up her pursuit. She assembled a nightclub act and, a few weeks later, headed to Las Vegas with her evening of song, dance, and impressions (while simultaneously discovering she was pregnant).

The search for Molly had by then begun anew. "In desperation," Weingarten divulged, "I went to see Debbie and her act. I was amazed at her virtuosity and her maturity."[7] Back in Culver City, Edens was first to hear the news that Reynolds had been hired. He immediately reached out to Deutsch, saying, "We didn't make a test of Carol Burnett. The New York office wouldn't go along with it. The powers-that-be have decided to postpone the picture until October or November when Debbie Reynolds will have her baby. That's it: DEBBIE REYNOLDS as MOLLY BROWN. Depressing thought, isn't it? Chuck is in San Francisco and hasn't heard this yet. I can promise you, he will be terribly depressed. It's all very sad."[8]

Weingarten's decision flummoxed both director and writer; it was a replay of the *I'll Cry Tomorrow* scenario, when Susan Hayward had conquered Weingarten. "When they told me that Debbie would cut her salary to a minimum to get the part, I cried," recalled Walters, "because I didn't think she was right for the part. And, of course, they let her know that I felt that way, which was no big help to me."[9] MacLaine was equally annoyed, as she still hoped Wallis would change his schedule and allow her to go to Metro. She phoned her replacement to demand, "What is this shit about *Molly Brown?* The role is mine. I signed for it. But you undercut my price. Larry Weingarten told me you'd do it for nothing."[10] Reynolds offered a few words in her defense but considered it pointless to argue the issue.

"Before the contracts were signed," recalled Reynolds, "Chuck . . . came to the house to visit me. It was a terribly rainy day in Los Angeles. The streets of Beverly Hills were flooded, and Chuck drove all the way from Malibu. His coming to see me in that kind of weather made me a little nervous. Although I had been told I had the part, I knew Chuck didn't want me; he wanted Shirley."[11]

"Debbie, I wish you'd turn this down," he said, "because you're totally wrong for it. You're much too short for the part."

"I'm too short for the part?" she slyly countered. "How short is the part?"

The director stared blankly for a moment, and then had to chuckle. "That's funny."

Having gotten her laugh, the actress offered a final remark: "You know, Chuck, it's possible that you could be wrong."

Several actors vied to play opposite Reynolds, with Robert Horton of NBC-TV's *Wagon Train* lobbying hardest. His main competition proved to be Presnell, who screen-tested on April 11, 1963; Weingarten was surprised "to hear women say that they thought he was quite handsome."[12] The big-voiced newcomer got the part, and another exceptional group of character actors was handpicked to bolster him, Reynolds, and the script. They included Ed Begley, Hermione Baddeley, and Jack Kruschen, with the regal Martita Hunt as Grand Duchess Elise Lupovinova. (Hunt's semi-secret on-set "nipping" gave her performance an added—if unintentional—amusing aura.) The small role of Lady Primdale was filled by Angela Lansbury's mother, Moyna MacGill, and Chuck was most pleased to provide his longtime friend Audrey Christie the plum role of Denver snob Mrs. McGraw. It had been twenty-five years since they'd partnered in *I Married an Angel*.

Peter Gennaro, the show's original choreographer, was brought to Metro to set new dances, while Chuck intended to supply the "intimate book numbers for Debbie and Harve." Gennaro hadn't really gotten to know the director during their aborted tenure with *By the Beautiful Sea*, but he remained grateful that Walters hadn't accepted Reynolds's original suggestion for choreographer. "Bob Sidney did *all* her things, [and] Debbie is very loyal to people she works with," he explained. "Chuck and the producers wanted someone else, so they got me."[13] Gennaro built his dance corps around a talented nucleus: Maria Karnilova (another *By the Beautiful Sea* escapee) as dance hall hostess Daphne, and high-spirited Gus Trikonis and Grover Dale as, respectively, Joe and Jam, Molly's rambunctious hillbilly stepbrothers. "Peter was the co-choreographer on *West Side Story*," explains Dale, "and I was the original Snowboy. I hadn't worked directly with him, though I'd gone to Peter's classes. So that's how it happened. *Molly* was my first major studio experience."

True to form, Walters remained an unobtrusive observer at Gennaro's rehearsals, plotting wide-screen framing and camera moves that would best complement the choreography. "Chuck and I got along very well," said Gennaro. "He just let me do what I wanted." Such lack of posturing surprised newcomer Dale, who thought a major Hollywood director would demand attention. "To me, Chuck seemed to be kind of shy," he recounted. "He was very quiet and unassuming. Roger was sort of the opposite; he was much more verbal—and participated. At times I didn't even know that Chuck was the director. He was just this nice guy, sitting and watching rehearsals. I wish I had known more about him when I was there. As years went by, and I started to learn his background, I was astonished."[14]

Reynolds's twofold elation over *Molly Brown* and her pregnancy was short-lived. The thirty-one-year-old actress lost the child she was carrying in May; it was the second time in less than two years she had endured such a tragedy. Taking a cue from the film's heroine, however, the unsinkable trouper—still fighting fatigue and depletion—reported to M-G-M on August 12, ready to tackle her first bravura routines: "Belly Up to the Bar, Boys," with Karnilova and company, and Molly's anthem, "I Ain't Down Yet," with Dale, Trikonis, and young Scott McCartor. According to Dale, there was no mention of the recent misfortune. "Debbie threw herself into rehearsals," he said admiringly. "She came dressed in sweat shirts and jeans. To me, she was like another gypsy, a real *worker*. She didn't pull the 'Okay, you're the featured player, and I'm the star' bit. It was always, 'Okay, here we are; we're sweating together.' Gus and I would throw Debbie around and treat her like a sister that we'd kick in the butt. The only time I had pause was when looking at her hand, because she had that diamond wedding ring on her finger. That ring was always the reminder . . . *she's a star*." (Reynolds was then married to millionaire shoe store magnate Harry Karl.)

Eight hours of song and dance rehearsal were just the beginning of Reynolds's daily schedule. She'd then meet with Metro acting coach Lillian Burns—the same Burns who'd snubbed Walters's talents in the past. But for Debbie, their one-on-one sessions provided a much-needed sounding board. "I wanted to be completely prepared by the time we began shooting," she explained. "I didn't expect to get any direction from Chuck Walters, and I didn't."[15] At least not at first.

By early September, the *Molly Brown* company was shooting in Montrose, Colorado. A productive first week on location included the scenes of Molly fishing and learning to read, plus three Presnell songs as staged by the director. Walters recounted: "For 'I'll Never Say No,' we rehearsed in the motel and then shot the day after. I did Harve's soliloquy ['Colorado, My Home'] on the mountain, and I like the way I shot it." As Presnell's voice rang through the air, Walters's clever camerawork showed only the Colorado terrain before swooping down to give the actor a surprise initial "entrance." Art director Preston Ames (who'd been on both *Torch Song* and *Jumbo*) remembers, "[Chuck] did a magnificent job on *Molly*. It was really a physical thing, tremendously physical, and sometimes a man of that nature isn't quite accustomed to jumping all over the mountains the way I am. He did it, and it was brilliant. You had all that beautiful scenery of Colorado—fantastic."[16] Ames also acknowledges that Walters was not always his usual amenable self while on location: "I ran into occasions where I suddenly realized I'd said the wrong word. There were sparks. But it was a joy working for the man, because he had great talent and great ability."

Reynolds felt the strain as well, whether she was recipient or cause or both. She cagily told *Seventeen* that she would only "talk to the director to make certain that we're not in conflict. . . . [H]e's got a million things to do without worrying about [my] role—the lights, the sets, the costumes."[17] Walters later confessed that their initial day-to-day friction was rather maddening: "All through the shooting of the picture, she'd say, 'I know you don't want me.'"

The company returned to M-G-M on schedule after their week in Colorado. "[Chuck] was starting to be a little nicer to me," admits Debbie. "Then the rushes started coming in, and we could see the film. One morning, Chuck came over to me on the set and gave me a kiss. 'Well, you were right,' he said. 'You're not too short for the part.'"[18]

Later, the director respectfully amended, "Debbie worked like the *blazes!*"[19]

With animosity between director and star having evaporated, there came new confrontations between Walters and Weingarten. Unlike the trusting Freed and Pasternak, *Molly*'s producer was a meddler and seemed to challenge Chuck's decisions at every turn. The rankled director received a defensive memo from Weingarten on October 15 in which the latter attempted to justify the re-editing of two scenes. He deemed the learning-to-read sequence between Johnny and Molly "unflattering photographically," and rationalized his extension of a long shot of Molly escaping Johnny after a scuffle: "It's one of the most beautiful and tender moments in the picture." At one point, Weingarten even attempted to counsel Reynolds in the interpretation of her role. Chuck found this particularly egregious, although the producer protested, "It was my impression you welcomed it, otherwise I should not have done it." He continued, "I am not insensible to the major contributions you have made to all our enterprises. I remember vividly your idea for the frame around *Tender*

Trap and now your conception of Harve's introduction into the picture. I am confident that you are on your way [to] getting a whopping picture, but I think we must work together happily if we are to have any joy in the process."[20]

Walters's fury lingered, however. Nearly a decade later, he told Freed biographer Hugh Fordin, "Weingarten went to Arthur—or asked to have lunch with him—and said, 'I am doing *Molly Brown* my way, and nobody is going to get in my way. Including Chuck Walters.'" When the director heard about this, he confronted his producer: "Why don't you shove *Molly Brown* up your ass? You do it *your* way—and fall on *your* ass.' . . . [Larry] had never done a musical, and how dare he say he's going to do it *his* way? And we had done three [*sic*] successful straight comedies together. *Charming* man."[21]

Such problems didn't seem to affect the overall mood of the company. "We weren't exposed to the tensions and the behind-the-scenes negotiating that was going on," remembers Dale. "The environment that happened on that set was something special; the atmosphere was very welcoming." During production, he and several other cast members were housed at the Chateau Marmont on Sunset Boulevard. "I used to drive Martita Hunt and Hermione Baddeley to the set. There were parties at night around the Marmont swimming pool with those two dames conducting the goings-on. It was hilarious."

The final production number to be filmed was a six-minute Peter Gennaro dance sequence, "He's My Friend." Written especially for the movie by Willson, it involved virtually the entire cast, and was destined to become *Molly*'s high point.

"With any other musicals I've ever been in," said Reynolds, "like *Singin' in the Rain,* you rehearsed and rehearsed the numbers for weeks until you had them all down cold before shooting. For some reason, ['He's My Friend'] was the exception."[22] Gennaro actually staged the routine while Debbie (who appeared virtually throughout the film) was on call elsewhere. When finally summoned to learn the dance, she realized, it had "*everything*—Irish jigs and hornpipes!"

Gennaro had you moving so your leg went out in one direction while your hip moved in another. . . . [I]t's practically impossible to do. It would have driven a ballet dancer crazy. I was supposed to shoot that number after three days of rehearsal. The boys I danced with, Grover and Gus, rehearsed it for sixteen weeks. *Sixteen weeks!* And I had three days! I went to Chuck and said, "*You've* been a dancer; *you* know what I'm up against. I've *got* to have more time! What's the use of shooting thirty or forty takes before I even get the steps right?" He said he couldn't help it. . . . Then I began to cry. I was tired and frustrated, and when I'm like that, I get angry—I cry. I said, "Well, you can go ahead and shoot that number tomorrow, but you can get Mae West and put *her* in there between the two boys because *I* won't be there!" And I stomped off the set.

Reynolds returned after additional rehearsal time was allocated, only to learn that "He's My Friend" was to be shot straight through in one extended take. "Chuck came up with the idea of filming the number with two cameras," she confirms, "something that had [rarely] been done in film. He shot the same way they filmed Spencer Tracy's great monologue in *Judgment at Nuremberg*—shooting it only one time."[23]

"I don't have the same memory," laughs Dale. "I remember five days working on that number. Debbie *was* correct in that there were long takes, and that once it got started, they would let us run the whole section. Because when we did it in a long take, our energies built as we were getting out of breath. And at the very end of the number, we do a dive and that *somersault.* That's pretty amazing. And Debbie did it in high heels!"[24]

Final days of filming were devoted to what should have been the most exciting moments of the plot: the climactic sinking of the *Titanic* and the ensuing lifeboat scenes as Molly uplifts fellow survivors. Instead, Metro chose that moment to reduce the picture's budget and invest its savings in the concurrent *Dr. Zhivago; Molly's* creative team had to make do. Despite such conditions, Walters wrapped the film shortly before Christmas. He then assembled an inexpensive—but highly effective—finale montage of footage during post-production that allowed audiences to re-experience the highs and lows of the Molly-Johnny relationship. A gradually burgeoning orchestral underscoring propelled the visuals, which climaxed with the embrace of the reconciled lovers.

The first preview, in San Francisco on February 7, 1964, was "extremely positive."[25] But it was topped a night later in Oakland. "It has been a long time since I have heard such a response from an audience," wrote producer Warner Toub, to the delight of the director.[26] Metro sprang into promotional overdrive, and M-G-M Records prepared a soundtrack album that disproved Weingarten's earlier predictions and sold well. The studio also circulated *The Story of a Dress,* a five-minute behind-the-scenes featurette with Edens, Reynolds, Weingarten, and a pipe-smoking Walters photographed as they viewed Morton Haack's costume sketches for the picture.

After Hollywood and Colorado premieres, *Molly Brown* broke an all-time record that August, bringing in nearly $30,000 on its first day at Radio City Music Hall. The total gross for the film's ten weeks at the venue hit $2 million (another record), and *Molly* went on to accumulate more than $11 million at box offices across the country.[27] The critics, however, were guarded in their recommendations, and the *New York Times* spoke for the majority when noting, "The screen, which is as wide as can be, is filled with vivid colors that help project the fact that this is merely a satisfying musical comedy and not an inspired subject."[28] The *Chicago Tribune* gave a wink to Walters's better-late-than-never coaching and observed that Reynolds "loses some of her frantic ferocity and becomes more appealing and more credible" throughout the film.[29] At the *New York Herald Tribune,* however, there was a snipe from the oft-withering Judith Crist, who was occasionally inaccurate in her perception of popular appeal: "Unfortunately what [Tammy] Grimes was able to do on stage Miss Reynolds cannot . . . and Miss Reynolds tries. She bounces and dashes and slams and flings her gams and warbles and wails. . . . [But] energy and enthusiasm are no substitutes for innate talent."[30]

Such swipes didn't prevent *Molly Brown* from netting a Golden Globe nomination for Best Picture/Musical or Comedy, and a satisfying six Academy Award nominations—for Adapted Score, Sound Mixing, Color Art Direction, Color Cinematography, Costume Design, and (perhaps most telling) Debbie Reynolds as Best Actress. She won public support for her first—and to date only—Academy recognition but lost the Oscar to Julie Andrews for *Mary Poppins.* (Fifteen years later, Walters wryly reflected: "Sometimes I'm asked, 'What do you think is your greatest contribution to the business?' If I could be honest, I'd say, 'Getting an Academy Award nomination for Debbie Reynolds.'")

The Unsinkable Molly Brown marked the last time the legendary Metro musical machine operated at full force. Grover Dale, fresh from

Broadway, found the whole enterprise astonishingly efficient. "The flow of how things got put together seemed so easy and natural," he said in 2008. "I never had an experience like that. In looking back—and having had some tough ones to deal with [later on]—it has reminded me how blessed I was to get that opportunity. I felt a freedom around me, for those months that we were rehearsing, that I could try anything. And I guess it starts at the top with Chuck Walters."[31]

27

After the Lion

As *Molly Brown* hit screens nationwide in summer 1964, the guard at M-G-M changed yet again. Robert O'Brien, vice president of Loew's, ascended to the presidency after the ambitious—if not always wise—Joseph Vogel stepped down. Guided by dictates of the board of directors, the compliant Robert Weitman remained in charge in Culver City.

Walters by then had seen four distinct and very different hierarchies come and go during his two decades under contract. Each in its own way managed to erode what was once considered an indestructible empire. "I got along fine enough with the Jews [Mayer and Schary]," he joked, "but when we got down to the Irish Catholics [O'Brien], forget it! It became all dollars and cents—nothing artistic. Whatever they could get the cheapest, they used."[1] The slate for M-G-M's 1964–1965 season included such eventual embarrassments as muscleman Steve Reeves's *Sandokan the Great,* Elvis Presley's *Harum Scarum,* and the George Maharis comedic misfire *Quick, Before It Melts.* "They were starting to send me real junk," Chuck remembered, "and I had two years to go on my contract."[2] John Darrow, still acting as agent, opted for a bluff: "We'll ask for a release. With *Molly* the big hit it is, they're not going to let you go. They'll just stop sending you crap. I'm going to write them a letter." According to the director, the plan backfired in a major way: "We got a letter back in a week, which said, 'We'd be happy to let Charles Walters go.' So that's how I got out."

Under the headline "Magna Cum Laude," good friend Hedda Hopper spread the news on June 11, 1964. "Chuck Walters has graduated from Metro after twenty-two years and twenty pictures. Asked for his release and got it. Now he'll have time to see *Molly Brown* at the Radio City Music Hall. Ten of his pictures have played that theater; he has yet to see one [there]. He was always working."[3]

There was no send-off at M-G-M for the man who'd turned a four-week option into a twenty-two-year career. But when driving off the lot for the final time, Walters stopped to take one last look at the brightly lit signboard positioned above the studio's main gate. Metro reserved this massive space for its designated hit picture of the year. "I finally made it with *Molly*," he said with a half smile. "My name in lights."[4]

The 1960s were fraught with challenges, turmoil, and new cultural forms. The Vietnam War, the civil rights movement, youth uprisings, and a developing drug culture contributed to an atmosphere in which a renegade moviemaker could thrive. Many contemporary films reflected a polarized society, and the studio system itself continued to implode. Walters, at age fifty-three, was daunted. The compartmentalized nature of M-G-M had always suited him, and he had been content to leave the rigors of pitching stories or haggling over budgets to the specialists. Thrust into the role of a freelance director-producer, he couldn't hide his unhappiness at the complexities he now faced.

"After twenty-two years at Metro," Chuck said, "I wanted at least a year off."

> Because, at fifty-two weeks a year, every time the phone rang, my stomach got in a knot. *"Oh, what now?"* Not that I didn't get time off; the studio was very reasonable . . . but there was always a heavy fear hovering over it all. And in that year I wanted off, the industry did a complete flop-over. The big studios changed, they just rented out space. And people said, "Chuck, all you do is find a script and put a package together." Well now, that sounds simple enough. But it made me feel like I'd been carried around on a pink pillow for twenty-two years. "Where the hell am I gonna find a script? And what do you mean put a package together? Do I go to a bank for financing?" I didn't have that kind of *energy* about it; I really didn't. I didn't have that drive. And truthfully I didn't like what I was seeing. Antonioni's *Blow-Up* threw me for an absolute loop. Everything we'd learned was just shit on.[5]

(Hinting there may have been other factors sabotaging Walters's self-confidence, Morrissey adds: "I think Chuck was drinking a little too much at this time.")[6]

Whatever his hesitations, the independent director announced purchase of the spy thriller *Sky High,* in which he would star Gia Scala. He additionally was rumored to helm Frank Sinatra in *Divorce American Style* at Columbia, and Dean Martin in *Community Property* at Warner Bros., though Chuck kidded that he'd need a guide to help him find either of those lots. He and Roger Edens discussed producing a Walters-directed television special for young singing sensation Barbra Streisand, and Chuck told Hedda Hopper, "What we should do is the story of her life. It's rags-to-riches and Cinderella all over again—and it happened before our eyes. Usually when they do someone's life story, half the people don't remember who they are. Barbra's current—and an exciting talent."[7] (The deal couldn't be made, but Streisand's *My Name Is Barbra* program ultimately possessed autobiographical overtones.)

Former M-G-M boss Sol Siegel requested that Walters come to Columbia for *Chautauqua* (alternately titled *Big America*), a Dick Van Dyke musical based on a traveling theatrical troupe. But when negotiations broke down, the producer suggested instead an update of the Jean Arthur–Joel McCrea comedy *The More the Merrier* (1943). Walters warily accepted, as "it was an amusing idea, but that's all." Sol Saks updated the original screenplay, and in his rewrite, the housing shortage in Washington, D.C., during World War II was replaced by Tokyo's lack of lodging during the 1964 Olympics. In the new film, renamed *Walk, Don't Run,* the protagonist became Sir William Rutland, a married British industrialist who bamboozles his way into an apartment share with both a young woman and an Olympic athlete, and then turns Cupid for the couple. Spencer Tracy was suggested for the lead, "but Cary Grant got interested," explained the director. "I like better that Cary—the great lover—would now play a matchmaker."[8] With Grant came both his Granley production company and a personal request for fledgling Samantha Eggar and Jim Hutton as co-stars. (Original contenders for those roles had been Julie Andrews and Jack Lemmon.)

Walters cast the film's minor roles, but sturdy Peggy Rea made it onto payroll without the "very fussy" director's approval. Rea remembered Chuck from her days as one of Arthur Freed's secretaries in the 1940s. "And *Walk, Don't Run* was in the 1960s," she recounted. "So Miss Peggy is twenty years older. I auditioned for the role of a Ukrainian lady shot-putter. I was certainly big enough to do it, but Chuck knew what he wanted—and he didn't want me at all." Rea won the role only when a consultant from the Russian Olympic committee saw her and shouted, "She's the spitting image of Tamara Press!" (Press had won three Olympic gold medals in distance throwing for the Soviet Union.) "Chuck was just flattened," Rea laughed, "and he kept his lips buttoned from then on."[9]

Walk, Don't Run evolved under Michael Frankovich, Columbia Pictures' vice president in charge of productions. Prior to principal photography, "there was a big meeting," recounted Walters, "with these assistants. Even though it was mid-summer, they were all dressed in black. You'd think they were from the mafia—or at MCA!" He went on:

> Frankovich and about a dozen of his men are all talking such bullshit, I can't believe it. Now, I'm not saying a word . . . but I am *smelling* what I'm stuck with. This went on for 45 minutes to an hour. Then there was a lull, and sensing they are just about through, I said, "May I say something?" [Frankovich] said, "Oh, yes, please Chuck, go ahead." All heads turned and I said, "If you don't take care of that plant over there, you're going to lose it in two weeks. Look how it's drooping." . . . Let them all guess what I'm thinking, right?[10]

Despite the perceived ineptitude at the top, the director anticipated a relatively uncomplicated shoot, as long as they could get the script in shape. ("I worked for eight months, with three sets of writers, but the whole thing wouldn't mix," Chuck would say later.) Frankovich and Grant wholeheartedly committed themselves to the picture, green-lighting a month of location work in Japan. Rea remembers the leading man telling the cast, "I have never had money in a picture before, and I do on this one. And I am very excited." Grant kept up public interest by announcing in advance that this film, his seventy-second, would be his last.

The *Walk, Don't Run* team arrived in Japan on the *President Roosevelt* in September 1965. Inclement weather plagued their schedule, which was further complicated by the challenges of the film's climatic Olympic race—a brisk heel-toe "walk" that reflected the film's title. Hutton started at Tokyo Stadium and made his way around Shimbashi Station at rush hour; Grant joined midway, wearing just a T-shirt and boxer shorts. Hidden cameras were positioned across thirty miles of the city, capturing spontaneous reactions from locals. "They got their shots all right," Philip K. Schuer later reported, "but Walters breaks out in a sweat at the recollection of the gamble involved. 'Murder!' he calls it."[11]

Filming wrapped in early 1966 on the Columbia lot, which was deemed by Chuck "a junkyard compared to M-G-M. Every day, five times a day, I said, 'I want to go home. This is a *studio*?' I was spoiled." Released in June, *Walk, Don't Run* was easily embraced by audiences and critics. Bosley Crowther credited the director for giving the comedy a "nimble locomotion and flavoring,"[12] and *Time* reported that Walters "shuffles words, pranks and players in and around greater Tokyo with a perfectly relaxed air . . . evidence that Hollywood's honorable high-comedy traditions are being well preserved."[13]

Walk, Don't Run fulfilled expectations as a pleasing final chapter to Cary Grant's distinguished thirty-four-year movie career. The actor's final celluloid moments, poignant and simple, were captured through the sympathetic eye of Walters's camera. Dapperly dressed, Grant stands beside a car waiting to take him to the airport. Smiling up at a pair of Japanese children, he blows a kiss and, with glistening eyes, waves his good-bye.

What wasn't obvious—or even imagined—was the fact that the slick romance marked Chuck's farewell to motion picture making as well. There was no slow fade, no announcement. It all just ended.

While working at Columbia, the director was hit by an ulcer attack. "It was the first time I ever missed a day of work," he admitted. The pain was so bad that Walters remained bedridden "from Friday night until Tuesday morning."[14] He refused an operation until the film was completed, thinking naysayers would assume he had been fired from his first job as an independent. But during his lengthy post-surgery convalescence, the fifty-five-year-old director brooded about the future. "I remembered what happened to the great Ernst Lubitsch, who was such a hero image to me. I heard that on his last films, he was able to work only half a day; he was down to six cigars a day instead of twelve. And I said, 'Oh, please, God, don't let it happen to me.'"[15] What did happen was a complete lull: there were no forthcoming job offers.

Letting go proved to be difficult. Gone were Chuck's ordered existence, creative stimulation, and the excitement to which he had grown accustomed in thirty-four nonstop years of employment. "The first year," he confessed, "I cried a lot."[16]

A twenty-four-year-old aspiring entertainer who worked at Columbia helped ease the transition. Given Joseph Anthony's age (and how swiftly he integrated himself into Walters's social environment and beach house), there are conflicting stories about the youngster's intentions. "I only met Joe once," says Morrissey. "Chuck invited me out to dinner, and Joe was dancing around the living room, doing a dance like those done in go-go cages in *Walk, Don't Run.* Chuck was saying, 'Isn't that cute? Isn't that cute?' I said, 'I can't take this.' I went home," and their relationship ended that night.[17]

Many of the director's intimate friends had similar reactions. Joe could be immature; his background was vague (although his natural father evidently died when Anthony was a child). Yet for all the inequality of their relationship, Walters was infatuated with the young man. He labeled him a protégé and designed showcases to kick-start Joe's performing career. Audrey Christie, who tolerated only so much, was among those who, when pressed by curious friends, would dismiss the youngster outright: "Oh, he's a gas station attendant."

The once-vital Chuck was now filling his time with worrisome pursuits. Debbie Reynolds had purchased a slice of his land on Carbon Beach, built a nearby home, and witnessed his ongoing lack of direction. "He partied . . . and he smoked like a fiend. You know, he just smoked, smoked, smoked. And everybody said, 'Chuck you smoke too much.' He'd say, 'Oh, it's my only vice.' And I'd say, 'Really? What about the booze?'"[18] But his charisma continued to pervade any association. "We'd sit on the beach and have drinks," the actress remembers. "Chuck would tell stories about his dancer days and about Joan Crawford. I loved hearing them; we had a lot of laughs."

Walters tried to reawaken his creativity by renovating a new Malibu condominium home, overlooking the Pacific. He kept the interior cool, simple, and white; only scattered signed photographs of Reynolds, Crawford, and Swanson gave any indication of his past career. (The main beach house, meanwhile, was leased to actor Burt Lancaster.)

Ironically, the director's somewhat self-imposed absence from filmmaking in the second half of the 1960s coincided with an unforeseeable resurgence of big-time movie musicals. Walt Disney's delightful *Mary Poppins* set in motion other equally British tales (*Doctor Dolittle, Chitty Chitty Bang Bang*), while the colossal profits from 20th Century-Fox's

The Sound of Music and Warner Bros.' *My Fair Lady* inspired major studios to unrestrainedly mount other contemporary Broadway hits (*Camelot, Oliver!, Funny Girl*) and previously overlooked past glories (*Finian's Rainbow, Paint Your Wagon*).

From the sidelines, Walters remained critical. In Bob Fosse's *Sweet Charity* (1969), he felt Shirley MacLaine's natural charm was buried by the edit-happy freshman director. "Fosse starred himself and was only concerned with movement; there was no heart."[19] Shortly thereafter, the buoyant efforts of such friends as Edens, Gene Kelly, and Michael Kidd were—in Chuck's estimation—undone by a movie's unrecoupable cost: "I'll tell you one thing, *Hello, Dolly!* at $20 million isn't the answer. [Musicals] should—and can—be done more modestly than that."[20]

Four years after *Walk, Don't Run*, Lucille Ball kicked across a concrete job offer. She then was in the third season of the top-rated *Here's Lucy* TV series and needed a fill-in director. Walters was eager to try television but wanted to master the three-camera filming technique before he would commit: "So I sat there for about two weeks and watched, and finally I had two of those mothers licked. . . . I just wished the other one would go home!"[21]

Produced at Paramount, Walters's episodes were typical television fare. "Lucy's House Guest Harry" (filmed September 17, 1970; aired January 25, 1971) was simple situation comedy; "Lucy and Aladdin's Lamp" (filmed April 6, 1970; aired February 1, 1971) had a more satisfying script, allowing for moments of broad physical comedy. "It was a new experience [for me]," he said, "because we filmed in front of an audience. . . . But I liked the intense rhythm of the work."[22] (In the show a week later, Ball played homage to their recent reunion by using the name Chuck Walters for an out-of-work performer who was a character in the script. She then joined the faux Chuck in a revue called *The Hollywood Unemployment Follies*.)

There was one more TV job—a directorial stint on one episode of Dan Dailey's series *The Governor and J.J.*—after which Walters self-deprecatingly joked about his "three weeks of work in the last five years."[23]

But Hollywood, he acknowledged, had changed beyond his recognition. A motion picture ratings system had been instituted to advise patrons of a film's content—"all that murder and violence and four-letter words. Who needs a musical comedy director for *that*?" he observed.[24] He also admitted it took him three days to recover after seeing Stanley

Kubrick's sadistic *A Clockwork Orange* (1971). "Obviously one can say it must be a great film if it could overwhelm me that way," he said. "But I reply: 'No thanks.'"

More to his liking was *Mame*. The touching and tuneful Jerry Herman stage musical triumphed on Broadway in 1966, and *Daily Variety* announced on July 13, 1970, that Warner Bros. would make the motion picture. Walters confessed to *Films and Filming* that he'd like to have a crack at it, "though not with Streisand. That's too easy. I'd go with Lucy Ball or Angela Lansbury."[25]

Warner Bros. seemed to agree. In spring 1972, *Here's Lucy* was winding down its fourth (though not final) season, and Ball signed to play Mame. The studio approached Vincente Minnelli to direct, but he found the property hackneyed. Lucy next opted for Walters, who she believed would keep both the musical and her performance on track. Ball was also fighting for Bea Arthur—then TV's *Maude*—to re-create her original role from *Mame*'s stage production, but her insistence backfired. "I wanted Bea so much that they rang in [her director-husband] Gene Saks on me without telling me," Lucy related in 1980. "I think Chuck would have done a great job . . . but [we] never got a chance. They hired [Saks]. . . . I said, 'I'm not going to argue with you, because I got Bea, and Gene Saks seems to be a nice guy.' But he never took the reins. He never took the reins. And he should [have]."[26]

For Walters it was another professional disappointment, another loss, just as his personal life seemed little more than a steady succession of final good-byes. On June 22, 1969—twelve days after her forty-seventh birthday—Judy Garland died of an accidental overdose of barbiturates. Chuck could not bring himself to attend her New York funeral. "The last time I saw her, she said to me, 'Of all the people I've worked with, no one ever treated me with more consideration, more respect, more understanding, than you did.'"[27] Roger Edens succumbed to cancer on July 13, 1970, although he lived long enough to see *Hello, Dolly!*, his final work (as associate producer), receive an Academy Award nomination for Best Picture. "Roger should have been a great producer," Chuck reflected. "It just didn't happen. I hope his spirit is out there and is going to be born into some other child—and his great talent will go on and on . . . and on."[28] Isobel Lennart died on January 25, 1971; his beloved Maw was backing out of her Malibu driveway on a particularly foggy day when her car was struck. Arthur Freed died on April 12, 1973, and less than three months later Betty Grable passed away at fifty-six, another victim of lung cancer.

The death of dear friends, the death of "Old Hollywood," the death of the past—all were overwhelming. But just as Chuck's own history seemed destined to remain a negligible, fractured memory, there came an affirming validation.

28

Final Ovation

By the early 1970s, Metro-Goldwyn-Mayer was in a state of collapse. There had been ever more disastrous changes in the hierarchy. The back lots had been sold for real estate. Costumes and props were auctioned or sold at thrift shop prices. Production files, orchestrations, department records, and film outtakes were banished to landfills or dumped in the Pacific Ocean. Only minimally a moviemaking entity, Metro released a scant five feature films in 1974.

One of these, surprisingly, became the sixth-highest-grossing film of the year, both domestically and abroad. In the process, it defied every popular movie trend—from disaster pictures to blaxploitation flicks to salty Mel Brooks satires. *That's Entertainment!* opened in May, anthologizing the studio's past musical triumphs with tidily excerpted moments from more than seventy motion pictures made between 1929 and 1958. With newly filmed introductions by star alumni Astaire, Kelly, Sinatra, Reynolds, and others, the homage took contemporary moviegoers on a wondrous and rousing journey to the dazzle that once was the M-G-M musical.

Bright moments from Walters's twenty-two years under contract were sprinkled throughout. Liza Minnelli hailed "Get Happy" as one of her mother's "very best" numbers, and—prior to clips of "Well, Did You Evah?" and "True Love"—Bing Crosby fondly recalled Chuck's direction "in a little pastiche called *High Society*." No better defense for the shuttered studio system could have been offered, and *Variety* raved, "While many may ponder the future of Metro-Goldwyn-Mayer, nobody can deny that it has one hell of a past!"[1]

Suddenly, Metro musicals (and those who had worked on them) were in vogue. *That's Entertainment, Part Two* (1976) included even more Walters material, and full-scale tributes followed. Chuck was honored with a seven-movie retrospective by Les Films Français in Marseilles in June 1976; closer to home, the Tiffany Theater on Sunset Boulevard selected *Good News* and *Lili* to close its well-attended M-G-M Film Festival in December 1977. Such retrospectives coincided with an avalanche of books and documentaries about Hollywood's Golden Age, and Chuck accommodated virtually every interviewer who sought information about Garland, Astaire, Crawford, Kelly (Gene, not Grace), et alia. As further proof that times had changed, however, Tyrone Power's young biographer pointedly asked if the famous actor had been homosexual. The ex-director was stunned and could offer only, "I know he went with a few gay guys. What happened, *I* don't know." Then, in a moment of honesty, he revealed what could be read as a quiet admission of the liability that his own homosexuality had caused him in Hollywood. "There was an element of secrecy to [Ty Power]. . . . I think that's what kept him under wraps," he said.

"It's an awful burden. You want the fame and fortune, and you have this awful load to carry."[2]

The much-anticipated, semi-sumptuous *Mame* also opened in movie theaters in 1974 and was instantly obliterated by brutal reviews. Pauline Kael in the *New Yorker* described Lucille Ball's singing voice as "somewhere between a bark and a croak" and rhetorically queried, "After more than forty years in movies and television, did she discover in herself an unfulfilled ambition to be a flaming drag queen?"[3] Such venom devastated the sixty-two-year-old star, but—never one to play victim—Ball valiantly headed back to work.

"The four TV specials were Lucy's idea," remembers Joseph Bologna, who co-wrote one production and co-starred in another. "She wanted to reinvent herself after *Mame* and prove those snarky critics wrong."[4] Former Metro choreographer Jack Donohue directed the first pair for the 1974–1975 season, and Ball's husband and producer Gary Morton tentatively approached Walters to do the next two. "I said, 'I'd love to,'" laughed Chuck. "I was hard to get." An hour-long teleplay, *What Now, Catherine Curtis?*, co-starred Bologna and Art Carney; it was the story of a recently divorced, middle-aged woman who romances a shy widower and a younger man in an attempt to reclaim her life. "If Lucy Ball is gonna come up with a special," Walters said at the time, "it better be *special,* and I felt this was: . . . a woman alone, after twenty years of marriage, lost and lonely. I said to Lucy, 'You haven't had to open your little trunk of guts and acting—the inside—for an awfully long time. You've been doing it off the top. But now I am going to insist you dig into your honest bag.' Well, since she *hadn't* done that for a long time, she was scared—which made me feel secure."[5]

Ball is at her most effective in the special's opening twenty-minute monologue. "Who the hell are you, Catherine Curtis?" she sharply asks her mirrored reflection. "For the last twenty-three years, I haven't lived one moment alone with you." There follows a cyclone of mixed emotions—sadness, embarrassment, seething hatred for her philandering husband—throughout which she painfully blames herself for the perceived failure of her life. Ball's final breakdown proved shattering in its authenticity, and daughter Lucie Arnaz ventures, "I think it is one of the very best dramatic performances of her career."[6] (When the special aired on CBS in March 1976, ratings were high but reviews were mixed. *Variety* found Lucy "outstanding,"[7] while the *Los Angeles Times* considered the whole affair unoriginal and dismissed the "stiff predictability" of Walters's direction.)[8]

The other Walters-Ball hour was filmed after—but broadcast before—*Catherine Curtis*. A triptych of comedy-dramas about marriage, *Three for Two* co-starred a hammy Jackie Gleason, and Walters "read it and hated it." Darrow convinced him to plunge in anyway, and the director just prayed the public would "kind of rush by" the program.

Despite the disparity in the two assignments, Chuck found the overall experience deeply gratifying, especially as happy congratulations arrived from old colleagues. "I saw your show last night," Helen Deutsch wrote. "It was a joy to see your name again."[9] Walters would later reflect, "Nobody knew if I was going to be slow, medium, or warm—and I was worrying myself. Am I going to remember how to direct? Is it all going to be there? You don't know where it [originally] came from. . . . But on the second day, I said, 'It's nice to be home again.' It was all there; you don't lose it. You can't drown once you know how to swim."[10]

Walters's resurgence was sadly interrupted by the death of his father at age eighty-eight. Joe Walter passed away in Anaheim on March 7, 1976, survived by his second wife, Amelia. Chuck's sorrow, however, was somewhat tempered by a concurrent offer from historian Arthur Knight, who asked the director to speak to his popular "Introduction to Film" class at the University of Southern California. On May 11, Walters arrived on the campus that he'd deserted (along with his law studies) in

1930. He didn't disappoint; indeed, the director's candid reminiscences palpably delighted the rapt students, and USC requested a major encore four years later. That invitation led to what was arguably the most rewarding period of Walters's later life.

His "Film Style Analysis" course met on Wednesday afternoons from February 6 to May 14, 1980, and provided students the opportunity to screen and discuss the Walters catalog of movies. Gifted graduate student Mary Whiteley was appointed his aide, and she proved an ideal comrade. "The first time I visited him at his home to really *start* our relationship," she remembers, "Chuck was kind of formal and tentative. He didn't seem 'Hollywood' to me. . . . At one point, I quite purposely used the word 'fuck.' He *really* reacted to that. He laughed and he said, '*Oh!* You're not one of those intellectuals from the university that's going to look down on me because I haven't been to college!' We were good friends from that point on. He said, 'I love an ass scratcher.'"[11]

The pair industriously plotted the course, with Whiteley advising which films would carry the weight of a lengthy discussion. "He wasn't a great judge of his own work," she said. "It was all good to him." Chuck, however, did not want an homage; he insisted that problem films be scheduled along with his successes and that genres should be alternated, telling her, "It's a better way to book the act!" Whiteley personally phoned Metro to obtain pristine 35mm prints. "Roger Mayer was the senior manager at that point," she recounted, and she kidded him about how good it was to speak with a Mayer at Metro-Goldwyn-Mayer. "Sometimes they sent all the way to Kansas for the only Technicolor print. It was just amazing how they came through.

"Usually Chuck would make some introductory remarks and place the film within his career life. People might have a pre-question. Then we'd run the film, and we had a good hour or hour and a half afterwards to talk about it. Sometimes, if things were really rocking and another class was coming in, we'd all go down the street to the hamburger joint, and Chuck would sit down with us and talk there."

The inquisitive USC students enjoyed their self-effacing professor's informality and easy humor. "They expected to hear theories," offers Whiteley, "but Chuck really didn't have any. Only: 'This is what worked here.' He remembered stories, not choices." Elated by the students' reception of his films throughout the course, Walters even grew misty-eyed over the ovation that greeted *Jumbo*. (He recovered in time to joke, "Where were you guys twenty years ago when this film needed an audience?")

"Then Chuck had to have a wrap party," recounts Whiteley. "He rented the entertainment suite at the Holiday Inn across the street, and anybody in the class who wanted could come over for a little cocktail party. That's how he was—very giving—and he wanted it to have a nice neat little ending."

He had already summarized his ambition for the semester in an interview offered midterm: "For openers I tell the kids, learn all you can. Then throw the book over your shoulder, and go from your guts. When I started, there was no such thing as a school or a book. It had to be on a gut level. There's only so much you can learn, [and] then it's up to you—your blood and guts."[12]

Teaching had become something of a salvation and a solace. He wrote Gloria Swanson, "School is going beautifully. Really think it is saving my life."[13] The underlying emotion in his phrasing reflected the fact that John Darrow had died on February 24, three weeks into Chuck's semester. He later told an interviewer, "I lost my . . . ," and there his voice trailed off. Their five and a half decades of companionship deserved more than a sterile "agent" or "manager," and he finally acknowledged softly, "I lost my best friend."

Understandably, USC invited the popular Walters to return in the fall. "I'm heading into my second season," he boasted—this time for evening sessions that were also open to the public. In turn, Chuck approached his famous friends to join in the post-screening talkbacks; George Cukor was one of the first to volunteer. "He said, 'I'd love to come to one of your classes . . . and fight!'" Chuck recalled with a laugh. Their plan was to alternate clips from Cukor's *The Philadelphia Story* and Walters's *High Society*. "We'll get into a big argument," Cukor chortled. "That'll be fun. Just give me first billing."[14] The irascible director never made it to class, as he was then immersed in filming *Rich and Famous* at M-G-M. But Nancy Walker turned up for *Best Foot Forward*, as did Lucy for *Du Barry Was a Lady*. On that night, when the floor was opened to questions, an audience member asked where *Du Barry* co-star Virginia O'Brien had been keeping herself, and a loud voice instantly rang out from the rear of the auditorium: "She's sitting back here in the cheap seats!" O'Brien thus won her own round of applause.

Future film producer and editor Les Perkins, then in his twenties and a participant in the class, fondly recalls another memorable moment:

One night I took in an audiocassette of "Mr. Monotony," sung by Judy Garland and deleted from *Easter Parade,* to ask Chuck about it. He was excited because he hadn't heard it in all those years since. The class listened intently to the rare recording. As the vamp started to build, I soon noticed Chuck, who had been sitting behind the students, had gotten up and was maneuvering down the aisle. [He was] strolling gracefully in time to the music, no doubt recalling his choreography: slowly stepping cat-like, forward and back, with occasional shoulder shrugs to accent Irving Berlin's catchy syncopation. I still smile as my mind visually recalls that moment.[15]

Walters would continue to play to his audience. He was forthright and frankly poked fun at contemporary Hollywood's misguided understanding of what makes a good musical director. Hearing that John Huston was directing the movie of *Annie,* he said, "My jaw dropped. Just like when I heard Sidney Lumet was doing *The Wiz.* That was another jaw-dropper. From *The Pawnbroker* to *The Wiz*! Come on."[16]

Whiteley continued as his teacher's aide that autumn, and by now their friendship had moved beyond the USC classroom. "Chuck was able to appreciate people," she says.

He would dish with everybody and have a good time. He took me to the theater a couple of times. We went to see *A Chorus Line,* which he loved. He loved that it was about dancers. We also saw *The Best Little Whorehouse in Texas,* and he loved the choreography. [In the process,] Chuck taught me where to sit. He had to be in the front row of the balcony—he said that's the only place to see a musical. From the front balcony, you get to see the shape of the movement, which is so much a part of the choreography. You don't get that from front-on in the orchestra.

Saluting Whiteley's selflessness on his behalf at USC, he surprised her with a one-of-a-kind gift. "I never told Chuck that Gene Kelly was my all-time favorite. It would come up that I liked his films, but I never *told* him I liked Kelly. In the end, Chuck figured it out, and he gave me Gene Kelly for a Christmas present. He had a party at his Malibu house, and he invited Gene. Gene came to talk with me and sort of be my date for five minutes. It was very generous—of both of them!"

Walters celebrated his sixty-ninth birthday during USC's second semester. His spirits were high, but he had begun to experience physical problems—a deepening cough, slight chest pains, and an inexplicable loss of weight. Much of the following year was spent with doctors.[17] By December 1981, he had been diagnosed with cancer. He would not live to see his next birthday.

Chuck's decades of chain smoking made the news almost an inevitability. The shock came when a biopsy confirmed mesothelioma—a rare, usually fatal cancer that attacks the linings of the lungs, heart, and abdominal cavity. Virtually all mesothelioma cases stem from exposure to asbestos, which puzzled Walters's doctors. Chuck searched his background for a possible cause and came to one probable conclusion: "The [movie] studio walls were lined, they were saturated with asbestos. The insulation was so old you could smell it. My God, I can't think of a place they didn't use it." (Actor Steve McQueen had been diagnosed with mesothelioma in late 1979, but this was attributed to his years working as a merchant mariner in asbestos-lined ships.)

Chuck sought counsel from lawyer Maury Gentile in March 1982. It was the first time that the film industry had been confronted with the possibility of a class action suit for work-related asbestos exposure. The ailing director asked for $60,000 in workman's compensation from M-G-M and Columbia Pictures for pain and suffering; Gentile later confirmed that the suit also included an additional $50,000 for medical bills and $15,000 for temporary disability.[18] "The poor man was really suffering," recalled KCOP–Channel 13 reporter Jackie Rich, who interviewed Chuck about the lawsuit. "He was very frustrated—frustrated that he couldn't work anymore."

As the gravity of mesothelioma settled in, Chuck realized that Joe Anthony—despite their fifteen years together—would have no legal claim to their shared property or any other portion of Walters's estate. Such assets passed to the surviving spouse, tax free, in a heterosexual marriage; at the time, those benefits were denied to gay couples. Whiteley summarizes

Chuck's solution to the problem: "He adopted Joe. . . . I think for the ease of settling his estate, whatever estate he was going to have left."[19]

Walters appeared that spring before a group of young attorneys, hired to hear class action depositions. "He was frail, but quite a character," recalls one anonymous witness. "We had been hearing many asbestos-related cases, mostly from old shipyard workers. Then Charles Walters came in, a colorful old guy, with two male nurses—and a son." He asked for a straight-backed chair and settled in to be questioned. When asked, "Mr. Walters, have you ever worked a shipyard?" the director rascally fell back on his candor and humor. "Oh, *honey*," he replied, his tone clearly indicating a negative response. "It was only mid-morning," continues the witness, "but the nurses had already pulled out a bottle of wine. They seemed more like playmates for the son. It all seemed very questionable. I don't recall if a lawsuit was even filed."[20]

The swift decline in Chuck's health during 1982 coincided with mainstream media reports about a curious "gay cancer" that was infecting homosexual men. Then known as GRID (gay-related immune deficiency) or GCS (gay compromise syndrome), it made headlines that June when a host of new cases were diagnosed in Southern California. The then-untreatable disease was renamed "acquired immune deficiency syndrome" in July, and some of Walters's closest colleagues would forever insist that he died of AIDS.

Chuck eventually was consigned to treatment at Cedars-Sinai Hospital. By pure coincidence, the adjoining room was occupied by Henry Fonda; it had been almost half a century since they crashed Broadway together in *New Faces*. Both men were battling cancer and realized they were losing the fight, but they took great pleasure in remembering their "Leonard Sillman days": the show's scores of auditions and their smashing opening night at the Fulton. That was where it had all begun.

Additional bolstering came from Walters's friends, whether in person or by phone. "I didn't go to see him," remembers Jimie Morrissey. "Our friend Manuel Alvarez wanted me to go, but I really didn't want to see him [in that condition]. I called instead, and Chuck said, 'Jim, thanks for calling. I'm going home. There's nothing they can do for me. It's all through my body.'"[21] After he returned to the condominium, Nancy Walker visited regularly, as did Lucille Ball.

Nurses were now required around the clock, and Joe said at the time, "I slept with that man day and night with the nurses right there."[22]

Through it all, "Chuck remained gracious," remembers Whiteley. "He tended to other people's needs, even when he was finally bedridden the last couple of weeks. He'd make sure Joe got a drink for me, or if there wasn't the right chair, he'd tell Joe to go get another one. He wouldn't have asked Joe before [he was sick]; Chuck would always get up and get something for me, or any of his guests. But now he couldn't walk around."

Walters's health took a decided turn for the worse in late summer. On Friday, August 13, 1982, just after eleven o'clock in the evening, he was gone. "He died in my arms," said Joe, "with his eyes wide open, and he said, 'Go for it, baby.'"[23]

By his request, Charles Walters was cremated, and there is no record of a funeral service. The cause of death was officially listed as "peritoneal mesothelioma with metastasis"; the coroner confirmed inhalation or ingestion of asbestos particles as the reason and gave 10202 Washington Boulevard in Culver City (the M-G-M studios) as the location of exposure.[24] "Walters is survived by an adopted son, Joseph," read the obituaries, and although Joe retained the Malibu condo, he soon moved to San Francisco. He also pursued his own lawsuit, asking for roughly $1 million from M-G-M and Columbia for loss of support. (He died at forty-three in 1986, a victim of alcohol poisoning.)[25]

Before Walters's passing, he'd stipulated that his set of twenty-one leather-bound, personalized shooting scripts be donated to USC, where they joined an archive that already held the papers of Arthur Freed and Roger Edens. Mary Whiteley also worked to pull together a Directors Guild tribute and confirmed the participation of Gene Kelly, Ann Miller, and Esther Williams, among others. But much as Joe would attempt to auction Chuck's scripts before USC claimed them, Whiteley found he also "seemed to get in the way" at every turn in the preparation for the DGA celebration, and it was canceled.

If there were no public posthumous honors afforded Charles Walters, his final life's chapter at least delivered other accolades. He took great satisfaction in the reactions he had received during his year at USC; that experience perhaps coalesced in a letter of thankful acknowledgment he received from student Les Perkins. Looking back, Perkins says, "I don't remember my exact wording. But I probably said something like, 'There were two men I most admired, Walt Disney and Frank Capra. Now there are three.' And I added that the difference with Chuck is that I also admired him as a person, [for] his kindness—not just for the work."[26]

Walters had the letter framed. It hung on his bedroom wall for the rest of his life.

Across his career, Charles Walters perpetually referred to himself as "a lucky, poor little son of a bitch from Anaheim who never had a dancing lesson." But a singular drive and inborn talent led him through a lifetime of often-joyous productivity and contribution. It's perhaps paradoxical that *The Belle of New York*—one of Walters's least favorite of his films—should yield an ideally worded final testament. Yet Johnny Mercer's "I Wanna Be a Dancin' Man," with its reflective, nonchalant lyric, seems an apt summation of a life quietly spent making entertainment, which, in the end, is the warm legacy of Charles Walters:

Let other men build mighty nations
Or buildings to the sky;
I'll leave a few creations
To show that I was dancin' by.

Appendix
The Works of Charles Walters

Stage Work: Performer

1931

Fanchon and Marco, U.S. tour, summer–fall.

1933

LOW AND BEHOLD, opening May 18 at the Pasadena Community Playhouse and July 19 at the Hollywood Music Box (California).

1934

NEW FACES OF 1934, opening March 15 at the Fulton Theater.
FOOLS RUSH IN, opening December 25 at The Playhouse. Songs introduced by Walters: "I Want to Dance," "Shoes" (danced and staged).

1935

Versailles Club, Fox and Walters, opening February. (Supper club appearances with Dorothy Fox.)
PARADE, opening May 20 at the Guild Theater.
JUBILEE, opening October 12 at The Imperial Theatre. Songs introduced by Walters: "Just One of Those Things," "A Picture of Me Without You," and "Begin the Beguine" (all with June Knight).

1936

TRANSATLANTIC RHYTHM, opening October 1 at the Adelphi Theater, London. Songs introduced by Walters: "I Heard a Song in the Taxi" (with

Dorothy Dare), "Finding You—Losing You" (with Ruth Etting), and "The Man Who Broke the Bank at Monte Carlo."

THE SHOW IS ON, opening December 25 at the Winter Garden. Songs introduced by Walters: "Little Old Lady" and "What Has He Got?" (both with Mitzi Mayfair).

1937

The Viennese Roof of the St. Regis Hotel, opening August 5. Solo engagement.

BETWEEN THE DEVIL, opening December 22 at The Imperial Theatre. Songs introduced by Walters: "You Have Everything" and "I'm Against Rhythm" (both with Vilma Ebsen).

1938

I MARRIED AN ANGEL, Opening May 11 at the Shubert Theatre. Song introduced by Walters: "How to Win Friends and Influence People" (with Audrey Christie).

1939

DU BARRY WAS A LADY, opening December 6 at the 46th Street Theater. Songs introduced by Walters: "Well, Did You Evah!" and "Ev'ry Day a Holiday" (both with Betty Grable).

Stage Work: Choreographer

1938

SING OUT THE NEWS, opening September 24 at the Music Box Theatre. Staged musical sequence: "Peace and the Diplomat."

1940

MANY A SLIP (Princeton Triangle Show), opening November 15 at Mc-Carter Theatre (New Jersey). Also played 44th Street Theatre, January 3–4, 1941 (New York).

SHE HAD TO SAY YES (also known as *MEET THE ELITE* and *LADY COMES ACROSS*), closed prior to Broadway.

1941

LET'S FACE IT, opening October 29 at the Imperial Theatre.
BANJO EYES, opening December 25 at the Hollywood Theatre.

1946

ST. LOUIS WOMAN, opening March 30 at the Martin Beck Theater.

1951

JUDY GARLAND AT THE PALACE, opening October 16 at the Palace Theater. Walters performed on stage with Garland opening night. Additionally, he supplied staging (in part or in whole) for Garland at the Palace (open: September 26, 1956), Chicago's Orchestra Hall (open: September 4, 1958), and the Los Angeles Cocoanut Grove (open: July 23, 1958).

Stage Work: Director

1954

BY THE BEAUTIFUL SEA, opening April 8 at the Majestic Theater. Walters left the show while it was on the road. Replaced by Marshall Jamison.

Film Work: Choreographer
(other than in his own movies)

1942

SEVEN DAYS' LEAVE. Studio: RKO Radio-Pictures. Choreographed all musical sequences.

1943

DU BARRY WAS A LADY. Studio: M-G-M. Choreographed all musical sequences.
PRESENTING LILY MARS. Studio: M-G-M. Musical sequence: "Where There's Music" finale.

BEST FOOT FORWARD. Studio: M-G-M. Choreographed all musical sequences with the exception of "Buckle Down Winsocki" (staged by Jack Donohue).

GIRL CRAZY. Studio: M-G-M. Musical sequences: "Embraceable You," "Bidin' My Time," "Could You Use Me," and (in part) "I Got Rhythm."

1944

SINCE YOU WENT AWAY. Studio: Selznick International Pictures. Uncredited. Staged "The Shadow Waltz."

GASLIGHT. Studio: M-G-M. Uncredited.

THE CANTERVILLE GHOST. Studio: M-G-M. Uncredited.

MEET THE PEOPLE. Studio: M-G-M. Musical sequence: "I Like to Recognize the Tune."

BROADWAY RHYTHM. Studio: M-G-M. Musical sequences: "Milkman, Keep Those Bottles Quiet" and "Brazilian Boogie."

THREE MEN IN WHITE. Studio: M-G-M.

MEET ME IN ST. LOUIS. Studio: M-G-M. Staged all musical sequences with the exception of "Have Yourself a Merry Little Christmas" (directed solely by Vincente Minnelli).

1945

THRILL OF A ROMANCE. Studio: M-G-M.

HER HIGHNESS AND THE BELLBOY. Studio: M-G-M. Musical sequence: "Dream."

WEEK-END AT THE WALDORF. Studio: M-G-M. Musical sequence: "Guadalajara."

BUD ABBOTT AND LOU COSTELLO IN HOLLYWOOD. Studio M-G-M. Musical sequence: "Fun on the Wonderful Midway."

1946

ZIEGFELD FOLLIES OF 1946. Studio: M-G-M. Musical sequences: "A Great Lady Has 'An Interview'" and (uncredited) "The Sweepstake Ticket." Deleted: "The Pied Piper" (director).

1948

SUMMER HOLIDAY. Studio: M-G-M. All musical sequences.

Film Work: Performer

1943

PRESENTING LILY MARS. Dances with Judy Garland in film's finale: "It's
Three O'Clock in the Morning" and "Broadway Rhythm."
GIRL CRAZY. Dances with Judy Garland in the "Embraceable You" sequence.

1945

BUD ABBOTT AND LOU COSTELLO IN HOLLYWOOD. Dances with
Frances Rafferty in "Fun on the Wonderful Midway."

1953

LILI. Doubles for actor Jean-Pierre Aumont in "Adoration Ballet."
EASY TO LOVE. Dances with Cyd Charisse. The couple is seen from the
waist down only.
TORCH SONG. Dances with Joan Crawford.

Film Work: Director

1945

SPREADIN' THE JAM (short subject). Metro-Goldwyn-Mayer Corp.
[Loew's Inc.]. (10 minutes) Also choreographed.

1947

GOOD NEWS. Metro-Goldwyn-Mayer Corp. [Loew's Inc.]. Producer: Arthur Freed. Associate Producer: Roger Edens. (95 minutes) Also choreographed: "Good News," "The Best Things in Life are Free," "Lucky in
Love," "Be a Ladies Man," "Just Imagine," and "The French Lesson."

1948

EASTER PARADE. Metro-Goldwyn-Mayer Corp. [Loew's Inc.]. Producer:
Arthur Freed. (103 minutes) Also choreographed: "A Couple of Swells"
(in part), "Better Luck Next Time," "A Fella with an Umbrella," "Easter

Parade," "I Want to Go Back to Michigan," "I Love a Piano" (opening). Deleted: "Mr. Monotony."

1949

THE BARKLEYS OF BROADWAY. Metro-Goldwyn-Mayer Corp. [Loew's Inc.]. Producer: Arthur Freed. (110 minutes) Also choreographed: "You'd Be So Hard to Replace," "A Weekend in the Country," "Manhattan Downbeat" (opening).

1950

SUMMER STOCK. Metro-Goldwyn-Mayer Corp. [Loew's Inc.]. Producer: Joe Pasternak. (109 minutes) Also choreographed: "Get Happy."

1951

THREE GUYS NAMED MIKE. Metro-Goldwyn-Mayer Corp. [Loew's Inc.]. Producer: Armand Deutsch. (91 minutes)
TEXAS CARNIVAL. Metro-Goldwyn-Mayer Corp. [Loew's Inc.]. Producer: Jack Cummings. (76 minutes)

1952

THE BELLE OF NEW YORK. Metro-Goldwyn-Mayer Corp. [Loew's Inc.]. Producer: Arthur Freed. Assistant Producer (and substitute director): Roger Edens. (82 minutes)

1953

LILI. Metro-Goldwyn-Mayer Corp. [Loew's Inc.]. Producer: Edwin H. Knopf. (81 minutes) Also choreographed, assisted by Dorothy Jarnac.
DANGEROUS WHEN WET. Metro-Goldwyn-Mayer Corp. [Loew's Inc.]. Producer George Wells. (95 minutes) Also choreographed, assisted by Billy Daniels. ("I Like Men" staged by Daniels.)
TORCH SONG. Metro-Goldwyn-Mayer Corp. [Loew's Inc.]. Producers: Henry Berman and Sidney Franklin Jr. (90 minutes). Also choreographed.
EASY TO LOVE. Metro-Goldwyn-Mayer Corp. [Loew's Inc.]. Producer: Joe Pasternak. (96 minutes) Also choreographed: "That's What a Rainy Day Is For," "Did'ja Ever," and "Easy to Love."

1955

THE GLASS SLIPPER. Metro-Goldwyn-Mayer Corp. [Loew's Inc.]. Producer: Edwin H. Knopf. (94 minutes)

THE TENDER TRAP. Metro-Goldwyn-Mayer Corp. [Loew's Inc.]. Producer: Lawrence Weingarten. (111 minutes) Also staged musical sequences.

1956

HIGH SOCIETY. Metro-Goldwyn-Mayer Corp. [Loew's Inc.]; Bing Crosby Productions; Sol C. Siegel Productions, Inc. Producer: Sol C. Siegel. (107 minutes) Also staged musical sequences.

1957

DON'T GO NEAR THE WATER. Metro-Goldwyn-Mayer Corp. [Loew's Inc.]; Avon Productions, Inc. Producer: Lawrence Weingarten. (102 minutes)

1959

ASK ANY GIRL. Metro-Goldwyn-Mayer Corp. [Loew's Inc.]; Euterpe Productions, Inc. Producer: Joe Pasternak. (101 minutes)

1960

PLEASE DON'T EAT THE DAISIES. Metro-Goldwyn-Mayer Corp. [Loew's Inc.]; Euterpe Productions, Inc. Producer: Joe Pasternak. Associate Producer: Martin Melcher. (111 minutes). Also staged musical sequences.

1961

TWO LOVES. Metro-Goldwyn-Mayer Corp. [Loew's Inc.]; Julian Blaustein Productions. Producer: Julian Blaustein. (100 minutes)

1962

BILLY ROSE'S JUMBO. Metro-Goldwyn-Mayer Corp. [Loew's Inc.]; Euterpe Productions, Inc.; Arwin Productions, Inc. Producer: Joe Pasternak and Martin Melcher. Associate Producer: Roger Edens. Second team: Busby Berkeley. (125 minutes) Also staged musical sequences.

1964

THE UNSINKABLE MOLLY BROWN. Metro-Goldwyn-Mayer Corp. [Loew's Inc.]; Marten Productions; A Lawrence Weingarten Production. Producer: Lawrence Weingarten. Associate Producer: Roger Edens. (128 minutes) Also staged musical sequences: "Colorado, My Home," "I'll Never Say No."

1966

WALK, DON'T RUN. Columbia Pictures; Walk Co.; Sol C. Siegel Productions. Producer: Sol C. Siegel. (114 minutes)

Uncredited Film Work: Director

1958

GIGI. Metro-Goldwyn-Mayer Corp. [Loew's Inc.]; Arthur Freed Productions, Inc. Director: Vincente Minnelli. Choreographed "The Night They Invented Champagne" and redirected (in part or in whole) various scenes and the musical sequences "The Parisians" and "She Is Not Thinking of Me."

1960

CIMARRON. Metro-Goldwyn-Mayer Corp. [Loew's Inc.]. Director: Anthony Mann. Redirected various scenes.

1961

GO NAKED IN THE WORLD. Metro-Goldwyn-Mayer Corp. [Loew's Inc.]. Director: Ranald MacDougall. Redirected various scenes, notably the beginning of the film.

Television Work: Director

1970

THE GOVERNOR AND J.J. "The Making of the Governor," aired November 25, 1970, on CBS.

1971

HERE'S LUCY. "Lucy and Aladdin's Lamp," filmed August 6, 1970, aired February 1, 1971, on CBS.
"Lucy's House Guest Harry," filmed September 17, 1970, aired January 25, 1971, on CBS.

1975

A LUCILLE BALL SPECIAL: THREE FOR TWO. Aired December 3, 1975, on CBS.

1976

A LUCILLE BALL SPECIAL: WHAT NOW, CATHERINE CURTIS? Aired March 30, 1976, on CBS.

Acknowledgments

Before laying down this lengthy (yet entirely warranted) record of acknowledgments, I'd like to paraphrase something Judy Garland once said she learned from legendary stage actress Laurette Taylor: one should go through life saying thank you. Well, in this case, this one cannot say thank you heartily or respectfully enough.

I begin by expressing my deep appreciation to two of Hollywood's most gracious women, Leslie Caron and Debbie Reynolds. They are truly in a class by themselves.

Ronald L. Davis has championed this book for years. What a treasure he has bestowed to students and scholars through his prolific Oral History Collection on the Performing Arts. I thank David Fantle and Tom Johnson, who gave me full access to their 1980 interview with Charles Walters, some of which appeared in their fine anthology *Reel to Real* (Oregon, WI: Badger Books, 2004). My kind appreciation to John Cutts, Hugh Fordin, Douglas McVay, and Paul Savauge for gathering Walters's words while it was possible—and for asking the right questions.

A biography with widely scattered source material can come about only with the skilled assistance of archivists nationwide. I am supremely indebted to Ned Comstock, who contributed far beyond the call of duty. Ned never tired in pointing me toward the treasures that are housed within the collections at USC's Cinema and Television Library. He is both a credit to his profession and a gift to any author. Additionally, I thank the devoted staffs at the Anaheim Historical Society, the Harry Ransom Humanities Research Center at the University of Texas at Austin, the Howard Gottlieb Archival Research Center at Boston University, the Margaret Herrick Library, the New York Public Library for the Performing Arts, the Palm Springs Historical Society, and the Seeley G. Mudd Manuscript Library at Princeton University.

While page limits make describing the services rendered by the volunteer army named below impossible, I bow to each of them for their assistance, knowledge, insight, effort, and/or inspiration: Woolsey Ackerman, John Angelo, Nita Bieber, Larry Billman, Saadia Billman, Craig Burke, Bryan Cooper, Grover Dale, David Engel, Harvey Evans (who selflessly works to save our dance heritage), Michael Feinstein, Peter Fitzgerald, Mark Griffin, Lee Hale (and the

Professional Dancers Society), Richard Schuyler Hooke, Sam Irvin, Mitchell Ivers, David Kaufman, Miles Krueger, Mark Levin, the late Don Liberto, Stanley Livingston, Caren Marsh-Doll, Bert May (what a blissfully, blizzardy afternoon that was), Dennis Millay (the prince of programming at TCM), Barry Monush, Jimie Morrissey, Miriam Nelson, Robert Osborne (whose wise counsel made a lasting impression on this eager novice), Les Perkins, Christine Peters, David Price, the late Peggy Rae, Scott Roberts, Donald Saddler, James Sheridan, Morgan Sills, Bobby Steggert, the late Gil Stratton, Elmer Thill, Lewis Turner, William Warren, Tom Watson, and the wonderfully helpful Mary Whiteley.

As a fellow film preservationist, I must acknowledge George Feltenstein and Richard P. May, for their years of service at Warner Bros., and Roger L. Mayer for his work at Turner Entertainment. Because of their painstaking efforts we continue to enjoy the Charles Walters legacy, luminously.

Thanks to Patrick McGilligan, Anne Dean Dotson, Debbie Masi, Sue Warga (copyeditor extraordinaire), Bailey E. Johnson, and the super-helpful staff at University Press of Kentucky, who agreed that the Charles Walters story needed to be shared.

I thank my rock-solid literary agent Kenneth Wright, who guided this book and gave sage advice freely. His kindness made all the initial rejection endurable. Thanks to the late Coyne Steven Sanders for our earliest conversations that prompted this project. I am also genuinely indebted to the unstinting Ranse Ransone for his never-flagging support, countless courtesies, and gentle nudges. He is a cherished friend.

Other personal thanks go to Dennis, Steven, and Owen Ballard-O'Neill (for free lodging and friendship) and to my treasured "second family" in Indiana: the Voelkers and the McCulloughs, with a special salute to Luke and Lydia.

As ever, my own loving family was a consistent support. I give further heartfelt mention to my imaginative nieces Caroline, Eleanor, and Madeleine and my bright nephews John and Nicholas. A posthumous blessing to my grandmother Bette, who I think would have liked this book, and my grandfather Glenn, who instilled in me many of the values I try to follow.

My utmost gratitude goes to the astoundingly generous John Fricke, for his keen critique and proactive support for this project—and his years of friendship. He is an unparalleled ally. ("Awww, nuthin' could be finer!")

But it all begins and ends with my partner, Frank McCullough, who convinced me that I could (and should) write this book. He has my appreciation for the essential role he played in its creation, and my love for the essential role he continues to play in my life.

Notes

In 1981, Charles Walters expressed a desire to pen his memoirs. This never happened, but I hope this biography has allowed him ample opportunity to recount (and comment upon) his own story. This wouldn't have been possible without the foresight and efforts of five outstanding oral historians who captured his words. Unless otherwise noted, all direct quotes from Charles Walters are derived from:

John Cutts, "On the Bright Side: An Interview with Charles Walters," *Films and Filming* 16, no. 11 (August 1970).

Ronald L. Davis Oral History Collection #215, De Golyer Library, Southern Methodist University, Dallas. Interview conducted in Malibu, California, August 21, 1980. (This stellar resource provided outstanding detail about Walters's pre-Hollywood days.)

David Fantle and Tom Johnson interview with Charles Walters, conducted in Malibu, California, September 1980, provided courtesy of David Fantle and Tom Johnson.

Pierre Sauvage, "Interview with Charles Walters," *Positif: Revue mensuelle de cinéma,* nos. 144–145 (November–December 1972).

Abbreviations

AMPAS = Margaret Herrick Library, Academy of Motion Pictures Arts and Sciences, Beverly Hills

BU = Howard Gotlieb Archival Research Center, Boston University

HRC = Harry Ransom Humanities Research Center, University of Texas at Austin

NYPL = New York Public Library for the Performing Arts, New York

SMU = De Golyer Library, Southern Methodist University

UGA = The Walter J. Brown Media Archive and Peabody Awards Collection, University of Georgia

USC = Cinema-Television Library, University of Southern California

Preface

1. David Quinlan, *The Illustrated Guide to Film Directors* (Totowa, NJ: Barnes and Noble Books, 1983), 311.

2. Conversation with Arthur Knight, May 11, 1976, audio reel at USC.

3. Leslie Caron, interview by the author, Los Angeles, October 12, 2008.

4. Jon Whitcomb, "Hollywood's Biggest Star," *Cosmopolitan*, October 1962.

5. Andrew Sarris, *Film Culture*, Spring 1963, 40. This appraisal was repeated in Sarris, *The American Cinema: Directors and Directions, 1929–1968* (New York: Dutton, 1968), 186–187. In the latter, Walters was referenced as "Lightly Likable."

6. Walters interview by Joseph McBride, *Variety*, November 5, 1975.

7. Eric Rohmer on Walters, *Cahiers du cinéma*, May 1981.

8. Walters 1976 interview in conjunction with the release of *That's Entertainment, Part 2*, AMPAS.

I. The Anaheim Hoofer

1. *New York Herald Tribune*, March 28, 1937.

2. Charles Powell Walter's birth certificate obtained from the Public Health Department, City of Pasadena.

3. Unidentified newspaper clipping, Anaheim History Room.

4. Howard Loudon, 1974 oral history, Anaheim History Room.

5. Anaheim phone directory from 1922, Anaheim History Room.

6. Elmer Thill, interview by the author, Anaheim, April 26, 2011.

7. The electrophone, in its simplest form, is an application of the telephone, including a system of transmitters and receivers—a transmitter being stationed at the theater and connected by a line (overhead or underground) with a receiver situated in the subscriber's house. The fact that Walters's childhood home had such a novelty apparatus is indication of how great a role the performing arts played in his family's life.

8. Thill interview, 2011.

9. *New York Herald Tribune*, March 28, 1937.

10. Thill interview, 2011.

11. Ibid.

12. *The Anoranco*, December 13, 1927. Despite the occasional grammatical error, the student-generated Anaheim Union High School newspaper offers additional evidence of the school's high standards. *The Anoranco* regularly featured articles aimed at developing students' positive deportment and behavior.

13. *The Anoranco*, February 1929.

14. *The Anoranco*, May 1929.

15. *The Anoranco*, 1929.

16. *New York Post,* April 17, 1937.

17. Louise Booth, *One to Twenty-Eight: A History of Anaheim Union School District,* Anaheim History Room. The school's newly appointed dramatics advisor, Faye Kern Schulz, purportedly lobbied for Walters's musical comedy ideas. Schulz, a plump, motherly teacher who sported a stylish permanent wave, offered philosophies of teaching and of life that were identical: "You can't please everyone, but if you feel you have pleased most people, you have accomplished something" (*Los Angeles Times,* June 9, 1963).

18. *The Anoranco,* November 19, 1929.

19. Ibid.

20. Ibid.

21. Richard Fischle Jr. oral history, Anaheim History Room.

22. Walters to Arthur Knight, 1976.

23. Walters letters to Leonard Sillman, circa 1931. All correspondence is from Box 190, Folder 6, Leonard Sillman Collection #280, BU.

24. Hector Arce, *The Secret Life of Tyrone Power* (New York: William Morrow, 1979), 72.

25. Ibid.

26. Leonard Sillman Collection #280, BU.

27. Ronald Davis, Oral History Collection (henceforth OHC) #154: Leonard Sillman. Interview conducted January 10, 1979, SMU.

28. From an early pitch for *Low and Behold.* Leonard Sillman Collection #280, BU.

29. Leonard Sillman, *Here Lies Leonard Sillman, Straightened Out at Last: An Autobiography* (New York: Citadel, 1959), 163.

30. Davis, OHC #154, SMU.

31. Ibid.

32. Arce, *Secret Life of Tyrone Power,* 72.

33. Early draft for *Here Lies Leonard Sillman,* Leonard Sillman Collection #280, BU. Throughout the original text, Sillman refers to Power, Walters, and the Rocky Twins as "beautiful"; an editor's pen is noticeable in the change to either "handsome" or "nice-looking."

34. Arce, *Secret Life of Tyrone Power,* 74.

35. *Los Angeles Times,* July 12, 1933.

2. A "New Face" in Town

1. Leonard Sillman Collection #280, BU.

2. Sillman, *Here Lies Leonard Sillman,* 159.

3. Arce, *Secret Life of Tyrone Power,* 73.

4. Sillman, *Here Lies Leonard Sillman,* 161.

5. Mary Whiteley, interview by the author, Los Angeles, August 2007. Per Sillman's memoir, he based salaries for the Los Angeles run of *Low and Behold* on an individual's contribution and importance to the show; Walters was on the high end of the scale—rating a 6 out of 10—while Tyrone Power (a 4) brought home only $5.81.

6. Frederick Nolan, *Lorenz Hart: A Poet on Broadway* (New York: Oxford University Press, 1994), 192.

7. Arce, *Secret Life of Tyrone Power,* 74.

8. Sillman, *Here Lies Leonard Sillman,* 162.

9. Early draft for *Here Lies Leonard Sillman,* Leonard Sillman Collection #280, BU.

10. Frederick Russell, "One Way to Broadway—and No Return to Hollywood for Charles Walters!" *American Dancer,* circa 1938, NYPL.

11. Ibid.

12. Early draft for *Here Lies Leonard Sillman,* Leonard Sillman Collection #280, BU.

13. Sillman, *Here Lies Leonard Sillman,* 167.

14. Ibid., 179.

15. Ibid., 180.

16. Conversation with Knight, 1976.

17. Davis, OHC #215, SMU. Walters recounted, "I'd get to my dressing room, [Coca's] dresser would come over and get the coat, and then I'd pick it up on my way out. I got ten dollars more a week, and that was great, because we were getting about $40."

18. Davis, OHC #6: Imogene Coca. Interview conducted December 3, 1974, SMU.

19. Leonard Sillman, "All in Fun," typed article, undated, Leonard Sillman Collection #280, BU.

20. *New Faces* program, Fulton Theatre, 1934.

21. *New York Sun,* March 16, 1934.

22. *New York Evening Journal,* March 29, 1934.

23. *New York World-Telegram,* March 16, 1934.

24. Sillman, *Here Lies Leonard Sillman,* 207.

25. *New York Sun,* December 2, 1938.

26. Ibid.

27. Davis, OHC #154, SMU.

3. Beginning the Beguine

1. *New York Sun,* December 2, 1938.

2. Virginia Volland, *Designing Woman: The Art and Practice of Theatrical Costume Design* (New York: Doubleday, 1966), 173–174.

3. Donald Saddler, interview by the author, New York, August 29, 2006.

4. Don Liberto, interview by the author, New York, February 23, 2008.

5. Ibid.

6. Lewis Turner, telephone interview by the author, New York, February 22, 2008.

7. *New York Times,* May 20, 1935. In *Parade,* the Fox and Walters team were featured in three prominent dance duets. One of these pairings, billed on opening night as "Decadence Dance," was retitled "Smart Set" a few days later. Also, their "Fear in My Heart" originally opened the second act but was shifted to another slot after the premiere. This allowed the large-scale "Bourgeois Processional"—where Walters portrayed a laborer—to greet audiences immediately after intermission.

8. Arthur Jacobson, interviewed by Irene Kahn Atkins, *A Directors Guild of America Oral History* (Metuchen, NJ: Scarecrow Press, 1991), 78–79.

9. For *Jubilee,* M-G-M supplied June Knight and Mary Boland, and it secretively bankrolled the production in order to secure the movie rights, fronting an estimated $125,000.

10. All conversations about Montgomery Clift come from Davis, OHC #215, SMU.

11. Russell, "One Way to Broadway."

12. The Albertina Rasch staging for "A Picture of Me Without You" began in the dark as a hand reaches up to turn on a lamp. The Prince and Karen are revealed lying together in a bed, and as evidenced in existing amateur film footage (held by the Institute of the American Musical in Los Angeles), the pajama-clad couple finish their bedroom frolic by executing a series of *chaîné* turns toward a French-style settee.

13. *New York World-Telegram,* October 14, 1935.

14. *Westchester County Times,* December 13, 1935. A Victor recording of "Just One of Those Things" by Richard Himber charted on November 30, 1935, and peaked at number ten.

15. Ethan Mordden, *Sing for Your Supper: The Broadway Musical in the 1930s* (New York: Palgrave Macmillan, 2005) 199. "Begin the Beguine" would not become a hit until three years after *Jubilee* closed. Bandleader and clarinetist Artie Shaw recorded his arrangement in 1938, which hit number one and remained there for six weeks. "Is it possible," Mordden muses, "that the song did not become immediately popular because the public was too entranced with the characters' [Knight and Walters] emotional transaction to absorb the music?"

16. Ronald Davis, OHC #159: Ralph Blane. Interview conducted March 12, 1979, SMU.

17. *Jubilee*'s Boston review from "Plays Out of Town," September 25, 1935, unidentified newspaper clipping, NYPL.

18. *Durham Times,* October 22, 1935.

19. *New York Herald Tribune,* March 29, 1937.

20. *New York Evening Journal,* October 14, 1935.

21. *Chicago Journal of Commerce,* October 14, 1935.

22. *New York Times,* October 14, 1935.

23. *Daily News Record,* October 15, 1935.

24. *Hollywood Reporter,* October 14, 1935.

25. *Women's Wear Daily,* October 14, 1935.

26. *New York Times,* November 24, 1935.

4. The Show Is On

1. *New York Times,* November 16, 1935.

2. Paramount Pictures publicity, John Darrow clippings file, NYPL.

3. Charles Higham, *Howard Hughes: The Secret Life* (New York: Putnam, 1993), 42.

4. Liberto interview, 2008.

5. Russell, "One Way to Broadway."

6. *New York Herald Tribune,* October 13, 1936.

7. *New York Herald Tribune,* October 2, 1936.

8. Ibid.

9. *London Times,* October 2, 1936.

10. Lucius Beebe, "Stage Asides," *New York Herald Tribune,* July 10, 1938.

11. Liberto interview, 2008.

12. New York Telephone Company advertisement, NYPL.

13. *New York Herald Tribune,* March 28, 1937.

14. Ibid.

15. Russell, "One Way to Broadway."

16. *New York Post,* April 17, 1937.

17. Ibid.

18. Russell, "One Way to Broadway."

19. *Variety,* August 25, 1937.

20. All of Gloria Swanson's quotes about her friendship with Walters are from an unpublished typescript for *Swanson on Swanson,* Gloria Swanson Papers, HRC.

21. Russell, "One Way to Broadway."

22. Rusty E. Frank, *Tap! The Greatest Tap Dance Stars and Their Stories, 1900–1955* (New York: William Morrow, 1990), 140.

23. Conversation between Vilma and Buddy Ebsen is from Walters's retelling to Davis, OHC #215, SMU.

24. *New York Herald Tribune,* December 23, 1937.

25. *Washington Post,* January 24, 1938.

26. *New York World-Telegram,* January 23, 1938.

27. Ibid.

28. Ibid.

29. *New York World-Telegram,* January 15, 1938.

30. Ibid.

31. Ibid.

32. Liberto interview, 2008.

33. Greg Lawrence, *Dance with Demons: The Life of Jerome Robbins* (New York: Putnam, 2001), 86.

34. Lucius Beebe, *New York Herald Tribune,* July 10, 1938.

35. 1940 United States Federal Census (Manhattan Borough), May 6.

5. Broadway's "Ranking Dancing Juvenile"

1. *Hartford News,* December 23, 1937.

2. Davis, OHC #215, SMU.

3. *New York Post,* May 13, 1938.

4. Josh Logan, *Josh: My Up and Down, In and Out Life* (New York: Delacorte, 1976), 122.

5. *Brooklyn Daily Eagle,* May 12, 1938. Amateur film footage of *I Married an Angel* held by the Institute of the American Musical in Los Angeles. For a finale to his Charlie McCarthy solo, Walters whipped off a series of *revoltades* (a difficult ballet jump encompassing a complete half aerial rotation) followed by consecutive sideways *jetés.*

6. *New York Times,* July 17, 1938.

7. *New York Herald Tribune,* July 10, 1938.

8. As *Angel* settled into its lengthy run, Walters and Christie quickly became Broadway's celebrated couple *du jour.* Darrow worked to keep the partnership in the public eye. On November 20, 1938, Chuck and Audrey appeared at the Astor Hotel, joining luminaries Walter Huston, Sophie Tucker, and Mary Martin for the first annual benefit show given for the Theatrical Managers, Agents, and Treasurers Association. One week later, the two returned to the hotel to entertain at City College's senior prom, where they reigned as prom king and queen.

9. *Brooklyn Daily Eagle,* May 12, 1938.

10. *Christian Science Monitor,* April 26, 1938.

11. *New York Times,* May 22, 1938.

12. *New York Journal-American,* May 12, 1938.

13. Lucius Beebe, "Stage Asides," *New York Herald Tribune,* July 10, 1938.

14. *Variety,* August 31, 1938.

15. In 1942, Metro-Goldwyn-Mayer delivered its movie of *I Married an Angel,* starring Jeanette MacDonald and Nelson Eddy. Comedy supplanted dancing as quavering character actor Edward Everett Horton (basically) essayed Walters's role.

16. It had been little more than a year since *Between the Devil,* but in that time Alton supplied dances for one musical play (*You Never Know*), two musical revues (*One for the Money, Streets of Paris*), two musical comedies (*Leave It to Me!, Too Many Girls*), and an aquacade.

17. Ethel Merman and George Eells, *Merman: An Autobiography* (New York: Simon and Schuster, 1978), 106–107. Johnny Barnes's services were retained in the minor role of Henri, which afforded him a specialty spot, "Danse Victoire."

18. Liberto interview, 2008.

19. Marge Champion, Turner Classic Movie Interview #73, 1995, UGA.

20. Davis, OHC #215, SMU.

21. *New York Evening Post,* "Two on the Aisle: Review of *Du Barry Was a Lady,*" December 7, 1939.

22. *New York Times,* December 7, 1939.

23. Stanley Green, *Ring Bells! Sing Songs!: Broadway Musicals of the 1930s* (New Rochelle, NY: Arlington House, 1971), 187.

24. Ibid.

25. *New York Daily Mirror,* May 13, 1940.

26. Turner interview, 2008.

27. John Lahr, *Notes on a Cowardly Lion: The Biography of Bert Lahr* (New York: Knopf, 1969), 333.

28. Turner interview, 2008.

29. Bert Lahr story from Davis, OHC #215, SMU.

30. *New York Journal,* circa 1939.

31. Turner interview, 2008.

32. Correspondence dated October 8, 1940, from Triangle Club Records, AC122, Seeley G. Mudd Manuscript Library, Princeton University.

33. *Chicago Daily Tribune,* December 29, 1940.

34. Davis, OHC #215, SMU.

6. Backstage

1. Davis, OHC #215, SMU.

2. *Friends* magazine, November 1941.

3. Fantle and Johnson interview with Walters, 1980. The *New York Times* reported on August 18, 1941, that Walters and Dorothy Fox were jointly hired to choreograph *Let's Face It.*

4. Robert Alton's rehearsal rules are cited by Agnes De Mille in her memoir *Dance with the Piper* (Boston: Little, Brown, 1952), 239.

5. *New York Times,* September 16, 1941.

6. Davis, OHC #215, SMU.

7. Miriam Nelson, interview by the author, New York, autumn 2010.

8. *Friends* magazine, November 1941.

9 Vivian Vance's memories about *Let's Face It* from Frank Castelluccio, *The Other Side of Ethel Mertz* (Manchester, CT: Knowledge, Ideas and Trends, 1998), 136.

10. *Boston Herald,* October 10, 1941. All other reviews, NYPL.

11. *Variety,* November 5, 1941.

12. Miriam Nelson, *My Life Dancing with the Stars* (Albany, GA: Bear Manor Media, 2009), 50.

13. Letter from the Virginia Mayo Collection, USC, Box 6:1.

14. *New York World-Telegram,* March 28, 1946.

15. *Billboard,* January 3, 1942.

16. *New York Times,* January 8, 1942.

7. "You Think Like a Director"

1. "Broadway Stars Sign for Duty," *Los Angeles Times,* October 17, 1940.

2. Liberto interview, 2008.

3. Gene Kelly interviewed in Jerome Delamater, *Dance in the Hollywood Musical* (Ann Arbor, MI: UMI Research Press), 13.

4. Ibid.

5. Sauvage, "Interview with Charles Walters."

6. Walters 1976 interview in conjunction with the release of *That's Entertainment, Part 2,* AMPAS.

7. Eleanor Powell in John Kobal, *People Will Talk* (New York: Knopf, 1985), 232.

8. Ibid., 626–627.

9. Fantle and Johnson interview with Walters, 1980.

10. Jack Cole quoted in Clive Hirschhorn, *Gene Kelly* (Chicago: Regnery, 1974), 100.

11. Kobal, *People Will Talk,* 635.

12. Ibid., 641.

13. Davis, OHC #215, SMU, and Fantle and Johnson interview with Walters, 1980. Walters told Davis that he charmed M-G-M's supreme couturier Irene Gibbons (known deferentially as Irene) into designing the girl dancers' costumes. "Don't do them like *chorus* clothes," he smiled. "Do them like . . . *Irene!*"

14. Walters interview with Hugh Fordin, December 1971, Hugh Fordin Collection, USC (audio reel).

15. I. H. Prinzmetal, M-G-M interoffice memo, August 2, 1942, Arthur Freed Collection, USC.

16. Maxine Barlett's column, *Los Angeles Times*, September 6, 1942.

17. Walters interview with Hugh Fordin, December 1971, Hugh Fordin Collection, USC (audio reel).

18. Kathleen Brady, *Lucille: The Life of Lucille Ball* (New York: Hyperion, 1995), 134.

19. Ronald Davis, OHC #197: Lucille Ball. Interview conducted August 21, 1980, SMU.

20. Seymour Felix, "What About Chorus Boys?" *The Dance*, February 1929.

21. John Kobal, *Gotta Sing, Gotta Dance: A History of Movie Musicals*, rev. ed. (New York: Exeter, 1983), 109.

22. L. K. Sidney, M-G-M interoffice memo to Roy Del Ruth, September 16, 1942, Arthur Freed Collection, USC.

23. Lucille Ball, *Love, Lucy* (New York: Putnam, 1996), 157.

24. Walters phone interview with William Warren about Roger Edens for Boston radio show, 1980.

25. Dorothy Tuttle Nitch interview, Arts and Entertainment Television, June 14, 1996.

26. Warren interview, 1980.

27. Walters interview with Hugh Fordin, December 1971, Hugh Fordin Collection, USC (audio reel).

28. A handful of cultural historians have expounded upon the perceived gay touch in M-G-M musicals in their (at times) insightful attempt to legitimize the "gay laborer" as a key reason for the artistic success of the Freed Unit. These include Steven Cohan in *Incongruous Entertainment: Camp, Cultural Value, and the MGM Musical* (Durham, NC: Duke University Press, 2005); Richard Dyer in "It's Being So Camp as Keeps Us Going," in *Camp: Queer Aesthetics and the Performing Subject*, edited by Fabio Cleto (Ann Arbor: University of Michigan Press, 1999); and Matthew Tinckerton in *Working Like a Homosexual: Camp Capital, Cinema* (Durham, NC: Duke University Press, 2002).

29. Charles Levin, M-G-M interoffice memo, October 20, 1942, Arthur Freed Collection, USC.

30. *Variety*, November 4, 1975.

8. Putting His *Best Foot Forward*

1. Larry Billman, *Film Choreographers and Dance Directors: An Illustrated Biographical Encyclopedia* (Jefferson, NC: McFarland, 1997).

2. Ibid.

3. Walters interview with Hugh Fordin, December 1971, Hugh Fordin Collection, USC (audio reel).

4. Kobal, *Gotta Sing,* rev. ed., 105.

5. Caren Marsh-Doll, telephone interview by the author, January 26, 2007.

6. Albert Johnson, "Conversation with Roger Edens," *Sight and Sound* 27, no. 4 (Spring 1958).

7. In *Girl Crazy,* "Treat Me Rough," a riotous specialty in which the debuting June Allyson put a stranglehold on Rooney, was delegated to Berkeley and Donohue.

8. Gil Stratton, *Best Foot Forward*'s wholesome-looking juvenile in New York, was among those set to reprise their roles, but instead Stratton was sent to play Rooney's roommate in the more prestigious *Girl Crazy.* (Given his physical similarity to Mickey, the youngster watched his screen time dramatically shorten, thanks to editor Albert Akst. "Pronounced *axed,*" the actor later joked.) "Poor Chuck Walters," Stratton recounted to the author in 2007. "For the dances in *Girl Crazy,* he had to put me in front, because my part was pretty big—or at least it was when we were filming. But Chuck knew what to do with us guys who couldn't dance. I was given simple things, basic stuff, and it all came off all right. I think I am seen doing more dancing than anything else in that picture."

9. Stanley Donen in Stephen M. Silverman, *Dancing on the Ceiling: Stanley Donen and His Movies* (New York: Knopf, 1996), 47.

10. Mary Whiteley, interview by the author, August 2007.

11. Davis, OHC #215, SMU.

12. June Allyson, Turner Classic Movie Interview #124, May 5, 1997, UGA.

13. Gloria De Haven in Silverman, *Dancing on the Ceiling,* 47.

14. Walters interview with Hugh Fordin, December 1971.

15. Walters interview, *Hooray for Hollywood* (BBC), circa 1976.

16. Nancy Walker's memories of *Girl Crazy* from Ronald Davis, OHC #144: Nancy Walker. Interview conducted August 18, 1978, SMU.

17. Albert Johnson, "Conversation with Roger Edens," *Sight and Sound* 27, no. 4 (Spring 1958).

18. Joseph Pasternak, *Easy the Hard Way* (New York: Putnam, 1956), 226–227.

19. *That's Entertainment, Part 2* interview, 1976, AMPAS.

20. *Chicago Tribune,* January 22, 1943.

21. *Hartford Courant,* April 18, 1943.

22. In the preceding twelve months, Garland had carried two major film musicals, contributed a guest song for another, begun *Girl Crazy,* continued her radio and recording work, and launched her World War II military camp tours. Dr. Marcus Rabwin, Garland's personal physician since childhood, recommended in a January 29, 1943, Metro interoffice memo that his patient "do no more dancing for six to eight weeks." Per that same memo, Garland's mother felt Judy would be able to work in three.

23. Walters interviewed for *Hooray for Hollywood* (BBC), circa 1976.

24. *Screen Guide,* June 1943.

25. *Modesto Bee,* April 9, 1943.

26. *Kingsport News,* April 27, 1943.

27. Plans to marry Garland from *The Magnificent Minnellis* (BBC), circa 1976.

28. Pasternak, *Easy the Hard Way,* 225.

29. *Presenting Lily Mars* rehearsal story primarily from Gerold Frank, *Judy* (New York: Harper and Row, 1975), 175.

30. Walters interview in *The Hollywood Greats: Judy Garland* (BBC), circa 1977.

31. Dorothy Tuttle Nitch interview, Arts and Entertainment Network, June 14, 1996.

32. Robert Hofler, *The Man Who Invented Rock Hudson: The Pretty Boys and Dirty Deals of Henry Willson* (New York: Carroll and Graf, 2005), 19.

33. *Chicago Tribune,* January 22, 1943.

34. Judy Garland telephone interview by Jack Wagner, *Silver Platter Service,* Capitol Records, 1965 (catalog nos. 163 and 164).

35. Conversation with Knight, 1976.

36. *Hollywood Reporter,* August 3, 1943.

37. *New York Times,* June 30, 1943.

38. Jerry Mason, "Sham Dancer?" *Los Angeles Times,* August 22, 1943.

9. A Company Man

1. Walters interview with Hugh Fordin, December 1971.

2. Jack Cole interviewed in Delamater, *Dance in the Hollywood Musical,* 195.

3. Davis, OHC #144, SMU.

4. Walters interview with Hugh Fordin, December 1971.

5. *New York Times,* April 23, 1944.

6. Walters interview with Hugh Fordin, December 1971.

7. The influence of *Oklahoma!* choreographer Agnes De Mille is apparent in Walters's "Skip to My Lou," from the stylized, De Mille–esque pair of wide-eyed eavesdroppers seen gossiping at the sequence's onset to the "girl-who-falls-down" nod that concludes the routine (evoking dancer Joan McCracken's star-making tumble in that show).

8. Walters's memories of staging "The Trolley Song" are from *Hooray for Hollywood* (BBC).

9. Dorothy Raye, Turner Classic Movie Interview #9, 1994, UGA.

10. John Fricke, interview by the author, New York, February 2011.

11. *Los Angeles Examiner,* November 1944.

12. M-G-M memo from Al Lewis, November 16, 1943, Arthur Freed Collection, USC.

13. Hugh Fordin, *The World of Entertainment: Hollywood's Greatest Musicals* (New York: Da Capo, 1975), 139.

14. Ibid., 140.

15. Gloria De Haven quoted in Silverman, *Dancing on the Ceiling,* 76–77.

16. Hedda Hopper's syndicated column, July 18, 1944.

17. Walters interview with Hugh Fordin, December 1971.

18. Steven Harvey, *Directed by Vincente Minnelli* (New York: Harper and Row, 1989), 61.

19. Walters interview with Hugh Fordin, December 1971. Besides Walters's contribution to "The Sweepstakes Ticket," he assisted Fanny Brice with the brief "I'm an Indian," which served as a live-action model for the picture's opening Louis Bunin puppet show. "But we had to photograph [Brice first]!" Chuck explained to Arthur Knight in 1976.

20. Bert May, interview by the author, South Dakota, January 2011.

21. Fordin, *The World of Entertainment,* 144.

22. Reviews for *Ziegfeld Follies* from John Fricke, *Judy: A Legendary Film Career* (Philadelphia: Running Press, 2011), 239.

23. Kobal, *Gotta Sing,* rev. ed., 214.

10. Good News

1. *That's Entertainment, Part 2* interview, 1976, AMPAS.

2. *New York Times,* October 7, 1945.

3. Hedda Hopper syndicated column, March 21, 1945: "Abbott and Costello's producer Martin Gosch tells me Dick Hayme's brother Bob [Stanton] gets the romantic lead . . . and Frances Rafferty, who used to understudy [ballerina Vera] Zorina, will dance with Chuck Walters. That sounds like they are whipping up a mighty good cast."

4. Davis, OHC #159, SMU.

5. *Defender,* March 2, 1946.

6. *New York World-Telegram,* March 28, 1946.

7. Ibid.

8. *New York Daily News,* April 1, 1946.

9. *Mirror,* April 1, 1946.

10. *New York Times,* April 1, 1946.

11. *Los Angeles Times,* March 18, 1946. In the mid-1950s, Freed tried once again to bring *St. Louis Woman* to the screen, this time hoping for a more faithful adaptation with stars Diahann Carroll and Sammy Davis Jr. Another version was announced for Frank Sinatra.

12. Fordin, *World of Entertainment,* 188.

13. John Kobal, *Gotta Sing, Gotta Dance,* 1st ed. (Feltham, NY: Hamlyn, 1970), 63.

14. Fordin, *World of Entertainment,* 202.

15. Donald Knox, *The Magic Factory: How M-G-M Made An American in Paris* (New York: Praeger, 1973), 21.

16. Arthur Freed Collection, USC. A twenty-three-page treatment for *Good News,* dated July 24, 1941 (submitted by Devery Freeman and Roger Edens), was intended for Judy Garland and Ray McDonald. In this version, a Hollywood movie company descends upon Tait College to film "Campus Queen," starring Enid Adams ("who looks a lot like Virginia Grey"). Garland was to play Connie Martin, the football coach's daughter, opposite McDonald's Pinky Wright, a "slim, engaging, swivel-hipped ball carrier." Pinky's father was a former vaudevillian—part of a duo act called Lefft and Wright—which would allow McDonald to dance throughout the picture. A romantic crisis occurs when Garland becomes jealous of McDonald's attentions toward the visiting Hollywood starlet.

17. J. G. Mayer memo, January 27, 1947. Arthur Freed Collection, USC.

18. Davis, OHC #215, SMU.

19. James Spada, *Peter Lawford: The Man Who Kept Secrets* (New York: Bantam, 1991), 114.

20. Ibid.

21. June Allyson, Turner Classic Movie Interview, May 5, 1997, UGA.

22. *Hollywood Reporter,* March 6, 1947.

23. Richard Kislan, *Hoofing on Broadway: A History of Show Dancing* (New York: Prentice Hall, 1987), 64.

24. Ethan Mordden, *The Hollywood Studios: House Style in the Golden Age of the Movies* (New York, Knopf, 1987), 166.

25. Warren interview, 1980.

26. Jennings interview transcript provided by Coyne Steven Sanders.

27. Walters interview with Hugh Fordin, September 5, 1972, Hugh Fordin Collection, USC (audio reel).

28. Ibid.

29. Walters interview with Hugh Fordin, December 1971.

30. *Milwaukee Journal,* December 28, 1947.

31. Originally budgeted at $1,754,930, *Good News* by day four was half a day ahead of schedule, due to completing the title number early; this decreased the budget by $8,545. Peter Lawford's illness soon obliterated that decrease, but by day fourteen the company had gained back another half day by finishing "Lucky in Love" early (lowering costs by $8,570). Walters delivered another save of $12,883 when three-quarters of a day were gained on Allyson's ballad "Just Imagine." Alton had "Pass That Peace Pipe" completely shot a day and a half early, which saved $26,202.

32. While production was under way on *Good News,* a purported wrongdoing had forced John Darrow into an unanticipated period of unemployment. In 1944, Actors' Equity in New York granted Darrow "inactive status" so that he could engage in war work in Burbank. As John explained, he "interrupted his duties at Lockheed-Vega Aircraft Corporation" to travel back east "in an effort to live up to my obligation as a franchised agent and provide an office where actors could be interviewed." Fred Steele was hired, and they opened the John Darrow–Fred Steele Agency at 9 Rockefeller Plaza. After the war, with his Equity status reactivated, Darrow turned his full attention to building the Darrow Agency in Beverly Hills, unaware that Steele was taking a 10 percent cut from client Danny Scholl, a *Call Me Mister* dancer, rather than the appropriate 5 percent. Equity was swift in handing down punishment. In April 1947, Darrow's license was revoked for half a year, even though he claimed no knowledge of the infraction. Actors' Equity Association Records, Tamiment Library and Robert F. Wagner Labor Archives, New York University.

33. *Good News* preview surveys, Arthur Freed Collection, USC.

34. *Good News* congratulatory letter from Freed, Charles Walters Collection, USC.

35. *Collier's,* December 1947.

36. *Hollywood Reporter,* December 2, 1947.

37. *Variety,* December 3, 1947.

38. *Milwaukee Journal,* December 28, 1947. When Gary Cooper's character in Frank Capra's *Mr. Deeds Goes to Town* (1936) was labeled the "Cinderella Man" by the press, he threatened to punch the paper's editor in the face.

11. A Swell Couple

1. Alan Jay Lerner, *The Street Where I Live* (New York: Norton, 1978), 138.

2. Fricke, *Judy Garland,* 100.

3. Kobal, *People Will Talk,* 649–650. An item in Hedda Hopper's September 22, 1947, column corroborates Freed's memories, telling that "Altho Garland asked for her husband, Vincente Minnelli, to direct *Easter Parade,* her doctor has decided he should not. Chuck Walters . . . will handle the megaphone on her new picture."

4. Fordin, *World of Entertainment,* 225.

5. Kobal, *People Will Talk,* 650.

6. *Easter Parade* script, page 73, dated September 17, 1947, Arthur Freed Collection, USC.

7. Sidney Sheldon in the DVD documentary *Easter Parade: On the Avenue* (Turner Entertainment), 2005.

8. Ann Miller, interview for *That's Entertainment III* (1994).

9. Ann Miller, interview, Arts and Entertainment Network, April 29, 1996.

10. *A Couple of Swells* staging appears to result from a conglomeration of creators, including Walters, Alton, Kelly, and Garland.

11. Sheldon, *Easter Parade*.

12. *The Fred Astaire Story* (BBC), date unknown.

13. Fred Astaire, *Steps in Time: An Autobiography* (New York: Harper), 292.

14. *That's Entertainment, Part 2* interview, 1976, AMPAS.

15. Walters interview, *The Magnificent Minnellis* (BBC), circa 1976.

16. Ibid.

17. Fordin, *World of Entertainment,* 233. Subsequently, Irving Berlin worked "Mr. Monotony" into his Broadway shows *Miss Liberty* and *Call Me Madam;* each time the number was dropped before opening night.

18. Quoted in Fricke, *Judy,* 260.

19. *Hollywood Reporter,* May 26, 1948.

20. *New York Herald Tribune,* [August] 1948.

21. *Tacoma Times,* August 27, 1948.

22. *Look* magazine, Charles Walters Papers, USC.

23. Astaire, *Steps in Time,* 293.

24. Ibid. In July 1948, the famed African American baseball pitcher Satchel Paige became the oldest man ever to debut in the major leagues.

25. Christopher Finch, *Rainbow: The Stormy Life of Judy Garland* (New York: Grosset and Dunlap), 159.

12. Fred and Ginger

1. Peter Levinson, *Puttin' on the Ritz: Fred Astaire and the Fine Art of Panache, a Biography* (New York: St. Martin's, 2009), 218.

2. Memos in the Arthur Freed Collection at USC reveal that the exact nature of Hermes Pan's involvement on *Barkleys* led to misunderstandings between the choreographer and Freed. In July 1948, executive F. L. Hendrickson informed Freed of the choreographer's contractual concerns wherein Pan insisted that Freed had agreed to an on-screen credit clause, placing his name alongside that of Bob Alton, who'd provide dances for Garland. As such, Alton's credit could not "be in greater prominence." Freed called Pan's billing clause "impossible." When Pan informed that he had directed "Shoes with Wings On," Freed declared that Walters was behind the camera. "Pan did not direct any number in whole," Freed reported, only "recommendations in connection" with the "Shoes" sequence, and "would not be entitled to screen credit." (In the end, screen credit was given to Pan for the sequence.)

3. Jennings on Garland: Jennings interview transcript provided by Coyne Steven Sanders.

4. "There'll Always Be an Encore," *McCall's,* January 1964, 143.

5. Arthur Freed Papers, USC.

6. Ginger Rogers, *Ginger: My Story* (New York: Harper Collins), 284.

7. *The Fred Astaire Story* (BBC), date unknown.

8. Fred Astaire, *Steps in Time,* 294.

9. *Los Angeles Times,* August 8, 1948.

10. Adolph Green quoted in Sam Kashner and Nancy Schoenberger, *A Talent for Genius: The Life and Times of Oscar Levant* (New York: Villard, 1994), 322.

11. Walters interview with Hugh Fordin, December 1971.

12. Ibid. In 1950, Robert Alton was given a second chance to direct when Freed launched his tropical Esther Williams–Howard Keel musical *Pagan Love Song.* Overwhelmed by problems on a Hawaiian location shoot, Alton never directed another feature film. Low on artistic merit, the film nevertheless performed well at the box office.

13. Unidentified Montreal paper, July 12, 1949, Charles Walters Papers, USC. The ever-oblivious Schary wrote to Freed on July 25: "Is there any way of cutting or switching . . . for French distribution? Did we do it in English? It's certainly something you should think about."

14. *Los Angeles Herald-Examiner,* September 29, 1948. Garland did return to the *Barkleys* set a few weeks later—this time announced—in wardrobe for her cameo in Freed's concurrent *Words and Music.* She and Ginger smiled amiably for a studio photographer recording the visit.

15. Astaire quoted in Levinson, *Puttin' on the Ritz,* 164.

16. Arthur Freed Collection, USC.

17. *Variety,* April 13, 1949.

18. *Washington Post,* May 12, 1949.

19. *New York Times,* May 13, 1949.

20. Charles Walters Collection, USC.

21. John Douglas Eames, *The M-G-M Story* (New York: Crown), 210.

13. Metro-Goldwyn-*Schary*

1. Esther Williams, *The Million Dollar Mermaid: An Autobiography* (New York: Simon and Schuster, 1999), 186.

2. Ibid.

3. Ronald Davis, OHC #82: Arlene Dahl. Interview conducted September 24, 1975, SMU.

4. Sauvage, "Interview with Charles Walters." Ironically, while preliminary work on *Annie* began in earnest under Berkeley's command, *Easter Parade* had its spectacular London premiere. That March, in its first three weeks at M-G-M's flagship theater in Leicester Square, the film pulled in more than 115,000 patrons.

5. Gloria Swanson Papers, HRC.

6. Howard Keel, interview in conjunction with the release of *That's Entertainment III,* circa 1994.

7. Walters interview with Hugh Fordin, September 5, 1972.

8. Sauvage, "Interview with Charles Walters."

9. Fricke, *Judy,* 288–289.

10. Fordin, *World of Entertainment,* 276.

11. Norman Borine, *Dancing with the Stars* (Paragon, IN: Fideli, 2007), 174.

12. Fricke, *Judy,* 288–289.

13. *Los Angeles Times,* May 19, 1949.

14. *New York Times,* May 29, 1949.

15. Kobal, *Gotta Sing,* 226.

16. Ibid., 226–227.

17. John Darrow letter dated December 5, 1949, Arthur Freed Collection, USC.

18. *Hollywood Reporter* on *Summer Stock* casting: Kelly-Garland (December 23, 1948) and Kelly-Allyson (February 3, 1949).

19. Walters's letter dated September 12, 1949, Charles Walters Collection, USC.

14. Get Happy

1. "Gene Kelly: Song and Dance Man," *Films Illustrated,* November 1947.

2. Clive Hirschhorn, *Gene Kelly: A Biography* (Chicago: Regnery, 1974), 190.

3. Ibid., 192.

4. "There'll Always Be an Encore," 144.

5. *Impressions of Garland* (BBC-TV), 1972.

6. Charles Walters Collection, USC.

7. Ibid.

8. Judy Garland, as told to Michael Drury, "My Story," *Cosmopolitan,* January 1951, 116.

9. *Hollywood Greats,* BBC Radio, circa 1976.

10. Pasternak, *Easy the Hard Way,* 229.

11. Hirschhorn, *Gene Kelly,* 192.

12. James Bawden, "Joe Pasternak," *Films in Review,* February 1985, 73.

13. Jennings interview transcript provided by Coyne Steven Sanders.

14. Carleton Carpenter, Turner Classic Movie Interview, circa 1995, UGA.

15. Jennings interview transcript provided by Coyne Steven Sanders.

16. Charles Walters Collection, USC.

17. Eddie Bracken, Turner Classic Movie Interview, circa 1995, UGA.

18. Dorothy Tuttle Nitch, interview, Arts and Entertainment Network, June 14, 1996.

19. Charles Walters Collection, USC.

20. Walters 1976 interview in conjunction with the release of *That's Entertainment, Part 2*, AMPAS.

21. John Cutts, "Dancer, Actor, Director," *Films and Filming* (London), August and September 1964.

22. Douglas McVay, "Charles Walters: A Case for Reassessment," *Focus in Film* 27 (1976).

23. Gerald Mast, *Can't Help Singin': The American Musical on Stage and Screen* (New York: Overlook Press, 1987), 245.

24. Cutts, "On the Bright Side."

25. Davis, OHC #215, SMU.

26. John Angelo, interview by the author, Los Angeles, August 2007.

27. *Hollywood Greats: Judy Garland*.

28. Carpenter, Turner Classic Movie Interview, UGA.

29. Frank, *Judy*, 273–274.

30. In a memo to Joe Pasternak dated April 5, 1950, Walters broached the subject of billing: "Dear Joe: Keep forgetting to mention this—would like to have billing credit for Judy's numbers in *Summer Stock*. Think it should read, 'Miss Garland's numbers staged by Mr. Walters.' Thanks."

31. *Hollywood Reporter*, August 4, 1950.

32. Roddy McDowall, *Double Exposure* (New York: Delacorte Press, 1966), 198–199.

33. Erskine Johnson, syndicated column, February 14, 1952.

34. McVay, "Charles Waters."

15. "A Dear Dame"

1. David Brown, *Let Me Entertain You* (New York: Morrow, 1990), 57.

2. William Mann, *Behind the Screen: How Gays and Lesbians Shaped Hollywood, 1910–1969* (New York: Viking, 2001), 247.

3. Michael Sidney Luft to Coyne Steven Sanders, as reported to author, Los Angeles, 1996.

4. Ibid.

5. Walters interview with Hugh Fordin, December 1971.

6. Ibid.

7. *Los Angeles Times*, May 25, 1950.

8. *Hollywood Greats: Judy Garland*.

9. Walters interview with Hugh Fordin, December 1971.

10. Garland's visits to Malibu: Frank, *Judy*, 274–276.

11. Hugh Martin, interview, Arts and Entertainment Network, June 3, 1996.

12. "Pug" Wells had spent one nonstop flight between Chicago and Los Angeles chatting about her experiences as a flight attendant to Hollywood director William A. Wellman; afterward, writer Ruth Brooks Flippen gathered her tales.

"She took words out of my mouth," Wells said, "twisted them around to make sense—and a story."

13. Sidney Sheldon, Turner Classic Movie Interview, circa 1995, UGA.

14. Armand Deutsch's memories of *Three Guys Named Mike* from Ronald Davis, OHC #270: Armand Deutsch. Interview conducted July 28, 1982, SMU.

15. *Chicago Daily Tribune*, September 26, 1950.

16. Charles Walters Collection, USC.

17. Walters's script, Charles Walters Collection, USC.

18. Walters on editing: Sauvage, "Interview with Charles Walters."

19. Charles Walters Collection, USC.

20. *New York Times*, March 2, 1951.

21. In 1979, M-G-M failed to renew the *Three Guys* copyright in its twenty-eighth year after "publication," and the film entered public domain status in the United States.

22. Jim Mahoney on-camera interview for Turner Entertainment TV mini-series *M-G-M: When the Lion Roars*, 1992.

23. Hedda Hopper, syndicated column, December 8, 1950.

24. "Dorothy Kingsley: The Fixer," interview by Patrick McGilligan in *Backstory 2: Interviews with Screenwriters of the 1940s and 1950s* (Berkeley: University of California Press, 1991), 122.

25. Erskine Johnson, syndicated column, March 23, 1951.

26. Ibid.

27. Williams, *Million Dollar Mermaid*, 196–197.

28. Howard Keel, interview in conjunction with the release of *That's Entertainment III*, circa 1994.

29. *Variety*, September 11, 1951.

30. *Los Angeles Times*, September 27, 1951.

31. *Daily News*, October 13, 1951.

32. Production Code Administration files, AMPAS.

33. M-G-M Press Book: *Texas Carnival*, 1951.

34. Ibid.

16. Playing the Palace

1. Scott Eyman, *Lion of Hollywood: The Life and Legend of Louis B. Mayer* (New York: Simon and Schuster, 2005), 462.

2. Ibid., 455.

3. *Los Angeles Times*, July 10, 1949.

4. Kobal, *People Will Talk*, 651.

5. Script work on *Belle* included three drafts by Chester Erskine (1943–1944), two drafts by Irving Brecher (1944–1947), a six-page outline by Fred Finklehoffe (1946), one draft by Sally Benson (1947), and two drafts by Jerry

Davis (1950–1951). Comden and Green—working on *Singin' in the Rain*—were approached in 1951, but the final script belonged to Robert O'Brien and Irving Elinson.

6. Astaire, *Steps in Time,* 300.

7. Ibid., 299.

8. Walters on Vera-Ellen primarily from Fantle and Johnson interview with Walters, 1980. Fred Astaire was admittedly "grateful" (his word) for Vera-Ellen's casting, pleased that he didn't have to reduce his own performance to accommodate another novice. Robert Alton adored Vera-Ellen, having employed her several times on Broadway in *Higher and Higher, Panama Hattie,* and *By Jupiter.* A year after *Belle,* their alliance would continue at 20th Century-Fox with *Call Me Madam* and then at Paramount for *Irving Berlin's White Christmas.*

9. Keenan Wynn, *Ed Wynn's Son* (New York: Doubleday, 1959), 147.

10. Astaire, *Steps in Time,* 299.

11. Oral history with Lela Simone, interviewed by Rudy Behlmer, AMPAS Oral History Program, 1994.

12. *The Fred Astaire Story* (BBC), date unknown.

13. *New York Post,* March 6, 1952.

14. *New York Herald Tribune,* March 6, 1952.

15. Astaire, *Steps in Time,* 300.

16. Douglas McVay, "The Belle of New York," *Velvet Light Trap* no. 14 (Winter 1975).

17. Warren interview, 1980.

18. Sid Luft to Sanders, 1996.

19. Warren interview, 1980.

20. Sid Luft to Sanders, 1996.

21. Bert May, interview by the author, South Dakota, January 2011.

22. Warren interview, 1980.

23. Frank, *Judy,* 334.

24. Primarily from Fantle and Johnson interview with Walters, 1980.

25. *Daily News,* October 17, 1951.

26. *Hollywood Greats: Judy Garland.*

27. *Billboard,* October 27, 1951.

28. Clifton Fadiman, "Where Lay the Magic?" *Holiday Magazine,* 1952, quoted in Fricke, *Judy Garland,* 138–139.

29. Fred McFadden, interview with author, October 2009.

30. Fantle and Johnson interview with Walters, 1980.

31. *Variety,* October 24, 1951.

32. Ed Sullivan, syndicated column, October 18, 1951.

33. *Movie Life,* February 1952.

34. Ibid.

35. *Variety,* September 10, 1958 (Orchestra Hall performance, Chicago). The Orchestra Hall and Cocoanut Grove concerts were forerunners to Garland's legendary one-woman concerts in the 1960s.

36. *Hollywood Greats: Judy Garland.*

17. Hi-Lili, Hi-Lo

1. Walters's memories of *Lili* primarily from Sauvage, "Interview with Charles Walters."

2. Censor warnings for *Lili,* Production Code Administration files, AMPAS.

3. Ibid.

4. Caron interview, 2008.

5. Davis, OHC #215, SMU.

6. Caron interview, 2008.

7. Dore Schary, *Heyday: An Autobiography* (Boston: Little, Brown, 1979), 212.

8. Martin Gottfried, *All His Jazz: The Life and Death of Bob Fosse* (New York: Bantam, 1990), 77.

9. *Lili* script, Helen Deutsch Papers, BU.

10. Schary, *Heyday,* 212–213.

11. Davis, OHC #215, SMU.

12. *Cue,* March 14, 1953.

13. Schary, *Heyday,* 213.

14. *Washington Post,* June 10, 1953.

15. Postcard in Charles Walters Collection, USC.

16. "1953's Ten Best," *Films in Review* 5, no. 1 (January 1954): 3. Among the personal accolades, Walters treasured a letter from casual acquaintance and Universal producer Ross Hunter: "The other evening I saw your picture, *Lili* and was so enchanted by its warmth and sincerity that I had to sit down to tell you about it. You are to be congratulated on a beautiful job of direction and you deserve so much credit for handling this picture the way you did. I can't begin to tell you how much I enjoyed it."

17. "Hi-Lili, Hi-Lo" was ineligible for a Best Original Song nomination due to a technicality: the lyric had come from a poem in a 1940 Helen Deutsch short story. The Caron-Ferrer soundtrack recording, however, peaked at number thirty on the charts.

18. John Anthony Gilvey, *Before the Parade Passes By: Gower Champion and the Glorious American Musical* (New York: St. Martin's, 2005), 95.

19. Davis, OHC #215, SMU.

18. "A Masterpiece of Modern Moisture"

1. Williams, *Million Dollar Mermaid,* 226.

2. *Los Angeles Times,* November 17, 1952.

3. Fernando Lamas's memories of *Dangerous When Wet* from Ronald Davis, OHC #220: Fernando Lamas. Interview conducted August 6 and 14, 1981, SMU.

4. *Chicago Daily Tribune,* June 25, 1953.

5. Davis, OHC #215, SMU.

6. Williams, *Million Dollar Mermaid,* 248.

7. Tony Martin's memories of *Easy to Love* from Turner Classic Movie Interview #118, 1997, UGA.

8. Williams, *Million Dollar Mermaid,* 244.

9. "Esther Williams: In the Swim" (May 1996), in David Fantle and Tom Johnson, eds., *25 Years of Celebrity Interviews from Vaudeville to Movies to TV, Reel to Real* (Oregon, WI: Badger Books, 2004), 103.

10. Davis, OHC #215, SMU.

11. *Washington Post,* December 24, 1953.

12. *Variety,* December 1953.

13. Cutts, "On the Bright Side."

14. Hedda Hopper's syndicated column, March 7, 1953.

15. Williams, *Million Dollar Mermaid,* 258.

19. "Two-Faced Woman"

1. Kobal, *People Will Talk,* 285.

2. Walters interview, *The Hollywood Greats: Joan Crawford* (BBC), 1978.

3. Joan Crawford with Jane Kesner Ardmore, *A Portrait of Joan: An Autobiography of Joan Crawford* (Garden City, NY: Doubleday, 1962), 159.

4. Ibid.

5. Ibid.

6. Sauvage, "Interview with Charles Walters."

7. Williams, *Million Dollar Mermaid,* 253.

8. Crawford, *Portrait of Joan,* 162.

9. *Chicago Tribune,* October 20, 1954.

10. Barry Norman, *The Hollywood Greats* (New York: F. Watts, 1980), 148.

11. Ibid.

12. Bob Thomas, *Joan Crawford: A Biography* (New York: Simon and Schuster, 1978), 186.

13. Crawford, *Portrait of Joan,* 162.

14. 1953 M-G-M pre-recording session, included as supplemental material on *Torch Song* 2008 DVD release, Warner Video/Turner Entertainment.

15. Christina Crawford on-camera interview for Turner Entertainment/ Warner Bros. Entertainment documentary, *Tough Baby: Torch Song,* 2007.

16. Hedda Hopper's syndicated column, November 29, 1953.

17. Walters interview, *Hollywood Greats: Joan Crawford.*

18. Crawford, *Portrait of Joan,* 159.

19. Davis, OHC #215, SMU.

20. Michael Wilding with Pamela Wilcox, *The Wilding Way: The Story of My Life* (New York: St. Martin's, 1982), 105–106.

21. Walters 1976 interview in conjunction with the release of *That's Entertainment, Part 2,* AMPAS.

22. Harrison Carroll's syndicated column, June 30, 1953.

23. Executive producer Charles Schnee memo, May 19, 1953, Charles Walters Collection, USC.

24. Charles Walters Collection, USC.

25. *Saturday Review,* October 1953.

26. *New York Herald Tribune,* October 1953.

27. *New Yorker,* October 24, 1953.

28. Thomas, *Joan Crawford,* 187.

29. Walters interview, *Hollywood Greats: Joan Crawford.*

30. Ibid.

20. Cinderella Stories

1. Gloria Swanson Papers, HRC.

2. Ezra Goodman, *The Fifty Year Decline and Fall of Hollywood* (New York: Simon and Schuster, 1961), 165–166.

3. *Hartford Courant,* January 31, 1954.

4. Donald Saddler, interview by author, New York, August 29, 2006.

5. *Variety,* February 17, 1954.

6. Saddler interview by author, 2006.

7. Unidentified Philadelphia newspaper clipping, March 19, 1954, NYPL.

8. *New York Times,* February 25, 1954.

9. Saddler interview by author, 2006.

10. *Variety,* November 18, 1959, and Roger Edens Collection, USC.

11. *The Glass Slipper* was partially inspired by a 1944 wartime morale booster of the same name, presented by actor-turned-producer Robert Donat at London's St James Theatre. M-G-M executive Kenneth MacKenna had seen the Herbert and Eleanor Farjeon "fairy tale with music" and sent a memo to the studio about a possible Cinderella movie. Metro "succeeded in wiping out the Farjeon credit" on the basis that the story itself was no longer under copyright—and the idea was eventually handed to Helen Deutsch.

12. All Helen Deutsch quotations on *The Glass Slipper:* Helen Deutsch Papers, BU.

13. Caron interview, 2008.

14. "It Seems That Michael Wilding Does Not Have Two Left Feet, After All," M-G-M press book for *The Glass Slipper,* 1955, USC.

15. Helen Deutsch Papers, BU.

16. Caron interview, 2008.

17. *New Yorker,* April 2, 1955.

18. Primarily from Sauvage, "Interview with Charles Walters."

19. Caron interview, 2008. Roland Petit's corps de ballet included venerated soloists Violette Verdy, Claire Sombert, and Lillian Montevecchi, each given a fifteen week guarantee.

20. "It Seems That Michael Wilding Does Not Have Two Left Feet."

21. Caron interview, 2008.

22. M-G-M press book for *The Glass Slipper,* 1955, USC.

23. Sauvage, "Interview with Charles Walters."

24. Charles Walters Collection, USC.

25. Memo to Dore Schary, January 10, 1955, Helen Deutsch Papers, BU.

26. *Films in Review,* March 1955, 132.

27. *Morning Globe,* February 25, 1955.

28. *Hollywood Reporter,* February 15, 1955.

29. Walters's annotated clipping of *The King's Thief* review is in Helen Deutsch Papers, BU.

30. M-G-M in the mid-1950s enjoyed bringing to the screen a spate of "suffering singer" sagas. In 1955 there was *Interrupted Melody,* in which Australia's Marjorie Lawrence fought polio, and *Love Me or Leave Me,* in which America's Ruth Etting endured domestic abuse. But *I'll Cry Tomorrow*—with its frank presentation of a woman alcoholic—was potentially the most riveting of them all.

31. Davis, OHC #215, SMU.

32. Mike Connolly syndicated column, December 11, 1955.

33. *New York Times,* March 4, 1955.

34. Louella Parsons, syndicated column, March 8, 1955.

35. May 16, 1955, letter to Theresa Helburn of the Theatre Guild, Helen Deutsch Collection, BU. Writer Jay Richard Kennedy continued to develop the *I'll Cry Tomorrow* screenplay, receiving joint on-screen credit with Deutsch. Daniel Mann directed. Deutsch, in an October 25, 1955, letter to columnist Radie Harris, mentions that Mann suggested Kennedy be brought to the project ("They are partners"). "[Chuck and I] never doubted [Hayward would] give a good performance. We just didn't like the way she treated us. This is absolutely not for publication, however."

21. In *High Society*

1. Mann, *Behind the Screen,* 282.

2. Jimie Morrissey, interview by the author, Los Angeles, August 2007.

3. Ibid.

4. Cutts, "On the Bright Side."

5. Walters on *The Tender Trap* is primarily from Davis, OHC #215, SMU, and Sauvage, "Interview with Charles Walters."

6. Alain Masson, *American Directors, Volume II*, ed. Jean-Pierre Coursodon with Pierre Sauvage (New York: McGraw-Hill, 1983), 359.

7. Sammy Cahn, *I Should Care: The Sammy Cahn Story* (New York: Arbor House, 1974), 152.

8. Dana Polan on-camera interview for *Frank in the Fifties,* Warner Bros. Entertainment, 2008.

9. Helen Deutsch Papers, BU.

10. Davis, OHC #215, SMU.

11. Debbie Reynolds, telephone interview by the author, July 25, 2012.

12. Ibid.

13. Nancy Sinatra, *Frank Sinatra: An American Legend* (Santa Monica, CA: General Publishing Group, 1995), 124.

14. Reynolds telephone interview, 2012.

15. *Los Angeles Times,* November 24, 1955.

16. *New York Times,* November 11, 1955.

17. Reynolds telephone interview, 2012.

18. *Walk on By: The Story of Popular Song (Episode 2: Stardust),* a BBC Production, 2001. As reported in this TV documentary series, Crosby and Armstrong enjoyed a friendship in the 1920s, taking in the jazz sounds coming from the clubs and speakeasies of Chicago (despite racial segregation). By the 1930s, they blended their talents and brought jazz phrasing and scatting to a wider audience over the radio.

19. Sinatra, *Frank Sinatra,* 126.

20. Donald Spoto, *High Society: The Life of Grace Kelly* (New York: Harmony, 2009), 238.

21. Masson, *American Directors, Volume II,* 358.

22. Charles Thompson, *Bing: The Authorized Biography* (New York: McKay, 1976), 185.

23. Ricky Riccardi, *What a Wonderful World: The Magic of Louis Armstrong's Later Years* (New York: Pantheon, 2011), 118.

24. Fantle and Johnson interview with Walters, 1980.

25. Saul Chaplin, *The Golden Age of Movie Musicals and Me* (Norman: University of Oklahoma Press, 1994), 163.

26. McVay, "Charles Walters."

27. Gwen Robyns, *Princess Grace: A Biography* (New York: McKay, 1976), 139.

28. Cole Porter letter dated June 6, 1956, M-G-M Music Department Collection, USC.

29. Thompson, *Bing,* 185.

30. George Eells, *The Life That Late He Led: A Biography of Cole Porter* (New York: Putnam, 1967), 305.

31. Chaplin, *Golden Age,* 158–159.

32. Sauvage, "Interview with Charles Walters."

33. Charles Schwartz, *Cole Porter: A Biography* (New York: Dial Press, 1977), 218.

34. Robyns, *Princess Grace,* 139–140.

35. Ronald Davis, OHC #416: Celeste Holm. Interview conducted March 30, 1988, SMU.

36. Spoto, *High Society,* 238.

37. Riccardi, *What a Wonderful World,* 118.

38. Chaplin, *Golden Age,* 162.

39. Fantle and Johnson interview with Walters, 1980.

40. Charles Walters Collection, USC.

41. Ibid.

42. Ibid.

22. Branching Out

1. *Variety*'s top five releases of 1956: (1) *Around the World in 80 Days,* (2) *The Ten Commandments,* (3) *Giant,* (4) Rodgers and Hammerstein's *The King and I,* and (5) *High Society.*

2. *New York Herald Tribune,* August 1956.

3. Jane Powell interviewed by Scott Eyman, *Palm Beach Post,* March 13, 2012.

4. Schary, *Heyday,* 248.

5. Morrissey interview, 2007.

6. Mike Connolly syndicated column, April 23, 1959.

7. Helen Deutsch Papers, BU.

8. All Morrissey recollections: interview, 2007.

9. Mann, *Behind the Screen,* 329.

10. M-G-M memo dated November 23, 1955, Helen Deutsch Papers, BU.

11. *Chicago Daily Tribune,* December 26, 1957.

12. *Variety,* November 13, 1957.

13. Walters's script, Charles Walters Collection, USC. Walters told Pierre Sauvage that the slapstick sequence depicting the construction of an officers' club, a high point of the film, was actually prepared and filmed separately by Johnny Waters with the movie's second unit crew.

14. Alton quote from 1952 in Richard Kislan, *Hoofing on Broadway: A History of Show Dancing* (New York: Prentice Hall, 1987), 63.

15. Davis, OHC #215, SMU.

16. Caron interview, 2008.

17. *Los Angeles Times,* October 27, 1957.

18. Delamater, *Dance in the Hollywood Musical*, 275.

19. Mark Griffin, *A Hundred or More Hidden Things: The Life and Films of Vincente Minnelli* (Cambridge, MA: Da Capo, 2010), 218.

20. Charles Walters Collection, USC.

21. Oral history with Lela Simone, interviewed by Rudy Behlmer, AMPAS Oral History Program, 1994.

22. Leslie Caron, *Thank Heaven: A Memoir* (New York: Viking, 2009), 135.

23. Primarily from Sauvage, "Interview with Charles Walters," and Walters 1976 interview in conjunction with the release of *That's Entertainment, Part 2*, AMPAS.

24. Retake schedule from M-G-M Production Department Collection, USC, and the Assistant Director Reports in the Arthur Freed Collection, USC.

25. Lerner, *Street Where I Live*, 170–180.

26. Caron, *Thank Heaven*, 133.

27. Minnelli's Oscar acceptance speech, April 6, 1959.

28. Sauvage, "Interview with Charles Walters."

23. A Virgin and a Housewife

1. Shirley MacLaine, *My Lucky Stars: A Hollywood Memoir* (New York: Bantam, 1995), 252.

2. Ibid., 232.

3. January 23, 1961, letter from MacLaine to Walters, Charles Walters Collection, USC.

4. *Christian Science Monitor*, March 15, 1960. When viewed today, that particular lunch counter scene plays out rather uncomfortably, given the film's archaic acceptance of female subservience. "You know," offers Elizabeth Frasier's character, "I used to think it was us girls who did all the shopping around. Nope. We're just pieces of merchandise on a shelf. Men come in, take a look, and if we have something they want, they take us home. All I know is I was getting pretty scared of staying on that shelf."

5. David Niven, *The Moon's a Balloon* (New York: Putnam, 1971), 340.

6. M-G-M memo to Howard Strickling from Dan Terrell dated April 29, 1959, Charles Walters Collection, USC.

7. *Los Angeles Times*, June 20, 1959.

8. *San Francisco News*, July 10, 1959.

9. Financial figures for *Ask Any Girl* from the Eddie Mannix Ledger, Howard Strickling Collection, AMPAS.

10. Morrissey interview, 2007.

11. Ibid.

12. Walters on Doris Day and *Daisies* primarily from Davis, OHC #215, SMU.

13. Ronald Davis, OHC #296: Doris Day. Interview conducted October 18, 1983, SMU.

14. Ronald Davis, OHC #225: Janis Paige. Interview conducted August 6 and 11, 1981, SMU.

15. *Los Angeles Examiner,* April 17, 1960.

16. Stanley Livingston, telephone interview by the author, March 2013.

17. Charles Walters Collection, USC.

18. Peter Howell, "The Sweet Day Turns Sour," *British Photoplay,* April 1965.

19. Martin Melcher memo to Walters and Pasternak, August 28, 1959, Joseph Pasternak Collection, USC.

20. Hedda Hopper's syndicated column, July 30, 1959.

21. Charles Walters Collection, USC.

22. Telegram from Pasternak to Walters, December 22, 1959, Joseph Pasternak Collection, USC.

23. Livingston, interview by the author, 2013.

24. *New York Times,* April 1, 1960.

25. *Washington Post,* April 14, 1960.

26. *Hollywood Reporter,* April 1960.

27. From a clipping in the Charles Walters Collection, USC, the American directors who made the most money in the 1959–1960 season: (1) Walter Lang, (2) Blake Edwards, (3) Charles Walters, (4) Michael Gordon, (5) Richard Brooks, (6) John Ford, (7) Vincente Minnelli, (8) Joseph L. Mankiewicz, (9) George Sidney, and (10) George Cukor.

24. Spoiled Spinster

1. Michael Singer, *A Cut Above: 50 Film Directors Talk about Their Craft* (Los Angeles: Lone Eagle, 1998), 144.

2. Hedda Hopper's syndicated column, June 28, 1960.

3. Financial figures for *Cimarron* from the Eddie Mannix Ledger, Howard Strickling Collection, AMPAS.

4. Sauvage, "Interview with Charles Walters."

5. Ibid.

6. Shelley Winters, *Shelley II: The Middle of My Century* (New York: Simon and Schuster, 1989), 284–291.

7. Morrissey interview, 2007.

8. Caron interview, 2008.

9. Production Code records on *Two Loves* dated February 2 and October 24, 1960, Production Code Administration files, AMPAS.

10. Sol Siegel memo dated November 9, 1960, Charles Walters Collection, USC.

11. *Time,* May 19, 1961.

12. Sol Siegel memo dated October 14, 1960, Charles Walters Collection, USC.

13. MacLaine, *My Lucky Stars,* 120.

14. *New York Times,* November 6, 1960.

15. Ibid.

16. Charles Walters Collection, USC.

17. Sauvage, "Interview with Charles Walters."

18. MacLaine, *My Lucky Stars,* 330.

19. Charles Walters Collection, USC.

20. Memo to Julian Blaustein, December 8, 1960, Charles Walters Collection, USC.

21. *Time,* May 19, 1961.

22. *Newsday,* [May 1961].

23. *Films in Review* 12, no. 6 (June–July 1961): 357–358.

24. *Daily Variety,* June 7, 2012.

25. Letter from MacLaine to Walters, January 23, 1961, Charles Walters Collection, USC.

25. *"What* Elephant?"

1. Walters interview with Hugh Fordin, December 1971.

2. Jon Whitcomb, "Hollywood's Biggest Star," *Cosmopolitan,* October 1962.

3. M-G-M exhibitor's campaign book for *Billy Rose's Jumbo,* 1962, USC.

4. Whitcomb, "Hollywood's Biggest Star."

5. *New York Times,* December 21, 1959.

6. Whitcomb, "Hollywood's Biggest Star."

7. Ibid.

8. Davis, OHC #296, SMU.

9. M-G-M exhibitor's campaign book for *Billy Rose's Jumbo,* 1962, USC.

10. Whitcomb, "Hollywood's Biggest Star."

11. Ibid.

12. M-G-M exhibitor's campaign book for *Billy Rose's Jumbo,* 1962, USC.

13. Cutts, "On the Bright Side."

14. *Los Angeles Times,* August 25, 1962.

15. *New York Times,* December 21, 1959.

16. Sauvage, "Interview with Charles Walters"; Cutts, "On the Bright Side."

17. Sauvage, "Interview with Charles Walters." Doubles Tina Davidson and Corquita Cristiani alternated Day's bareback riding, while the venerable Danish clown Linon performed in long shot for Durante's tattered-tramp-on-a-tight-wire act.

18. Whitcomb, "Hollywood's Biggest Star."

19. McVay, "Charles Walters," 31–32.

20. Warren interview, 1980.

21. *Oakland Tribune,* December 23, 1962.

22. Sheldon letter to Walters, May 23, 1962, Charles Walters Collection, USC.

23. *Los Angeles Times,* November 25, 1962.

24. *Variety,* December 12, 1962.

25. *Time,* December 12, 1962.

26. *Saturday Review,* [December 1962].

27. *New Yorker,* December 15, 1962.

28. *New York Times,* 1962.

29. James Bawden, "Joe Pasternak," *Films in Review,* February 1985, 76.

26. Ain't Down Yet

1. Hedda Hopper's syndicated column, August 2, 1962.

2. Helen Deutsch Papers, BU.

3. Weingarten letter to Deutsch, March 28, 1963, Helen Deutsch Papers, BU.

4. Ibid.

5. Deutsch letter to Weingarten, 1963, Helen Deutsch Papers, BU.

6. Debbie Reynolds with David Patrick Columbia, *Debbie: My Life* (New York: Morrow, 1988), 264.

7. Weingarten letter to Deutsch, March 28, 1963, Helen Deutsch Papers, BU.

8. Roger Edens letter to Deutsch, 1963, Helen Deutsch Papers, BU.

9. Primarily Davis, OHC #215, SMU.

10. Reynolds, *Debbie,* 266.

11. Ibid., 267, and Reynolds telephone interview with author, 2012.

12. Weingarten letter to Deutsch, March 28, 1963, Helen Deutsch Papers, BU.

13. Ronald Davis, OHC #347: Peter Gennaro. Interview conducted June 2, 1986, SMU.

14. Grover Dale, telephone interview by the author, September 23, 2008.

15. Reynolds, *Debbie: My Life,* 270.

16. Preston Ames interviewed in Delamater, *Dance in the Hollywood Musical,* 238.

17. *Seventeen,* July 1964.

18. Reynolds telephone interview by the author, 2012.

19. Cutts, "On the Bright Side."

20. Weingarten M-G-M memo to Walters, October 15, 1963, in Roger Edens Collection, USC.

21. Walters interview with Hugh Fordin, December 1971.

22. *Seventeen,* July 1964.

23. Reynolds, *Debbie,* 271.

24. Dale telephone interview with author, 2008. *Molly Brown* production records for "He's My Friend" indicated that the forty-fifth through forty-eighth days of shooting were devoted to rehearsing, the forty-ninth day to pre-recording the

number, the fiftieth day to dress rehearsal and lighting, and the fifty-first and fifty-second days to film. Besides "He's My Friend," the ensuing brawl sequence was also staged and shot during these seven days.

25. *Molly* first preview report from Warfield Theatre, San Francisco, February 7, 1964, in Roger Edens Collection, USC.

26. Toub letter to Walters, February 1964, viewed in Roger Edens Collection, USC.

27. Lawrence Weingarten Collection, USC.

28. *New York Times,* [June] 1964.

29. *Chicago Tribune,* June 25, 1964.

30. *New York Herald Tribune,* [June] 1964, viewed in Charles Walters Collection, USC.

31. Dale telephone interview with author, 2008.

27. After the Lion

1. Davis, OHC #215, SMU.

2. Ibid. Actor George Hamilton told the author that he wanted Walters to direct *The Hank Williams Story:* "We knew if we got Chuck to direct, the picture would get made." The uninterested director passed on the honky-tonk biopic, despite Gloria Swanson's intervention on behalf of Hamilton. (Production was later realized as *Your Cheatin' Heart,* directed by dancer-turned-director Gene Nelson.)

3. Hedda Hopper syndicated column, June 11, 1964.

4. Davis, OHC #215, SMU.

5. Fantle and Johnson interview with Walters, 1980.

6. Morrissey interview, 2007.

7. *Los Angeles Times,* December 24, 1964.

8. Other actors considered to play William Rutland included George C. Scott, Fredric March, Fred Astaire, and Bing Crosby.

9. Peggy Rea, telephone interview by the author, July 25, 2012.

10. Sauvage, "Interview with Charles Walters."

11. *Los Angeles Times,* January, 11, 1966.

12. *New York Times,* August 25, 1966.

13. *Time,* July 15, 1966.

14. Davis, OHC #215, SMU.

15. *Variety,* November 5, 1975.

16. Walters interview with Richard Hack, *Hollywood Reporter,* March 30, 1976.

17. Morrissey interview, 2007.

18. Reynolds telephone interview, 2012.

19. *Variety,* November 4, 1975.

20. Cutts, "On the Bright Side."

21. Fantle and Johnson interview with Walters, 1980.

22. Sauvage, "Interview with Charles Walters." The episode "Lucy and Aladdin's Lamp" also contains a gentle jab at friend Joan Crawford when Lucy dons a suit jacket allegedly worn by the actress in *Mildred Pierce*. "From the looks of those shoulder pads," cracks Desi Arnaz Jr., "she could have worn it in *The Spirit of Notre Dame*."

23. Sauvage, "Interview with Charles Walters."

24. Walters interview with Richard Hack, *Hollywood Reporter*, March 30, 1976.

25. Cutts, "On the Bright Side."

26. Ronald Davis, OHC #197: Lucille Ball. Interview conducted August 21, 1980, SMU. Gene Saks was also the original director of *Mame* on Broadway.

27. Sauvage, "Interview with Charles Walters."

28. Warren interview, 1980.

28. Final Ovation

1. After viewing *That's Entertainment!*, Walters said he marveled at the efficiency and craftsmanship of the M-G-M factory, virtues "he did not fully appreciate" during his tenure at the studio. He mentioned to *Variety* journalist Joseph McBride that the studio's strength was its "meshing of talents—nobody said, 'I did this,' 'I did that'—it was the movie itself that counted, the entertainment." But that didn't deter other Metro vets from grabbing credit. Joyce Haber of the *Los Angeles Times* reported on September 12, 1974, that Donen "implied" he was most responsible for Kelly's *Singin' in the Rain* and the dancing in *Seven Brides for Seven Brothers*; Jack Cummings said he felt shafted for his decades of contributions; producer Mervyn LeRoy contacted Haber to make sure the journalist recognized that he, not Arthur Freed, was responsible for *The Wizard of Oz*. When asked to comment on the unanticipated bitterness, Walters modestly brushed the question aside. "You know where the credit is?" he answered, touching his heart. "It's in here."

2. Arce, *Secret Life of Tyrone Power*, 73.

3. *New Yorker*, March 11, 1974, 122.

4. Joseph Bologna on-camera interview for *The Lucille Ball Specials: Happy Anniversary and Goodbye* and *What Now, Catherine Curtis?*, produced by GAB Entertainment (MPI Home Video), 2010.

5. Primarily from interview with Richard Hack, *Hollywood Reporter*, March 30, 1976.

6. Lucie Arnaz on-camera interview for *Lucille Ball Specials*. Rehearsal and filming on *Two for Three* was fraught with tacit tension. Per Gleason: "Lucy's a bear for rehearsals, I hate 'em." *Los Angeles Times*, October 5, 1972.

7. *Variety*, [March] 1976.

8. *Los Angeles Times*, March 30, 1976.

9. Helen Deutsch Papers, BU.

10. Hack, *Hollywood Reporter,* March 30, 1976.

11. All Mary Whiteley quotes are from interview by the author, Los Angeles, August 2007. At USC, Walters was willing to step out of the spotlight. He broke from the syllabus to pay attention to Bob Fosse's *All That Jazz* (1980), which was playing in theaters. "Fosse's film was controversial, granted, but a beautifully done piece," he told David Fantle and Tom Johnson in September 1980. "I told the class, 'Forget I'm here. This is au courant. It's the current thing.' But it's amazing how many students liked the oldies better."

12. Fantle and Johnson interview with Walters, 1980.

13. Gloria Swanson Papers, HRC.

14. Ibid.

15. Les Perkins, email correspondence with author, October 2013.

16. Fantle and Johnson interview with Walters, 1980.

17. In early 1981, Walters met with Judy Garland's ex-husband to discuss Sid Luft's plans for a multimedia film and live-action production in which Chuck would "return" Judy to the New York Palace Theatre. The director politely declined.

18. Details of Walters's lawsuit, Joe Anthony's lawsuit, and all quotes: *Evening Outlook,* March 31, 1982, and the USC *Daily Trojan,* September 23, 1982. Although Walters worked at Columbia for only a year, it provided the site of his last alleged exposure to asbestos, and so it became the legally prescribed target of the worker's compensation claim, reported Walters's lawyer Maury Gentile.

19. On one occasion Joe told a reporter that he had been adopted as early as 1966, which seems improbable, as he and Chuck had just met. More likely he meant their relationship dated back to that year.

20. This eyewitness asked to remain anonymous; phone conversation with author, 2008.

21. Morrissey interview, 2007.

22. USC *Daily Trojan,* September 23, 1982.

23. Ibid.

24. Charles Powell Walter death certificate, State of California, Department of Health Services, originally signed August 18, 1982. Cremation: August 19, 1982.

25. Joseph Anthony Walters death certificate, State of California, Department of Health Services, originally filed October 2, 1986.

26. Les Perkins, email correspondence with author, October 2013.

Index

choreographer (CW), critics on: *Brazilian Boogie*, 78; *Girl Crazy*, 73, 74; *Good News*, 91; *A Great Lady Has 'An Interview,'* 82, 84; *Heigh-Ho*, 6; *Her Highness and the Bellboy* dream sequence, 85; *Let's Face It*, 52–53; *St. Louis Woman*, 86–87; "The Trolley Song," 80

A Chorus Line (stage), 249

Christie, Audrey, 18, 39, 40, 41, 53, 56, 228, 240, 256

Chuck Walters Presents, 195

Cimarron (film), 210, 262

Cinderella stories, 173

Cinderfella (film), 173

cine-dance, 65

CinemaScope, 182

cinematographer (CW): critics on, 108, 133; diversity in style as, xi; elaborate and subtle treatments, 221–222; innovation as a, 73, 108, 182; risk taking as a, 73; single shot takes, 99–100,123, 232; talent as a, 82–83; use of color, 81, 149, 233

Cinerama, 219

Clark, Fred, 197

Clayton, Jan, 85

Cleopatra (film), 157, 219

Clift, Montgomery ("Monty"), 24–25

Clift, Sunny, 25

A Clockwork Orange (film), 242

Clyde Beatty show, 218

Coca, Imogene, 15–18, 19

Cody, Lew, 13

Coe, Richard L., 109, 152, 160

Cohan, George M., 137

Cole, Jack, 55, 57, 75, 83

Coleman, Ronald, 114

Colette, 198

collaborate, CW's ability to, 52, 63, 67–68, 75, 92, 97, 160, 188

"Colorado, My Home," 262

Columbia Pictures, 75, 237, 239

Comden, Betty, 89, 91, 103, 109, 141

Come Back, Little Sheba (film), 171

"Command Performance," 36

Community Property (film), 237

Connolly, Mike, 178, 194, 195

Cooper, Melville, 24

"Copperfield Street," 175

Corbin, Joe, 205

Corcoran, Donna, 155

"Could You Use Me," 73, 258

Count Me In (stage), 57

"A Couple of Swells," 99–100, 140, 141, 143, 259

"The Courtin' of Elmer and Ella," 106

The Courtship of Eddie's Father (film), 204

Coyne, Jeanne, 125

The Cradle Snatchers (stage, later *Let's Face It*), 50

Crawford, Christina, 165

Crawford, Joan, 18, 26, 58, 162–169, 172, 202, 240, 259

Crewe, Regina, 46

Crist, Judith, 233

Crosby, Bing, ix, 101, 173, 184, 185, 186, 187–191, 244

Crowther, Bosley, 78, 109, 132, 184, 209, 224, 239

Cukor, George: after-hours socializing, 29; CW screen test and, 13; Darrow friendship, 29, 35; guest at CW's film class, 248; moneymaker, 209; reputation, 196; Sunday afternoon soirees, 29; at Swanson party, 114; works of referenced, 75, 152, 167–168, 175, 184, 199

Cummings, Jack, 76, 133, 291n35

Cutts, John, 109, 123

Dahl, Arlene, 112

Dailey, Dan, Jr. (later Dan Dailey), 42, 56, 241

Dale, Grover, 228–229, 231, 232, 233–234

dance as social commentary, CW on, 22–23

dance director, 64

dance lessons (CW), 3, 25

Dangerous When Wet (film, was *Everybody Swims*), 155–158, 161, 196, 260

Daniel, Billy, 157, 260

Daniels, Lisa, 175

Darcel, Denise, 155, 157

D'Arcy, Richard, 37

Screen Classics

Screen Classics is a series of critical biographies, film histories, and analytical studies focusing on neglected filmmakers and important screen artists and subjects, from the era of silent cinema to the golden age of Hollywood to the international generation of today. Books in the Screen Classics series are intended for scholars and general readers alike. The contributing authors are established figures in their respective fields. This series also serves the purpose of advancing scholarship on film personalities and themes with ties to Kentucky.

Series Editor

Patrick McGilligan

Books in the Series